iMac® FOR DUMMIES®

A Wiley Brand

8th Edition

by Mark L. Chambers

FOR DUMMIES®
A Wiley Brand

iMac® For Dummies, 8th Edition

Published by: **John Wiley & Sons, Inc.,** 111 River Street, Hoboken, NJ 07030-5774, www.wiley.com

Copyright © 2014 by John Wiley & Sons, Inc., Hoboken, New Jersey

Media and software compilation copyright © 2014 by John Wiley & Sons, Inc. All rights reserved.

Published simultaneously in Canada

No part of this publication may be reproduced, stored in a retrieval system or transmitted in any form or by any means, electronic, mechanical, photocopying, recording, scanning or otherwise, except as permitted under Sections 107 or 108 of the 1976 United States Copyright Act, without the prior written permission of the Publisher. Requests to the Publisher for permission should be addressed to the Permissions Department, John Wiley & Sons, Inc., 111 River Street, Hoboken, NJ 07030, (201) 748-6011, fax (201) 748-6008, or online at http://www.wiley.com/go/permissions.

Trademarks: Wiley, For Dummies, the Dummies Man logo, Dummies.com, Making Everything Easier, and related trade dress are trademarks or registered trademarks of John Wiley & Sons, Inc. and may not be used without written permission. iMac is a registered trademark of Apple, Inc. All other trademarks are the property of their respective owners. John Wiley & Sons, Inc. is not associated with any product or vendor mentioned in this book.

For general information on our other products and services, please contact our Customer Care Department within the U.S. at 877-762-2974, outside the U.S. at 317-572-3993, or fax 317-572-4002. For technical support, please visit www.wiley.com/techsupport.

Wiley publishes in a variety of print and electronic formats and by print-on-demand. Some material included with standard print versions of this book may not be included in e-books or in print-on-demand. If this book refers to media such as a CD or DVD that is not included in the version you purchased, you may download this material at http://booksupport.wiley.com. For more information about Wiley products, visit www.wiley.com.

Library of Congress Control Number: 2013956847

ISBN 978-1-118-86237-7 (pbk); ISBN 978-1-118-86451-7 (ebk); ISBN 978-1-118-86452-4 (ebk)

Manufactured in the United States of America

10 9 8 7 6 5 4 3 2 1

Table of Contents

Introduction

Skeptical about your new anodized aluminum iMac, with that super-charged Intel quad-core processor? Perhaps you're thinking it's too dog-gone thin, or you're wondering where all the buttons are. Shouldn't there be places to plug in cables?

Ladies and gentlemen, I have great news for you: Not only did you make The Right Decision about which computer to buy — you shot a hole in one! The latest incarnation of the iMac has everything a computer power user could want: speed, the latest in hardware and standards, a top-of-the-line LED screen, and all the connectors you need to add just about any device meant for today's computers.

I wrote this book especially for the proud Intel iMac owner who wants to make the most of this new stunning aluminum computer, so this book is a guide to both the iMac hardware and *Mavericks,* Apple's superb OS X operating system. I start by describing the basics that every iMac owner should know. Then I move on to chapters devoted to the software that comes with your iMac. Along the way, you come across a generous sprinkling of power-user tips and tricks that save you time, effort, and money.

Foolish Assumptions

So who is the target audience for this book? As in past editions, I make no assumptions about your previous knowledge of computers and software. I figure you've either just bought a brand-new iMac or you're considering buying one — perhaps you've found a great bargain on a gently-used older iMac model, and you'd like guidance as you learn the ropes. Those are the **only** assumptions I make. . . and unlike other books that require all sorts of technical experience to understand, the only requirement between these covers is your desire to become an iMac *power user* (someone who produces the best work in the least amount of time and has the most fun doing it)!

By the way, if your friends and family told you that you're going to spend half your life savings on software — or that no "decent" software is available for Mac computers — just smile quietly to yourself! The iMac comes complete with about a ton more software than any Windows box, and the iLife and iWork software suites are better than anything available on a PC!

This book was written using the latest Intel quad-core iMac computer, so owners of older iMac computers might not be able to follow along with everything I cover. However, if you've upgraded an older Intel iMac with OS X Mavericks (and the iLife and iWork application suites), you should be able to use most of the book with no problem.

About This Book

In writing about the iMac, I've kept one precept firmly in mind: OS X Mavericks, the operating system you'll run, is just as important as the actual iMac computer itself. Therefore, you'll find that *iMac For Dummies* is just as much about familiarizing you with all the software you get as it is with introducing you to hardware features like your keyboard and mouse. After all, it's relatively easy to connect an entire forest of cables and turn on any new computer — what comes *next* is the challenging part!

As in my other *For Dummies* titles, I respect and use the same English language you do, avoiding jargon, ridiculous computer acronyms, and confusing techno-babble whenever possible.

If you're upgrading from a PC running the Windows operating system, I've got tips, tricks, and entire sections devoted to those hardy pioneers called *Switchers!* You'll discover both the similarities and differences between the iMac running Mavericks and the PC running Windows. I also show you how to make the switch as easy and quick as possible.

A word about the conventions I use: Even with an absolute minimum of techno-speak, this book needs to cover the special keys that you have to press or menu commands that you have to choose to make things work. Therefore, please keep this short list of conventions in mind as you read:

- ✔ **Stuff you type:** If I ask you to type (or enter) something, such as in a text box or field, that text appears in bold, like this:

  Type me.

  If I ask you to type a command within an application, that text appears like this (and note that you usually have to press the Return key before anything happens):

  ```
  Type me.
  ```

- ✔ **Menu commands:** I list menu paths and commands using another format. For example, this instruction indicates that you should click the Edit menu and then choose the Copy menu item:

  Edit⇨Copy

- ✔ **Web addresses:** No up-to-date book on a computer would be complete without a bag full of web addresses for you to check out. When you see these in the text, they look like this: www.mlcbooks.com.

- ✔ **For the technically curious:** Tangential techy stuff is presented in sidebars, and you don't have to read them unless you want to know what makes things tick.

Icons Used in This Book

Like other technology authors, I firmly believe that important nuggets of wisdom should **stand out on the page!** With that in mind, this *For Dummies* book includes a number of margin icons for certain situations:

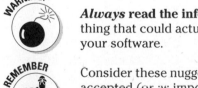

This is the most popular icon in the book, and you find it parked next to suggestions that I make to save you time and effort (and even cash!).

You don't have to know this stuff, but the technologically curious love high-tech details. (Of course, we're great fun at parties, too.)

Always **read the information before you take action!** I'm discussing something that could actually harm your hardware or throw a plumber's helper into your software.

Consider these nuggets to be highlighter stuff — not quite as universally accepted (or as important to the author) as a Mark's Maxim (described next), but good reminders nonetheless. I use these icons to reinforce what you should remember.

These gold-plated truisms are easily spotted; just look for the likeness of my rugged, iMac-lovin' mug. These are *MFRs* (short for My Favorite Recommendations). In fact, I'll bet just about any iMac power user would tell you the same. Follow my Maxims to avoid the quicksand and pitfalls that I've encountered with all sorts of Macs for well over two decades!

Beyond the Book

Thanks to my good friends at Wiley, there's a ton of extra content to accompany this book that you won't find between the covers! Fire up your Safari browser and go online to find the following:

- ✔ **Cheat Sheet:** I've created a number of Cheat Sheet pages that cover things like common keystrokes and maintenance procedures that every iMac owner should follow on a regular basis, and you'll find them on the web at www.dummies.com/cheatsheet/imac.

- ✔ **Dummies.com online articles:** At the beginning of each major section of the book, you'll find links to Dummies.com and articles that extend the content covered in this book. This additional content includes all sorts of different topics: tips on network troubleshooting, a discussion of the Unix foundation that supports OS X, information on managing and expanding your iCloud storage, and even my history of Data Elves! (You'll have to read online to learn more about the Elves.) These articles appear on the book's Extras page (www.dummies.com/extras/imac).

- ✔ **Bonus Chapters:** If you're dying to find out how to share data among wireless devices via Bluetooth technology, check out the handy Bluetooth bonus chapter at the Wiley website (www.dummies.com/extras/imac) as well as at my website (www.mlcbooks.com). You'll also find a spiffy bonus chapter dedicated to running Windows on your iMac using Boot Camp!

- ✔ **Updates to this book, if we have any, are at**

  www.dummies.com/extras/imac

Where to Go from Here

Each chapter in this book is written as a reference on a specific hardware or software topic. You can begin reading anywhere you like because each chapter is self-contained. However, I recommend that you read the book from front to back because the order of this book makes a great deal of sense.

Part I

Know Your iMac

getting started with iMac

Learn how OS X Mavericks uses a Unix foundation at www.dummies.com/extras/imac.

In this part . . .

- ✔ Introduce yourself to the important hardware features of your iMac
- ✔ Unpack and set up your iMac The Right Way
- ✔ Check your iMac for shipping damage and proper operation
- ✔ Familiarize yourself with OS X Mavericks and your Desktop

Chapter 1

Okay, This Machine Looks Really, Really Weird

. . . .

In This Chapter

▶ Identifying the important parts of your iMac

▶ Locating the right home for your computer

▶ Plugging stuff in and getting hooked up

▶ Playing with your bundled software

▶ Buying additional stuff that you might need

. . . .

*Y*ou bought a brand-new iMac, and there it sits, in the box. Waiting. Waiting for you.

If you're a little nervous about unpacking that shiny aluminum and glass rectangle, I completely understand. Face it: The latest iMac follows in the footsteps of many revolutionary iMac designs that have come before it. In other words, it doesn't *look* like a computer at all, and that can be a bit disconcerting. And if you're switching from a Windows PC to the Apple universe, you might find yourself floating weightlessly in your office or your living room without a familiar bulky PC case to anchor yourself. Hence, the reluctance you might be feeling.

However, dear reader, let me assure you that you've indeed made The Right Choice. I commend you! Today's Intel iMac is the fastest, leanest, and easiest-to-use self-contained all-in-one computer ever built. Practically everything's in one shining panel (except for your keyboard and mouse). You've got one of the best backlit LED screens on the planet, a super-fast processor, room for a ton of RAM (memory), and a regular laundry list of the latest technology. Best of all, you don't have to be a techno-nerd to use all that power!

In this chapter, I introduce you to your new dream machine, giving you an overview of the more important locations within iMac City. I show you how to unpack your new computer, what wires go where, and where your iMac should set up housekeeping. I preview the awesome software that's waiting within that powerful panel. Finally, I list the accessories that help keep both you *and* your new iMac computing smoothly.

An Introduction to the Beast

The Intel iMac might look like a sculpture straight out of a museum of modern art, but it still sports everything that it needs to function as a computer. In this section, I identify the important stuff that you need to live your life — you know, write a term paper in Pages, hear the music you downloaded, or manage the affairs of those lazy Sims.

Major parts of your major appliance

Every computer requires some of the same gizmos. Figure 1-1 helps you track them down. Of course, as you'd expect, a computer has a "body" of sorts in which all the innards and brains are stored (the screen, in this case), a display screen, a keyboard, a mouse/pointing device, and ports for powering and exchanging data with peripherals.

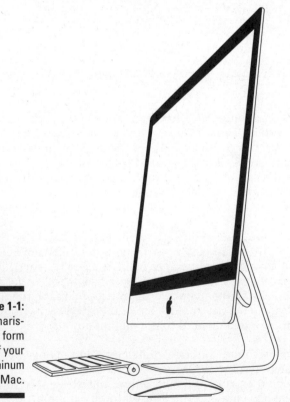

Figure 1-1:
The charismatic form of your aluminum Intel iMac.

That magnificent screen

What a view you've got! An aluminum iMac is graced with either a 21.5" or 27" LED display, complete with backlighting for outstanding color and brightness.

LED screens use far less electricity than their antique CRT ancestors, and they emit practically no radiation (less, in fact, than even the LCD screens Apple once used).

Both sizes of iMac screens offer a *widescreen* aspect ratio (the screen is considerably wider than it is tall), which augurs well for those who enjoy watching movies. (A favorite editor of mine loves it when I use the antique word *augur,* meaning *to predict or foretell.*) For example, the 27" screen boasts a whopping 2560 x 1440 resolution.

That reminds me: Throw away your printed dictionary! You won't need it because OS X Mavericks includes both a handy Dictionary widget and a fantastic Dictionary application! (Each one uses the Internet to retrieve definitions.) More on launching applications in Chapter 4, and I describe widgets in Chapter 5 . . . and yes, both do contain the word *augur.*

The keyboard and mouse

Hey, here's something novel for the Intel iMac — something *external* (outside the computer's case). Gotta have a keyboard and mouse, right? And you gotta love the options with iMac: You'll go nomadic . . . um, that is, wireless and free.

The iMac comes standard with a truly 21st century combo of an Apple wireless keyboard and either a Magic Mouse or a Magic Trackpad! This dynamic duo lets you sit back and relax with your keyboard in your lap, without being tied down by a cord. (Say it with me: "Death to cords, death to cords.") Just stay within about 30 feet of your iMac screen, and sweet freedom is yours. You can also feel safe using these wireless peripherals because they offer secure 128-bit, over-the-air encryption, which helps keep sensitive information safe while you type and click away. One downside of the wireless keyboard, though: Unlike older wired keyboards, the wireless model doesn't include any USB ports, and you will need a supply of batteries. (Go rechargeable!)

The keyboard layout is a particular favorite of mine because from here

- ✔ You can either control the sound volume (using the volume control buttons F11 and F12) or mute all that noise completely (using the Mute button F10).

- ✔ Mission Control, Launchpad, and Dashboard — three outstanding features of OS X Mavericks that you learn about later in the book — are each available with a single keystroke.

- ✔ A handy-dandy Media Eject key lets you eject a CD or DVD (if you have an external optical drive).

The latest iMac models don't have a built-in optical drive. If you have one of these machines, don't drive yourself batty looking for a disc slot!

Both the wireless Magic Mouse and Magic Trackpad need a flat surface, but that's what TV trays are for, right?

Yes, your computer has a foot . . . just one

You and I — normal human beings — would say that the iMac is supported by a sturdy aluminum *stand,* but Apple calls it a *foot.* The foot lets you tilt the iMac panel up and down for the best viewing angle. Most important, though, the foot minimizes the computer's desk space requirements (or its *footprint*). (Engineers . . . sheesh.) And yes, that foot is perfectly balanced and quite stable, so there's no danger of your treasured iMac taking a dive.

If you decide to get really snazzy and mount your 27" iMac to the wall, you can remove the foot and install the VESA mounting adapter (available separately for about $40). You can use any VESA standard mounting bracket on your wall, too. You can be positioned within 30 feet or so of your wall-mounted iMac with a wireless Apple keyboard and mouse (or trackpad).

Hey, Hewlett-Packard or Dell, can you mount one of those monolithic desktop PCs to the wall? *I think not.*

Food for your ears

A machine this nice had better have great sound, and the iMac doesn't disappoint. You have a couple of options for iMac audio:

✔ The iMac sports built-in stereo speakers (and a microphone to boot).

✔ Built-in ports connect your iMac audio to either

- More powerful (and more expensive) external speaker systems
- A set of headphones (including the Apple iPhone headset)
- A home stereo system

The power cable

Sorry, but you can't get a wireless power system . . . yet. (Apple's working hard on that one.) With the wireless keyboard and mouse/trackpad setup, though, the power cable is actually the only required cable that you need to run your computer! Now that's *sassy.*

The power button

Yep, you've got one of these, too. It's on the back of the case (if you're looking at the screen, it's at the lower-left corner).

Those holes are called ports

Our next stop on your tour of Planet iMac is Port Central — that row of holes on the back of your computer (see Figure 1-2). Each port connects a different type of cable or device, allowing you to easily add all sorts of extra functionality to your computer.

Figure 1-2:
Only slightly less sexy — it's the back end of an iMac.

One of the holes is an exception to the Rule of Ports: The iMac's SDXC card slot accepts the same type of SD memory cards as most of today's digital cameras and video cameras. (In other words, that hole is not for connecting a cable; you insert the card instead.) The SDXC slot appears as a tiny vertical slot.

Each of these stellar holes is identified by an icon. Here's a list of what you'll find as well as a quick rundown on what these ports do:

✔ **USB:** Short for *Universal Serial Bus,* the familiar USB port is the jack-of-all-trades in today's world of computer add-ons. Most external devices (such as portable hard drives, scanners, or digital cameras) that you want to connect to your iMac use a USB port. The current iMac sports four USB 3.0 ports on its back. USB 3.0 connections are much faster than the old USB 2.0 standard, but you can still use your USB 2.0 devices with the faster ports (at the slower speed, of course).

For the specs on connecting your keyboard and mouse, see the upcoming section "Absolutely essential connections."

For more on USB ports — as well as the FireWire ports included on older iMac models — get the lowdown in Chapter 23.

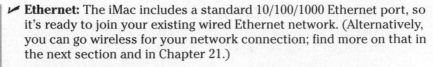

✔ **Ethernet:** The iMac includes a standard 10/100/1000 Ethernet port, so it's ready to join your existing wired Ethernet network. (Alternatively, you can go wireless for your network connection; find more on that in the next section and in Chapter 21.)

Apple doesn't include a built-in modem on the iMac, so if you need a dialup connection to the Internet, you need an external 56K v.92 USB modem that's compatible with OS X Mavericks (version 10.9).

✔ **Thunderbolt:** Yes, I know, it's a dumb name, but it really *is* that fast. Thunderbolt ports offer the absolute speediest connection between external devices and your iMac, including the fastest (and most expensive) external hard drives and storage systems. Thunderbolt's appeal doesn't end there, though: In case that splendid screen isn't quite big enough, you can add an adapter or cable to this port and send the video signal from your iMac to an Apple Thunderbolt monitor, a standard LCD/LED monitor, or a flat-screen TV. (Apple also offers different adapters that can connect your iMac to standard VGA monitors and projectors.) All iMac models sport two Thunderbolt ports.

Connections for external audio

Your iMac comes equipped with two pretty powerful stereo speakers on the bottom of the case, but you're certainly not limited to them. Apple provides an Audio Line Out jack, allowing you to send the high-quality audio from your rectangular beast to a set of standard headphones or to an optical digital audio device, such as a high-end home theater system. (Unlike older iMac models, note that the newest iMac has no audio Line In jack.)

You can also connect Mavericks-compatible USB speakers to your iMac.

Important Hidden Stuff

When you bought your new digital pride and joy, you probably noticed a number of subtle differences between the low-end iMac and the über-expensive top-end model. I call these differences the *Important Hidden Stuff* (or IHS, in case you're addicted to acronyms), and they're just as important as the parts and ports that you can see:

✔ **Hard drive:** The current iMac can be equipped with either a traditional serial ATA (SATA) hard drive or flash storage (also called a *solid state drive,* or SSD). Apple also offers a *Fusion Drive*, which is essentially a combination of a SATA drive and flash storage (offering the larger capacity of a SATA drive and the improved performance of flash storage).

As I type these words, the iMac product line offers a number of different storage capacities, depending on the processor speed and screen size you choose: anywhere from a standard 1TB SATA drive to an immense 3TB Fusion Drive. (Yes, friends and neighbors, *TB* means *terabyte,* or 1,000GB.) The bigger, the better. Alternatively, you can opt for anywhere from 256GB to 1TB of flash storage instead. (Remember, though, that the iMac has room for only one internal drive.)

✔ **Wireless Ethernet:** "Look, Ma, no wires!" As I mention earlier, your iMac can join an existing wireless Ethernet network with its built-in wireless hardware. With wireless connectivity, you can share documents with another computer in another room, share a single high-speed Internet connection amongst several computers, or enjoy wireless printing. Truly *sassy!*

Although Apple would want you to build your wireless wonderland with an Apple AirPort Extreme Base Station or a Time Capsule unit — go figure — you can actually use your iMac with any standard 802.11g, 802.11n, or 802.11ac wireless network. And yes, PCs and Macs can intermingle on the same wireless network without a hitch. (Scandalous, ain't it?)

✔ **Bluetooth:** Let's get the old "digital pirate" joke out of the way: "Arrgg, matey, I needs me a wireless parrot." (Engineers again . . . sheesh.) Although strangely named, Bluetooth is actually another form of wireless connectivity. This time, however, the standard was designed for accessories like your keyboard and mouse, and devices like your tablet and smartphone. Bluetooth is built into every Intel iMac.

✔ **SDXC card slot:** As I mention earlier, this slot allows your iMac to read photos and video directly from standard SD memory cards — photographers and video junkies, rejoice!

✔ **FaceTime HD camera:** The iMac built-in video and still camera appears as a tiny lens and activity light at the top of your computer.

✔ **Video card:** If your applications rely heavily on high-speed 3D graphics, you'll be pleased as punch to find that your iMac comes equipped with either Intel Iris Pro or NVIDIA GeForce graphics hardware. The three high-end NVIDIA GeForce cards are well suited for 3D modeling, video editing, and, well, honestly, blasting the enemy into small, smoking pieces with aplomb.

Choosing a Home for Your New Pet

If you pick the wrong spot to park your new iMac, I can guarantee that you'll regret it later. Some domiciles and office cubicles obviously don't offer a choice — you've got but one desk at work, for example, and nobody's going to hand over another one — but if you can select a home for your iMac, consider the important placement points in this section.

Picking the right location

You know the mantra: Location, location, location.

✔ **There's always the wall.** Your iMac can disguise itself as a particularly interesting digital picture frame. With the right mounting adapter, you can hang your computer right on the wall and snub your desk altogether.

This wall-mounted solution has three big problems:

- Your VESA mounting plate must be installed safely and correctly (for example, using the studs within your walls).

  The iMac is slim and trim, but it's no lightweight, and it doesn't bounce well. You don't want it to take a high dive!

- You may have to remove your iMac from the wall mount to connect or disconnect cables from the ports on the back.

- External peripherals aren't happy campers, that includes any Thunderbolt and USB devices, which must either camp out on the floor or on a nearby (and conspicuous) shelf. (Personally, I think the cables for external devices tend to spoil the appearance of a wall-mounted computer, so if you're using a wall mount, I recommend using an AirPort Time Capsule device for your backups!)

Your iMac must be mounted at the proper height on the wall. It's not good ergonomic practice to sit more than two feet away from your iMac screen, and the screen should be placed at (or slightly below) eye level.

My solution? Don't plan on using any external devices. Instead, opt for a wireless network with a remote printer and remote backup storage space, like a Time Capsule unit on your network.

✔ **Keep things cool.** Your new iMac is nearly silent, but that super-fast Intel quad-core processor generates quite a bit of heat. Fans inside the case draw the heat away. (Nothing like an overheated processor to spoil an evening of *BioShock Infinite*.)

Follow these three rules to keep your cool. Make sure that

- The location you choose is far from heating vents.

- The location you choose is shielded from direct sunlight.

- You allow plenty of room below the machine (where the air enters the case) and above the machine (where heated air escapes from the slot at the top of the case).

  Hot air from a wall-mounted iMac can discolor the wall.

Considering the convenience factor

Technology is nothing if you can't make it convenient:

- **Outlets, outlets, outlets!** Your computer needs a minimum of at least one nearby outlet, and perhaps as many as three or four:

  - *A standard AC outlet*

    I discuss surge protectors and uninterruptible power supplies (UPS) at the end of this chapter.

  - *A telephone jack* (if you use a Mavericks-compatible external USB modem for connecting to the Internet or sending and receiving faxes)

  - *A nearby Ethernet jack* (if you use the iMac's built-in Ethernet port for connecting to a wired Ethernet network)

     If you prefer to send your data over the airwaves, consider using wireless networking for your iMac. I discuss everything you need to know about wireless networking in Chapter 21.

- **Don't forget the lighting.** Let me act as your mom. (I know that's a stretch, but bear with me.) She'd say, "You can't possibly expect to work without decent lighting! You'll go blind!" She's right, you know. At a minimum, you need a desk or floor lamp.

- **Plan to expand.** If your iMac hangs out on a desk, allow an additional foot of space on each side. That way, you have space for external peripherals and more powerful speakers.

Unpacking and Connecting

You are going to love this section. It's short and sweet because the installation of an aluminum iMac on your desktop is a piece of cake. (Sorry about the cliché overload, but this really *is* easy.)

Unpacking your iMac For Dummies

Follow these guidelines when unpacking your system:

- **Check for damage.** I've never had a box arrive from Apple with shipping damage, but I've heard horror stories from others (who claim that King Kong must have been working for That Shipping Company). Check all sides of your box before you open it.

Take a photograph of any significant damage (just in case).

✔ **Search for all the parts.** When you're removing those chunks o' foam, make certain that you check all sides of each foam block for parts that are snuggled therein or taped for shipment.

✔ **Keep all those packing materials.** Do *not* head for the trash can with that box and those packing materials. Keep your box intact, complete with all the packing materials, for at least a year until your standard Apple warranty runs out. If you have to ship it to an Apple Service Center, the box with the original packing is the only way for your iMac to fly.

And now, a dramatic Mark's Maxim about cardboard containers:

Smart computer owners keep their boxes far longer than a year.

For example, if you sell your iMac or move across the country, you'll want that box. *Trust me on this one.*

✔ **Store the invoice for safekeeping.** Your invoice is a valuable piece of paper indeed.

Save your original invoice in a plastic bag, along with your computer's manuals and original software, manuals, and other assorted hoo-hah. Keep the bag on your shelf or stored safely in your desk, and enjoy a little peace of mind.

✔ **Read the iMac manual.** "Hey, wait a minute, Mark — why do I have to read the manual from Apple along with this tome?" Good question, and here's the answer: There might be new and updated instructions in the documentation from Apple that override what I tell you in this book. (For example, *"Never* cut the red wire. Cut the blue wire instead." Or something to that effect.)

Besides, Apple manuals are rarely thicker than a restaurant menu.

Connecting cables like a true nerd

The iMac makes all its connections really simple, but your computer depends on you to place the outside wires and thingamabobs where they go.

Absolutely essential connections

After your new iMac is resting comfortably in its assigned spot (I assume that's a desktop or a wall), you need to make a minimum of one connection: the power cable. Plug the cable into the corresponding socket on the iMac first; then plug 'er into that handy AC outlet.

Apple has already installed your batteries in your wireless keyboard and mouse (or trackpad). How thoughtful! If you ordered your iMac with a wired Apple keyboard, of course, you have no batteries to worry about at all.

Adding the Internet to the mix

If you have Internet access or a local computer network, you need to make at least one of the following connections.

If you don't already have *any* Internet service, you may want to start with local dialup Internet access (assuming that you have an external USB modem for your iMac; see the next section). If you decide to investigate your high-speed options immediately, your local cable and telephone companies can provide you more information on cable or DSL Internet service.

Dialup Internet access

If you get on the Internet by dialing a standard phone number, you'll need an external USB modem that's compatible with OS X 10.9 to connect your iMac. Follow these steps:

1. **Plug your external USB modem into one of the USB ports on the back of your iMac.**

2. **Plug one of the telephone cable's connectors into your modem's line port.**

3. **Plug the other telephone cable connector into your telephone line's wall jack.**

Networks and high-speed Internet access

If you have high-speed Internet service, or if you're in an office or school with a local computer network, you can probably connect through the iMac's built-in Ethernet port. You make two connections:

1. **Plug one end of the Ethernet cable into the Ethernet port on the iMac.**

2. **Plug the other end of the Ethernet cable into the Ethernet port from your network.**

    It's probably one of the following:

    • An Ethernet wall jack

    • An Ethernet switch

    • A cable or DSL Internet router (or sharing device)

Will you be joining a wireless network? If so, look to Chapter 21 to find all the details you need to configure Mavericks for wireless networking.

Discovering All the Cool Things You Can Do

This section answers the most common of all novice computer questions: "What the heck will I *do* with this thing?" You find additional details and exciting factoids about the software that you get for free, software you'll want to buy, and stuff you can do on the Internet.

What software do I get?

Currently, all iMac computers ship with these major software applications installed and ready to use:

✔ **The iLife suite:** You know you want these applications! They turn your iMac into a digital hub for practically every kind of high-tech device on the planet, including DV camcorders, digital cameras, portable music players, tablets, and even smartphones.

Chapters 13–16 of this book focus on the four major applications that make up iLife: iTunes, iPhoto, iMovie, and GarageBand.

✔ **The iWork suite:** Apple's powerful office productivity suite can be downloaded for free from the App Store. You can create documents, spreadsheets, and presentations within Pages, Numbers, and Keynote. It's much like that Other Office Suite from those guys in Redmond.

Figure 1-3 illustrates a flyer under construction in Pages.

Figure 1-3: Pages is a great tool for home and office.

The installed software on your iMac might change as new programs become available.

Looking forward to fun on the Internet

What is a modern computer without the Internet? Apple gives you great tools to take full advantage of every road sign and off ramp on the Information Superhighway, right out of the box:

- ✔ **Web surfing:** I use the Safari web browser every single day. It's faster and better designed than other browsers (although I might be biased). Safari includes tabbed browsing and offers shared bookmarks through iCloud.

  If *tabbed browsing* and *shared bookmarks* sound like ancient Aztec to you, don't worry. Chapter 10 is devoted entirely to Safari.

- ✔ **Web searches:** Your Dashboard widgets can search the entire Internet for stocks, movie listings, business locations, and dictionaries.

- ✔ **FaceTime:** You can videoconference with someone using another Mac, or even with those using iOS devices like the iPhone 4 (or later) and the iPad. You'll find more on FaceTime in Chapter 12.

- ✔ **Messages:** *Messages* lets you use your iMac to chat with others around the world for free via the Internet — by keyboard, voice, or (with your iMac's built-in FaceTime HD web camera) full-color video. This is awesome stuff straight out of Dick Tracy and Buck Rogers. If you've never seen a video chat, you'll be surprised by just how good your friends and family look!

  Always wear a shirt when videoconferencing.

- ✔ **E-mail:** Soldier, Apple's got you covered. The Mail application is a full-featured e-mail system, complete with defenses against the torrent of junk mail awaiting you. (Imagine a hungry digital saber-toothed tiger with an appetite for spam.) Send pictures and attached files to everyone else on the planet, and look doggone good doing it.

Applications that rock

Dozens of useful applications are included with OS X. I mention the most important of them in later chapters, but here are three good examples to whet your appetite:

- ✔ **Calendar:** Keep track of your schedule and upcoming events, and even share your calendar online with others in your company or your circle of friends. Figure 1-4 illustrates Calendar in action.

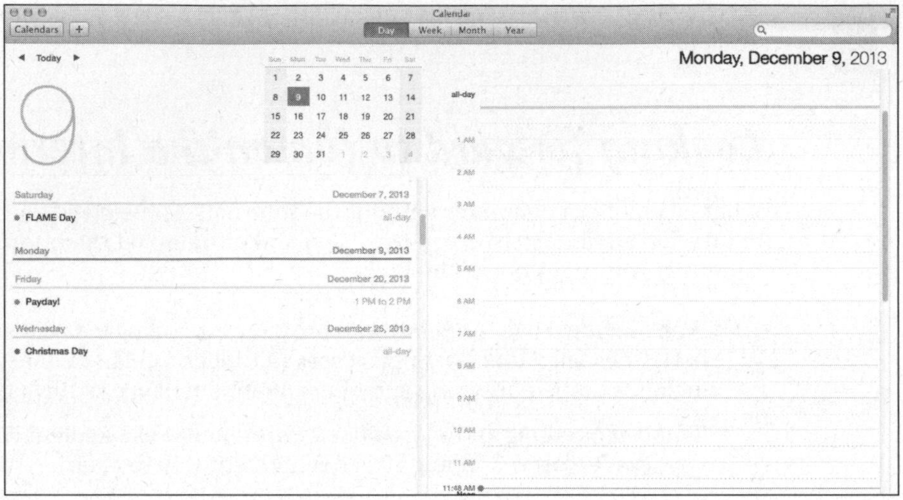

Figure 1-4:
Hey,
isn't that
Calendar
running on
your iMac?
You are
iTogether!

✔ **DVD Player:** Got an external optical drive for your iMac? Put all that widescreen beauty to work and watch your favorite DVD movies with DVD Player! You have all the features of today's most expensive stand-alone DVD players, too, including a spiffy onscreen control that looks like a remote.

✔ **Contacts:** Throw away that well-thumbed collection of fading addresses. The OS X Contacts application can store, search, and recall just about any piece of information on your friends, family, and acquaintances.

You can use the data you store in your Contacts in other Apple applications that are included with Mavericks, such as Apple Mail and Messages.

Would you like to play a game?

"All productivity and no play . . ." Hey, even a hard-working person like yourself enjoys a good challenging game, so you can look forward to playing Chess on your iMac right out of the box — ah, but this isn't the chessboard your dad used! Play the game of kings against a tough (and configurable) opponent — your iMac — on a beautiful 3D board. Heck, your iMac even narrates the game by speaking the moves!

Stuff You Oughta Buy Right Now

No man is an island, and no computer is, either. I always recommend the same set of stuff for new PC and Mac owners. These extras help keep your new computer clean and healthy (and some make sure you're happy as well):

- ✔ **Surge suppressor or uninterruptible power supply (UPS):** Even an all-in-one computer like your iMac can fall prey to a power surge. I recommend one of these:

    - A *basic surge suppressor* with a fuse can help protect your iMac from an overload.

    - A *UPS* costs a little more, but it does a better job of filtering your AC line voltage to prevent brownouts or line interference from reaching your computer.

      A UPS also provides a few minutes of battery power during a blackout so that you can save your documents and safely shut down your iMac.

- ✔ **Screen wipes:** Invest in a box of premoistened screen wipes. Your iMac's screen can pick up dirt, fingerprints, and other unmentionables faster than you think.

    Make sure your wipes are especially meant for flat-panel monitors or laptop computer screens.

- ✔ **Blank CDs and DVDs:** Most folks still consider an optical drive important, so if you'll miss watching DVD movies and importing/recording audio CDs, I'll bet you've already bought one. Depending on the type of media you're recording — like computer data CDs, DVD movies, or audio CDs — you'll want blank discs for

    - CD-R (record once)

    - CD-RW (record multiple times)

    - DVD-R (record once)

    - DVD-RW (record multiple times)

- ✔ **Cables:** Depending on the external devices and wired network connectivity you'll be using, these are

    - A standard Ethernet cable (for wired networks or high-speed Internet)

    - Thunderbolt or USB cables for devices you already have

Most hardware manufacturers are nice enough to include a cable with their products, but there are exceptions, especially USB printers. *Shame on those cheapskates!*

✔ **A wrist rest for both your keyboard and mouse:** You might have many reasons to buy a new iMac, but I know that a bad case of carpal tunnel syndrome is *not* one of them. Take care of your wrists by adding a keyboard and mouse rest (even for a wireless keyboard/mouse combo, even on a TV tray).

Chapter 2

Life! Give My iMac Life!

*I*f you've already been through Chapter 1, you got as far as unpacking your iMac and connecting at least one cable to it. And unless you bought this computer solely as a work of modern art, it's time to actually turn on your iMac and begin living The Good iLife. (Plus you still get to admire that Apple design whilst using iTunes.) After you get your new beauty powered on, I help you here with an initial checkup on your iMac's health.

I also familiarize you with the initial chores that you need to complete — such as using OS X Setup as well as moving the data and settings from your existing computer to your iMac — before you settle in with your favorite applications.

In this chapter, I assume that OS X Mavericks (version 10.9) was preinstalled on your iMac or that you just completed an upgrade to Mavericks. (If you're upgrading, your iMac is already turned on — and you can skip the next section!)

Throwing the Big Leaf Switch

Your iMac's power switch is located on the back of the computer, at the lower-left corner of the case (as you look at the screen). Press it now to turn on your iMac, and you hear the pleasant startup tone that's been a hallmark of Apple computers for many years now. Don't be alarmed if you don't immediately see anything onscreen because it takes a few seconds for the initial Apple logo to appear.

In my experience, a simple, quick press of the power button on some iMacs sometimes just doesn't do it. Instead, you actually have to hold down the button for a count of two or so before the computer turns on.

While the Apple logo appears, you see a twirling, circular high-tech progress indicator appear that looks like something from a *Star Wars* movie. That's the sign that your iMac is loading Mavericks. Sometimes the twirling circle can take a bit longer to disappear. As long as it's twirling, though, something good is happening — after all, Mavericks has to load file sharing, networking, and printing components (and such).

At last, your patience of a whole 10 to 15 seconds is rewarded, and after a short (but neat) video, you see the Mavericks Setup Assistant appear.

Mark's Favorite Signs of a Healthy iMac

Before you jump into the fun stuff, don't forget an important step — a quick preliminary check to make sure that your iMac survived shipment intact and happy. Although the shipping box that Apple uses for the iMac series is one of the best I've ever encountered in 30 years of swapping computer hardware, your computer could still have met with foul play from its shipping travels.

If you can answer Yes to each of these questions, your iMac likely made the trip without serious damage:

1. **Does the computer's chassis appear undamaged?**

   It's pretty easy to spot damage to your iMac's svelte metal and glass design. Look for scratches, puncture damage, and misalignment of the screen.

2. **Does the LED screen work, and is it undamaged?**

   I'm talking about obvious scratches or puncture damage to your screen. Additionally, you should also check whether any individual dots (or *pixels*) on your LED monitor are obviously malfunctioning. Bad pixels either appear black or in a different color from everything surrounding them.

   Techs call these irritating anarchists *dead pixels*. Unfortunately, many new LED screens include one or two. After all, a 21.5" iMac screen sports literally more than 1 million pixels.

3. **Can you feel a flow of air from the vent on top?**

   Your iMac's Intel processor, hard drive, and power supply generate quite a bit of heat, so the fan system never turns off completely. If you don't feel warm air from the fan system after your iMac has been on for a minute or two, you might have a problem.

4. Do the keyboard and mouse work?

Check your iMac's Bluetooth connection by moving the mouse or running your finger across the trackpad; the cursor should move on your screen. To check the keyboard, press the Caps Lock key and observe whether the green Caps Lock light turns on and off. (Don't forget to check for good batteries in all your wireless input devices and make sure they're turned on.)

If you do notice a problem with your iMac (and you can still use your Safari browser and reach the web), you can make the connection to an Apple support technician at www.apple.com. If your iMac is lying on its back with its foot in the air and you can't get to the Internet, you can check your phone book for a local Apple service center, or call the AppleCare toll-free number at 1-800-275-2273. Chapter 22 also offers troubleshooting information.

Harriet, It's Already Asking Me Questions!

After your iMac is running and you've given it the once-over for obvious shipping damage, your next chore is to set up your iMac. Unlike other tasks in this book, I don't cover the setup process step by step. Apple "tweaks" the questions that you see during setup on a regular basis, and the questions are really very easy to answer. Everything is explained onscreen, complete with onscreen Help if you need it.

However, I do want you to know what to expect as well as what information you need to have at hand. I also want you to know about support opportunities, such as the AppleCare Protection Plan and Apple's iCloud Internet services — hence, this section. Consider it a study guide for whatever your iMac's setup procedure has to throw at you.

Setting up OS X Mavericks

After you start your iMac for the first time — or if you just upgraded from an earlier version of OS X — your iMac will likely automatically launch the Mavericks setup procedure. (Note that some custom install options, like the Archive and Install option, might not launch the Setup procedure.) The setup process takes care of a number of different tasks:

✔ **Setup provides Mavericks with your personal information.**

As I mention in Chapter 1, your iMac ships with a bathtub full of applications, and many of those use your personal data (like your address and telephone number) to automatically fill out your documents.

If that personal stored information starts you worrying about identity theft, I congratulate you. If you're using your common sense, it *should*. However, Apple doesn't disseminate this information anywhere else, and the applications that use your personal data won't send it anywhere, either. And the Safari web browser fills out forms on a web page automatically only if you give your permission.

✔ **Setup configures your language and keyboard choices.**

OS X Mavericks is a truly international operating system, so Setup offers you a chance to configure your iMac to use a specific language and keyboard layout.

✔ **Setup configures your e-mail accounts within Apple Mail.**

If you already have an e-mail account set up with your Internet service provider (ISP), keep that e-mail account information handy to answer these questions. (The list should include the incoming POP3/IMAP and outgoing SMTP mail servers you'll be using, your e-mail address, and your login name and password. Don't worry about those crazy acronyms, though, because your ISP will know exactly what you mean when you ask for this information.) Mavericks can even automatically configure many e-mail accounts for you — including web-based services such as Google Mail, Yahoo! Mail, and AOL Mail — if you supply your account ID and password. *Sweet.*

✔ **Setup allows you to sign up for an Apple ID and Apple's iCloud service.**

iCloud makes it easy to share data automatically between your iMac and iOS 5 (or later) devices (like an iPhone, iPad, or iPod touch), along with Apple e-mail accounts (through both web mail and the Apple Mail application). I go into all these in detail in Chapter 9. For now, just create your Apple ID, sign up for iCloud, and take the opportunity to feel smug about owning an Apple computer.

✔ **Setup sends your registration information to Apple.**

As a proud owner of an iMac, take advantage of the year of hardware warranty support and the free 90 days of telephone support. You have to register to use 'em, but rest assured that all this info is confidential.

✔ **Setup launches Migration Assistant.**

This assistant guides you through the process of *migrating* (an engineer's term for *copying*) your existing user data from your old Mac or PC to your new iMac. Naturally, if your iMac is your first computer, you can skip this step with a song in your heart! (Read more on Migration Assistant in the section "Importing Documents and Data from Your Old Mac.")

Registering your iMac

I'll be honest here: I know that many of us (myself included) don't register every piece of computer hardware we buy. However, your iMac is a different kettle of fish altogether, and I *strongly* recommend that you register your purchase with Apple during the setup process. You spent a fair amount of moolah on your computer, and it's an investment with a significant number of moving parts.

Even the hardiest of techno-wizards would agree with this important Mark's Maxim:

If you don't register your iMac, you can't receive support.

Rest assured that Apple is not one of those companies that constantly pesters you with e-mail advertisements and near-spam. I've registered every Apple computer I've owned, and I've never felt pestered. (And I have an extremely low tolerance for pester.) However, just in case your tolerance is even lower than mine, Apple's registration process allows you to disable this e-mail communication.

Importing Documents and Data from Your Old Mac

If you're upgrading from an older Mac computer running OS X to your new iMac, I have great news for you: Apple includes the Migration Assistant utility application that can help you copy (whoops, I mean, *migrate*) all sorts of data from your old Mac to your new machine. The list of stuff that gets copied over includes

- ✔ **User accounts:** If you set up multiple user accounts (so that more than one person can share the computer), the utility ports them all to your new iMac.

- ✔ **Network settings:** Boy, howdy, this is a real treat for those with manual network settings provided by an ISP or network administrator! Migration Assistant can re-create the entire network environment of your old Mac on your new iMac.

- ✔ **System Preferences settings:** If you're a fan of tweaking and customizing OS X to fit you like a glove, rejoice. Migration Assistant actually copies over all the changes that you've made within System Preferences on your old Mac! (Insert sound of angelic chorus of cherubim and seraphim: *Hallelujah!*)

✔ **Documents:** The files in your Documents folder(s) are copied to your new iMac.

✔ **Applications:** Migration Assistant tries its best to copy over the third-party applications that you've installed in your Applications folder on the older Mac. I say *tries its best* because you might have to reinstall some applications, anyway. Some developers create applications that spread out all sorts of files across your hard drive, and Migration Assistant just can't keep track of those nomadic files. Too, some other applications make the trek just fine, but you might have to re-enter their serial numbers.

Setup launches Migration Assistant automatically if you indicate that you need to transfer stuff during the setup process, but you can also launch Migration Assistant manually at any time. Click the Launchpad icon on the Dock (which bears a rocket ship icon); then click the Utilities icon (which, depending on your installation, can also be called Other). Click the Migration Assistant icon to launch the application.

To use Migration Assistant to copy your system from your older Mac, you need one of the following:

✔ **FireWire cable** (compatible with most Macs made within the last five years or so): If you don't already have one, you can pick up a standard FireWire cable at your local Maze o' Wires electronics store or at your computer store. Current iMac models do not have FireWire ports, so if you have the latest model — and you're connecting to an older Mac with FireWire ports — you'll need to use another method in this list or buy an Apple Thunderbolt to FireWire adapter for $30 at the Apple Store (http://store.apple.com).

Some recent iMac models included only a FireWire 800 port. If you're upgrading from an older Mac that has only FireWire 400 ports to a more recent iMac with a FireWire 800 port, you'll need a FireWire cable and a 400-to-800 adapter, which you can typically get at any large computer store (or through Amazon or eBay).

✔ **Thunderbolt cable** (compatible with the most recent iMac, Mac mini, and MacBook laptops): A Thunderbolt connection will transfer your data between the two computers at lightning speed! (Bad pun intended.) Apple sells a Thunderbolt cable that's perfect for the job for $49 at the Apple Store.

✔ **Wired or wireless network connection between the computers:** If you've already hooked up your new iMac to your wired or wireless Ethernet network while using Setup Assistant, eschew cables completely and click Use Network instead! (Note, however, that a Wi-Fi migration will be much slower than migrating with either a direct cable connection or a wired network connection.)

> ✔ **Time Machine external drive or an AirPort Time Capsule backup**
> **unit:** If you're using Time Machine on the older Mac with an external
> drive, you can migrate directly from your most recent backup. The same
> option applies if you've invested in Apple's AirPort Time Capsule wire-
> less backup device.

If you'll be using a FireWire or Thunderbolt cable, make sure that the two
machines are connected with the cable first. If you're using a network connection, both computers should be connected to the network. Typically,
you'll also have to load Migration Assistant on the source Mac (or a free
Windows program downloaded from `www.apple.com`, if the source
computer is a PC.)

After the two computers are connected, simply follow the onscreen instructions displayed within the Migration Assistant window. The application will
lead you through the process step by step. If you need to return to the previous step at any time, click the Back button that appears at the bottom of the
screen.

Manually Importing Documents and Data from Windows

If you're a classic Windows-to-Mac *Switcher,* you made a wise choice, especially if you're interested in the creative applications within the iLife suite!
Although you can choose to start your Apple computing life anew, you probably want to migrate some of your existing documents and files from that
tired PC to your bright, shiny new iMac.

If you're switching from a PC to a Mac, you can use the Windows Migration
Assistant on your PC (available from Apple's website) to automatically
handle most of your migration tasks for you, and you should witness the
miracle of your PC's photos, video, music, and documents suddenly appearing on your iMac. Unfortunately, you'll have some exceptions. Some stuff
won't make the move because the Windows Migration Assistant simply can't
recognize and transfer files and folders from some nonstandard locations.
For example, folders you created yourself at the root of your PC's hard drive
likely won't be recognized.

Here's the good news, though: You can easily copy those files that weren't
transferred! Moving items manually from a USB flash drive or over a network
is easy. (If the target iMac is an older model with a SuperDrive, you can also
move items by using DVDs.)

Switching from a PC to . . . an Apple PC?

With the Mavericks Boot Camp feature, you can actually create a full Windows XP, Vista, Windows 7, or Windows 8 system on your Intel iMac. Yup, Windows and Mavericks coexist peacefully *on the same computer*. However, you have to reboot your computer to use your iMac as a Windows system, and you can't install Windows at all without retaining at least a basic OS X system. (All this is covered in detail in Bonus Chapter 2, which you can download at www.dummies.com/extras/imac.)

This capability brings a whole new meaning to the term *Switcher* because some iMac owners are moving their stuff from Windows (running on their old PC) to . . . well, Windows (running on their new iMac) rather than Mavericks. If you do decide to create a Windows system on your iMac by using Boot Camp, the files and folders on your existing PC can be copied directly by using a good old-fashioned Windows wizard.

The OS X Help system contains an entire subsection on specific tricks that you can use when switching from Windows to Mac, including how to connect to a Windows network and how to directly connect the two computers.

In general, you can move documents, movies, photos, and music without a problem. Table 2-1 illustrates what can be moved between Windows and OS X as well as the application that you use in Mavericks to open those files and documents.

Table 2-1	Moving Media and Documents betwixt Computers		
File Type	*Windows Location*	*OS X Location*	*Mac Application*
Music files	My Music folder	Music folder	iTunes
Video and movie files	My Videos folder	Movies folder	QuickTime/DVD Player/iTunes
Digital photos	My Pictures folder	Pictures folder	iPhoto
Office documents	My Documents folder	Documents folder	Mac Office/iWork

Chapter 3

Introducing the Apple of Your iMac

. . . .

. . . .

*I*n the other books that I've written about OS X Mavericks, I use all sorts of somewhat understated phrases to describe my operating system of choice, such as *elegantly reliable, purely powerful,* and *supremely user friendly.*

But *why* is Mavericks such a standout? To be specific, why do creative professionals and computer techno-wizards across the globe hunger for the very same OS X that runs your iMac? Why is Mavericks so far ahead of both Windows 7 and 8 in features and performance? Good questions, all!

In this chapter, I answer those queries and satisfy your curiosity about your new surfing spot. I introduce the main elements of the Mavericks Desktop, and I show you the fearless Unix heart that beats underneath the sleek exterior of OS X. I also point out the most important similarities between Mavericks and Windows 8, and I outline the resources available if you need help with OS X.

Oh, and I promise to use honest-to-goodness English in my explanations, with a minimum of engineer-speak and indecipherable acronyms. (Hey, you've got to boast about Mavericks in turn to your family and friends. Aunt Harriet might not be as technologically savvy as we are.)

A Quick Tour of the Premises

Mavericks is a special type of software called an *operating system*. You know, *OS,* as in *OS X?* That means that Mavericks essentially runs your iMac as well as allows you to run all your other applications, such as iTunes or Adobe Photoshop. It's the most important computer application — or *software* — that you run.

Think of a pyramid, with Mavericks as the foundation and other applications running on top of it.

You're using the OS when you aren't running a specific application, such as these actions:

- Copying files from a CD to your hard drive
- Choosing a different screen saver

Sometimes, Mavericks even peeks through an application while it's running. For example, Mavericks also controls actions such as these:

- The Open and Save As dialogs that you see when working with files in Photoshop
- The Print dialog that appears when you print a document in Microsoft Word

In this section, I escort you personally around the most important hotspots in Mavericks, and you meet the most interesting onscreen thingamabobs that you use to control your iMac. (I told you I wasn't going to talk like an engineer!)

The Mavericks Desktop

This particular desktop isn't made of wood, and you can't stick your gum underneath. However, your Mavericks Desktop does indeed work much like the surface of a traditional desk. You can store things there, organize things into folders, and take care of important tasks like running other applications. Heck, you've even got a clock and a trash can.

Gaze upon Figure 3-1 and follow along as you venture to your Desktop and beyond.

Meet me at the Dock

The Dock is the closest thing to the pilot's cabin of a jumbo jet that you're likely to find on a Macintosh. It's a pretty versatile combination: one part organizer, one part application launcher, and one part system monitor. From the Dock, you can launch applications, see what's running, and display or hide the application windows.

Apple Menu — Finder Menu Bar

Wolfgang
315.35 GB, 35.72 GB free

Johann
381.73 GB, 203.13 GB free

Ludwig
301.48 GB, 251.69 GB free

Time Machine Backups
499.76 GB, 4.47 GB free

59M-final.pdf

Figure 3-1:
Everything
Mavericks
starts
here — the
OS X
Desktop.

Dock   Application Icon   Application Window   Trash

Each icon in the Dock represents one of the following:

- ✔ An application that you can run (or that is running)
- ✔ An application window that's *minimized* (shrunk)
- ✔ A web page
- ✔ A document or folder on your system
- ✔ A network server or shared folder
- ✔ Your Trash

I cover the Dock in more detail in Chapter 5.

The Dock is highly configurable:

- ✔ It can appear at different sides of the screen.
- ✔ It can disappear until you move your mouse pointer to the edge to call it forth.
- ✔ You can resize it larger or smaller.

Dig those crazy icons

By default, Mavericks always displays at least one icon on your Desktop. Typically, it's the icon representing your iMac's internal hard drive. To open the hard drive and view or use the contents, you double-click the icon. Depending on the preferences you choose, other icons that might appear on your Desktop can include

- ✔ CDs and DVDs
- ✔ An iPod, iPhone, or iPad
- ✔ External hard drives or USB flash drives
- ✔ Applications, folders, and documents
- ✔ Files you downloaded from the Internet
- ✔ Network servers you access

Chapter 4 provides the good stuff on icons and their uses within Mavericks.

There's no food on this menu

The Finder menu bar isn't found in a restaurant. You find it at the top of the Desktop, where you can use it to control your applications. Virtually every application that you run on your iMac has a menu.

To use a menu command, follow these steps:

1. **Click the menu title (like File or Edit).**
2. **Choose the desired command from the list that appears.**

Virtually every Macintosh application has some menu titles, such as File, Edit, and Window. You're likely to find similar commands under these titles. However, only two menu titles are in *every* OS X application that displays a menu bar:

- ✔ The *Apple menu* (which is identified with that jaunty Apple Corporation icon,).
- ✔ The *application menu* (which always bears the name of the active application). For instance, the DVD Player menu title appears when you run the Mavericks DVD Player, and the Word menu group appears when you launch Microsoft Word.

I cover these two common titles in more detail in Chapters 4 and 5.

You can also display a contextual menu — regular human beings call it a *right-click menu* or shortcut menu — by right-clicking (or, as Apple calls it, *secondary-clicking*) your Mavericks Desktop or an application, a folder, or a file icon. I discuss right-click menus in detail in Chapter 4.

There's always room for one more window

You're probably already familiar with the ubiquitous window itself. Both Mavericks and the applications that you run use windows to display things like

- ✔ The documents that you create
- ✔ A web page
- ✔ The contents of your hard drive

Mavericks gives you access to the applications, documents, and folders on your system through Finder windows.

Windows are surprisingly configurable. I cover them at length in Chapter 4.

What's going on underneath?

How the core of your operating system is designed makes more of a difference than all the visual bells and whistles, which tend to be similar between Windows and OS X Mavericks (and Linux as well, for that matter). Time for a Mark's Maxim:

Sure, the elegant exterior is a joy to use, but OS X is a better OS than Windows because of the unique Unix muscle that lies underneath!

Isn't Windows 8 the latest thing?

You've seen highly customized "pocket rocket" compact cars with the flashy paint jobs, huge noisy mufflers, and aerodynamic fiberglass stuff. You might think that these cars are real road racers, but what's underneath is different. The four-cylinder engine that you *don't* see is completely stock. These cars don't perform any better than mundane models straight from the factory.

The same holds true for Microsoft Windows 8 — another attempt by the folks at Redmond to put a modern face on an antique OS. Forget the new Start screen and that doggone disappearing Start button: Windows 8 is simply more of the same. Sure, it's optimized for touchscreen tablets and PCs with support for gestures, but you won't find a boatload of new performance features in 8; instead, Microsoft focused on making Windows 8 simpler to use. (Unfortunately, if you're running PC hardware, the only other practical choice for a computing novice is Linux, which is still regarded as too complex by major manufacturers like Dell and Hewlett-Packard. Therefore, with a PC, you're usually stuck with Windows 7 or Windows 8 — or you've picked up a very expensive paperweight.)

So what should you and I look for in an OS? Keep in mind that today's computer techno-wizard demands four requirements for a truly high-powered software wonderland — and OS X Mavericks easily meets all four:

- ✔ **Reliability:** Your OS has to stay up and running reliably for as long as necessary — I'm talking *months* here — without lockups or error messages. If an application crashes, the rest of your work should remain safe, and you should be able to shut down the offending software.

- ✔ **Performance:** If your computer has advanced hardware, your OS must be able to use those resources to speed things up big time. The OS has to be highly configurable, and it has to be updated often to keep up with the latest in computer hardware.

"Mark, what do you mean by advanced hardware?" Well, if you're already knowledgeable about state-of-the-art hardware, examples include

  - • True 64-bit computing

  - • Multicore processors (like the Intel chip in the latest iMacs, which have four "virtual" processors on one chip)

  - • A huge amount of RAM (32GB on the iMac)

  - • Multiple hard drives used as a RAID array

  If all that sounds like ancient Sumerian, gleefully ignore this technical drabble and keep reading.

- ✔ **Security:** You want your stuff to remain your own — which is why Mavericks offers a strong level of security across your local network and the Internet. If you share your iMac with others, you'll be happy to know that Mavericks keeps track of your personal information and private files, and prevents others from accessing them. Heck, Mavericks even provides parental controls to help safeguard kids using your iMac!

- ✔ **Ease of use:** All the speed, security, and reliability in the world won't help an OS if it's difficult to use.

DOS was the PC OS of choice before the arrival of Windows. It was doomed because it wasn't intuitive or easy to master, requiring a PC owner to remember all sorts of commands that looked like hieroglyphics. (This is one of the reasons that the Macintosh was so incredibly popular in the days of DOS-based PCs. Macs had a mouse, and they were far easier to master and use.)

Similarities with that Windows behemoth

You might have heard of the *Windows Switcher:* a uniquely intelligent species that's becoming more and more common these days. Switchers are former PC owners who have abandoned Windows and bought a Macintosh, thereby joining the Apple faithful running OS X. (Apple loves to document this migration on its website.) Because today's Macintosh computers are significantly faster than their PC counterparts — and you get neat software, such as Mavericks, the iLife suite, and the iWork suite when you buy a new Mac — switching makes perfect sense.

Switchers aren't moving to totally unfamiliar waters. Windows 7/8 and Mavericks share a number of important concepts. Familiarizing yourself with Mavericks takes far less time than you might think.

Here's an overview of the basic similarities between the two operating systems:

- **The Desktop:** The Mavericks Desktop is a neat representation of a real physical desktop, and Windows uses the same idea:

    - You can arrange files, folders, and applications on your Desktop to help keep things handy.

    - Application windows appear on the Desktop.

- **Drives, files, and folders:** Data is stored in files on your hard drive(s), and those files can be organized in folders. Both Mavericks and Windows use the same file/folder concept.

- **Specific locations:** Both Windows and Mavericks provide every user with a set of folders to help keep various types of files organized. For example, the My Videos folder that you can use in Windows 7 and 8 corresponds to the Movies folder that you find in your Home folder within Mavericks.

- **Running programs:** Both Mavericks and Windows run programs (or applications) in the same manner:

    - Double-clicking an application icon launches that application.

    - Double-clicking a document runs the corresponding application and then automatically loads the document.

- **Window control:** Yep, both operating systems use windows, and those windows can be resized, hidden (or minimized), and closed in similar fashions. (Are you starting to see the connections here?)

- **Drag-and-drop:** One of the basics behind a GUI (a ridiculous acronym that stands for *graphical user interface*) like Windows and Mavericks is the ability to drag documents and folders around to move, delete, copy, and open them. Drag-and-drop is one of the primary advantages of both of these operating systems because copying a file by dragging it from one window to another is intuitive and easy enough for a kid to accomplish.

- **Editing:** Along the same lines as drag-and-drop, both Mavericks and Windows offer similar cut-and-paste editing features. You've likely used Cut, Copy, and Paste for years, so this is familiar stuff.

But what if you feel homesick for your Windows Desktop from time to time? No worries — you can actually run Windows effortlessly on your iMac! To find out how to use Apple's Boot Camp feature, you can go to `www.dummies.com/extras/imac` and download Bonus Chapter 2.

Calling for Help

You can call on these resources if you need additional help while you're discovering how to tame the Mavericks.

Some of the help resources are located on the Internet, so your web browser will come in handy.

The Mavericks built-in Help Center

Sometimes the help you need is as close as the Help title on the menu bar. You can get help for either

- **A specific application:** Just click Help. Then click in the Search box and type a short phrase that sums up your query (such as *startup keys*). You'll see a list of help topics appear on the menu. Just click a topic to display more information.

- **Actions and functions (topics):** Click a Finder window and then click Help on the menu bar. Again, you'll see the Search box, and you can enter a word or phrase to find within the Help system. To display the Help Center window, click the Help Center item under the Search box.

The Apple web-based support center

Apple has online product support areas for every hardware and software product that it manufactures. Visit www.apple.com and click the Support tab at the top of the web page.

The Search box works just like the Mac OS Help system, but the Knowledge Base that Apple provides online has a *lot* more answers.

Magazines

Many magazines (both in print and online) offer tips and tricks on using and maintaining OS X Mavericks.

My personal online favorites are Macworld (www.macworld.com) and MacLife (www.maclife.com).

Mac support websites

Numerous private individuals and groups offer support forums on the web, and you can often find help from other Mac owners on these sites within a few hours of posting a question.

I'm very fond of the CNET forum MacFixIt (www.macfixit.com) and Mac OS X Hints (http://forums.macosxhints.com).

Local Mac user groups

I'd be remiss if I didn't mention your local Mac user group. Often, a user group maintains its own website and discussion forum. If you can wait until the next meeting, you can even ask your question and receive a reply from a real-live human being in real time . . . quite a thrill in today's web-riffic world!

Part II
Shaking Hands with Mac OS X

Find out how to add and import contacts easily at www.dummies.com/extras/imac.

In this part . . .

- ✔ Master common tasks within OS X Mavericks
- ✔ Customize your OS X Desktop
- ✔ Use System Preferences to fine-tune how Mavericks works
- ✔ Use Spotlight to search your entire system in seconds
- ✔ Keep track of all your stuff using Notes, Reminders, and Contacts
- ✔ Locate places and navigate with the Maps application

Chapter 4

Opening and Closing and Clicking and Such

In This Chapter

▶ Introducing the highlights of the Finder

▶ Discussing that missing button on your pointing device

▶ Launching and quitting applications

▶ Identifying and selecting icons

▶ Using keyboard shortcuts to speed things up

▶ Managing windows in Mavericks

*A*h, the Finder — many admire its scenic beauty, but don't ignore its unsurpassed power nor its many moods. And send a postcard while you're there.

Okay, so the OS X Finder might not be *quite* as majestic as the mighty Mississippi River, but it's the basic toolbox that you use every single day while piloting your iMac. The Finder includes the most common elements of Mavericks: window controls, common menu commands, icon fun (everything from launching applications to copying files), network connections, keyboard shortcuts, and even emptying the Trash. In fact, one could say that if you master the Finder and find how to use it efficiently, you're on your way to becoming a power user! (My editor calls this the Finder "window of opportunity." She's a hoot.)

That's what this chapter is designed to do: This is your Finder tour guide, and we're ready to roll.

Working within the Finder

This is a hands-on tour, with none of that "On your right, you'll see the historic Go menu" for you! Time to get off the bus and start the tour with Figure 4-1, in which I show you around the most important elements of the Finder. (In the upcoming section "Performing Tricks with Finder Windows," I give you a close-up view of window controls.)

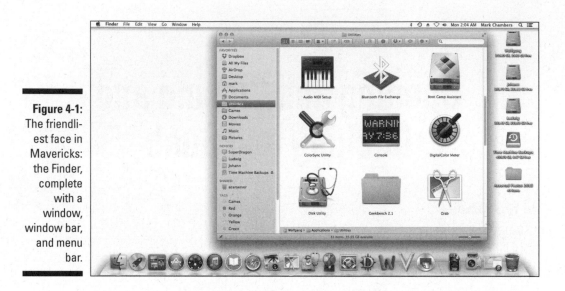

Figure 4-1:
The friendliest face in Mavericks: the Finder, complete with a window, window bar, and menu bar.

The popular attractions include

✔ **The Apple menu (⌘):** This is a special menu because it appears both in the Finder and within every application menu that you run. It doesn't matter whether you're in iTunes or Adobe Photoshop or Microsoft Word: If you can see a menu bar, the Apple menu is there. The Apple menu contains common commands to use no matter where you are in Mavericks, such as Restart, Shut Down, and System Preferences.

✔ **The Finder menu bar:** Whenever the Finder is ready to use (or, in Mac-speak, whenever the Finder is the *active* application, rather than another application), the Finder menu bar appears at the top of your screen. You know the Finder is active and ready when the word *Finder* appears at the left of the menu bar (just to the right of the Apple menu).

In case you're brand-new to computers, a *menu* is simply a list of commands. For example, you click the File menu and then choose Save to save a document. When you click a menu, it extends down so that you can see the commands it includes. While the menu is extended, you can choose any enabled menu item (just click it) to perform that action. You can tell that an item is enabled if its name appears in black. Conversely, a menu command is disabled if it is grayed out — clicking it does nothing.

When you see a menu path, like this example — File⇨Save — it's just a visual shortcut that tells you to click the File menu and then choose Save from the drop-down menu that appears.

✔ **The Desktop:** Your Desktop serves the same purpose as your physical desktop: You can store stuff here (files, folders, alias icons, and so on), and it's a solid, stable surface where you can work comfortably. Application windows appear on the Desktop, for example, as do other applications, such as your Stickies notes and your DVD player. Just double-click an application or document icon on the Desktop to launch it.

You can easily customize your Desktop. For example, you can use your own images to decorate the Desktop, organize it to store new folders and documents, arrange icons how you like, or put the Dock in another location. Don't worry — I cover all this in other areas of the book — I just want you to know that you don't have to settle for what Apple gives you as a default Desktop.

✔ **All sorts of icons:** This is a Macintosh computer, after all, replete with tons of make-your-life-easier tools. Icons can appear on your Desktop as well as within the Finder window itself. Each icon is a shortcut to a file, folder, network connection, or device in your system, including applications that you run and documents that you create. Refer to Figure 4-1 to see the icon for my iMac's internal hard drive (named Wolfgang) at the upper-right corner of the Desktop.

Sometimes you click an icon to watch it do its thing (like icons in the Dock, which I cover next), but usually you double-click an icon to make something happen.

If you're using a late-model iMac, you may be able to share files with other Macs on your local network using the AirDrop feature in Mavericks. For the full scoop on AirDrop, visit Chapter 21.

✔ **The Dock:** The Dock is an organizational tool for your favorite applications, documents, folders, network connections, and websites. You can also refer to it to see what applications are running. Click an icon there to open the item. For example, the postage-stamp icon represents the Apple Mail application, and clicking the spiffy compass icon launches your Safari web browser.

✔ **The Finder window:** Finally! The basic Finder window in Figure 4-1 displays the contents of my Utilities folder. You use Finder windows to launch applications; perform disk chores, such as copying and moving files; and navigate your hard drive.

Pointing in a Mac World

Mavericks takes a visual approach to everything, and what you see in Figure 4-1 is designed for point-and-click convenience. You click (or double-click) an item, it opens, you do your thing, and life is good. If you've grazed on the other side of the fence — one of Those Who Were Once Windows Users — you're probably accustomed to using a mouse with at least two buttons. This brings up the nagging question: "Hey, Mark! Where the heck are my mouse buttons?" Or perhaps you're thinking even farther out of the box, and you ordered a Magic Trackpad as your pointing device of choice — again, no buttons!

In a nutshell, the "buttons" on your iMac's Magic Mouse (or Magic Trackpad) are the entire top surface! Although you won't see any separate buttons for clicking, your Magic pointing device can tell when you tap with one finger (to single-click). Owners of a Magic Trackpad should think "tap" whenever they read "click" in the Apple world. If you've used an iPhone, iPad, or iPod touch, the idea of *tapping* something onscreen makes perfect sense.

To configure everything Magic Mouse — including all your buttons and your double-click/tracking/scrolling speeds — visit the Mouse pane within System Preferences. You can also configure your wireless mouse from here as well. Similarly, you can configure your wireless Magic Trackpad using the Trackpad pane. (More on the System Preferences window in the next section.)

Speaking of right-clicking, you can easily configure your Apple pointing device to recognize a right-click (also called a *secondary click*) within System Preferences. Tapping the top-right corner (of a Magic Mouse) or tapping with two fingers (on the Magic Trackpad) performs the same default function in Mavericks that clicking the right mouse button does in Windows. Namely, when you right-click most items — icons, documents, even your Desktop — you get a *shortcut menu* of things. That is, you get more commands specific to that item. (To keep familiar things familiar, I call it the "right-click menu," and I promise to refer to it as such for the rest of the book.)

If you're using a Magic Trackpad with your iMac, never use any object other than your finger (or a trackpad stylus) on the trackpad surface! That means no pencils (no, not even the eraser end), pens, or chopsticks; they can damage your trackpad in no time at all. And no, that doesn't bode well for ladies with long fingernails.

Figure 4-2 illustrates a typical convenient right-click menu within a Finder window.

But that's not all. Apple's series of Multi-Touch gestures for your Magic Mouse or Trackpad includes all sorts of handy time-saving commands! Depending on the changes you make within the Mouse and Trackpad panes in System Preferences, these gestures can include

Figure 4-2:
Well-
adjusted
folks call
this a right-
click menu.

✔ **Double-clicking:** Tap twice with one finger to double-click.

✔ **Scrolling:** To move in any direction within a document window, just swipe two fingers across the surface in that direction.

✔ **Two-finger paging:** Swipe your thumb and first fingertip to the left or right across the surface to page through a document or move to the next or previous image in a set (like web pages in Safari or photos in your iPhoto library).

✔ **Two-finger zooming:** Pinching your thumb and first fingertip toward each other on the surface zooms in on a document or image. The reverse (moving your fingertips away from each other) zooms out. You can also enable zooming with a modifier key.

✔ **Three-finger full-screen switching:** Swipe your thumb and first two fingertips to the left or right across the surface to move between open applications in full-screen mode.

✔ **Rotate:** Place your thumb and index finger on the trackpad and turn clockwise (or counterclockwise) to rotate a photo.

✔ **Perform actions within OS X itself:** Using the combination of thumb and fingers you specify, you can configure the display and operation of many features within Mavericks.

I know all these gestures sound like a kids' gymnastics meet, but they'll soon become second nature to you. I recommend that you visit the Mouse and Trackpad panes in System Preferences and simply experiment with the possibilities of Multi-Touch — each gesture is demonstrated with a video clip, making the gestures very easy to learn!

Launching and Quitting for the Lazy iMac Owner

Now it's time for you to pair your newly found mouse and trackpad acumen with the Mavericks Finder window. Follow along this simple exercise. Move your cursor over the iTunes icon on the Dock (the round blue icon bearing a musical note), and click once. Whoosh! Mavericks *launches* (or starts) the iTunes application, and you see a window much like the one in Figure 4-3.

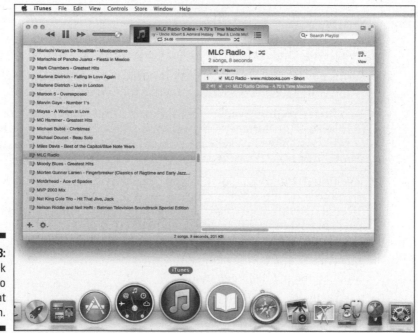

Figure 4-3: Click a Dock icon to launch that application.

If an application icon is already selected (which I discuss in the next section), you can simply press ⌘+O to launch it. The same key shortcut works with documents, too.

Dig that crazy Launchpad!

You can customize your Launchpad display by dragging icons to display in the order you prefer. For example, I have all the applications I use the most on the first Launchpad page. Drag an application icon to the right or left side of the screen to move it to another page.

Just as a Finder window does, Launchpad allows you to create folders to help you organize your applications. To create a folder within Launchpad, drag one application icon on top of another and then add other icons by dragging them to the folder (or remove them by dragging them out of the folder). To run an application within a folder, click the folder icon to display the icons within it and then click the desired application.

Oh, and there's no need to stick with the boring folder names assigned by Launchpad. To change a folder name, click the folder to open it and then click the folder name to display a text-editing box. Type the new moniker for the folder and press Return.

If you want to remove an application from Launchpad — **which also deletes the application from your iMac entirely** — click the icon and continue pressing on the trackpad until the icons start to wiggle. (Yes, you read that correctly; I said wiggle. iPhone and iPad owners know what I mean.) Click the tiny Delete button that appears next to the icon — the one with the *x* — and the icon disappears. Press Esc to stop all that wiggling. (Note that the applications supplied with Mavericks can't be deleted this way.)

Besides the Dock, you have several other ways to launch an application or open a document in Mavericks:

- **Using Launchpad:** Click the Launchpad icon on the Dock (it's the second one to the right of the Finder icon, sporting a rocket-ship icon) to display all your application icons in a full-screen display. If you have more than one screen (or *page*) worth of applications, press the arrow keys to move between Launchpad pages (with a Magic Trackpad or Magic Mouse, swipe two fingers to the left or right). To launch an application, just click the icon. (If you're a proud owner of an iPhone, iPad, or iPod touch, you'll be very familiar with Launchpad because it corresponds directly to the Home screen on those devices.)

- **From the Apple menu (🍎):** A number of applications can always be launched anywhere within Mavericks from the Apple menu:

  - *System Preferences:* This is where you change all sorts of settings, such as your display background and how icons appear.

  - *Software Update:* This uses the Internet to see whether update patches are available for your Apple software, as I discuss in Chapter 24.

  - *App Store:* This launches the App Store and displays software that you can download for your iMac.

✔ **From the Desktop:** If you have a document that you created, an application icon, or an application *alias* (shortcut) on your Desktop, you can launch or open it here by double-clicking that icon (tapping with one finger twice in rapid succession when the cursor is on top of the icon).

Double-clicking a device or network connection on your Desktop opens the contents in a Finder window. This trick works for CDs and DVDs that you've loaded as well as for external hard drives and USB flash drives. Applications and documents launch from a CD, a DVD, or an external drive just the same as they launch from your internal drive (the one that's named Macintosh HD), so you don't have to copy stuff from the external drive just to use it. (You can't change the contents of most CDs and DVDs; they're read-only, so you can't write to them.)

✔ **From the Recent Items selection:** When you click the Apple menu (🍎) and hover your mouse over the Recent Items menu item, the Finder displays all the applications and documents that you used over the past few computing sessions. Click an item in this list to launch or open it.

✔ **From the Login Items list:** Login Items are applications that Mavericks launches automatically each time you log in to your user account.

I cover Login Items in detail in Chapter 20.

✔ **From the Finder window:** You can also double-click an icon within the confines of a Finder window to open it (for documents), launch it (for applications), or display the contents (for a folder).

The Quick Look feature can display the contents of just about any document or file — without actually opening the corresponding application! *Sweet.* To use Quick Look from a Finder window, click a file to select it, click the Action button (which bears an eye icon) on the Finder window toolbar, and then choose Quick Look. My favorite method of using Quick Look? Just click a file to select it and press the spacebar!

After you finish using an application, you can quit that application to close its window and return to the Desktop. Here are a number of ways to quit an application:

✔ **Press ⌘+Q.** This keyboard shortcut quits virtually every Macintosh application on the planet. Just first make sure that the application that you want to quit is active!

✔ **Choose the Quit command from the application's menu.** To display the Quit command, click the application's name — its menu — from the menu bar. This menu is always to the immediate right of the Apple (🍎) menu. For example, Safari displays a Safari menu, and that same spot in the menu is taken up by Calendar when Calendar is the active application. In Figure 4-3, look for the iTunes menu, right next to 🍎.

128986

✓ **Choose Quit from the Dock.** You can right-click an application's icon on the Dock and then choose Quit from the right-click menu that appears.

A running application displays a small blue ball under its icon in the Dock.

✓ **Click the Close button on the application window (refer to Figure 4-8).** Some applications quit entirely when you close their window, like the System Preferences window or the Apple DVD Player. Other applications might continue running without any window, like Safari or iTunes; to close these applications, you have to use another method in this list.

✓ **Choose Force Quit from the Apple menu.** *This is a last-resort measure!* Use this only if an application has frozen and you can't use another method in this list to quit. Force-quitting an application doesn't save any changes to any open documents within that application!

Juggling Folders and Icons

Finder windows aren't just for launching applications and opening the files and documents that you create. You can also use the icons within a Finder window to select one or more specific items or to copy and move items from place to place within your system.

A field observer's guide to icons

Not all icons are created equal. Earlier in this chapter, I introduce you to your iMac's hard drive icon on the Desktop, but here is a little background on the other types of icons that you might encounter during your iMac travels:

✓ **Hardware:** These are your storage devices (such as your hard drive) as well as external peripherals (such as your iPod, DVD drive, USB flash drive, and printer).

✓ **Applications:** These icons represent the applications (or programs) that you can launch. Most applications have a custom icon that incorporates the company's logo or the specific application logo, so they're very easy to recognize, as you can see in Figure 4-4. Many applications written for Mavericks will automatically load any open documents you were working on when you last closed the application; otherwise, you typically get a new blank document or an Open dialog from which you can choose the existing file you want to open.

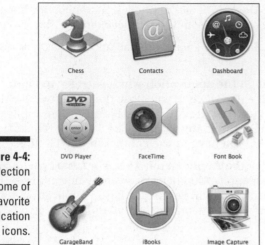

Chess   Contacts   Dashboard

DVD Player   FaceTime   Font Book

GarageBand   iBooks   Image Capture

Figure 4-4:
A collection
of some of
my favorite
application
icons.

✔ **Documents:** Many of the files on your hard drive are documents that can be opened within the corresponding application, and the icon usually looks similar to the application's icon. Double-clicking a document automatically launches the required application (that is, as long as OS X recognizes the file extension or associated application).

✔ **Files:** Most of the file icons on your system are mundane things (such as preference and settings files, text files, log files, and miscellaneous data files), yet most are identified with at least some type of recognizable icon that lets you guess what purpose the file serves. You also come across generic file icons that look like a blank sheet of paper (used when Mavericks has no earthly idea what application opens that type of file).

✔ **Aliases:** An *alias* acts as a link to another item elsewhere on your system. For example, to launch Adobe Acrobat, you can click an Adobe Acrobat alias icon that you can create on your Desktop rather than click the actual Acrobat application icon. The alias essentially acts the same way as the original icon, but it doesn't take up the same space — only a few bytes for the icon itself, compared with the size of the actual application. Plus, you don't have to go digging through folders galore to find the original application icon. (Windows switchers know an alias as a *shortcut,* and the idea is the same although Macs had it first. Harrumph.) You can always identify an alias by the small curved arrow at the base of the icon, and the icon might also sport the tag `alias` at the end of its name.

You have three ways to create an alias. Here's one:

    a. *Select the item.* The following section has details about selecting icons.

    b. *Choose File➪Make Alias, or press ⌘+L.*

    Figure 4-5 illustrates a trio of typical alias icons.

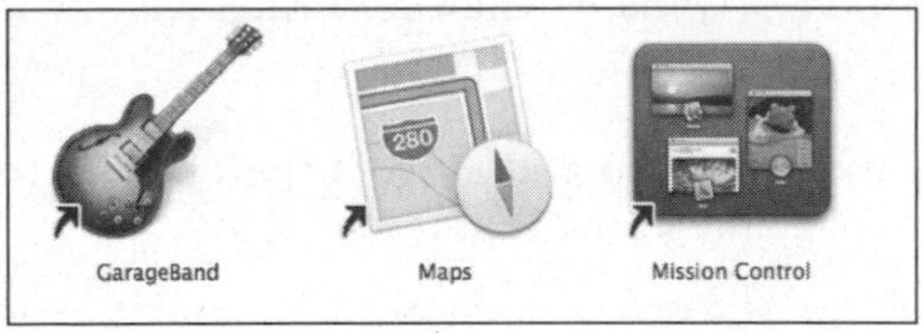

Figure 4-5:
No, not the famous girl-spy TV show. These are alias icons in Mavericks.

GarageBand   Maps   Mission Control

Here's another way to create an alias:

a. Hold down ⌘+Option.

b. Drag the original icon to the location where you want the alias.

Note that this funky method doesn't add the alias tag to the end of the alias icon name (unless you drag it to another location in the same directory)!

Another option for creating an alias is to right-click the original icon and choose Make Alias.

So why bother to use an alias? Three good reasons:

✓ **Launch an application or open a document from anywhere on your drive.** Organization *and* convenience . . . life is good.

✓ **Add aliases wherever you need them.** Aliases take up very little hard drive space, and that tiny size allows you to add multiple aliases (and mucho convenience) for a single application without gulping down hard drive real estate.

✓ **Send an alias to the Trash without affecting the original item.** When that work project is finished, you can safely delete a Pages alias without worrying about deleting the actual application icon.

If you move or rename the original file, Mavericks is actually smart enough to update the alias, too! However, if the original file is deleted (or if the original is moved to a different volume, such as an external hard drive), the alias no longer works. (Go figure.)

Selecting items

Often, the menu commands or keyboard commands that you perform in the Finder need to be performed on something: Perhaps you're moving an item to the Trash, or getting more information on the item, or creating an alias for that item. To identify the target of your action to the Finder, you need to select one or more items on your Desktop or in a Finder window. In this section, I show you how to do just that.

Selecting one thing

Mavericks gives you a couple of options when selecting just one item for an upcoming action:

- ✔ **Move your pointer over the item and click.** A dark border (or *highlight*) appears around the icon, indicating that it's selected.

- ✔ **Type the first few letter of the icon's name.** After you type a letter, OS X highlights the first icon that matches that character.

- ✔ **If an icon is already highlighted on your Desktop or within a window, move the selection highlight to another icon in the same location by using the arrow keys.** To shift the selection highlight alphabetically, press Tab (to move in order) or press Shift+Tab (to move in reverse order).

Selecting items in the Finder doesn't actually *do* anything to them by itself. You have to perform an action on the selected items to make something happen.

Selecting a whole bunch of things

You can also select multiple items with aplomb by using one of these methods:

- ✔ **Adjacent items**

  - *Drag a box around them.* In case that sounds like ancient Sumerian, here's the explanation: Click a spot above and to the left of the first item; then hold down your finger on the surface of the mouse and drag the mouse down and to the right. If you're using a track-pad, just hold down your finger while moving it down and to the right. (This is *dragging*, in Mac-speak.) A box outline like the one in Figure 4-6 appears, indicating what you're selecting. Any icons that touch or appear within the box outline are selected when you release the mouse button.

  - *Click the first item to select it and then hold down the Shift key while you click the last item.* Mavericks selects both items and everything between them.

- ✔ **Nonadjacent items:** Select these by holding down the ⌘ key while you click each item.

If you turn it on, the status bar displays additional information on what you're doing within a Finder window. (To check it out, choose View⇨Show Status Bar from the Finder menu.) The status bar tells you how much space is available on the drive you're working in as well as how many items are displayed in the current Finder window. When you select items, it shows you how many you highlighted.

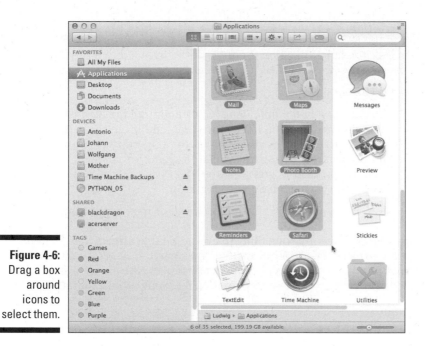

Figure 4-6: Drag a box around icons to select them.

Copying items

Want to copy items from one Finder window to another, or from one location (like a CD) to another (like your Desktop)? *Très* easy. Just use one of these methods:

✔ **On the same drive**

- *To copy one item to another location:* Hold down the Option key (you don't have to select the icon first) and then click and drag the item from its current home to the new location.

  To put a copy of an item within a folder, just drop the item on top of the receiving folder. If you hold the item that you're dragging over the destination folder for a second or two, Mavericks opens a new window so that you can see the contents of the target — this feature is called *spring-loaded folders*, and you can turn it on by clicking Finder➪Preferences.

- *To copy multiple items to another location:* Select them all first (see the earlier section "Selecting a whole bunch of things"), hold down the Option key, and then drag and drop one of the selected items where you want it. All the items that you selected follow the item you drag. (Rather like lemmings. Nice touch, don't you think?)

To help indicate your target when you're copying files, Mavericks highlights the location to show you where the items will end up. (This works whether the target location is a folder or a drive icon.) If the target location is a window, Mavericks adds a highlight to the window border.

✔ **On a different drive**

• *To copy one or multiple items:* Click and drag the icon (or the selected items, if you have more than one) from the original window to a window you open on the target drive. (No need to hold down the Option key whilst dragging.) You can also drag one item (or a selected group of items) and simply drop the items on top of the drive icon on your Desktop.

The items are copied to the top level, or *root,* of the target drive.

If you try to move or copy something to a location that already has an item with the same name, Figure 4-7 illustrates the answer: You get a confirmation dialog that prompts you to decide whether to replace the file or to stop the copy/move procedure and leave the existing file alone. Good insurance, indeed.

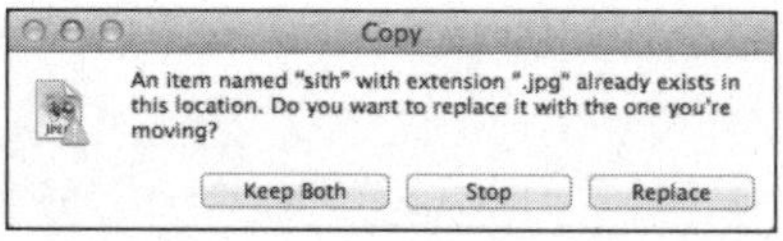

Figure 4-7:
Replace
the existing
file only if
you're sure.

Moving things from place to place

Moving things from one location to another location on the same drive is the easiest action you can take. Just drag the item (or selected items) to the new location. The item disappears from the original spot and reappears in the new spot.

Duplicating in a jiffy

If you need more than one copy of the same item within a folder, use the Mavericks Duplicate command. I use Duplicate often when I want to edit a document but ensure that the original document stays pristine, no matter what. I just create a duplicate and edit that file instead.

To use Duplicate, you can

- ✔ **Click an item to select it and then choose File➪Duplicate.**
- ✔ **Right-click the item and choose Duplicate from the menu.**
- ✔ **Hold down the Option key and drag the original item to another spot in the same window.** When you release the mouse button, the duplicate file appears like magic!

The duplicate item has the word copy appended to its name. A second copy is named copy2, a third is copy3, and so on.

You can also hold down the Option key while dragging the item to a different Finder window, and the duplicate is created there (but without the word copy appended.)

Duplicating a folder also duplicates all the contents of that folder, so creating a duplicate folder can take some time to create if the original folder was stuffed full (or contained very large files). The duplicate folder has copy appended to its name, but the contents of the duplicate folder keep their original names.

Keys and Keyboard Shortcuts to Fame and Fortune

Your iMac keyboard might not be as glamorous as your mouse, but any Macintosh power user will tell you that using keyboard shortcuts is usually the fastest method of performing certain tasks in the Finder, such as saving or closing a file. I recommend committing these shortcuts to memory and putting them to work as soon as you begin using your iMac so that they become second nature to you as quickly as possible.

Special keys on the keyboard

The Apple standard keyboard has a number of special keys that you might not recognize — especially if you've made the smart move and decided to migrate from the chaos that is Windows to OS X! Table 4-1 lists the keys that bear strange hieroglyphics on the Apple keyboard as well as what they do.

Table 4-1		Too-Cool Key Symbols
Action	**Symbol**	**Purpose**
Media Eject	⏏	Ejects a CD or DVD from your optical drive (if you have one)
Audio Mute	🔈	Mutes (and restores) all sound produced by your iMac
Volume Up	🔊	Increases the sound volume
Volume Down	🔉	Decreases the sound volume
Command	⌘	Primary modifier for menus and keyboard shortcuts
Control	⌃	Modifier for shortcuts
Option	⌥	Modifier for shortcuts

Using Finder and application keyboard shortcuts

The Finder is chock-full of keyboard shortcuts that you can use to take care of common tasks. Some of the handiest shortcuts are included in the online Cheat Sheet for this book, which you'll find at

www.dummies.com/cheatsheet/imac

But wait, there's more! Most of your applications also provide their own set of keyboard shortcuts. While you're working with a new application, display the application's Help file and print a copy of the keyboard shortcuts as a handy cheat sheet.

If you've used a PC before, you're certainly familiar with three-key shortcuts — the most infamous being Ctrl+Alt+Delete, the beloved shutdown shortcut nicknamed the Windows Three-Finger Salute. Three-key shortcuts work the same way in Mavericks (but you'll be thrilled to know that you won't need to reboot your iMac using that notorious Windows shortcut)! If you're new to computing, just hold down the first two keys simultaneously and then press the third key to activate a three-key shortcut.

You're not limited to the keyboard shortcuts listed previously, either. Within System Preferences, visit the Keyboard pane and click the Keyboard Shortcuts button to change an existing shortcut or add another.

Performing Tricks with Finder Windows

In this section of your introduction to OS X, I describe basic windows management within Mavericks: how to move things around, how to close windows, and how to make 'em disappear and reappear like magic.

Scrolling in and resizing windows

Can you imagine what life would be like if you couldn't see more than a single window's worth of stuff? Shopping would be curtailed quite a bit — and so would the contents of the folders on your hard drives!

That's why Mavericks adds *scroll bars* that you can click and drag to move through the contents of the window. By default, scroll bars don't appear until you move your pointer close to them, but when they're visible, you can either

- ✔ Click the scroll box and drag it. (For the uninitiated, that means clicking the darker portion of the bar and holding down your finger on the surface of your pointing device while you move in the desired direction.)
- ✔ Click anywhere in the empty area above or below the box to scroll pages one at a time.
- ✔ Hold down the Option key and click anywhere in the empty area above or below the bar to scroll to that spot in the window.

Of course, you can also scroll by moving one finger on the surface of your Magic Mouse or Magic Trackpad in the desired direction (both vertically and horizontally). To set the scroll gesture behavior, open System Preferences and click the Mouse pane (or Trackpad pane, depending on which one you're using).

Figure 4-8 illustrates both vertical and horizontal scroll bars in a typical Finder window.

Often, pressing your Page Up and Page Down keys moves you through a document one page at a time. Also, pressing your arrow keys moves your insertion cursor one line or one character in the four compass directions.

Close

Minimize/Restore

Zoom

Tabs

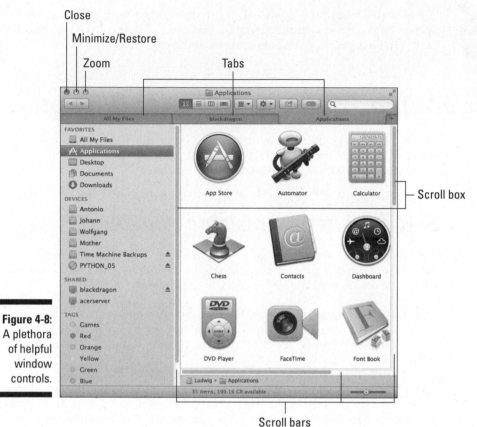

Scroll box

Scroll bars

You can also resize most Finder and application windows by enlarging or reducing the window frame itself. Move your pointer over any edge of the window and then drag the edge in any direction until the window is the precise size you need. You can also drag a corner of the window diagonally to resize two dimensions at once.

Minimizing and restoring windows

Resizing a window is indeed helpful, but maybe you simply want to banish the doggone thing until you need it again. That's a situation for the Minimize button, which also appears in Figure 4-8. A *minimized* window disappears from the Desktop but isn't closed; by default, it simply reappears in the Dock as a miniature icon. Minimizing a window is easy: Move your pointer over the Minimize button at the top-left corner of the window — a minus sign appears in the button to tell you that you're on target — and then click.

Only one can be active at one time

Yes, here's a very special Mark's Maxim in the OS X universe.

> **Only one application window can be active in Mavericks at any time.**

You can always tell which window is active:

✔ **The active window is on top of other windows.**

Some applications provide smaller *floating* windows that offer additional controls and information. Floating windows are subsets of their parent applications, but they may appear on top of the parent window.

Tip: You can still use a window's Close, Minimize, and Zoom buttons when it's inactive.

✔ **Any input you make by typing or by moving your mouse appears in the active window.**

✔ **OS X *dims* inactive windows that you have not minimized.**

Hold down the Shift key whilst you minimize, and prepare to be amazed when the window shrinks in slow motion like Alice in Wonderland!

To restore the window to its full size again (and its original position on the Desktop), just click its window icon in the Dock.

Moving and zooming windows

Perhaps you want to move a window to another location on the Desktop so that you can see the contents of multiple windows at the same time. Click the window's *title bar* (that's the top frame of the window, which usually includes a document or application name) and drag the window anywhere you like. Then lift your finger. (Don't click the icon in the center of the title bar, though. You won't move the window, just the icon itself.)

Many applications can automatically arrange multiple windows for you. Choose the Window⇨Arrange All menu item (if it appears).

To see all that a window can show you, use the Zoom feature to expand any Finder or application window to its maximum practical size. Note that a zoomed window can fill the entire screen, or (if that extra space isn't applicable for the application) the window might expand only to a larger part of the Desktop. To zoom a window, move your pointer over the button (as shown in the earlier Figure 4-8) at the top-left corner of the window. When the plus sign appears in the Zoom button, click to claim the additional territory on your Desktop. (You can click the Zoom button again to automatically return the same window to its previous dimensions.)

Toggling toolbars the Mavericks way

Time to define a window control that's actually *inside* the window for a change. A *toolbar* is a strip of icons that typically appears under the window's title bar (or at the bottom of the window). These icons typically perform the most common actions within an application; the effect is the same as if you use a menu or press a keyboard shortcut. Toolbars are very popular these days. You see 'em within everything from the Finder window to most application windows.

Most windows that include a toolbar also include some method of hiding the toolbar (to save screen real estate for your document). For example, you can toggle the display of the toolbar on and off in a Finder window from the View menu, or you can use the convenient ⌘+Option+T key shortcut to toggle the toolbar display on and off.

Closing windows

When you're finished with an application or no longer need a window open, move your pointer over the Close button at the top-left corner of the window. When the X appears in the button, click it. (And yes, I can get yet another reference out of Figure 4-8, which I'm thinking of nominating as Figure of the Year.)

If you have more than one window open in the same application and you want to close 'em all in one swoop, hold down the Option key whilst you click the Close button in any of the windows.

If you haven't saved a document and you try to close that document's window, Mavericks gets downright surly and prompts you for confirmation. "Hey, human, you don't really want to do this, do you?" If you answer in the affirmative — "Why, yes, machine. Yes, indeed, I do want to throw this away and not save it." — the application discards the document that you were working on. If you decide to save the current state of your document (thereby saving your posterior from harm), you can use the File⇨Save a Version menu command. (For those applications that don't support the OS X Version feature, the menu command is File⇨Save As.)

Using Finder Tabs

With the introduction of Mavericks, OS X now has a powerful new feature you can use to display multiple locations in the same window: *Finder Tabs,* which work just like the tabs in Safari (as well as other popular browsers for both Macs and PCs). To open a new tab in a Finder window, you have a wealth of choices:

- ✔ Click the desired location and press ⌘+T.
- ✔ Right-click the location and choose Open in New Tab.

Doing the full-screen dance

Mavericks provides system-wide support for *full-screen* operation — which means that a single application fills the entire screen without displaying a window frame or traditional Finder menu bar.

The method you use to switch to full-screen mode varies within applications, so there's no One Menu Command or One Keyboard Shortcut that will always do the deed. Most of the applications that are included with OS X Mavericks use View⇨Enter Full Screen, and many applications have a button you can click in the window to switch back and forth. You may also see a button with a double-diagonal arrowhead icon in the upper-right corner of the window.

So how do you switch among applications if they're all in full-screen mode?

✔ If you use a mouse, you can move your pointer to the bottom of the screen to display the Dock, where you can click another application to switch to it.

✔ You can invoke Mission Control and choose another application from there.

✔ If you're working with a Magic Trackpad or Magic Mouse, swipe three fingers to the left or right across the surface.

✔ From the keyboard, use the ⌘+Tab shortcut to cycle through the applications you have running.

✔ Select the location and click the New Tab button (which bears a plus sign) at the right side of the window.

✔ Click the Action icon (which bears a gear icon) in any Finder window toolbar and choose New Tab.

For example, if you're working on an iMovie project, you might create tabs using the Applications item in the Finder window sidebar and a folder (or even a DVD disc or shared drive) named Work that contains your video clips. The location appears as a new tab immediately under the toolbar. You can open as many tabs as you like. To close a tab, hover your cursor over it and click the X button that appears. And you guessed it, the incredibly hardworking Figure 4-8 illustrates three Finder Tabs at work.

So why all the hullaballoo? Think about switching between multiple locations on your Mac *instantly,* and you start to understand why this crusty old Mac fanatic is so excited! Just click a tab to switch to that location; you can even drag files and folders from tab to tab. You can drag the Finder Tabs themselves to reorder them as you like.

You can also set new folders to open in tabs instead of windows. Just click the Finder menu at the top of your Desktop, choose Preferences, and then select the Open Folders in Tabs Instead of New Windows check box to enable it.

Chapter 5

A Plethora of Powerful Fun

*W*hen you're no longer a novice to Mavericks and the basics of the Finder, turn your attention to a number of more advanced topics 'n tricks to turn you into an iMac power user — which, after all, is the goal of every civilized consciousness on Planet Earth.

Consider this chapter a grab bag of Mavericks knowledge. Sure, I jump around a little, but these topics are indeed connected by a common thread: They're all surefire problem-solvers and speeder-uppers. (I can't believe the latter is really a word, but evidently it is. My editors told me so.)

Home, Sweet Home Folder

Each user account that you create within Mavericks is actually a self-contained universe. For example, each user has a number of unique characteristics and folders devoted just to that person, and Mavericks keeps track of everything that a user changes or creates. (In Chapter 20, I describe the innate loveliness of multiple users living in peace and harmony on your iMac.)

This unique universe includes a different system of folders for each user account on your system. The top-level folder uses the short name that Mavericks assigns when that user account is created. Naturally, the actual folder name is different for each person, so Mac techno-types typically refer to this folder as your *Home folder.* (Mine is called mark, as you'll see in upcoming figures.)

Each account's Home folder contains a set of subfolders, including

- ✔ Movies
- ✔ Music
- ✔ Pictures
- ✔ Downloads (for files you download via Safari and Mail attachments that you save to disk)
- ✔ Sites (for web pages created by [or provided to] the user)
- ✔ Documents (created by the user)

Although you can store your stuff at the *root* (top level) of your hard drive, that gaggle of files, folders, and aliases can get very crowded and confusing very quickly. Here's a Mark's Maxim to live by:

Your Home folder is where you hang out and where you store your stuff. Use it to make your computing life *much* easier!

Create subfolders within your Documents folder to organize your files and folders even further. For example, I always create a subfolder in my Documents folder for every book that I write so that I can quickly and easily locate all the documents and files associated with that book project.

I discuss security within your Home folder and what gets stored where in Chapter 20. For now, Figure 5-1 shows how convenient your Home folder is to reach because it appears in the Finder window Sidebar (on the left). One click of your Home folder, and all your stuff is within easy reach.

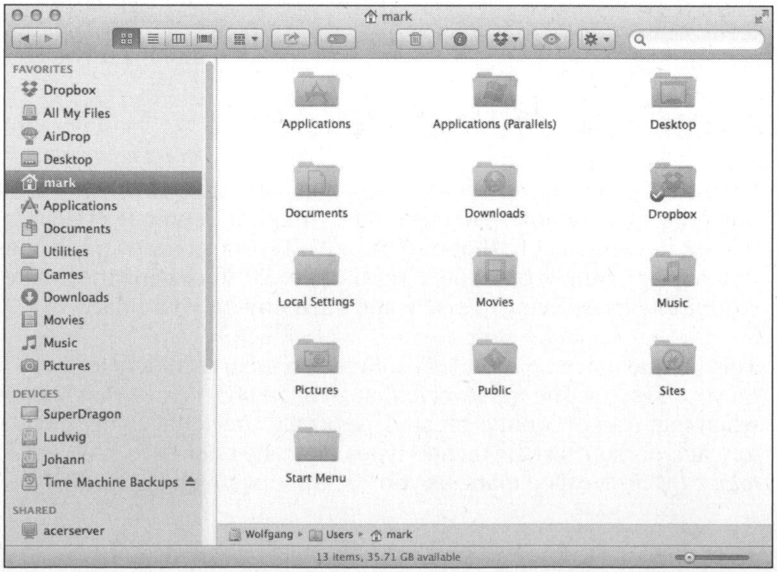

Figure 5-1:
Your Home folder is the central location for all your stuff on your iMac.

In addition to the Finder window Sidebar, you can reach your Home folder in other convenient ways:

- ✔ **From the Go menu:** Choose Go➪Home to display your Home folder immediately from the Finder window. Alternatively, you can press ⌘+Shift+H to accomplish the same thing.

- ✔ **From within Open and Save dialogs:** The standard File Open and File Save dialogs displayed by Mavericks also include the same Home folder (and subfolder) icons as the Finder window Sidebar.

- ✔ **Within any new Finder window you open:** If you like, you can set every Finder window that you open to open automatically within your Home folder.

    a. *Choose Finder➪Preferences and click the General button on the toolbar to display the dialog that you see in Figure 5-2.*

    b. *Click the arrows at the right side of the New Finder Windows Show pop-up menu.*

    A menu pops up (hence the name).

    c. *Click your Home folder entry in the menu.*

    d. *Click the Close button at the top-left corner of the dialog.*

    You're set to go. From now on, every Finder window you open displays your Home folder as the starting location!

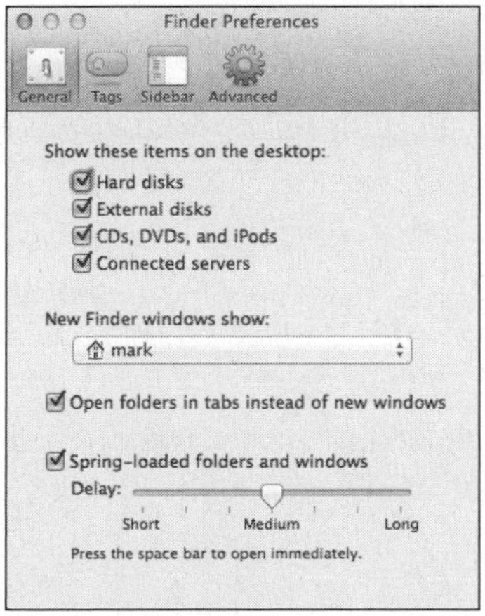

Figure 5-2:
Set
Mavericks
to open
your Home
folder within
new Finder
windows.

Here's another reason to use your Home folder to store your stuff: Mavericks expects your stuff to be there when you migrate your files from an older Mac to a new Mac.

Arranging Your Desktop

Many folks put all their documents, pictures, and videos on their Mavericks Desktop because the file icons are easy to locate! Your computing stuff is right in front of you . . . or *is* it?

Call me a finicky, stubborn fussbudget — go ahead, I don't mind — but I prefer a clean Mavericks Desktop without all the iconic clutter. In fact, my Desktop usually has just three or four icons even though I use my iMac several hours every day. It's an organizational thing; I work with literally hundreds of applications, documents, and assorted knickknacks daily. Sooner or later, you'll find that you're using that many, too. When you keep your stuff crammed on your Desktop, you end up having to scan your screen for one particular file, an alias, or a particular type of icon, which ends up taking you more time to locate it on your Desktop than in your Documents folder!

Plus, you'll likely find yourself looking at old icons that no longer mean anything to you, or stuff that's covered in cobwebs that you haven't used in years. Stale icons . . . *yuck.*

I recommend that you arrange your Desktop so that you see only a couple of icons for the files or documents that you use the most. Leave the rest of the Desktop for that cool image of your favorite actor or actress.

Besides keeping things clean, I can recommend a number of other favorite tweaks that you can make to your Desktop:

✔ **Keep Desktop icons arranged as you like.**

a. *Close all windows and right-click any open space within your Desktop to display the Finder menu.*

b. *From the right-click menu, choose Show View Options.*

c. *From the Sort By pop-up menu, choose the criteria that Mavericks uses to automatically arrange your Desktop icons, including the item name, the last modification date, or the size of the items.*

I personally like things organized by name. You can also quickly change your sorting criteria by right-clicking any open space and choosing Sort By.

✔ **Choose a favorite background.**

a. *Tap two fingers on the surface of your Magic Mouse (or Magic Trackpad) over any open spot on your Desktop. (Or, if you use an older pointing thing with a right mouse button, click that instead.)*

b. *From the right-click menu that appears, choose Change Desktop Background.*

You see the Desktop & Screen Saver pane within System Preferences, as shown in Figure 5-3. Browse through the various folders of background images that Apple provides, a range of solid colors, or use an image from your iPhoto library or Pictures folder.

✔ **Display all the peripherals and network connections on your system.**

> a. *Click any open space on your Desktop to switch to the Finder menu.*
>
> b. *Choose Finder➪Preferences.*
>
> c. *Make sure that all four of the top check boxes (Hard Disks; External Disks; CDs, DVDs, and iPods; and Connected Servers) are selected.*
>
> Any external networks, hard drives, or devices to which you're connected show up on your Desktop. You can double-click the Desktop icon to view your external stuff.

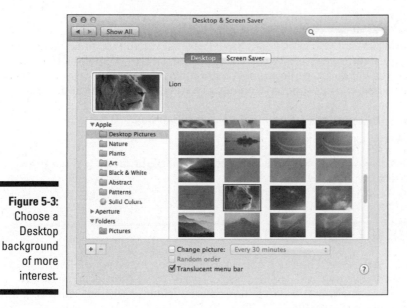

Figure 5-3: Choose a Desktop background of more interest.

Putting the Dock to the Test

If the Dock seems like a nifty contraption to you, you're right again. It's like one of those big control rooms that NASA uses. From the *Dock* — that icon toolbar at the bottom of the Mavericks Desktop — you can launch an application, monitor what's running, and even use the pop-up menu commands to control the applications that you launch. (Hey, that NASA analogy is even better than I thought!)

By default, the Dock hangs out at the bottom of your screen, but you can move it to another edge, change the size of the icons, or even hide it until it's necessary. (You can find more details on customizing the Dock using System Preferences in Chapter 6.)

When you launch an application — either by clicking an icon on the Dock, clicking an icon within Launchpad, or double-clicking an icon in a Finder window or the Desktop — the icon begins to bounce hilariously in the Dock to indicate that the application is loading. (So much for my NASA analogy.) After an application is running, the application icon appears in the Dock with a shiny blue dot underneath. Thus, you can easily see what's running at any time just by glancing at the Dock.

You can hide most applications by pressing ⌘+H. Although the application itself is still running, it might not appear on the Dock.

Some applications run in the *background* — that is, they don't show up on the Dock. You generally don't even know that these applications are working for you. However, if you need to see in detail what's going on, you can always use the Activity Monitor utility to view everything that's happening on your iMac. (For example, an Apple support technician might ask you to run Activity Monitor to help troubleshoot a problem.) To run the Activity Monitor

1. **Click the Spotlight icon on the Finder menu bar.**

2. **Type** Activity Monitor.

3. **Click the Activity Monitor entry in the Spotlight menu (or just press Return).**

Adding Dock icons

Ah, but there's more: The Dock can offer more than just a set of default icons! You can add your own MIS (or *Most Important Stuff*) to the Dock, making it the most convenient method of taking care of business without cluttering up your Desktop. You can add

✔ **Applications:** Add any application to your Dock by dragging the application icon into the area to the left of the *separator line* (the vertical line in the Dock that appears between applications and folders or documents). The existing Dock icons move aside so that you can place the new neighbor in a choice location.

Do not try to add an application anywhere to the right of the separator line. You can't put applications there because Mavericks might think that you want the application dumped in the Trash!

✔ **Folders:** Here's where you want to add things to the area to the right of the separator line. A folder or volume icon that you drag to the Dock is called a *stack* in Mavericks, and you can display the contents with a single click. (The contents of the folder "fan out" into a half-circle or grid arrangement, depending on the number of items in the folder. In fact, if you have enough items in the stack, scroll bars will appear.) To open or launch an item, just click it in the stack display.

Mavericks already includes two stacks on the Dock by default: your Documents folder and your Downloads folder.

✔ **Web URLs:** Sure, you can add your favorite website from Safari! Drag it right from the Safari Address bar into the area to the right of the separator line. When you click the URL icon, Safari opens the page automatically.

Removing Dock icons

You can remove an icon (okay, almost any) from the Dock at any time as long as the application isn't running. In fact, I always recommend that every Mavericks user remove the default icons that never get used to make more room available for your favorite icons. The only two icons you can't remove are the Finder and Trash icons. To remove an icon from the Dock, just click and drag it off the Dock. You're rewarded with a ridiculous puff of smoke straight out of a Warner Brothers cartoon! (One of the OS X developers was in a fun mood, I guess.)

When you delete an icon from the Dock, all you delete is the Dock icon: The original application, folder, or volume is not deleted, and you can even add that banished icon back to the Dock in the future.

Using Dock icon menus

From the Dock menu, you can open documents, open the location in a Finder window, set an application as a Login Item, control the features in some applications, and other assorted fun, depending on the item.

To display the right-click Dock menu for an icon

1. **Move your cursor over the icon.**

2. **Right-click.**

   Note that you can also press the Control key and click the icon, or even hold down the left mouse button (or tap and hold on a trackpad) for a second or two.

I cover the Dock settings that you can change within System Preferences in Chapter 6. You can also change the same settings from the Apple menu if you hover your mouse over the Dock item, which displays a submenu with the settings.

What's with the Trash?

Another sign of an iMac power user is a well-maintained Trash bin. It's a breeze to empty the discarded items you no longer need, and you can even rescue something that you suddenly discover you still need!

The Mavericks Trash bin resides on the Dock, and it works just like the Trash has always worked in OS X: Simply drag selected items to the Trash to delete them.

Note one very important exception: If you drag an external device or removable media drive icon on your Desktop to the Trash (such as an iPod, an iPhone, a DVD, or an external hard drive), the Trash bin icon automagically turns into a giant Eject icon, and the removable device or media is ejected or shut down — **not** erased. Repeat, *not erased.* (That's why the Trash icon changes to the Eject icon — to remind you that you're not doing anything destructive.)

Here are other methods of chunking items you select to go to the wastebasket:

- Choose File➪Move to Trash.
- Click the Action button on the Finder toolbar and choose Move to Trash from the list that appears.
- Press ⌘+Delete.
- Right-click the item and choose Move to Trash from the right-click menu.

You can always tell when the Trash contains at least one item because the basket icon is full of crumpled paper! However, you don't have to unfold a wad of paper to see what the Trash holds: Just click the Trash icon in the Dock to display the contents of the Trash. To rescue something from the Trash, drag the item(s) from the Trash folder to the Desktop or to any other folder in a Finder window. (If you're doing this for someone else who's not familiar with Mavericks, remember to act as though it were a lot of work, and you'll earn big-time DRP, or *Data Rescue Points.*)

When you're sure that you want to permanently delete the contents of the Trash, use one of these methods to empty the Trash:

- **Choose Finder⇨Empty Trash.**

- **Choose Finder⇨Secure Empty Trash.**

  If security is an issue around your iMac, and you want to make sure that no one can recover the files you've sent to the Trash, using the Secure Empty Trash command takes a little time but helps to ensure that no third-party hard drive repair or recovery program could resuscitate the items you discard.

- **Press ⌘+Shift+Delete.**

- **Right-click the Trash icon on the Dock and then choose Empty Trash from the right-click menu.**

Working Magic with Dashboard, Mission Control, and Spaces

iMac power users tend to wax enthusiastic over the convenience features built into Mavericks. In fact, we show 'em off to our PC-saddled friends and family. Three of the features that I've demonstrated the most to others are the OS X Dashboard display and the amazing convenience of Mission Control. In this section, I show 'em off to you as well. (Then you can become the Mavericks evangelist on *your* block.)

Using Dashboard

The idea behind Dashboard is deceptively simple, yet about as revolutionary as it gets for a mainstream personal computer operating system. *Dashboard* is an alternative Desktop that you can display at any time by using the keyboard or your pointing device (by swiping upward with three fingers and clicking Dashboard); the Dashboard desktop holds *widgets* (small applications that each provides a single function). Examples of default widgets that come with Mavericks include a calculator, a world clock, weather display, and a dictionary/thesaurus. (Think of the apps you can download for an iPhone or iPad, and you're in the same territory.)

Oh, did I mention that you're not limited to the widgets that come with Mavericks? Simply click the plus button at the bottom of the Dashboard display and drag new widgets to your Dashboard from the menu at the bottom of the screen. To remove a widget, click the minus button at the bottom of the Dashboard display, and then click the X icon that appears next to the offending widget. When you're done with your widgets — that sounds a bit strange, but I mean no offense — press the Dashboard key again to return to your Desktop.

Widgets can also be rearranged any way you like by dragging them to a new location.

Simple applications like these are no big whoop. After all, OS X has always had a calculator and a clock. What's revolutionary is how you *access* your widgets. You can display and use them anywhere in Mavericks, at any time, by simply pressing the Dashboard key. The default key on most late-model iMacs is F4, although you can change the Dashboard key via the Mission Control pane within System Preferences (or even turn it into a key sequence, like Option+F4).

A WebClip widget can include text, graphics, and links, which Dashboard updates every time you display your widgets. Think about that for a second: Dynamic displays, such as weather maps, cartoons, and even the Free Music Download image from the iTunes Store are all good sources of WebClip widgets! (That last one is a real time saver.)

Follow these steps to create a new WebClip Dashboard widget from your favorite website:

1. **Run Safari and navigate to the site you want to view as a widget.**

2. **Choose File⇨Open in Dashboard.**

   If you've added the Open in Dashboard button to the Safari toolbar (which bears a pair of scissors and a dotted box), you can click it instead.

3. **Select the portion of the page you want to include in your widget.**

   This step allows you to choose the section with the desired content.

4. **Drag the handles at the edges of the selection border to resize your widget frame to the right size and then click Add.**

   Bam! Mavericks displays your new WebClip widget within Dashboard.

When you click a link in a WebClip widget, Dashboard loads the full web page in Safari, so you can even use WebClips for surfing chores with sites you visit often.

Switching between apps with Mission Control

In Chapter 4, I mention using the ⌘+Tab keyboard shortcut to switch between your open applications. If you've moved to the iMac from a PC running Windows, you might think this simple shortcut is all there is to it. Ah, dear reader, you're in Mavericks territory now!

Mission Control is a rather complex-sounding feature, but (like Dashboard) it's really all about convenience. If you typically run a large number of applications at the same time, Mission Control can be a real time saver, allowing you to quickly switch among a forest of different application windows (or display your Desktop instantly without those very same windows in the way). The feature works in three ways:

✓ **Press F3 (or Control+↑, depending on your keyboard) to show *all* open windows using Mission Control, grouped by application; then click the one you want.** Figure 5-4 illustrates the tiled All Window display on my iMac after I press F3. Move the cursor on top of the window you want to activate (the window border turns blue when it's selected) and click once to switch to that window. You can specify which keys you want to use within the Mission Control pane in System Preferences.

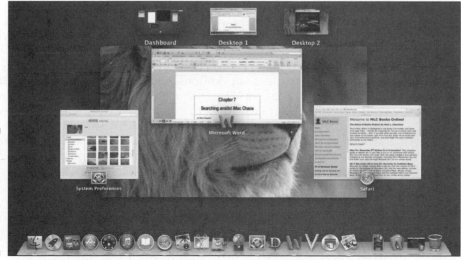

Figure 5-4: Mission Control is the Desktop manager within Mavericks.

✔ **Press Control+F3 (or Control+↓, depending on your keyboard) to show all open windows from the application that you're currently using; then click the one that you want to activate.** This Mission Control function is great for choosing from all the images that you've opened in Adobe Photoshop or all the Safari web pages littering your Desktop!

✔ **Press ⌘+F3, and all your open windows scurry to the side of the screen (much like a herd of zebras would if you dropped a lioness in the middle).** Now you can work with drives, files, and aliases on your Desktop — and when you're ready to confront those dozen application windows again, just press the keyboard shortcut a second time.

Although the Mission Control screen appears automatically when necessary, you can also launch it at any time from your iMac's Launchpad display, from the Mission Control icon in the Dock (which looks like a tiny Desktop with three windows), or by pressing the Mission Control/F3 key on your keyboard. From a Magic Trackpad, display the Mission Control screen by swiping up with three fingers.

Switching between desktops with Spaces

Ah, but what if you want to switch to an entirely different *set* of applications? For example, suppose that you're slaving away at your pixel-pushing job, designing a magazine cover with Pages. Your page-design desktop also includes Photoshop and Apple's Aperture, which you switch between often, using one of the techniques I just described. Suddenly, however, you realize that you need to schedule a meeting with others in your office using the OS X Calendar application, and you also want to check your e-mail in Apple Mail. What to do?

Well, you could certainly open Launchpad, launch those two applications on top of your graphics applications, and then minimize or close them. With Mission Control's *Spaces* feature, though, you can press the Control+← or Control+→ sequences to switch to a completely different "communications" Desktop, with Calendar and Apple Mail windows already open and in your favorite positions! Figure 5-4, shown in the previous section, illustrates two available Spaces desktops, labeled Desktop 1 and Desktop 2, as well as my Dashboard screen. (If you're using a trackpad, you can swipe to the left or right using three fingers to switch Spaces.)

After you're done setting up your meeting and answering any important e-mail, simply press Control+← or Control+→ to switch back to your "graphics" desktop, where all your work is exactly as you left it! (And yes, Virginia, Spaces does indeed work with full-screen applications.)

Now imagine that you've also created a custom "music" Desktop for GarageBand and iTunes . . . or perhaps you joined Safari and iPhoto as a "webmaster" Desktop. See why everyone's so excited?

To create a new Desktop for use within Spaces, click the Mission Control icon on the Dock, or press F3. Now you can set up new Spaces desktops. Move your cursor to the top-right corner of the Mission Control screen and click the Add button (with the plus sign) that appears. (If you've relocated your Dock to the right side of the screen, the Add button shows up in the upper-left corner instead.) Spaces creates a new, empty, Desktop thumbnail. Switch to the new Desktop by clicking the thumbnail at the top of the Mission Control screen and open those applications you want to include. (Alternatively, you can drag the applications from Mission Control onto the desired Desktop thumbnail.) That's all there is to it!

To switch an application window between Spaces desktops, drag the window to the edge of the Desktop and hold it there. Spaces will automatically move the window to the next Desktop. (Applications can also be dragged between desktops within the Mission Control screen.) You can also delete a Desktop from the Mission Control screen: Just hover your pointer over the target Spaces thumbnail and then click the Delete button (with the X) that appears.

You can jump directly to a specific Spaces Desktop by clicking its thumbnail within your Mission Control screen — or you can hold down the Control key and press the number corresponding to that Desktop. Additionally, you can always use the Control+← or Control+→ shortcuts to move among desktops and full-screen applications.

You can even activate Mission Control, Spaces, and Dashboard by using your cursor instead of the keyboard:

1. **Click the System Preferences icon on the Dock.**

2. **Click the Mission Control icon to display the settings.**

3. **Click the Hot Corners button.**

4. **Click the desired Screen Corner pop-up menu to choose what function that screen corner will trigger.**

5. **Press ⌘+Q to save your changes and then exit System Preferences.**

   When you move your pointer to that corner, the feature you've specified automatically kicks in. *Sweet!*

Printing within OS X

Mavericks makes document printing a breeze. Because most Mac printers use a Universal Serial Bus (USB) port, setting up printing couldn't be easier. Just turn on your printer and connect the USB cable between the printer and your iMac; Mavericks does the rest.

Printer manufacturers supply you with installation software that might add cool extra software or fonts to your system. Even if Mavericks recognizes your USB printer immediately, I recommend that you still launch the manufacturer's OS X installation disc. For example, my new Epson printer came with new fonts and a CD/DVD label application, but I wouldn't have 'em if I hadn't installed the Epson software package.

After your printer is connected and installed, you can use the same procedure to print from within just about every OS X application on the planet! To print with the default page layout settings — standard 8½-x-11" paper, portrait mode, no scaling — follow these steps:

1. **Within the active application, choose File⇨Print or press the ⌘+P shortcut.**

   OS X displays the Print dialog.

2. **From this dialog, you can**

   • *Print from a different printer connected to your iMac or print over a network connection to a shared printer on another computer (or a printer with built-in Ethernet networking).*

   Open the Printer pop-up menu to display all the printers that you can access.

   • *Print multiple copies.*

   For more than one copy, click in the Copies field and type the number of copies that you need.

   • *Check what the printed document will look like.*

   Use the left- and right-arrow keys under the Preview display to look at each page of your document as it will appear when printed.

   If you have to make changes to the document or you need to change the default print settings, click Cancel to return to your document. (You have to repeat Step 1 again to display the Print dialog again.)

If everything looks good at this point and you don't need to change any settings (like choosing a different page size or to print only a portion of the document), click Print — and you're done! Or, to change settings, click the Show Details button at the bottom of the sheet. Now you can make a number of optional changes to your print job:

✔ To print a range of selected pages, select the From radio button and then enter the starting and ending pages.

   To print the entire document, leave the default Pages option set to All.

✔ To select a different paper size, click the Paper Size pop-up menu.

✔ To choose application-specific settings (like collating and grayscale printing), click the pop-up menu in the center of the Print dialog and choose the desired settings pane that you need to adjust.

When you're set to go, click Print.

You can also save an electronic version of a document in the popular Adobe Acrobat PDF format from the Print dialog — without spending money on Adobe Acrobat. *(Slick.)*

1. **Click the PDF button to display the destination pop-up menu.**

2. **Choose Save as PDF.**

   Mavericks prompts you with a Save As dialog, where you can type a name for the PDF document and also specify a location on your hard drive where the file should be saved.

Heck, if you like, you can even fax a PDF (with an external USB modem or a multifunction printer), add the PDF to iBooks, or send it as a Messages or an Apple Mail e-mail attachment! Just choose these options from the destination list rather than Save as PDF.

Chapter 6

A Nerd's Guide to System Preferences

Remember the old TV series *Voyage to the Bottom of the Sea?* You always knew you were on the bridge of the submarine *Seaview* because it had an entire wall made up of randomly blinking lights, crewmen darting about with clipboards, and all sorts of strange and exotic-looking controls on every available surface. You could fix just about anything by looking into the camera with grim determination and barking out an order. After all, you were On The Bridge. That's why virtually all the dialogue and action inside the sub took place on that one (expensive) set: It was the nerve center of the ship and a truly happenin' place to be.

I devote this entire chapter to the System Preferences window and all the settings within it. After all, if you want to change how Mavericks works or customize the features within our favorite operating system, this one window is the nerve center of OS X and a truly happenin' place to be. (Sorry, no built-in wall of randomly blinking lights, but there *are* exotic controls just about everywhere.)

A Not-So-Confusing Introduction

The System Preferences window (as shown in Figure 6-1) is a self-contained beast, and you can reach it in a number of ways:

✔ Click the Apple menu (🍎) and choose the System Preferences menu item.

✔ Click the System Preferences icon on the Dock.

✔ Click most of the Finder menu status icons and then choose the Open Preferences menu item. (This trick works with the Bluetooth, Wi-Fi, Display, Input Source, Time Machine, Modem, and Clock icons.)

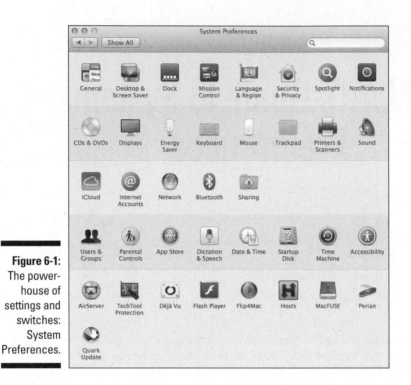

Figure 6-1:
The power-
house of
settings and
switches:
System
Preferences.

When the System Preferences window is open, you can click any of the group icons to switch to that group's pane, and the entire window morphs to display the settings for the selected pane. For example, Figure 6-2 illustrates the Sound pane, where you can set a system alert sound, configure your iMac's built-in microphone, and choose from among several output options.

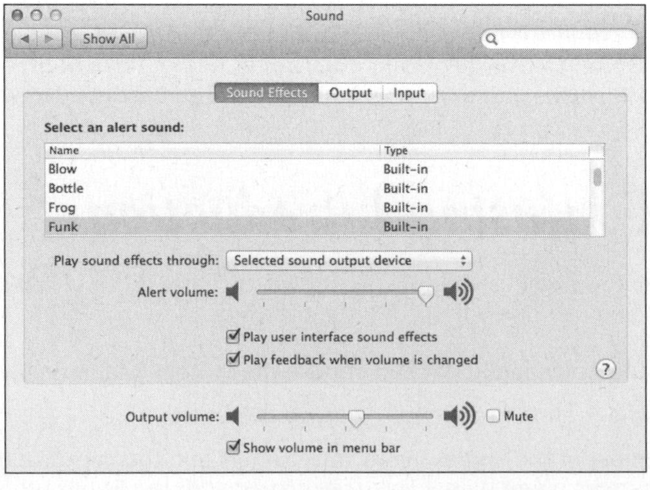

Figure 6-2:
The Sound
pane,
proudly
showing off
the Sound
Effects
panel.

Hey, I got bonus icons in my window!

Some third-party applications and media plug-ins can actually install their own icons within your once-pristine System Preferences window. You'll see them at the bottom of the window in Figure 6-1. (A good example is Flash Player from Adobe.) Naturally, I can't document these invited guests in this chapter, but they work the same way as any other group within System Preferences. Click the icon, adjust any settings as necessary, and then close the System Preferences window to save your changes.

Many panes also include tabbed buttons at the top. For example, the Sound pane sports Sound Effects, Output, and Input tabs. You can click these tabs to switch to another pane within the same pane. Many panes within System Preferences have multiple subpanes. This design allows our friends at Apple to group a large number of related settings in the same pane (without things getting too confusing).

To return to the top-level System Preferences window from any pane, just click the Show All button (top left) or press ⌘+L. You can also click the familiar Previous and Next buttons to move backward through the panes you've already visited and then move forward again, in sequence. (Yep, these buttons work just like the browser controls in Safari. Sometimes life is funny that way.)

If a System Preference pane is locked, you can't modify any of the settings on that pane unless you unlock the pane. If that's the case, click the padlock icon (lower left) and, if prompted, type your admin-level account password to unlock the pane. After you finish your tweaking, you can protect the settings from inadvertent changes by clicking the padlock icon again to close the pane.

Your changes to the settings in a pane are automatically saved when you click Show All or when you click the Close button on the System Preferences window. You can also press ⌘+Q to exit System Preferences and save all your changes automatically . . . a favorite shortcut of mine.

If you see an Apply button in a pane, you can click it to immediately apply any changes you make, without exiting the pane. This is perfect for some settings that you might want to try first before you accept them, like many of the controls on the Network pane. However, if you're sure about what you changed and how those changes will affect your system, you don't have to click Apply. Just exit the System Preferences window or click Show All as you normally would, and your tweaks are accepted.

Searching for Settings

Hey, wouldn't it be great if you could search through all the different panes in System Preferences — with all those countless radio buttons, check boxes, and slider controls — from one place? Even when you're not quite sure exactly what it is you're looking for?

Figure 6-3 illustrates exactly that kind of activity taking place. Just click in the System Preferences Spotlight Search box (upper right, with the magnifying glass icon) and type in just about anything. For example, if you know part of the name of a particular setting you need to change, type that. Mavericks highlights the System Preferences panes that might contain matching settings. And if you're a *Switcher* from the Windows world, you can even type in what you might have called the same setting in Windows!

The System Preferences window dims, and the group icons that might contain what you're looking for stay highlighted. *Slick.*

If you need to reset the Search box to try again, click the X icon that appears at the right side of the box to clear it.

Figure 6-3:
Searching for specific settings is a breeze with the Search box.

Popular Preference Panes Explained

Time to get down to brass tacks. Open the most-often-used panes in System Preferences to see what magic you can perform! I don't discuss all the panes because I cover many of them in other chapters. (In fact, you might never need to open some System Preferences panes at all, such as Language & Text.) However, this chapter covers just about all the settings that you're likely to use on a regular basis.

The Displays pane

If you're a heavy-duty game player or you work with applications like video editing and 3-D modeling, you probably find yourself switching the characteristics of your monitor on a regular basis. To easily accomplish switching, visit the Displays pane (see Figure 6-4), which includes two panes:

✔ **Display:** To allow Mavericks to choose the best resolution for your display, select the Best for Display radio button. To manually select a resolution, select the Scaled radio button and then choose the resolution that you want to use from the Resolutions list on the left. (In most cases, you want to use the highest resolution.) If you have an external monitor connected to your iMac, click the Detect Displays button that appears to scan for that monitor. Drag the Brightness slider to manually change the brightness level of your display, or select the Automatically Adjust Brightness check box to allow Mavericks to dim or brighten your display as necessary.

Select the Show Mirroring Options in the Menu Bar When Available check box if you'll be using multiple monitors or a projector with your iMac. If you're using multiple monitors, each display has a dedicated Finder menu bar, and the Dock appears on whichever display you're using!

Ready to stream content to your TV directly from your iMac — *without cables*? You can use the wireless AirPlay Mirroring feature to send the display from your Mac to your HD-TV. AirPlay Mirroring requires an Apple TV unit that supports this feature. You can also send the audio from your iMac directly to an AirPlay-enabled receiver or speaker system.

✔ **Color:** Your iMac can use a *color profile* file that controls the colors on your display. This setting comes in handy for graphic artists and illustrators who need color output from their printers that closely matches the colors displayed by the iMac. Click the Calibrate button to launch the Display Calibrator, which can create a custom ColorSync profile and calibrate the colors that you see on your monitor.

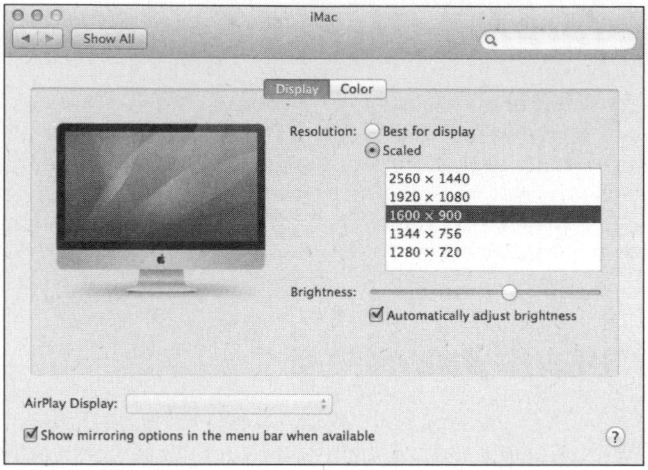

Figure 6-4:
The
Displays
pane
allows you
to change
monitor
resolutions
in a jiffy.

The Desktop & Screen Saver pane

Hey, who doesn't want to choose their own background? And what about that nifty screen saver you just downloaded from that movie website? You can change both your background and screen saver by using these options on the Desktop & Screen Saver pane.

The settings on the Desktop tab (as shown in Figure 6-5) include

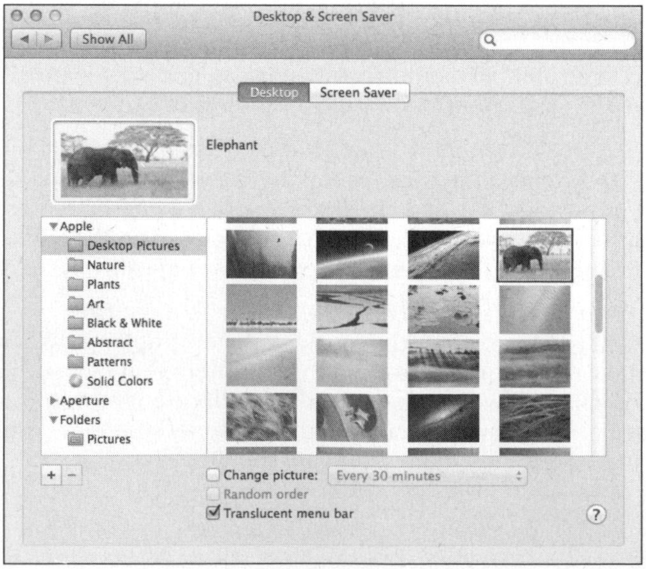

Figure 6-5:
Show
The Man
who's boss
and pick
your own
Desktop
background.

✔ **Current Desktop picture:** To change your Desktop background, click a thumbnail. You can also drag a picture from a Finder window or the desktop and drop it into the *well* (the fancy technical name for the square box with the sunken look). Mavericks automatically updates your Desktop so that you can see the results. To open another collection of images from Apple, click the desired collection folder from the list on the left of the pane. If you want to open a different folder with your own images, click the Add button (which bears a plus sign) at the lower left of the pane and then navigate to that folder. Click Choose to select a folder and display the images it contains.

✔ **Layout:** You can automatically fit an image to your screen, *tile* your background image (repeat it across the Desktop), center it, and stretch it to fill the screen. Because the images from Apple are all sized correctly already, the Layout pop-up menu appears only when you're using your own pictures (so it's not visible in this figure).

✔ **Change Picture:** If you like a bit of automatic variety on your Desktop, select the Change Picture check box. You can click the pop-up menu to set the delay period. The images in the current collection or folder are then displayed in the sequence in which they appear in the thumbnail list.

✔ **Random Order:** Select this check box to throw caution utterly to the wind and display random screens from the current collection or folder!

✔ **Translucent Menu Bar:** When enabled, this feature turns your Finder and application menu bars semi-opaque, allowing them to blend in somewhat with your Desktop background. If you'd rather have a solid-color menu bar, deselect this check box.

The settings on the Screen Saver tab include

✔ **Screen Savers:** From the Screen Savers list at the left, click any screen saver to preview it (on the right). To try out the screen saver in full-screen mode, click the Test button. (You can end the test by moving your cursor.) If the screen saver module that you select has any configurable settings, you can set them from the pane on the right (or, depending on the screen saver, you can also click the Screen Saver Options button to display them). Choose the Random screen saver to display a different screen saver module each time the screen saver is activated.

✔ **Start After:** Drag this slider to choose the period of inactivity that triggers the screen saver. Choose Never if you want to disable the screen saver entirely. (***Note:*** The Start After delay you set should be less time than the Display Sleep delay you set in the System Preferences Energy Saver pane, or you won't see the great screen saver at all. I discuss the Energy Saver pane later in this chapter.)

✔ **Show with Clock:** Select this check box, and Mavericks adds a clock display to your screen saver (a great help for those of us who spend many minutes on the phone).

✔ **Hot Corners:** Click this button to display a drop-down sheet and then click any of the four pop-up menus at the four corners of the screen to select that corner as an *activating hot corner.* (Moving your mouse pointer to a hot corner immediately activates the screen saver.) You can also specify a corner as a *disabling hot corner;* that is, as long as the mouse pointer stays in that corner, the screen saver is disabled. Note that you can also set the Dashboard and Mission Control activation corners from here. (Read on for the entire lowdown.)

For additional security, check out the Security & Privacy pane in System Preferences. On the General pane, you'll find the Require Password After Sleep or Screen Saver Begins check box. Select the check box and choose the desired delay.

The Mission Control pane

Figure 6-6 illustrates the Mission Control, Spaces, and Dashboard settings that you can configure in this group. You can use Mission Control to view all the application windows that you're using at one time so that you can select a new active window. Or you can move all windows aside so that you can see your Desktop. Dashboard presents a number of *widgets* (mini-applications), which you can summon and hide with a single key. (Find more on Mission Control, Spaces, and Dashboard in Chapter 5.)

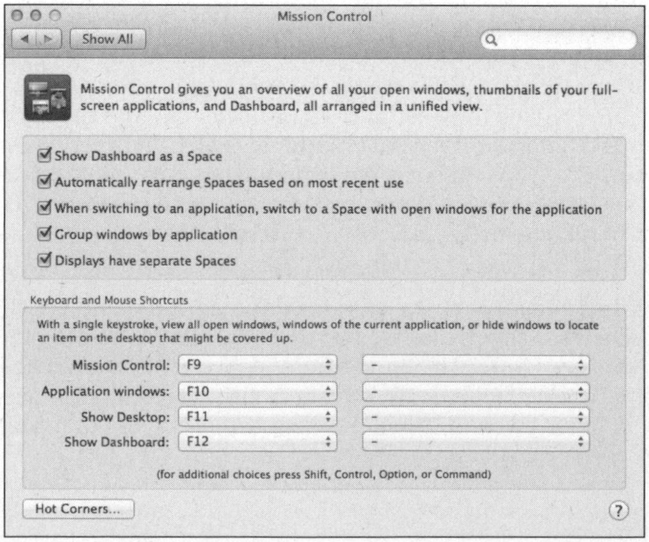

Figure 6-6:
Tweak the operation of Mission Control from this pane.

Mission Control gives you an overview of all your open windows, thumbnails of your full-screen applications, and Dashboard, all arranged in a unified view.

☑ Show Dashboard as a Space
☑ Automatically rearrange Spaces based on most recent use
☑ When switching to an application, switch to a Space with open windows for the application
☑ Group windows by application
☑ Displays have separate Spaces

Keyboard and Mouse Shortcuts
With a single keystroke, view all open windows, windows of the current application, or hide windows to locate an item on the desktop that might be covered up.

Mission Control: F9
Application windows: F10
Show Desktop: F11
Show Dashboard: F12

(for additional choices press Shift, Control, Option, or Command)

Hot Corners…

Here's what you can control about Mission Control (horrible pun not intended but accepted nonetheless):

✔ **Hot Corners:** Click the button at the lower left to specify your hot corner settings. These four pop-up menus operate just like the Hot Corners/ Active Screen Corners of the Desktop & Screen Savers pane, but they control the operation of the OS X screen management features. Click one to specify that corner as

- *All Windows corner:* Displays all windows on your Desktop

- *Application Windows corner:* Displays only the windows from the active application

- *Desktop corner:* Moves all windows to the outside of the screen to uncover your Desktop

- *Dashboard corner:* Displays your Dashboard widgets

- *Notification Center corner:* Displays the Notification Center strip at the right side of your Desktop

Choose Launchpad to activate the Launchpad screen. Note that you can also set the Screen Saver Start and Disable corners from here, as well as put your display to sleep.

✔ **Keyboard and Mouse Shortcuts:** Use each pop-up menu to set the key sequences (and mouse button settings) for Mission Control, Application windows, Show Desktop, and the Dashboard.

You're not limited to just the keyboard and mouse shortcuts on the pop-up menus. Press the Shift, Control, Option, and ⌘ keys while a pop-up menu is open, and you see these modifiers appear as menu choices! (Heck, you can even combine modifiers, such as ⌘+Shift+F9 instead of just F9.)

By default, Mavericks displays your Dashboard as a Space within the Mission Control screen. If you prefer your Dashboard widgets to appear as an overlay (as they did in previous versions of OS X), deselect the Show Dashboard as a Space check box.

✔ **Automatically Rearrange Spaces Based on Most Recent Use:** If this check box is selected, Mission Control presents your most recently used Spaces first within the thumbnails at the top of the screen.

✔ **When Switching to an Application:** When selected, this check box allows you to switch applications between Spaces desktops using the ⌘+Tab shortcut. Mavericks jumps to the desktop that has an open window for the application you choose, even if that desktop is not currently active.

✔ **Group Windows by Application:** When selected, this check box automatically arranges windows in the Mission Control screen by the application that created them.

✔ **Displays Have Separate Spaces:** If you have multiple monitors connected to your iMac, you can select this check box to create a separate Spaces display for each monitor.

The General pane

The talented General pane (shown in Figure 6-7) determines the look and operation of the controls that appear in application windows and Finder windows. It looks complex, but I cover each option here.

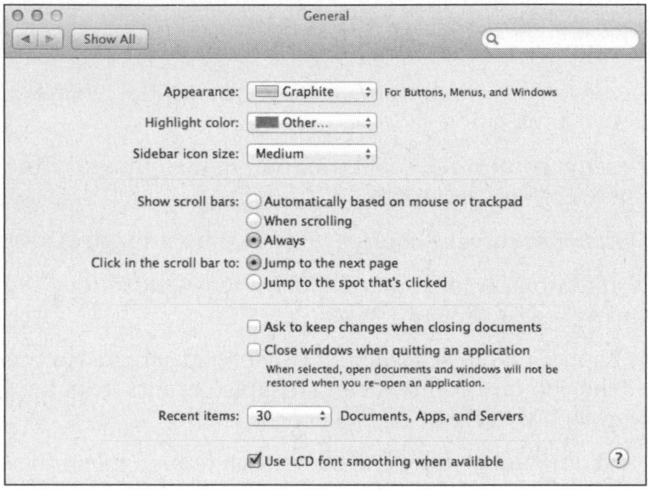

Figure 6-7:
Appear-
ances might
not be
everything,
but they're
easy to
find on the
General
pane.

The settings include

- **Appearance:** Open this pop-up menu to specify the color Mavericks uses for buttons, menus, and windows.

- **Highlight Color:** Open this pop-up menu to choose the color that highlights selected text in fields, pop-up menus, and drop-down list boxes.

- **Sidebar Icon Size:** Select the size of the icons in the Finder window *Sidebar,* which is the strip to the left of the Finder window that displays your devices and favorite locations on your system. If you have a large number of hard drives or you've added several folders to the sidebar, reducing the size of the icons will allow you to display more of them without scrolling.

- **Show Scroll Bars:** Use these radio buttons to specify when Mavericks should display scroll bars within a window. By default, they're placed automatically when necessary, but you can choose to display scroll bars always, or only when you're actually scrolling through a document.

- **Click in the Scroll Bar To:** By default, OS X jumps to the next or previous page when you click in an empty portion of the scroll bar. Select the Jump to the Spot That's Clicked radio button to scroll the document to the approximate position in relation to where you click.

✔ **Ask To Keep Changes When Closing Documents:** If you select this check box, Mavericks prompts you for confirmation if you attempt to close a document with unsaved changes. If the check box is deselected, Mavericks will allow the unsaved document to be closed without saving a new version.

✔ **Close Windows When Quitting an Application:** If this check box is selected, the Resume feature built in to Mavericks automatically saves the state of an application when you quit. When you launch the application again, Mavericks restores all the application windows and opens the documents you were working on when you quit. In effect, you can continue using the application just as if you had never quit. If you deselect the check box, Mavericks will not restore your work, and you'll have to load your document again; this is the same action taken by earlier versions of OS X.

✔ **Recent Items:** By default, Mavericks displays ten recent applications, documents, and servers within Recent Items in the Apple menu. Need more? Just open the corresponding pop-up menu and specify up to 50 items.

✔ **Use LCD Font Smoothing:** By default, this check box is selected, making the text on your iMac's LED display appear more like the printed page.

The Energy Saver pane

I'm an environmentalist (it's surprising how many techno-types are colored green), so this pane (as shown in Figure 6-8) is pretty doggone important. When you use them correctly, you not only save electricity but also even invoke the Power of Mavericks to automatically start and shut down your iMac whenever you like!

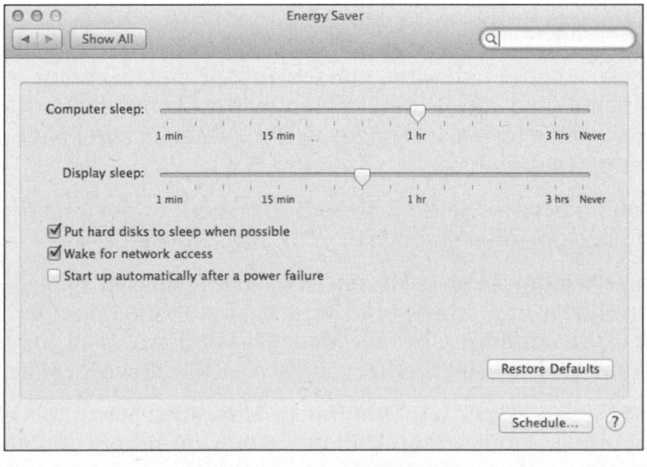

Figure 6-8: Reduce your iMac's power consumption from the Energy Saver pane.

To save electricity, drag the Computer Sleep slider to a delay period that triggers sleep mode when you're away from the keyboard for a significant period of time. (I prefer 30 minutes.) If your iMac must always remain alert and you want to disable sleep mode entirely, choose Never. You can set the delay period for blanking your monitor separately from the sleep setting with the Display Sleep slider.

To conserve the maximum juice and cut down on wear, select the Put Hard Disks to Sleep When Possible check box to power-down your hard drives when they're not needed. (This might cause a delay of a second or two while loading or saving files because the drives must spin back up — if you're sharing files with others on your network, sleeping hard drives can also significantly slow file transfers.)

You can set Mavericks to start or shut down your iMac at a scheduled time. Click the Schedule button and then select the desired schedules (the Start Up or Wake check box and the Shut Down/Restart/Sleep pop-up menu) to enable them. Set the trigger time by clicking the up and down arrows next to the time display for each schedule. Click OK to return to the Energy Saver pane.

Select the Wake for Network Access check box to wake your iMac from sleep mode whenever your computer is accessed remotely across your network. Mavericks can restart your iMac automatically after a power failure — a good feature for those running their iMac as a server, because your server will automatically come back online after power is restored.

The Dock pane

You can use the settings shown in Figure 6-9 to configure the Dock's behavior until it fits your personality like a glove:

- **Size:** Pretty self-explanatory. Just drag the slider to change the scale of the Dock.

- **Magnification:** When you select this check box, each icon in your Dock swells like a puffer fish when you move your mouse cursor over it. (Just how much it magnifies is determined by the Magnification slider.) I really like this feature because I resize my Dock smaller, and I have a large number of Dock icons.

- **Position on Screen:** Select a radio button here to position the Dock on the left, bottom, or right edge of your iMac's Desktop.

- **Minimize Windows Using:** Mavericks includes two cool animations that you can choose from when shrinking a window to the Dock (and expanding it back to the Desktop). Open the Minimize Windows Using pop-up menu to specify the genie-in-a-bottle effect or a scale-up-or-down-incrementally effect.

- **Double-Click a Window's Title Bar to Minimize:** Select this check box to minimize a Finder or application window by simply double-clicking the window's title bar.

✓ **Minimize Windows into Application Icon:** If this check box is not selected, minimized application windows appear as thumbnail icons at the right side of the Dock. To minimize application windows into the application icon in the Dock — which can save space on your Dock — select this check box. (To restore a window that's been minimized into the application icon, right-click the icon on the Dock and choose Restore from the menu that appears.)

✓ **Animate Opening Applications:** Are you into aerobics? How about punk rock and slam dancing? Active souls who like animation likely get a kick out of the bouncing application icons on the Dock. They indicate that you've launched an application and that it's loading. You can turn off this bouncing behavior by deselecting this check box.

✓ **Automatically Hide and Show the Dock:** Select this check box, and the Dock disappears until you need it. (Depending on the size of your Dock, the Desktop real estate that you gain can be significant.) To display a hidden Dock, move your mouse pointer over the corresponding edge of the Desktop.

✓ **Show Indicator Lights for Open Applications:** OS X indicates which applications are running in the Dock with a small blue dot in front of the icon. To disable these indicators, deselect this check box.

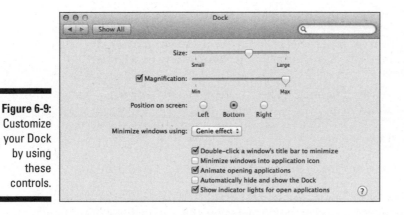

Figure 6-9:
Customize
your Dock
by using
these
controls.

The Sharing pane

So you're in a neighborly mood and want to share your toys with others on your local wired or wireless network. Perhaps you'd like to start your own website or protect yourself against the Bad Guys on the Internet. All these fun diversions are available from the Sharing pane in System Preferences, as shown in Figure 6-10.

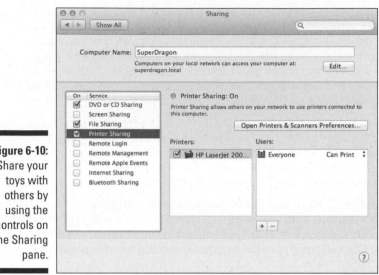

Figure 6-10:
Share your
toys with
others by
using the
controls on
the Sharing
pane.

Click the Edit button to change the default network name assigned to your iMac during the installation process. Your current network name is listed in the Computer Name text field.

Each entry in the services list controls a specific type of sharing. To turn on any of these services, select the On check box for that service. To turn off a service, click the corresponding On check box to deselect it.

From a security standpoint, I highly recommend that you enable only those services that you actually use, because each service that you enable automatically makes your Mavericks firewall open to allow that service. A Mark's Maxim to remember:

Poking too many holes in your firewall is *not* A Good Thing.

When you click one of the services in the list, the right side of the Sharing pane changes to display the settings you can specify for that particular service. To display all the details on these options, click the Help button (the question mark) at the lower-right corner of the System Preferences dialog.

The Time Machine pane

Mac users are justifiably proud about the Time Machine automatic backup feature that's built in to Mavericks. You can easily configure how Time Machine handles your backups from the pane shown in Figure 6-11. Of course, you'll need an external hard drive (or an AirPort Time Capsule wireless backup station) for the best backup security. Note that Time Machine won't work with an internal or external DVD drive: It's got to be a hard drive. (Note, however, that if your Wi-Fi network uses an AirPort Extreme base station, you can connect an external hard drive to the base station's USB port for use with Time Machine. Your iMac will back up wirelessly to the base station's drive, just like Apple's AirPort Time Capsule device!)

Figure 6-11: Put Time Machine to work, and your data is always backed up.

To enable Time Machine, click the On switch and then click the Select Disk button to choose a disk to hold your Time Machine backup data. Time Machine backs up all the hard drives on your system. However, to save time and hard drive space, Time Machine allows you to exclude specific drives and folders from the backup process. Click the Options button, click the Add button (with the plus sign) to select the drives or folders you want to exclude, and they appear in the Exclude list.

To remove an excluded item, select it in the list and click the Delete button (with the minus sign). Note that the Estimated Size of Full Backup figure increases, and Time Machine adds the item you deleted from the list to the next backup.

By default, Mavericks warns you when deleting older backup files, but you can turn this warning off from the Options sheet as well.

If you enable the Show Time Machine in Menu Bar check box, you can elect to back up your Mac immediately by clicking the Time Machine icon in the Finder menu bar and then choosing Back Up Now.

Chapter 7

Searching amidst iMac Chaos

*W*hat would you say if I told you that you could search your entire system for virtually every piece of data connected with a person — and in only the short time it takes to type that person's name? And I'm not just talking about files and folders that might include that person's name. I mean *every* e-mail message and *every* Calendar event that references that person — and even that person's Contacts card, to boot? Heck, how about if that search could dig up every occurrence of the person's name inside PDF documents? What if it could even search folders shared on other Macs across your network?

You'd probably say, "That makes for good future tech — I'll bet I can do that in five or ten years. It'll take Apple at least that long to do it . . . and just in time for me to buy a new iMac! (Harrumph.)"

Don't be so hasty: You can do all this right now. The technology is the OS X feature named *Spotlight,* built right into Mavericks. In this chapter, I show you how to use it like an iMac power guru.

Doing a Basic Search

Figure 7-1 illustrates the Spotlight search field, which is always available from the Finder menu bar. Click the magnifying glass icon once (or press ⌘+Spacebar), and the Spotlight search box appears.

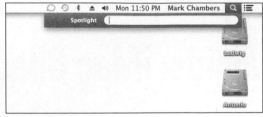

Figure 7-1:
A lot of
power purrs
behind
this single
Spotlight
search box.

To run a search, simply click in the Spotlight box and begin typing. (The words you type that you want to match are *keywords*.) Matching items start appearing as soon as you type, and the search results are continually refined while you type the rest of your search keywords. In other words, you don't need to press Return to begin your search.

The results of your Spotlight search appear in the Spotlight menu, which is updated automatically in real time while you continue to type. The top 20 most-relevant items are grouped into categories — such as Messages, Definitions, Documents, Folders, Images, PDFs, and Contacts, right on the Spotlight menu. Spotlight takes a guess at the item that's most likely the match you're looking for (based on your Search Results list in System Preferences, which I cover later in the chapter) and presents it in the special Top Hit category that always appears first.

Hover your cursor over an item in the Spotlight menu, and *shazam!* — Spotlight uses the Quick Look technology built into Mavericks to display either a thumbnail image of a document or information on the item. If the item is a song, you can even move your cursor on top of the thumbnail in the Quick Look display and click to play it — all without leaving the Spotlight menu.

To open the Top Hit item like a true Mavericks power user, just press Return. (My brothers and sisters, it just doesn't get any easier than that.)

Literally any text string is acceptable as a Spotlight search. However, here's a short list of the common search criteria I use every day:

✔ **Names and addresses:** Because Spotlight has access to the Contacts application in Mavericks, you can immediately display contact information using any portion of a name or an address.

✔ **E-mail message text:** Need to open a specific e-mail message you've already received, but you'd rather not launch Mail and spend time digging through the message list? Enter the person's e-mail address or any text string contained in the message you're looking for.

✔ **File and folder names:** A simple item name is the classic search favorite. Spotlight searches your entire system for that one file or folder in the blink of an eye.

✔ **Events and Reminder items:** Yep, Spotlight gives you access to your Calendar events and those all-important Reminders you've created.

✔ **System Preferences:** Now things start to get *really* interesting! Try typing the word **background** in the Spotlight field. Some of the results will be System Preference panes! Every setting in System Preferences is referenced in Spotlight. (For example, the Desktop background setting resides in the Desktop & Screen Saver pane in System Preferences.)

✔ **Web pages:** *Whoa.* Stand back, Google. You can use Spotlight to search the web pages you've recently displayed in Safari! (Note, however, that this feature doesn't let you search through all the Internet like Google does. Instead, you can search only the pages stored in your Safari web cache and any HTML files you've saved to your iMac's hard drive.)

✔ **Metadata:** This category is a pretty broad, but it fits. If you're not familiar with the term *metadata*, think of the information stored by your digital camera each time you take a photo: exposure setting, time and date, and even the location where the photo was taken, which are also transferred to iPhoto when you import. Here's another example: I like to locate Word documents on my system using the same metadata that's stored in the file, such as the contents of the Comments field in a Word document. Other supported applications include Adobe Photoshop images, Microsoft Excel spreadsheets, Keynote presentations, iTunes media, and other third-party applications that offer a Spotlight plug-in that you've installed.

To reset the Spotlight search and try another text string, click the X icon that appears at the right side of the Spotlight box. Of course, you can also backspace to the beginning of the field, but that's a little less elegant, so try pressing ⌘+A to select the entire contents and then press Delete.

After you find the item you're looking for, you can click it once to

✔ Launch it (if the item is an application).

✔ Open it in System Preferences (if it's a setting or description on a Preferences pane).

✔ Open it within the associated application (if the item is a document or a data item).

✔ Display it in a Finder window (if the item is a folder).

Here's another favorite timesaver: You can display all the files of a particular type on your system by using the file type as the keyword. For example, to provide a list of all images on your system, just use *images* as your keyword — the same goes for *movies* and *audio*, too.

How Cool Is That!? Discovering What Spotlight Can Do

Don't get fooled into simply using Spotlight as another file-'n-folder-name search tool. Sure, it can do that, but Spotlight can also search *inside* PDF, Pages, Word documents, and HTML files, finding matching text that doesn't appear in the name of the file. To wit: A search for *Mavericks* on my system pulls up all sorts of items not only with *Mavericks* in their names but also files with *Mavericks* in them. For example

- ✔ `Apple Store SF.ppt`: A PowerPoint presentation with several slides containing the text *Mavericks*

- ✔ `bk01ch03.doc`: A rather cryptically named Microsoft Word file chapter of another *For Dummies* book of mine that mentions Mavericks in several spots

- ✔ Conference Call with Bob: A Calendar event pointing to a conference call with my editor about upcoming Mavericks book projects

---

Is Spotlight secure?

So how about all those files, folders, contacts, and events that you *don't* want to appear in Spotlight? What if you're sharing your iMac as a multiuser computer or accessing other Macs remotely? Can others search for and access your personal information through Spotlight?

Definitely not! The results displayed by Spotlight are controlled by file and folder permissions as well as your account login, just as the applications that create and display your personal data are. For example, you can't access other users' calendars using Calendar, and they can't see your Mail messages. Only

you have access to your data, and only after you've logged in with your username and password. Spotlight works the same way. If a user doesn't normally have access to an item, the item simply doesn't appear when that user performs a Spotlight search. (In other words, only you get to see your stuff.)

However, you can hide certain folders and disks from your own Spotlight searches if necessary. Check out the final section of this chapter for details on setting private locations on your system.

Not one of these three examples actually has the word *Mavericks* occurring anywhere in the title or filename, yet Spotlight found them because they all contain the text *Mavericks* therein. That, dear reader, is the true power of Spotlight, and how it can literally guarantee you that you'll never lose another piece of information that Spotlight can locate in the hundreds of thousands of files and folders on your hard drive!

Heck, suppose that all you remember about a file is that you received it in your mail last week or last month. To find it, you can actually type time periods, such as *yesterday, last week,* or *last month,* to see every item that you saved or received within that period. (Boy, howdy, I *love* writing about TGIs — that's short for Truly Good Ideas.)

Be careful, however, when you're considering a search string. Don't forget that (by default) Spotlight matches only those items that have *all* the words you enter in the Spotlight box. To return the highest number of possible matches, use the fewest number of words that will identify the item; for example, use *horse* rather than *horse image,* and you're certain to be rewarded with more hits. On the other hand, if you're looking specifically for a picture of a knight on horseback, using a series of keywords — such as *horse knight image* — shortens your search considerably. It all depends on what you're looking for and how widely you want to cast your Spotlight net.

To allow greater flexibility in searches, Apple also includes those helpful Boolean friends that you may already be familiar with: AND, OR, and NOT. For example, you can perform Spotlight searches, such as

- ✔ **Horse AND cow:** Collects all references to both those barnyard animals into one search

- ✔ **Batman OR Robin:** Returns all references to either Batman or Robin

- ✔ **Apple NOT PC:** Displays all references to Apple that don't include any information on dastardly PCs

Because Spotlight functions are a core technology of OS X Mavericks — in other words, all sorts of applications can make use of Spotlight throughout the operating system, including Finder — the Finder window's Search box now shares many of the capabilities of Spotlight. In fact, you can use the time period trick that I mention earlier (entering *yesterday* as a keyword) in the Finder window Search box.

Expanding Your Search Horizons

I can just hear the announcer's voice now: "But wait, there's more! If you click the Show in Finder menu item at the beginning of your search results, we'll expand your Spotlight menu into the Spotlight window!" (Fortunately, you don't have to buy some ridiculous household doodad.)

Keyboard mavens will appreciate the Spotlight window shortcut key, and I show you where to specify this shortcut in the final section of this chapter.

Figure 7-2 illustrates the Spotlight window (which is actually a Finder window with extras). To further filter the search, click one of the buttons on the Spotlight window toolbar or create your own custom filter. Click the button with the plus sign (upper right) to display the search criteria bar and then click the pop-up menus to choose from criteria, such as the type of file, the text content, or the location on your system (for example, your hard drive, your Home folder, or a network server). You can also filter your results listing by the date when the items were created or last saved. To add or delete criteria, click the plus and minus buttons at the right side of the search criteria bar. To save a custom filter that you've created, click the Save button.

Icon view

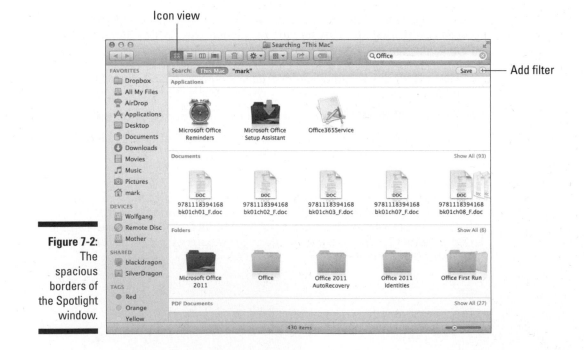

Add filter

Figure 7-2:
The spacious borders of the Spotlight window.

Images appear as thumbnail icons, so you can use that most sophisticated search tool — the human eye — to find the picture you're looking for. (If you don't see thumbnail images, click the Icon view button on the toolbar.) Don't forget that you can increase or decrease the size of the icons by dragging the slider at the bottom right of the window.

To display the contents of an item in the list (without leaving the comfortable confines of the Spotlight window), click the item to select it and press the spacebar for a better view. Note that Mavericks must recognize the format of the file (and it must be supported by at least one application) for this display feature to work.

Again, when you're ready to open an item, just double-click it in the Spotlight window.

As I mention earlier, Spotlight can look for matching items on other Macs on your network only if those remote Macs are configured correctly. To allow another Mac running OS X Tiger 10.5 (or later) to be visible to Spotlight on your system, enable File Sharing on the other Mac. (Oh, and remember that you need an admin-level account on that Mac — or access to a good friend who has an admin-level account on that Mac.)

Follow these steps to enable file sharing on the other Mac:

1. **On the Dock, click the System Preferences icon (look for the gears).**

2. **Click the Sharing pane.**

3. **In the service list on the left side of the Sharing pane, select the On check box next to the File Sharing item to enable it.**

4. **Click the Close button in the System Preferences window.**

You can search only those items for which you have rights and permissions to view on the remote Mac (such as the contents of the Public folders on that computer). I discuss more about these limitations earlier in this chapter, in the "Is Spotlight secure?" sidebar.

Customizing Spotlight to Your Taste

You might guess that such an awesome OS X feature has its own pane in System Preferences — and you'd be right again. Figure 7-3 shows off the Spotlight pane in System Preferences: Click the System Preferences icon on the Dock and then click the Spotlight icon to display these settings.

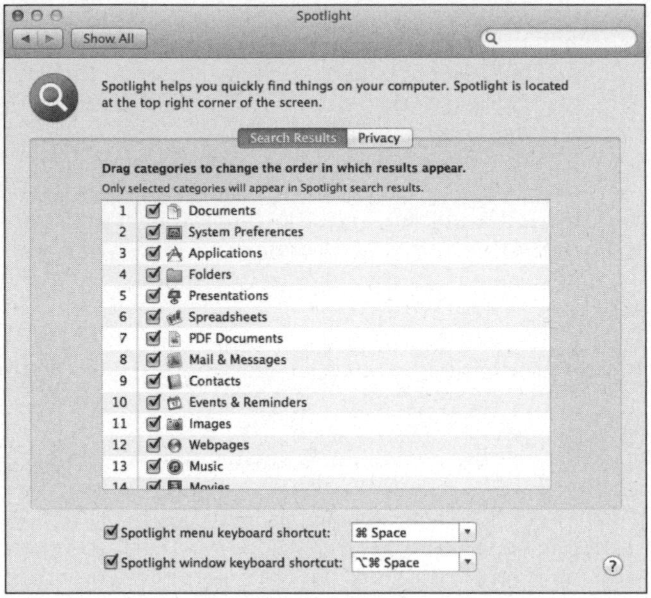

Figure 7-3:
Fine-tune
your
Spotlight
menu and
Results
window
from System
Preferences.

Click the Search Results tab to

- ✔ **Determine which categories appear in the Spotlight menu and Results window.** For example, if you don't use any presentation software on your iMac, you can clear the check box next to Presentations to disable this category (thereby making more room for other categories that you will use).

- ✔ **Determine the order that categories appear in the Spotlight menu and Results window.** Drag the categories to the order in which you want them to appear in the Spotlight menu and window. For example, I like the Documents and System Preferences categories to appear higher in the list because I use them most often.

- ✔ **Specify the Spotlight menu and Spotlight Results window keyboard shortcuts.** You can enable or disable either keyboard shortcut and choose the key combination from the pop-up menu. By default, the menu keyboard shortcut is ⌘+Space, and the results window keyboard shortcut is ⌘+Option+Space.

Click the Privacy tab (shown in Figure 7-4) to specify disks and folders that should never be listed as results in a Spotlight search. I know, I know — I said earlier that Spotlight respected your security, and it does. However, the disks and folders that you add to this list won't appear even if *you* are the one performing the search, so the exclusion is absolute. This is a great idea for folders and removable hard drives that you use to store sensitive information, such as medical records.

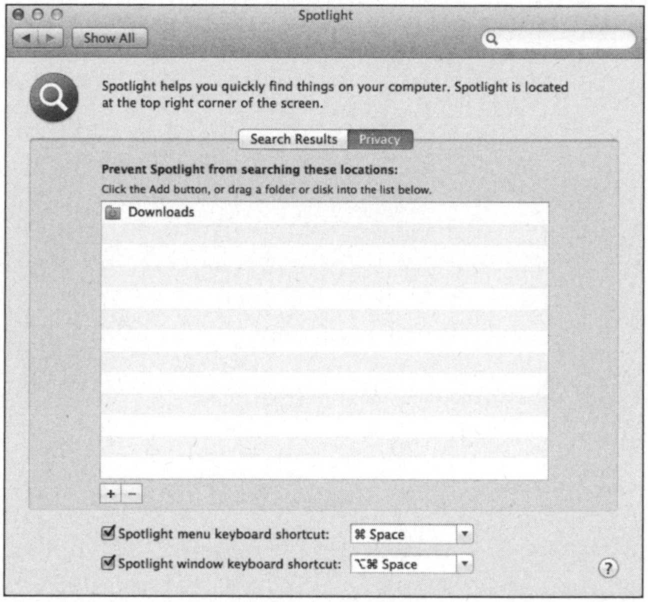

Figure 7-4:
When locations must remain private during a search (even from you!), add them to this list.

To add locations that you want to keep private, click the Add button (bearing a plus sign) and navigate to the desired location. Click the location to select it, and then click Choose. Alternatively, you can drag folders or disks directly from a Finder window and drop them into the pane.

Chapter 8

Using Reminders, Notes, and Notifications

As I've said many times before in my books, "If it works in one place, it's likely to show up in another." In this case, three popular timesaving (and headache-preventing) apps have crossed over from the world of iOS devices — namely, the iPhone, iPad, and iPod touch — and have securely landed on your iMac Desktop! Those apps are Reminders, Notes, and Notification Center.

That's not the only good news, though: These three Mac applications work seamlessly with an iCloud account you've already set up, so if you also use an iOS device (with the same Apple ID), the notes you take and the reminders you make are automatically synchronized among all your Apple computers and devices.

Because all three applications have a similar goal — namely, to keep you in touch with the information, daily tasks, and digital events that matter to you — I'm going to cover them in one shiny chapter. Consider this chapter a guide that demonstrates how you can note, remind, and notify like a power user!

Remind Me to Use Reminders

You don't need to look far to find the Reminders application on your Mac. Just click the Reminders icon on the Dock to display the main window, as shown in Figure 8-1.

Reminders sidebar   Add Reminder

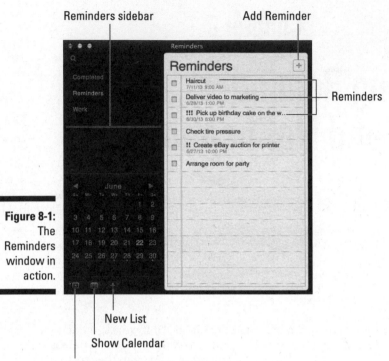

Reminders

Figure 8-1:
The
Reminders
window in
action.

New List

Show Calendar

Hide/Show Reminders Sidebar

The highlights of the Reminders window include

- **Search box:** Click here and type a phrase or name to search for it among your reminders.

- **Reminders sidebar:** You can add as many separate Reminder lists as you like in the application (one for work, for example, and another for your Mac user group). In the sidebar, you can switch quickly between your lists. (Note that two lists, Reminders and Completed, already appear.)

- **Hide/Show Reminders Sidebar button:** Click this button (lower left) to hide or show the Reminders sidebar. You save a significant amount of screen real estate when the display is hidden.

- **Calendar:** This handy calendar indicates which days of the current month already have reminders pending: They're displayed with a dot under the date. You can jump to any date by clicking it. To move forward and backward through the months, click the Previous (left arrow) and Next (right arrow) buttons next to the month name. (Note that this calendar does not sync or exchange reminder dates with the Calendar application.)

✔ **New List button:** Click this button (bottom left) to add a new Reminder list to the sidebar; or, from the keyboard, press ⌘+L. The list name is highlighted in a text box, where you can simply type the new name and then press Return.

✔ **Reminders:** These entries are the reminders themselves. In its simplest form, a reminder is just a short phrase or sentence. Each is prefaced by a check box that you select when the reminder is complete, thereby moving that reminder automatically to the Completed list. And yes, conversely, if you select the Completed list in the sidebar and deselect the check box for a reminder, it returns (like a bad penny) to the original list.

✔ **Add Reminder button:** Click this button (upper right) to add a new reminder to the currently selected list; or, from the keyboard, press ⌘+N. Press Return afterward to save it to your list.

Adding a reminder is straightforward. First, click a date in the calendar display to jump to that date, and then click the Add Reminder button. Type a few words and press Return to create a basic reminder. Now for the fun part: Hover your cursor over the reminder you just created, and an Info button (the lowercase *i* in a circle icon) appears next to the text. The game is afoot! Click that Info button to display the settings you see in Figure 8-2.

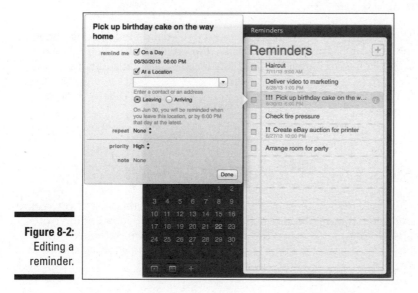

Figure 8-2:
Editing a
reminder.

The fields on the Edit sheet are

- ✔ **Reminder text:** Click this text to edit the reminder text itself.

- ✔ **On a Day:** Enable this check box if the reminder should appear in Notification Center on a particular day. By default, the date is the one selected when you created the reminder. You can click the Date and Time fields to change them.

- ✔ **At a Location:** Here's a powerful feature. Enable this check box, and you can choose a card from your Contacts application that includes an address (or simply type an address into the box). Now Reminders will monitor your current location on your cellular-enabled iOS device (using Location Services) and notify you when you're leaving or arriving at that location (and optionally, on the date and time you specify in the On a Day field). For example, you could create a reminder that notifies you on your iPhone when you're arriving at the mall on September 15 to pick up the watch that's being repaired. *Shazam!*

- ✔ **Repeat:** Set this reminder to automatically repeat every day, week, two weeks, month, or year at the same time. To disable repeat, choose None.

- ✔ **Priority:** You can assign one of four priorities to the reminder: Low, Medium, High, or None. Assigning a priority prefaces the reminder text with one (Low), two (Medium), or three (High) red exclamation points so that the reminder stands out from the crowd.

- ✔ **Note:** Click next to the Note field to enter a free-form text note along with the reminder.

Click the Done button on the Edit sheet when you've finished making changes. You can edit a reminder as often as you like. For example, I sometimes have to change the date on a reminder multiple times as my schedule changes.

To delete a reminder from the list, right-click it and choose Delete from the menu that appears.

Taking Notes the Mavericks Way

Imagine a notepad of unlimited pages that's always available whenever you're around your iMac, iPhone, iPod touch, or iPad. That's the idea behind Notes, and it's superbly simple! To open the application, click the Notes icon on the Dock, which resembles a familiar yellow notepad. The window shown in Figure 8-3 appears.

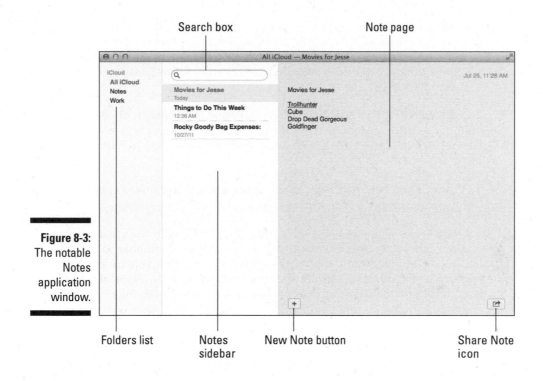

Search box   Note page

Folders list   Notes   New Note button   Share Note
                sidebar   icon

Figure 8-3:
The notable
Notes
application
window.

The salient stuff in the Notes window includes

- **Search box:** If you're hunting for a specific note, click in this box and type a phrase or name to search for it.

- **Folders list:** You can create new folders to hold specific kinds of notes. In Figure 8-3, for example, I added a Work folder. To add a new folder, choose File⇨New Folder or press ⌘+Shift+N, and then type the new folder name. To switch between folders, display the Folders list and click the desired folder.

- **Notes sidebar:** Each Note you create appears as a separate entry in the sidebar. You can click a Note to switch to it immediately.

- **New Note button:** Click this button to add a new Note. You can also right-click the sidebar and choose New Note from the contextual menu. Notes uses the first line of text that you type as the title of the Note, which appears in the sidebar.

- **Note page:** This free-form pane is where you type the body of your note. You can also drag images from a Finder window and include them in the body of the note and even attach files by dragging them from a Finder window as well.

✔ **Share Note icon:** Open this pop-up menu to share the contents of the current note, just like the Share button that appears on the Finder window toolbar. Sharing options can include a new e-mail message, a new message in the Messages application, and new postings to Twitter and Facebook.

To edit a note, click it to select it in the sidebar, and then simply make your changes or additions in the Note page. You can format the text from the Format menu — everything from different fonts and colors to inserting bulleted and numbered lists.

To delete a note you no longer need, right-click it in the sidebar and choose Delete from the menu that appears.

If a note is particularly important and you'd like to keep it "front and center" on your Mavericks Desktop, double-click the note in the sidebar to open it in a separate window and then choose Window⇨Float on Top. Now the note window will stay visible on your Desktop until you quit the Notes application. Even if other application windows are active and would normally be *on top* of the note window, it's downright stubborn, and refuses to be hidden from view!

Staying Current with Notification Center

Unlike Reminders and Notes, Notification Center isn't an application you launch. Instead, the Notification Center icon appears at the far right side of the Finder menu bar, and it's always running.

Click the icon (or, if you're using a trackpad, swipe from the right edge to the left) to display your notifications, as shown in Figure 8-4. These notifications can be generated by a whole host of Mavericks applications and functions, including Calendar, Mail, FaceTime, Reminders, Game Center, Photo Stream, Messages, Safari, Facebook, and even the Apple App Store.

I love how Notification Center doesn't interfere with open applications. It simply moves the entire Desktop to the left so that you can see your notifications. You can close Notification Center at any time by clicking anywhere on the Desktop to the left, clicking the Notifications icon on the Finder menu bar again, or swiping in the opposite direction.

Notification entries that appear in Notification Center are grouped under the application that created them. Many entries can be deleted from the Notification Center by clicking the Delete button that appears next to the application heading (the button bears an X symbol). Other entries, such as Calendar alerts, remain in Notification Center until a certain time has elapsed.

Quick Message buttons

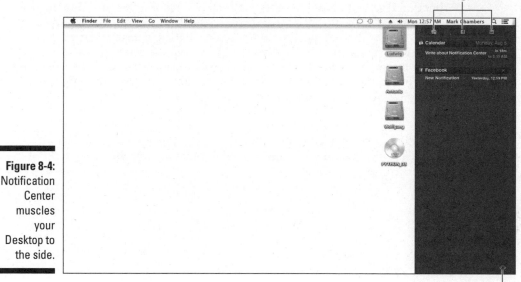

Figure 8-4:
Notification
Center
muscles
your
Desktop to
the side.

System Preferences icon

At the top of Notification Center is a Quick Message button. Just click it to display a pop-up dialog where you can specify the recipients of the message, type your message text, and then click Send — all without having to even launch the Messages application. Depending on the Internet accounts you've added in System Preferences, you may see Facebook and LinkedIn Quick Message buttons at the top of Notification Center as well.

But wait, there's more to Notification Center than just a strip of happenings! Depending on the settings you choose, notifications can also appear without Notification Center being open at all. These notifications are displayed as pop-up *banners* (which disappear in a few seconds) and *alerts* (which must be dismissed by clicking a button). Figure 8-5 illustrates a typical alert notification.

Figure 8-5:
An alert
notification
appears
on your
Desktop.

Mavericks allows *actions* in notifications. Depending on the application or function that generated the notification, you may see buttons on a banner or an alert that allow you to take care of business (without requiring the application to be running). For example, if a new e-mail message is received in Apple Mail, you can choose to reply to or delete the message. Websites can display updates as notifications, and you can answer a FaceTime call directly from the notification. You'll also receive notifications from the App Store indicating the applications that need updating.

You can configure the notifications for all your applications from the Notifications pane in System Preferences, which you can reach easily if Notification Center is open. Just click the gears icon at the lower right of the screen.

Chapter 9

Keeping Track with Contacts and Maps

*A*re you still struggling with a well-thumbed address book stuck in a drawer of your office desk or an archaic folded map in your glove box? Are you fighting a wallet or purse crammed with sticky notes and odd scraps of paper, each of which bears an invaluable e-mail address, phone number, or scribbled directions? If so, you can finally set yourself free and enjoy the "Paperless Lifestyle" of the new millennium with the revolutionary new Rauncho Digital Buddy! Only $29.95 — and it doubles as an indestructible garden hose! But wait! There's more! And if you order in the next 10 minutes, we'll also send you. . . .

Of course, you and I would tune that stuff out as soon as we heard it, but believe it or not, the digital Address Book and Road Map does exist (after a fashion), and you already have both on your iMac — Contacts and Maps. In this chapter, I show you how to store and retrieve all your contact data, including Internet contact information, photographs, and much more. You'll also learn how to view and print travel directions and virtually tour a city!

(And before you ask, operators are *not* standing by.)

Hey, Isn't Contacts Just a Part of Mail?

In early versions of OS X, Contacts (then called Address Book) was relegated to the minor leagues and usually appeared only when you asked for it in Mail. Although it could be run as a separate application, many Mac owners never launched it as a standalone.

Now, however, the Contacts application appears in the limelight, earning a default location on the Dock and available whenever you need it. Although Contacts can still walk through a meadow hand-in-hand with Mail, it also flirts with other OS X applications.

Figure 9-1 illustrates the default face of the Contacts application, complete with a personal address card: your contact information, which you enter during the initial setup of your iMac. This card carries a special me tag on your thumbnail image (indicating that it's your personal card) as well as your user thumbnail next to your name. Other OS X applications use the data in your card to automatically fill out your personal information in all sorts of documents. (In Figure 9-1, I added a number of well-known friends as well . . . a composer or two. You know the drill.)

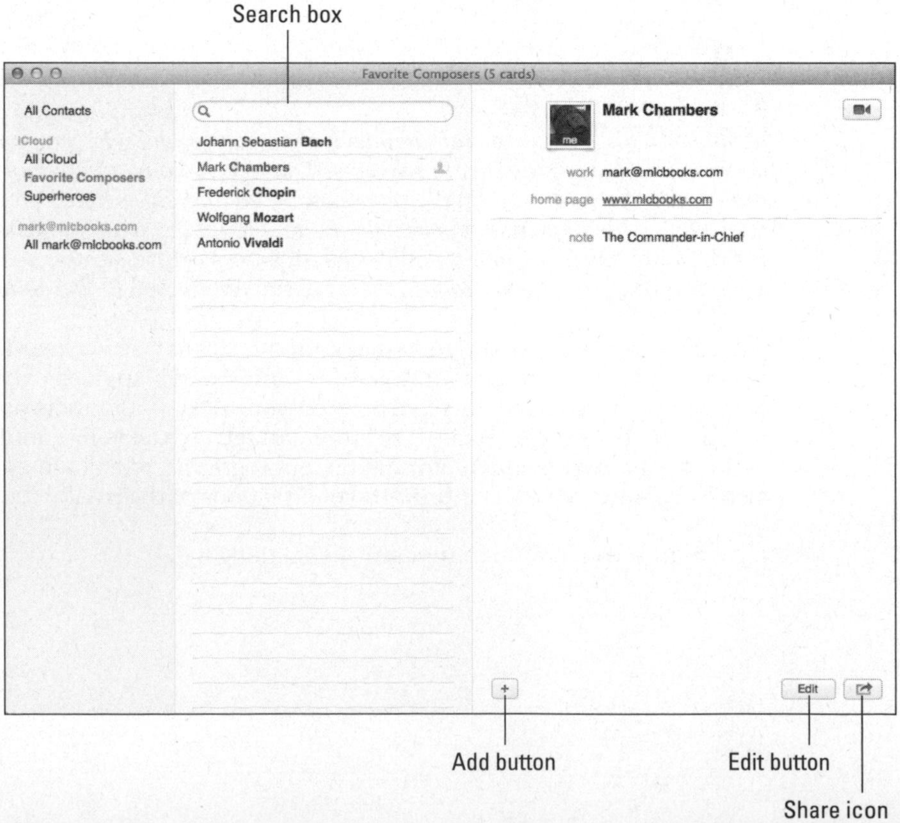

Search box

Figure 9-1:
Greetings
from the
OS X
Contacts
application!

Add button   Edit button

Share icon

Entering Contact Information

Unless you actually meet and hire a group of Data Elves, you do have to either add contacts to Contacts manually or import your contacts from another existing address book application. Allow me to demonstrate here how to create a new contact card:

1. **From the Dock, launch Contacts by clicking its icon.**

   The icon looks like an old-fashioned paper address book with an @ symbol on the cover.

2. **Press the ⌘+N shortcut to create a new contact.**

   Alternatively, choose File⇨New Card, or click the Add button (which carries a plus sign) at the bottom of the window and then click New Contact from the menu that appears.

   Contacts displays the template that you see in Figure 9-2, with the First (name) field highlighted and ready for you to type.

3. **Enter the contact's first name and press Tab to move to the Last name field.**

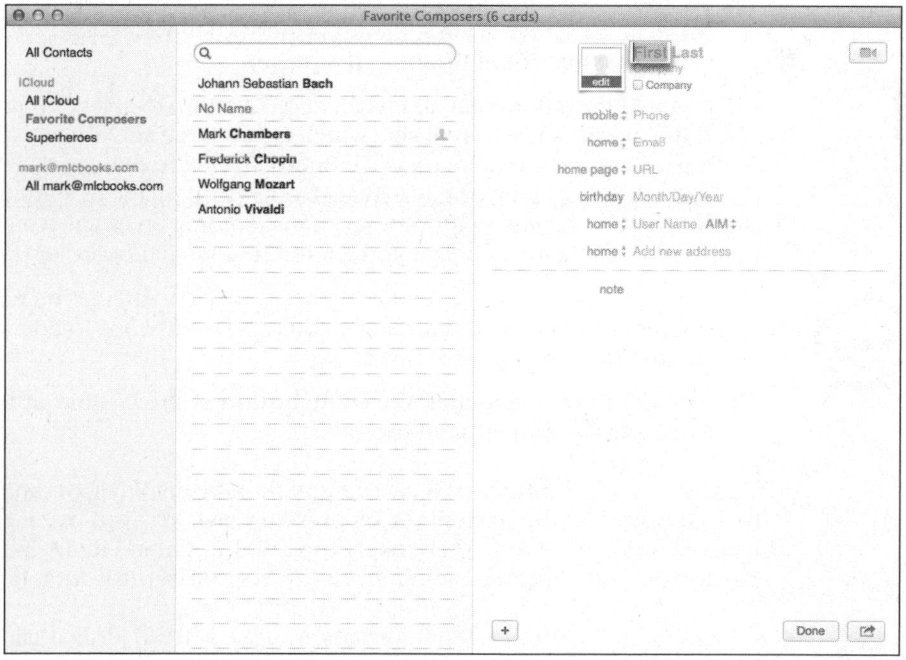

Figure 9-2: "Hey, I don't know anyone named *First Last!*"

4. **Continue entering the corresponding information in each field, pressing Tab to move through the fields.**

If a field isn't applicable (for example, if a person has no home page), just press Tab again to skip it. (Note that when you're browsing your contacts, fields show up within a card only if you've already entered a value — in other words, the fields you skip won't appear unless you add them later.) You can press Return to add extra lines to the Address field.

Note the up- and down-arrow icons next to each field. When you see those, Contacts is telling you that there are additional versions of the field that you can enter as well. (Think home and work addresses.) Click the up/down arrow, and a pop-up menu appears, allowing you to choose which version of the field will be displayed. Depending on the field, Contacts may automatically display an additional version; for example, if you enter a work address for the contact, another field for the contact's home address appears. Click this new field and then you can enter the contact's home address, too.

You can also add new fields to a card, such as web addresses (URLs), birthdays, and maiden names. To add a new field, choose Card⇨Add Field and then choose the field you want to add from the menu that appears. You can also click the Add button at the bottom of the window to display the same menu.

5. **To add a photograph to the card, choose Card⇨Choose Custom Image (or drag an image from a Finder window, Mail message, web page, or iPhoto on top of the thumbnail square).**

If you choose to assign an image, click Defaults to select an image from the Mavericks thumbnail set (which is the same set you get when assigning a user account image). Click Photo Stream to choose an image from your Photo Stream, or click Faces to select an image of someone's face that you've tagged in iPhoto. You can also drag an image from a Finder window or paste an image you copied to your Clipboard earlier.

Because your iMac has a built-in FaceTime HD camera, you can click the Camera tab to take a new image. You can also choose to add a Photo Booth effect to your new image.

6. **When you're done, click the Done button at the bottom of the Contacts window to save the card.**

You can edit the contents of a card at any time by displaying it and clicking the Edit button at the bottom (or by pressing ⌘+L, or even by clicking Edit on the Contacts menu bar and choosing the Edit Card menu item). When you're finished editing the card, click Done at the bottom of the Contacts window.

No need to edit a card to add information to the Note field. Just click and type.

You can also add contact cards directly to Contacts from the OS X Mail application as well as a number of third-party e-mail applications (go figure). In Mail, click the message (to highlight it) from the person whom you want to add, click the friendly Message menu, and then choose Add Sender to Contacts. However, adding contacts this way doesn't add their supporting information — just their name and e-mail address — and, if they used Mail on their end to send the message and they have a photo attached to their personal card, their photo gets imported as well. Once again, your nimble fingers have to manually enter the rest.

"Mark, I never use the Home Page field when I add a contact. Can't I get rid of it completely?" Indeed you can, good reader! To customize the default fields that appear when you create a new contact card, open the Contacts menu, choose Preferences, and then click the Template tab. Each field has a Delete icon (the red minus sign) and some have an Add icon (the green plus sign). To remove a field from your template, click the Delete icon. To add a new version of a field (for example, a home e-mail address), click the Add icon next to the existing field of the same type, and then click the up/down arrow icon to select the field name. To add a completely new field (such as Middle or Maiden Name), click the Add Field drop-down menu.

Don't forget to add those fax numbers! If you have an external USB analog modem that's compatible with OS X Mavericks (or a multifunction printer that supports faxing), you can fax from any application. Just choose File⇨Print (or press ⌘+P), click the PDF button at the bottom of the Print dialog, and choose Fax PDF. OS X automatically fills in the address for you but only if the contact has a fax number entered as part of the contact card.

If someone sends you an e-mail message with a vCard (look for an attachment with a .vcf extension), consider yourself lucky. Just drag the vCard from the attachment window in Mail and drop it in your Contacts; any information that the person wants you to have is added automatically. Sweet!

To delete a card, right-click the unlucky name and then choose Delete Card.

Using Contact Information

Okay, after you have your contact information in Contacts, what can you actually *do* with it? Often, all you really need is a quick glance at an address. To display the card for any contact in Contacts, just click the desired entry in the Name column. You can move to the next and previous cards by using the up- and down-arrow keys on your keyboard. (Oh, and don't forget that you can right-click many items in a card to display menu commands specific to those items.)

But wait, there's more! You can also

- ✔ **Copy and paste.** The old favorites are still around. You can copy any data from a card (press ⌘+C) and paste it into another open application (press ⌘+V).

- ✔ **Visit a contact's home page.** Click the contact entry to select it, and then click the page link displayed in the card. Safari dutifully answers the call, and next thing you know, you're online and at the home page specified in the entry.

- ✔ **Send an e-mail message.** Click and drag to select any e-mail address on a card; then choose Contacts➪Services➪New Email to Address. Bingo! Depending on the information that you select, other services might also be available.

- ✔ **Add a Messages buddy.** From Messages, choose Buddies➪Add Buddy. From the dialog that appears, you can select a contact card that has an Instant Messenger address and add it to your Buddy list.

- ✔ **Export contacts.** From Contacts, select the contacts that you want to export and then choose File➪Export➪Export vCard. Contacts displays a Save sheet. Navigate to the location where you want to save the cards and click Save.

- ✔ **Send a contact through Mail or Messages.** Click the Share a Contact button (it looks like a box with an arrow) at the bottom of the Contacts window, and choose either Email Card or Message Card. The Contacts application automatically creates a new Mail message (or Messages conversation) with the contact information attached as a vCard.

- ✔ **Search amongst your contacts.** If you're searching for a specific person and all you have is a phone number or a fragment of an address, click in the Search field (which bears a magnifying glass icon) and type the text. While you continue to enter characters, Contacts shows you how many contact cards contain matching characters and displays just those entries in the Name column. Now that's *sassy!* (And convenient. And fast as all get-out.) Check out Figure 9-3; a couple of familiar folks share the same address in Gotham City, and I found them by using the Search field.

Speaking of searching using a contact card in Contacts, Spotlight is also at your beck and call. Click a contact to select it and then choose Edit➪Spotlight. *Whoosh!* Mavericks searches your entire system for everything related to that contact and displays it in the familiar Spotlight window. (Find more on Spotlight in Chapter 7.)

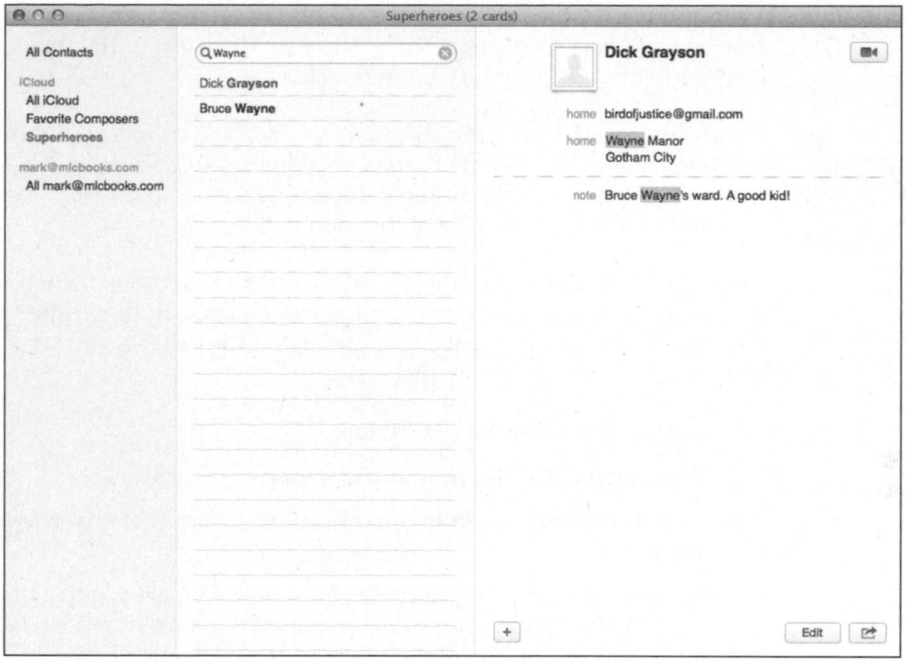

Superheroes (2 cards)

All Contacts

iCloud
All iCloud
Favorite Composers
Superheroes

mark@mlcbooks.com
All mark@mlcbooks.com

Q Wayne

Dick Grayson
Bruce Wayne

Dick Grayson

home birdofjustice@gmail.com
home Wayne Manor
         Gotham City

note Bruce Wayne's ward. A good kid!

Edit

Figure 9-3:
Holy text
match,
Batman!

Arranging Your Contact Cards

Contacts also provides you with a method of organizing your cards into groups. Use a *group* to identify folks with a common link, such as family, friends, co-workers, or folks who enjoy yodeling. For example, you could set up a Cell Phone group that you can use when syncing data with your Bluetooth smartphone. You can hide or display the Groups list at the left of the Contacts window by choosing View➪Hide/Show Groups (or by pressing ⌘+1).

To create and name a group, click the Add button at the bottom of the window and click New Group. (You can also choose File➪New Group or press ⌘+Shift+N.) Contacts adds a highlighted text box where you can type the group name. Then press Return to save it.

Then, with your new (empty) group created, just add folks manually. From the group list, click the All Contacts link to see a list of everyone in Contacts database, and then click and drag the entries that you want to add to the desired group name.

Or, you can first select the entries for those contacts you want to add to the group, and then choose File➪New Group from Selection instead. This saves you a step because the group is created and the members are added automatically simultaneously.

After you create a New Group, you can instantly display members of that group by clicking its name in the group list. To return to the display of all your contacts, click the All Contacts link.

To further organize your groups, you can drag and drop a group on top of another group. The "dropped" group becomes a subgroup, which is handy for organizing things, such as branch offices in your company or perhaps relatives to whom you're not speaking at the moment.

Need an even harder-working group? Create a *smart group,* which — get this — automatically adds new contacts you create to the proper group or removes them from the group, depending on the criteria you specify! To create a smart group, follow these steps:

1. **Choose File⇨New Smart Group.**

2. **Type a name for the new smart group.**

3. **From the Card pop-up menu, choose the item that will trigger the action.**

   For example, you can choose to automate a smart group according to the contents of each new card, a company name, or a particular city or state.

4. **From the Contains pop-up menu, choose the criteria for the item.**

   You can set an item to contain (or not contain) a specific string of characters, or change it in a certain amount of time. To illustrate, one of my hardest-working smart groups automatically checks the Company field in every new card for my publisher's company name and adds that contact card to my Wiley Publishing group if a match occurs.

   • *To add another criteria line:* Click the button with the plus sign at the end of the first text field.

   • *To delete a criteria line:* Conversely, if you decide you have one criteria line too many, click the button with the minus sign next to the offending rule.

5. **After your smart group criteria are correct, click OK.**

   The smart group name appears in your group list. *Voilà!*

Here's another handy feature of a Contacts group: You can send all the members of a group the same e-mail message at one time. In Mail, simply enter the Group name in the To field of the Compose window, and the same message is sent to everyone. Even Gandalf couldn't do that (but my copy editor bets that Dumbledore could).

Using Network Directories

I know, I know. I said earlier that you'd have to enter all your contacts yourself (or import them, if possible), but I was talking about your personal contacts. You can also access five types of external directories from Contacts:

- ✔ iMac users working in a Windows network environment can use Exchange 2007 (or later) or Outlook network directories.

- ✔ If you're a member of a company NetInfo network — and if you don't know, ask your wizened network administrator — you can search network directory servers from Contacts. These servers are available automatically, so no configuration is necessary. Sweet.

- ✔ OS X Mavericks Server — a separate purchase from the App Store — offers a Contacts server feature for sharing directories across your network, using the CardDAV standard.

- ✔ Contacts can share contact information using your iCloud, Google, Facebook, LinkedIn, or Yahoo! account.

- ✔ You can search Internet-based LDAP directories. Again, suffice it to say that your network guru can tell you whether LDAP servers are available to you. (In another blazing display of techno-nerd acronym addiction, LDAP stands for *Lightweight Directory Access Protocol*.) With LDAP, you can search a central company directory from anywhere in the world as long as you have an Internet connection. Your network administrator or the LDAP server administrator can supply you with these settings.

To search any network directory, you need to create a corresponding directory account. Follow these steps to add a directory account:

1. **Choose Contacts⇨Preferences to display the Preferences window.**

2. **Click the Accounts tab.**

3. **Click the Add button at the bottom of the Accounts list to launch the Add Account assistant.**

4. **If you're using an Exchange directory, click Exchange from the list. If you're connecting to a CardDAV or LDAP directory, choose Other Contacts Account from the list.**

5. **Click Continue.**

   Type the required information in the fields that appear. (Your network administrator should be able to provide you with the necessary values.)

6. **Click Create.**

   You'll see the blue network directory entry appear in the Group column.

The rest is easy! Click the desired directory link in the group display and use the Search field as you normally would. Matching entries display the person's name, e-mail address, and phone number.

"But hey, Mark, what if I'm not online? My company's LDAP directory isn't much good then, right?" Normally, that's true. LDAP information is available to you only when you're online and the LDAP server is available. To make a person's information always available (even if your network is unavailable), search the LDAP database and drag the resulting entry from the contacts list to the desired group (or the All Contacts link) on the group display. You'll import the information to your local Contacts database — and you'll see it even when you're not online! (You should repeat this import step on a regular basis, since the import is a "snapshot" of the current database and doesn't automatically update with any changes made later.)

Printing Contacts with Flair

For those moments when you need an archaic hard copy of your contacts, Contacts offers a whopping four formats: mailing labels, envelopes, lists, and even a snappy pocket address book.

By default, Contacts prints on standard U.S. letter-size paper (8½ x 11") in portrait orientation. You can change these settings to, for example, legal-size paper or landscape orientation, right from the Print dialog (choose File⇨Print or press ⌘+P).

Follow these steps to print your contacts:

1. **Press ⌘+P.**

    Contacts displays the Print dialog. To show all the settings, click the Show Details button at the bottom of the sheet.

    If you need more than one copy, click in the Copies field to specify the desired number.

    Need labels? We've got 'em! From the Style pop-up menu, choose Mailing Labels and then specify what type of label stock you're using on the Layout pane. Click the Label button to sort your labels by name or postal code, choose a font, select a text color, and add an icon or image to your labels. To switch to a standard contact list, click Style again and then click Lists. (You can also print envelopes and pocket address book pages in a similar manner; just choose the desired entry from the Style pop-up menu.)

2. **Select the desired Attributes check boxes to specify which contact card fields you want to appear in your list.**

    The Attributes list appears only if you're printing contacts in either the Lists style or the pocket address book style.

3. **Click the Print button to send the job to the selected printer.**

   Alternatively, you can create a PDF file in a specified location, which is a handy trick to use if you'd rather not be burdened with paper, but you still need to consult the list or give it to others. (*PDF files* are a special document display format developed by Adobe; they are displayed like a printed document but take up minimal space.) To display the contents of a PDF file in OS X, you need only double-click it in the Finder window, and the built-in Preview application is happy to oblige. Even faster, select the PDF file in the Finder window and press the spacebar for a Quick Look.

Swapping Bytes with vCards

A *vCard* is a standard file format for exchanging contact information between programs such as Contacts, Microsoft Entourage, Microsoft Outlook, Eudora, and the Android operating system. (Heck, if you're sharp enough to have an iPod, iPhone, or iPad, you can even store vCard data there.) Think of a vCard as an electronic business card that you can attach to an e-mail message, send via File Transfer Protocol (FTP), or exchange with others by using your smartphone and tablet computer. vCard files end with the extension .vcf.

In Contacts, you can create a single vCard containing one or more selected entries by choosing File⇨Export⇨Export vCard. Then, like with any other OS X Save dialog, just navigate to the spot where you want the file saved, give it a name, and click Save.

Here are two ways to import vCards into Contacts:

✔ Drag the vCard files to Contacts and drop them in the application window.

✔ Choose File⇨Import (or press ⌘+O). From the Open dialog, navigate to the location of the vCard files that you want to add, select them, and then click Open.

The vCard tab in the Contacts Preferences window allows you to choose the format of your exported vCard files. Older devices work only with vCard 2.1 format, while newer applications recognize the improved vCard 3 format. You can also specify whether your exported vCard files will contain the contents of the Notes field and also whether they will include any photos you've attached. If you'd rather not provide the private data on your personal (or Me) card in a vCard, make sure that you select the Enable Private Me Card check box.

Introducing the Maps Window

If you're an owner of an iPad, iPhone, or iPod touch, prepare yourself for a joyful state: With the arrival of OS X Mavericks, your beloved Maps application now resides on your Dock! As long as you have a connection to the

Internet, Maps is ready to display locations, provide directions, and even allow for informal views of important sites worldwide! (Recognize the grand dame in Figure 9-4?)

Displaying an overhead view of an address is one of the simplest chores in all of OS X. From the Maps window, just click in the Search box at the top-right corner, type the address, and press Return. Maps displays the address with a red pushpin to help you locate it.

TIP

Depending on the location you've chosen, you may also see a tiny Info icon (which looks like a lowercase "*i*" within a circle) next to the name. To view more information, click the Info icon.

3D view   View buttons   Search box

Figure 9-4:
The Statue of Liberty shines in the Maps application.

Zoom Out

Zoom In

Compass

You can quickly map your current location. Just choose View↪Go to Current Location, or press ⌘+L.

Ah, but why stop with just a simple address? You can also enter information such as

- ✔ The name of a landmark, monument, or building (for example, *Statue of Liberty*).

- ✔ The name of a business or restaurant (or even a genre of food, such as *Chinese*) followed by the city name. Maps displays matching sites with pushpins (complete with reviews), and you can click any of the pushpins to find out more information on that location. Figure 9-5 illustrates a search for *pizza*. You can see the Info pop-up that appeared when I clicked the Info icon next to the restaurant name, complete with a link to its website and reviews a-plenty.

- ✔ Attractions and services, followed by the city name. You can search for a gas station, movie theater, or a local park.

If you need to zoom in or zoom out on a Maps display, use the scroll function on your mouse, click the plus and minus buttons at the bottom-right corner of the Maps window, or use the ⌘+plus and ⌘+minus shortcuts. To move around the Maps window, click and drag the map in the desired direction.

Figure 9-5: Looks like this pizza joint is highly rated.

Switching Views in Maps

A traditional printed map offers you only one view, which may be perfectly fine for determining a route, but provides no visual interest. (The word *banal* comes to mind.) Maps, on the other hand, offers three types of views, each of which offers certain advantages:

✔ *Standard mode* is a familiar line map, with streets and highways marked. Standard mode is best for planning a road trip, just like your father's old-fashioned paper map.

✔ *Satellite mode* is a photographic overhead view without streets or high-ways marked, which is great for panoramic views of your neighborhood or a location and its surroundings.

✔ *Hybrid mode* is a photographic overhead view with streets and highways marked. (A friend of mine who's a realtor loves Hybrid mode because she can display an overview of a neighborhood with identified streets.)

To select your view, click one of the three buttons at the top of the Maps window, or press ⌘+1 for Standard, ⌘+2 for Hybrid, or ⌘+3 for Satellite. Figure 9-4 illustrates Satellite view mode, while Figure 9-6 shows off Standard view.

Figure 9-6: Standard view reminds me of an auto GPS unit.

For additional visual thrills, you can angle the Maps display with a slight 3D effect — nothing quite as grand as a 3D TV, but it does help add depth to Satellite and Hybrid views. To toggle 3D on and off, press ⌘+0, or press the button with the buildings icon in the upper-left corner of the Maps window (refer to Figure 9-4).

By default, Maps is oriented with north at the top of the screen. To change the orientation, click the compass at the bottom-right corner of the screen and drag in the desired direction. To immediately return to north at the top of the screen, press ⌘+up or choose View⇨Snap to North.

Getting Directions over Yonder

My primary use for a map is getting directions from one point to another, and Maps doesn't disappoint when it comes to navigation. Click the Directions button to display the panel you see in Figure 9-7, and you're ready to plot your course.

Figure 9-7: The Directions panel is ready to provide directions to your next clambake.

Follow these steps to get directions between two addresses:

1. **In the Start box, type the starting address.**

   As you type, Maps provides a pop-up list of suggestions taken from your recent locations, as well as addresses from your Contacts database and matching streets from around the globe. To choose one of these suggestions, just click it. To clear the contents of the field, click the X button that appears at the right side of the box.

2. **Press Tab to move to the End box.**

3. **In the End box, type the destination address.**

   Note that your destination doesn't have to be a specific address — for example, **Memphis, TN** works just fine.

4. **Click the Car button (which carries a car icon) for road directions, or the Walk button (which sports a pedestrian icon) for walking directions.**

5. **Press Return to generate your directions or Clear to start over.**

As you can see in Figure 9-7, Maps usually offers more than one route for your trip. The first route suggested is typically the fastest or shortest, and it appears as a bright blue line. To view one of the other routes (light blue), just click it, and it turns bright blue to indicate it's now the selected route. You can see the approximate mileage and time for the currently selected route at the top of the turn list. The turn-by-turn list provides approximate mileage for each leg of the journey.

You can easily print the route map and directions by choosing File⇨Print (or by pressing ⌘+P), and then clicking the Show Details button at the bottom of the Print sheet to display all the options.

If you'd rather create a PDF document with your map and directions, choose File⇨Export as PDF.

Finally, Maps also allows you to share your maps and directions using Mail, Messages, Twitter, or Facebook. Click the Share button at the top of the window, and then select the desired sharing method.

Part III
Connecting and Communicating

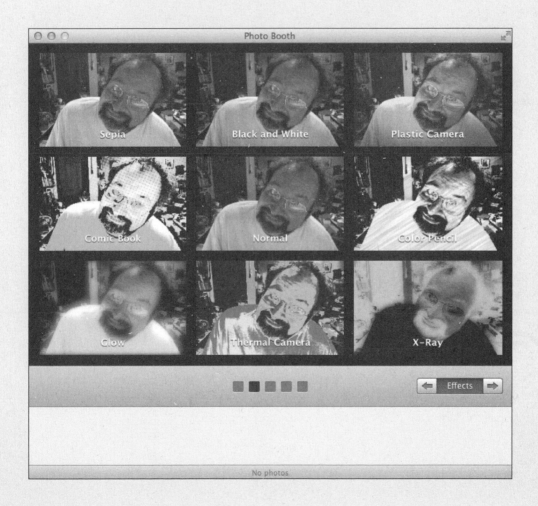

In this part . . .

- ✔ Surf the web with ease using Apple's Safari browser
- ✔ Sync documents and data automatically using iCloud
- ✔ Make video calls to friends and family using FaceTime

Chapter 10

Going Places with Safari

I proudly surf the web via a lean, mean — and fast — browser application. That's Safari, of course, and it just keeps getting better with each new version of OS X. Safari delivers the web the right way, without the wait. You'll find that new features have been added to Safari that no other browser offers, such as the Reading List (which allows you to easily select articles and pages for later perusal).

If you need a guide to Safari, this is your chapter. Sure, you can start using Safari immediately, but wouldn't you rather read a few pages so that you can surf like a power user?

Within these pages, I show you how to use those other controls and toolbar buttons in Safari — you know, the ones in addition to the Forward and Back buttons — and you discover how to keep track of where you've been and where you'd like to go.

Pretend You've Never Used This Thing

Figure 10-1 illustrates the Safari window. You can launch Safari directly from the Dock, or you can click the Safari icon from Launchpad.

Sidebar

Top Sites

iCloud tabs

Share

Favorites bar

Tab bar

Downloads

New Tab

Reload

Address box

Toolbar

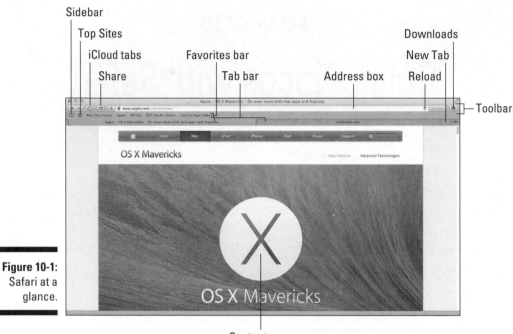

Figure 10-1:
Safari at a
glance.

Content pane

Major sections of the Safari window are

✔ **The toolbar:** Here are the most often-used commands for common tasks such as navigation, adding bookmarks, and searching Google (or Yahoo!, or Bing). Plus, here you can type or paste the address for websites that you'd like to visit. You can easily hide the toolbar to provide more real estate in your browser window for web content. To toggle hidden mode, choose View⇨Hide/Show Toolbar.

✔ **The Favorites bar:** Consider this a toolbar that allows you to jump directly to your favorite websites with but a single click or two. I show you later (in the section "Adding and Using Bookmarks") how to add and remove sites from your Favorites bar. For now, remember that you can toggle the display of the Favorites bar by choosing View⇨Hide/Show Favorites Bar or by pressing ⌘+Shift+B.

✔ **The Tab bar:** This toolbar allows you to quickly switch between multiple web pages that you've loaded, using what appear to be old-fashioned filing folder tabs (something familiar — familiar is good). To hide or display the Tab bar, press ⌘+Shift+T or choose View⇨Hide/Show Tab Bar.

✔ **The Safari sidebar:** The sidebar pane allows you to organize and read your bookmarks, your reading list, and your shared links. To hide or display the sidebar, press ⌘+Shift+L or choose View⇨Hide/Show Sidebar.

✔ **The Content pane:** Congratulations! At last, you've waded through the pregame show and reached the area where web pages are displayed. The Content pane can be scrolled, and when you minimize the Safari window to the Dock, you get a *thumbnail* (minimized) image of the Content pane.

The Content pane often contains underlined (or colored) text and graphics that transport you to other pages when you click them. These underlined words and icons are *links,* and they zip you right from one area of a site to another or to a different site. You can tell when your cursor is resting on a link because the cursor changes to that reassuring pointing-finger hand. Handy!

✔ **The status bar:** The status bar displays information about what the cursor is resting upon, such as the address for a link or the name of an image; it also updates you on what's happening while a page is loading. To hide or display the status bar, press ⌘+/ (forward slash) or choose View➪Hide/Show Status Bar.

Visiting Websites

Here's the stuff that virtually everyone over the age of five knows how to do . . . but I get paid by the word, and some folks might just not be aware of the many ways to visit a site. You can load a web page from any of the following methods:

✔ **Type (or paste) a website address in the Address box on the toolbar and then press Return.** If you're typing in an address and Safari recognizes the site as one that you've visited in the past, it "helps" by autocompleting the address for you. Press Return if you want to accept the suggested site. If this is a new site, just keep typing.

The Safari Address box also acts as a *smart address* field, displaying a new pop-up menu of sites that match the text you entered. Safari does this by using sites taken from your History file and your bookmarks, as well as sites returned from Google, Yahoo!, or Bing. If the site you want to visit appears in the list, click it to jump there immediately.

✔ **Click a Bookmarks entry in Safari.**

✔ **If the Home button appears on your toolbar, click the button to go to the home page that you specify.** Read more on this in the upcoming section, "Setting Up Your Home Page."

✔ **Click the Show Top Sites button on the toolbar.** Safari displays a wall of preview thumbnail pages from your most frequently visited sites, and you can jump to a site just by clicking the preview. You can anchor a thumbnail to keep it onscreen permanently by clicking the pin icon next to the desired thumbnail. Click the Edit button on the Top Sites screen to delete a preview thumbnail (click the X). You can also choose the size of the preview thumbnails in Edit mode.

Because each thumbnail is updated with the most current content, the Top Sites wall makes a great timesaver. Quickly make a visual check of all your favorite haunts from one screen!

✔ **Click an item you saved earlier in the sidebar's Reading list.**

✔ **Click a link in the sidebar's Shared Links list.**

✔ **Click a page link in Apple Mail or another Internet-savvy application.** Some Mac applications require you to hold down ⌘ while clicking to open a web page.

✔ **Click a page link in another web page.**

✔ **Select a web address in a document, click the Services menu, and choose Open Page in Safari.**

✔ **Type a search term in the Address box.** By default, Safari uses Google as a search engine, but you can also use Yahoo! or Bing if you prefer. To set the default search engine, choose Safari⟶Preferences; then, on the General tab, open the Default Search Engine drop-down menu. (You can immediately switch to another engine from the bottom of the menu that appears as you're typing into the Address box.)

Click in the Address box, type the contents that you want to find, and then press Return. Safari presents you with the search results page on Google for the text that you entered.

✔ **Click a Safari page icon on the Dock or in a Finder window.** Drag a site from your Favorites bar (or drag the icon from the left side of the Address box) and drop it on the right side of the Dock. Clicking the icon that you add launches Safari and automatically loads that site.

This trick works only on the side of the Dock to the right of the vertical line. More on that all-important divider in a bit.

If you minimize Safari to the Dock, you'll see a thumbnail of the page with the Safari logo superimposed on it. Click this thumbnail on the Dock to restore the page to its full glory.

Speaking of full glory, Safari supports the same full-screen mode as many other Mavericks applications. Click the Full Screen icon at the top-right corner of the Safari window to switch to full-screen mode, or press the Control+⌘+F short-cut (a good shortcut to memorize because it works with virtually all Mavericks-compatible applications). To make things convenient for you, the Address box remains, as do the iCloud Tabs, Share, Reader, Downloads, Back, and Forward icons. To exit full-screen mode, press Esc or the Control+⌘+F shortcut again.

Navigating the Web

A typical web surfing session is a linear experience. You bop from one page to the next, absorbing the information that you want and discarding the rest. However, after you visit a few sites, you might find that you need to return to where you've been or head to the familiar ground of your home page. Safari offers these navigational controls on the toolbar:

- ✔ **Back:** Click the Back button (the left-facing arrow) on the toolbar to return to the last page you visited. Additional clicks take you to previous pages, in reverse order. The Back button is disabled if you haven't visited at least two sites. If you right-click the Back button, you see a pop-up menu with the pages you've visited — click any entry in the menu to return there immediately!

- ✔ **Forward:** If you've clicked the Back button at least once, clicking the Forward button (the right-facing arrow) takes you to the next page (or through the pages) where you originally were, in forward order. The Forward button is disabled if you haven't used the Back button and haven't navigated to another page.

Safari supports a number of trackpad gestures. For example, you can swipe in either direction with two fingers to move backward and forward, just as you would move with the Forward and Back buttons. To zoom in and out on the Content pane, you can either double-tap the trackpad or pinch with two fingers — yes, just like an iPhone. (Ever get the notion that someday we'll just have a single box called "The Device" that does it all?)

- ✔ **Home:** Click this button (look for the little house) to return to your home page.

Not all these buttons and controls must appear on your toolbar. You may never see many of these toolbar controls unless you add them yourself. To display or hide toolbar controls, choose View⇨Customize Toolbar. The sheet that appears works just like the Customize Toolbar sheet in a Finder window: Drag the control you want from the sheet to your Safari toolbar or drag a control that you don't want from the toolbar to the sheet.

- ✔ **New Tab:** Click this button (it looks like a little tab with a plus sign) to open a new tab in the tab bar. I'll get knee-deep into tabbed browsing later in the chapter.

- ✔ **AutoFill:** If you fill out a lot of forms online — when you're shopping at websites, for example — you can click the AutoFill button (which looks like a little text box and a pen) to complete these forms for you. You can set what information is used for AutoFill by choosing Safari⇨Preferences and clicking the AutoFill toolbar button.

To be honest, I'm not a big fan of releasing *any* of my personal information to *any* website, so I don't use AutoFill often. If you do decide to use this feature, make sure that the connection is secure (look for the padlock icon in the Address box) and read the site's Privacy Agreement page first to see how your identity data will be treated.

✔ **Top Sites:** Click this button to display the Top Sites screen I discuss earlier. If you're having trouble finding it, the button bears a tiny, fashionable grid of squares.

✔ **Zoom:** Shrink or expand the size of text on the page, offering smaller, space-saving characters (for the shrinking crowd) or larger, easier-to-read text (for the expanding crowd) by clicking the Zoom button, which is labeled with a small and large letter *A*. (From the keyboard, you can press ⌘++(plus sign) to expand and ⌘+− (minus sign) to shrink.

✔ **Favorites bar:** Click this button (which carries the Bookmarks symbol sandwiched between two horizontal lines) to display or hide the Favorites bar.

✔ **Stop/Reload:** Click Reload (which has a circular arrow in the Address box) to *refresh* (reload) the contents of the current page. Although most pages remain static, some pages change their content at regular intervals or after you fill out a form or click a button. By clicking Reload (look for the curvy arrow in the Address box), you can see what's changed on these pages. (I use Reload every hour or so with CNN.com, for example.) While a page is loading, the Reload button turns into the Stop button — with a little X mark — and you can click it to stop the loading of the content from the current page. This feature is a real boon when a download takes *foorrevverr,* which can happen when you're trying to visit a popular or slow website (especially if you're using a dial-up modem connection to the Internet). Using Stop is also handy if a page has a number of very large graphics that are likely to take a long time to load.

✔ **Bookmarks:** Click this toolbar button (which carries an open book icon) to hide or display the Safari sidebar. You'll find the complete description of the sidebar in an upcoming section.

✔ **History:** Click this button (which bears a clock symbol) to display or hide the History list, which I discuss later in this chapter.

✔ **Downloads:** Click this toolbar button to display the files you've downloaded recently. Click the Clear button to clear the contents of the Download list. Note that clearing the list does not delete the files you've downloaded; it simply cleans things up. You can also double-click a completed download in the list to open it immediately. (More on downloading in a couple pages.)

When you're downloading a file, a tiny progress bar appears in the Downloads button on the toolbar to show you how much you've received. Now that, good reader, is *progress!* (Let's see whether my editor allows such a horrible pun to remain.)

✔ **Open in Dashboard:** Click this button to create a Dashboard widget using the contents of the currently displayed web page. Safari prompts you to choose which clickable section of the page to be included in the widget's borders (such as the local radar map on your favorite weather website). Click Add, and Dashboard loads automatically with your new widget.

✔ **Mail:** Click this button (bearing an envelope icon) to send an e-mail message with a link to the current page, just as if you clicked the Share button and chose Email This Page. Safari automatically opens Apple Mail (or whatever you're using as your default email application) and creates a new message with the link already in the body. *Shazam!*

✔ **Add Bookmark:** Click this toolbar button (which carries a plus sign) to add a page to your Bookmarks bar or Bookmarks menu. (More on this in a tad.)

✔ **Print:** Click this convenient button to print the contents of the Safari window. (Dig that crazy printer icon!)

✔ **Share:** If you have an iPhone, iPod touch, or iPad, you're probably already familiar with this button, which carries a rectangle and curved arrow symbol. Click the Share button to send the current page (or a link to it) to a number of different destinations, including your reading list, an e-mail message, your Messages application, Facebook, or Twitter. You can also add a bookmark to the current page using the Share button. Figure 10-2 illustrates the Share button in action.

Figure 10-2:
The Share button makes it easy to spread goodness and light!

Setting Up Your Home Page

Choosing a home page is one of the easiest methods of speeding up your web surfing, especially if you're using a dial-up modem connection. However, a large percentage of the Mac owners whom I've talked with have never set their own home page; instead, they simply use the default home page provided by their browser. Declare your independence! With Safari running, take a moment to follow these steps to declare your own freedom to choose your own home page:

1. **In Safari, navigate to the web page that you want to become your new home page.**

   I recommend selecting a page with few graphics, or a fast-loading popular site.

2. **Choose Safari⇨Preferences or press ⌘+, (comma).**

3. **Click the General button.**

   You see the settings shown in Figure 10-3.

4. **Click the Set to Current Page button.**

5. **Click the Close button to exit the Preferences dialog.**

Alternatively, open the New Windows Open With pop-up menu and choose Empty Page if you want Safari to open a new window with a blank page. This choice is the fastest one for a home page.

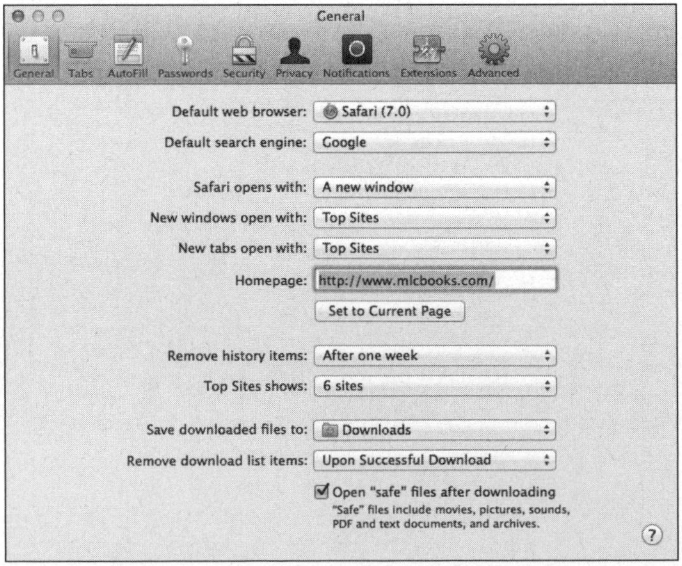

Figure 10-3:
Adding your own home page is an easy change you can make.

Visit your home page at any time by pressing the Home button on the toolbar. If it doesn't appear on your toolbar, you can add it by choosing View⇨ Customize Toolbar.

Adding and Using Bookmarks

No doubt about it: Bookmarks make the web a friendly place. As you collect bookmarks in Safari, you're able to immediately jump from one site to another with a single click of the Bookmarks menu or the buttons on the Favorites bar.

To add a bookmark, first navigate to the desired page and then do any of the following:

✔ **Choose Bookmarks⇨Add Bookmark.**

✔ **Press the ⌘+D keyboard shortcut.**

   Safari displays a sheet where you can enter the name for the bookmark and also select where it appears (on the Favorites bar, Top Sites display, Bookmarks folder, or Bookmarks menu).

✔ **Drag the icon next to the web address from the Address field to the Favorites bar.**

   This trick also works with other applications besides Safari, including in a Mail message or Messages conversation. Drag the icon from the Safari Address field to the other application window, and the web page link is added to your document.

You can also drag a link on the current page to the Favorites bar, but note that doing this adds a bookmark only for the page corresponding to the link — not the current page.

To jump to a bookmark

✔ **Choose it from the Bookmarks menu.** If the bookmark is contained in a folder, which I discuss later in this section, hover your cursor over the folder name to show its contents and then click the bookmark.

✔ **Click the bookmark on the Favorites bar.**

   If you've added a large number of items to the Favorites bar, click the More icon on the edge of the Favorites bar to display the rest of the buttons.

✔ **Click the Show Sidebar button (which looks like a small, opened book) on the Favorites bar, click the Bookmarks icon in the sidebar, and then click the desired bookmark.** The sidebar that you see in Figure 10-4 appears, where you can review each collection of bookmarks at your leisure.

✔ **Choose Bookmarks⇨Show Bookmarks (or press Option+⌘+B) to open the Bookmark list.** For those who prefer more information (and more onscreen elbow room) while selecting or organizing their bookmarks, the Bookmark list is the cat's meow. It displays both the name and web address for each bookmark in your collection.

The more bookmarks you add, the more unwieldy the Bookmarks menu and the sidebar can become. To keep things organized, choose Bookmarks⇨Add Bookmark Folder and then type a name for the new folder. With folders, you can organize your bookmarks into *collections,* which appear in the column at the left of the sidebar, as folders in the Bookmark list, and as menus on the Bookmarks bar. (Collections also appear as separate submenus in the Bookmarks menu on the Safari menu bar.) You can drag bookmarks into the new folder to help reduce the clutter.

To delete a bookmark or a folder from any of these locations, right-click it and then choose Delete.

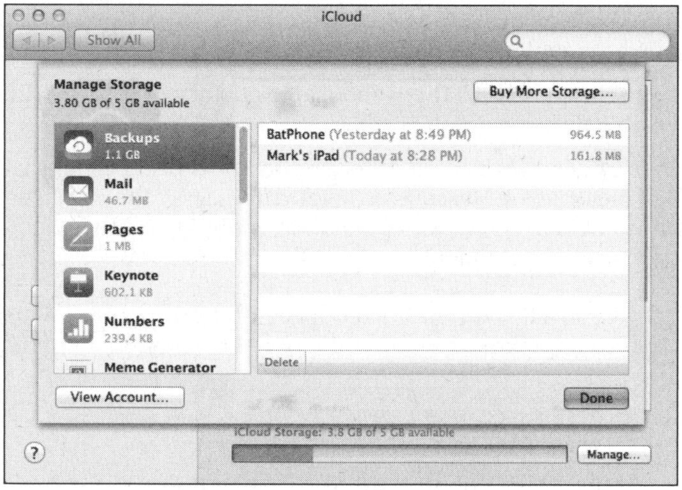

Figure 10-4:
The sidebar puts all your bookmarks in easy reach.

Working with the Reading List and Shared Links

Here are two other methods of loading, saving, and retrieving specific pages in Safari — and they're both hiding in the now-familiar confines of the Safari sidebar! These two sidebar celebrities are the reading list and your shared links.

Saving pages for later with the Reading List

The sidebar's Reading List pane allows you to save entire pages for later perusal — unlike a bookmark (which displays only the current contents of a page), a page saved to your Reading List is retained (with its original content) until you can read it. From the keyboard, press ⌘+Shift+L to display the sidebar, and then click the Reading List button. Choose Bookmarks⇨Add to Reading List or press ⌘+Shift+D to add the current page to the list; you can quickly add a snapshot of that page to the list by holding down the Shift key and clicking the link. (Oh, and don't forget that you can click the Sharing icon in the toolbar and choose Add to Reading List to achieve the same victory.)

Ah, but when you click one of those entries in the Reading List and then click the blue Reader button that appears at the right side of the Address box, the real magic begins! The Reader panel appears to display text articles free of advertisements and silly pop-ups. And if an article is continued over multiple web pages, the Reader panel automatically stitches them together to form a continuous block of text. (Think of an e-book shown within iBooks on your iMac, and you get the idea.) You can also print or e-mail the article from in the Reader panel.

If the Reader button is blue in Safari's Address box — and you're *not* using the Reading List — don't panic! Because the page you're reading contains text articles, Safari is offering to display it in the Reader panel. (If a page has nothing to display in the Reader panel, the button remains gray.) To display the page in the Reader panel, click the blue Reader button in the Address box. To return to your mundane browsing experience, click the Reader icon again.

Visiting pages recommended by friends

If you're a fan of the Twitter or LinkedIn social media sites, listen up: Mavericks introduces shared links to Safari! After you add your Twitter and LinkedIn account information in the Internet Accounts pane in System Preferences, Safari automatically adds links posted by your friends on both services on the sidebar's Shared Links pane.

To visit a shared link, just click it. To search for a specific shared link, click in the Search Links box at the top of the Shared Link list and type a portion of the link (or just type the person's name to see all the links he or she has posted).

The Shared Links pane won't appear in the sidebar unless you successfully add your Twitter or LinkedIn account information in System Preferences.

Downloading Files

A huge chunk of the fun that you'll find on the web is the capability to download images and files. If you've visited a site that offers files for downloading, typically you just click the Download button or the download file link, and Safari takes care of the rest. While the file is downloading, feel free to continue browsing or even download additional files; the Downloads status list helps you keep track of what's going on and when everything will be finished transferring. To display the Download status list from the keyboard, press ⌘+Option+L. You can also click the Download button at the upper-right corner of the window to display the Download list.

By default, Safari saves any downloaded files to the Downloads folder on your Dock, which I like and use. To specify the location where downloaded files are stored — for example, if you'd like to scan them automatically with an antivirus program — follow these steps:

1. **Choose Safari⇨Preferences or press ⌘+, (comma).**

2. **Click the General tab (refer to Figure 10-3) and then open the Save Downloaded Files To pop-up menu.**

3. **Choose Other.**

4. **Navigate to the location where you want the files stored.**

5. **Click the Select button.**

6. **Click the Close button to exit Preferences.**

To download a specific image that appears on a web page, move your cursor over the image, right-click, and then choose Save Image As from the menu that appears. Safari prompts you for the location where you want to store the file.

You can choose to automatically open files that Safari considers safe — things like movies, text files, and PDF files that are *very* unlikely to store a virus or a damaging macro. By default, the Open "Safe" Files after Downloading check box is selected on the General pane. However, if you're interested in preventing *anything* you download from running until you've manually checked it with your antivirus application, you can deselect the check box and breathe easy.

Luckily, Safari has matured to the point that it can seamlessly handle most multimedia file types that it encounters. However, if you've downloaded a multimedia file and Safari doesn't seem to be able to play or display it, try loading the file in QuickTime Player. *QuickTime Player* is like a Swiss Army knife that can recognize a huge number of audio, video, and image formats.

Using Subscriptions and History

To keep track of where you've been, you can display the History list by clicking the History menu. To return to a page in the list, just choose it from the History menu. Note that Safari also arranges older history items by the date you visited the site so you can easily jump back a couple of days to that page you forgot to bookmark!

Safari also searches the History list automatically, when it fills in an address that you're typing. That's the feature I mention in the earlier section, "Visiting Websites."

To view your Top Sites thumbnail screen, press ⌘+Option+1 or choose Show Top Sites from the History menu. You can also click the Top Sites button on the toolbar.

You can add a site manually to your Top Sites by dragging a bookmark from the sidebar to the Top Sites icon in the Favorites bar, or by dragging a link or URL address from another application to the Top Sites icon in the Favorites bar. (You'll see a plus sign appear next to your cursor to indicate the addition.) To rearrange screens in the Top Sites display, just drag a screen thumbnail to the desired location. If you prefer that a specific thumbnail remain in the same place, hover your cursor over the thumbnail and click the gray pushpin icon, which will turn blue to indicate that the thumbnail is pinned in place.

If you're worried about security and would rather not keep track of where you've been online, find out how to clear the contents of the History file in the upcoming section, "Handling ancient history."

Tabs Are Your Browsing Friends

Safari also offers *tabbed browsing,* which many folks use to display (and organize) multiple web pages at one time. For example, if you're doing a bit of comparison shopping for a new piece of hardware among different online stores, tabs are ideal. (Heck, tabbed browsing is so popular, Apple added tabs to Finder windows with the release of OS X Mavericks!)

When you hold down the ⌘ key and click a link or bookmark using tabs, a tab representing the new page appears at the top of the Safari window. Just click the tab to switch to that page. By holding down Shift+⌘, the tab is both created and opened. (If you don't hold down ⌘, things revert to business as usual, and Safari replaces the contents of the window with the new page.)

You can also open a new tab by clicking the plus sign that appears at the upper-right corner of the Safari window, or by pressing ⌘+T.

Trackpad owners will appreciate Safari's two new gestures that control tabs. With multiple tabs active, you can

- ✔ Pinch to display them all in a new *Tab view* (as shown in Figure 10-5).
- ✔ Swipe to switch between tabs.

To display your tabs in Tab view without a trackpad, click the Show All Tabs button that appears at the right side of the Safari window (next to the Open a New Tab button). From Tab view, you can click the white dots that appear below the thumbnails to view your tabs, and click any tab thumbnail to switch immediately to that tab. To close a tab in Tab view, click the Close button at the top of the thumbnail.

To fine-tune your tabbed browsing experience, choose Safari⇨Preferences to display the Preferences dialog; then click Tabs. From here, you can specify whether a new tab or window automatically becomes the active window in Safari.

Close button

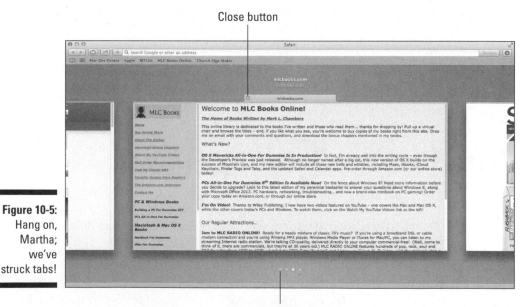

Figure 10-5:
Hang on,
Martha;
we've
struck tabs!

Tab navigation buttons

Done with a page? You can remove a tabbed page by hovering your cursor over the tab and then clicking the X button that appears to the left of the title.

Printing Web Pages

If you've encountered a page that you'd like to print, follow these steps:

1. **Display the desired page.**

2. **Choose File⇨Print or press ⌘+P.**

3. **In the Save As text field, type a name for the saved page.**

4. **Select the number of copies and specify whether you'd like to print the entire page, only the current page or a range of pages.**

5. **Click Print.**

   After the Save file has been created, double-click it to load it in Safari.

 A quick word about printing a page in Safari: Some combinations of background and text colors might conspire to render your printed copy worthless. In a case like that, use your printer's grayscale setting (if it has one) or click the Show Details button and deselect the Print Backgrounds check box in the Print dialog (which can save you quite a bit of ink or toner). Alternatively, you can simply click and drag to select the text on the page, press ⌘+C to copy it, and then paste the text into TextEdit, Word, or Pages, where you can print the page on a less offensive background (while still keeping the text formatting largely untouched). You can also save the contents of a page as an electronic PDF file by choosing File⇨Export as PDF.

 If you'd rather mail the contents of a web page to a friend, click the Share button and choose Email This Page. (If you've added the Mail button to your toolbar, one click does the job.) Mail loads automatically, complete with a prepared e-mail message. Just address it to the recipients and then click Send.

Protecting Your Privacy

No chapter on Safari would be complete without a discussion of security, against both outside intrusion from the Internet and prying eyes around your iMac. Hence this last section, which covers protecting your privacy.

 Although diminutive, the padlock icon that appears at the left side of the Address box when you're connected to a secure website means a great deal! A *secure site* encrypts the information that you send and receive, making it much harder for those of unscrupulous ideals to obtain private data, such as credit card numbers and personal information. You can click the padlock icon (next to the site name) to display the security certificate in use on that particular site. A secure site web address begins with the prefix `https:` instead of `http:`. (The extra *s* stands for *secure.* A Good Thing.)

Yes, there are such things as bad cookies

First, a definition of this ridiculous term: A *cookie,* a small file that a website automatically saves on your hard drive, contains information that the site will use on your future visits. For example, a site might save a cookie to preserve your site preferences for the next time or — like shopping at Amazon.com — to identify you automatically and help customize the offerings that you see.

In and of themselves, cookies aren't bad things. Unlike a virus, a cookie file isn't going to replicate itself or wreak havoc on your system, and only the original site can read the cookie that it creates. However, many folks don't appreciate acting as a gracious host for a slew of little snippets of personal information. (Not to mention that some cookies have highly suggestive names, which can lead to all sorts of conclusions. End of story.)

You can choose to accept some or all cookies, or you can opt to disable cookies altogether. You can also set Safari to accept cookies only from the sites you choose to visit. To change your *Cookie Acceptance Plan* (or CAP, for those who absolutely crave acronyms), follow these steps:

1. **Choose Safari⇨Preferences.**

2. **Click the Privacy toolbar button.**

   Safari displays the preference settings shown in Figure 10-6.

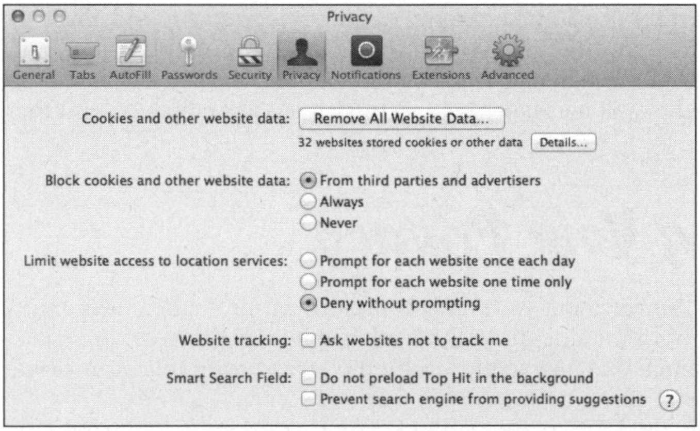

Figure 10-6: Specifying who's welcome in my cookie jar.

3. **Choose how to block cookies via these radio button choices:**

   • *From Third Parties and Advertisers:* I use this option, which allows sites such as Amazon.com to work correctly without allowing a barrage of superfluous cookies.

- *Always:* Block cookies entirely.

- *Never:* Accept all cookies.

4. **To view the cookies currently on your system, click the Details button.**

   If a site's cookies are blocked, you might have to take care of things manually, such as by providing a password on the site that used to be read automatically from the cookie.

5. **Click the Close button to save your changes.**

Feeling nervous about the data stored by the websites you visit? You can always delete *all* that stored information with a single click. From the Privacy pane in the Safari Preferences window, click the Remove All Website Data button. You'll be asked to confirm your draconian decision.

The Privacy pane also includes the Ask Websites Not to Track Me check box, which works . . . *sometimes.* Unfortunately, it's up to a particular web-site whether to honor Safari's request for privacy. (Also, some sites — such as Amazon.com — use tracking legitimately, to keep track of your likes and purchases each time you return.) If you're especially worried about leaving a trail of breadcrumbs behind you on the web, however, I recommend selecting this check box.

Cleaning your cache

Safari speeds up the loading of websites by storing often-used images and multimedia files in a temporary storage, or *cache,* folder. The files in your cache folder can be displayed (hint), which can lead to assumptions (hint, hint) about the sites you've been visiting (hint, hint, hint). (Tactful, ain't I?)

Luckily, Safari makes it easy to dump the contents of your cache file. Just choose Safari⇨Reset Safari, deselect all but the Clear History check box, and then click Reset to confirm that you want to clean up your cache.

Banishing pesky iCloud Keychain passwords

Time for a confession: I am the world's biggest critic of *keychains*, which Mavericks uses to automatically provide all sorts of login information throughout the system. In Safari, for example, the password information is automatically entered for you whenever a website you've approved requires you to log in.

To be more specific, I'm sure many readers will adopt the new *iCloud Keychain*, which stores password and credit card information for Safari and wirelessly distributes that information automatically to other Macs and iOS devices using the same Apple ID. (Apple even says the passwords generated by iCloud Keychain are more complex and harder to crack, which *sounds* more secure, right?)

I'd rather keep a pet piranha in a cereal bowl than use this feature! Why? Whenever you're logged in, *anyone* using your iMac gets control of your online persona (in the form of your passwords to secure websites). Safari, like an obedient puppy, will automatically provide access to sites with stored keychain passwords, no matter *who* is sitting in front of your iMac. Nervous yet?

If you'd like to take the far-less-convenient-but-**much**-safer, old-fashioned route of remembering your passwords yourself, follow my lead: Visit the iCloud pane in System Preferences and deselect the Keychain check box to turn the iCloud Keychain feature off.

Now that I've warned you thoroughly, I feel better about mentioning the Passwords tab in Safari Preferences for those who *do* decide to use iCloud Keychain. From the Passwords tab, you can view the iCloud Keychain information that Safari uses, and either remove a specific password (or all passwords) from your iCloud Keychain.

Handling ancient history

As you might imagine, your History file leaves a very clear set of footprints indicating where you've been on the web. To delete the contents of the History menu, choose History⇨Clear History (at the very bottom of the History menu).

Safari also allows you to specify an amount of time to retain entries in your History file. Open the Safari Preferences dialog, click the General tab (refer to Figure 10-3), and then open the Remove History Items pop-up menu to specify the desired amount of time. Items can be rolled off daily, weekly, biweekly, monthly, or yearly.

Setting notifications

In Mavericks, Safari can allow websites you've approved to send you messages using Notification Center — you can control which sites have been given this functionality from the Notifications tab in Safari's Preferences dialog. To prevent a website from sending notifications, click the site in the list and click the Remove button.

Avoiding those @!^%$ pop-up ads*

I hate pop-up ads, and I'm sure you do, too. To block many of those pop-up windows with advertisements for everything from low-rate mortgages to "sure-thing" Internet casinos, open the Safari Preferences dialog, click the Security tab, and verify that Block Pop-Up Windows is selected.

Chapter 11

Expanding Your Horizons with iCloud

*I*f you ask the average iMac owner what's available on the Internet, you likely hear benefits such as e-mail, photo storage, web surfing, and Google searches. What you may *not* hear is "instant syncing and document sharing among all my Apple iOS devices, Macs, and even PCs."

If you have an iPhone, iPad, or iPod touch, you may have experienced what I like to call the "Synchronizing Blues": When you took a photo with your iPhone or created a new document with your iPad, your new additions just *sat* there (in their original location) until you had a chance to sync your device with your iMac. Ah, but with Apple's iCloud functionality, your stuff gets automatically synchronized across the Internet!

In this chapter, I show you what's *really* exciting about your iMac and that fancy Internet connection. With iCloud, you can automatically synchronize your stuff, access your documents with any Internet connection, and manage online backups of all your contacts, calendars, mail, bookmarks, and documents!

So How Does iCloud Work, Anyway?

Today's Apple iOS devices can all display or play the same media: photos, music, books, TV shows, and such. Heck, some iOS devices (such as your iPhone and iPod touch) can even share applications that you install. Therefore, it makes sense to effortlessly share all your digital media across these devices, and that's what iCloud is all about. Apple calls this synchronization "pushing."

Here's a look at how the pushing process works. Imagine that you just completed a Pages document on your iMac (an invitation for your son's birthday party), but you're at the office, and you need to get the document to your family so that they can edit and print it using your son's iPad.

Before iCloud, you had to attach the document to an e-mail message or upload it to some type of online storage (such as Dropbox or Microsoft SkyDrive), and then a family member had to download and save the document to the iPad before working with it. With iCloud, you simply save the document on your iMac to your iCloud Library, and OS X automatically pushes the document to the iPad! Your document appears on the iPad, ready to be opened, edited, and printed — and it appears on any other devices running iOS 5 or later (using the same Apple ID) as well. Figure 11-1 gives you an idea of what's happening in the background when one of your devices pushes data using iCloud.

Figure 11-1: iCloud works by pushing data among all your iOS devices.

| A new Pages document you've created and saved on your iMac | Uploaded | Stored in iCloud | Pushed to other iOS devices such as your iPhone and iPad | The Pages document automatically appears on your iPad |

And iCloud isn't limited to just digital media. Your iMac can also automatically synchronize your e-mail accounts, Calendar calendars and events, and Contacts entries with other iOS 5 or later devices across the Internet, so staying in touch is much easier no matter where you are, or which device you happen to be using at the moment.

Apple also throws in 5GB of free online storage that you can use for all sorts of things: not only digital media files but also documents that you'd like to save online for safekeeping. Items you buy through the iTunes Store — music, video, and applications — and the images in your Photo Stream do not count against your free 5GB limit. (More on how you can expand that 5GB limit later in the chapter.)

To join the iCloud revolution, you first need an Apple ID. If you didn't create one during the initial Mavericks setup, you can create an Apple ID from the App Store.

You can also access your documents through the web at www.icloud.com. Log in with your Apple ID and password to send mail, access your contacts and calendar, edit your notes and reminders, locate your devices, and use online versions of Pages, Numbers, and Keynote. (Don't forget that you can access those web-based, online iWork applications at any time, even when you're using a PC!)

Saving and Opening iCloud Documents

iCloud online storage for your documents is definitely neat. However, if you're used to using Dropbox, you'll find that the functionality of saving and opening files is somewhat different with iCloud. Dropbox allows you to use Finder to access your online Dropbox files (just like your iMac's internal drive), but iCloud allows you to save, open, move, and delete files only from within Mavericks applications.

In other words, you can't copy a Numbers project from your iCloud Library directly to a Finder window. You can open it, delete it, or move it by dragging it from the Open dialog to your iMac's drive, but otherwise that document remains firmly entrenched in your iCloud Library. You also can't copy files (such as an image file you create with Disk Utility) directly into your iCloud Library. You can save documents to your iCloud Library only from applications that support iCloud.

Figure 11-2 illustrates an iCloud Library Open dialog in action — in this case, the Open dialog from Pages.

Figure 11-2:
I've stored three Pages documents in my iCloud Library.

Configuring iCloud

You control all the settings for iCloud from Mavericks' iCloud pane in System Preferences (shown in Figure 11-3). Click the System Preferences icon on the Dock and then click the iCloud icon. At the sign-in prompt, enter your Apple ID and your password. System Preferences will then guide you through basic iCloud configuration.

Figure 11-3:
The iCloud pane appears within System Preferences.

Most of the check boxes on the iCloud Preferences pane control whether a particular type of data — such as a Contacts entry, password, Mail account, Keychain password, or calendar in Calendar — is pushed among all your iOS devices. You can also disable the Documents & Data check box to return to the original File Open dialog, with no access to your iCloud Library. (Alternatively, you can specify which applications will have access to your iCloud Library by clicking the Options button.)

Note, however, that you can enable three other unique features from this pane as well:

✔ **Photos:** Click the Options button here and enable the My Photo Stream check box to allow your Mac to automatically receive photos from your iOS devices. Take a photo with your iPhone, for example, and that image is immediately pushed to your Mac, iPad, and iPod touch. On the Mac, however, Photo Stream goes one step further: The photos appear automatically in iPhoto or Aperture in a special album titled Photo Stream.

To turn on Photo Stream in iPhoto, choose iPhoto⇨Preferences, click the Photo Stream button, and then select all three check boxes. My Photo Stream must also be selected in the iCloud Preferences pane.

✔ **Back to My Mac:** If you enable Back to My Mac, you can remotely control your iMac from another Mac computer (or vice versa) using Mavericks' Screen Sharing feature. You can also transfer files between the two computers. Back to My Mac works over a broadband Internet connection or a local network (LAN). Available Mac computers show up in the Shared section of the Finder window sidebar. Note that you must manually turn on Screen Sharing in the System Preferences Sharing pane before you can remotely control another Mac.

✔ **Find My Mac:** Talk about Buck Rogers! Imagine locating a lost or stolen iMac from your iPhone or iPad. Now think about this: With Find My Mac, you can even lock or completely wipe your iMac's hard drive *remotely,* preventing unauthorized use or erasing your private data! After you access your iMac from another iOS device, you can play a sound, send a message to be displayed onscreen, remotely lock the machine, or remotely wipe the drive.

If you ever opt to lock or wipe the drive, though, you can't locate your iMac again. Use this protection maneuver as a last resort.

Chapter 12

Hooking Up with Handy Helpers

*T*his chapter is all about getting interesting things into — and out of — your iMac. Some of the devices I mention are common (almost mundane these days) and pretty easy to take care of, such as scanners and printers. Then I might surprise you with something new to you, like your iMac's built-in FaceTime HD video camera.

I also show you how to turn your iMac into a photo booth. Heck, I even describe how you can pull that fancy satellite or cable TV signal into your iMac.

It's perfectly okay to tell everyone else that you're watching the financial channel. But watching a little football never hurt anyone. . . .

Connecting Printers

All hail the USB port! It's the primary connection point for all sorts of goodies. In this section, I concentrate on adding a local USB printer and the basics of adding a network printer to your system. (Find more on connecting a wireless Bluetooth printer in Bonus Chapter 1 at www.dummies.com/extras/imac.)

USB printers

Connecting a USB printer to your iMac is duck soup. Don't you wish all things in life were this easy? You might very well be able to skip most of the steps in this section entirely, depending on whether your printer came with an installation disc. (Virtually all do, of course, but you might have bought yours used, say, from eBay.)

Your printer needs to be fully supported within OS X:

✔ If the software is designed for earlier versions of OS X (say, 10.7 or 10.8), it probably works with Mavericks.

✔ I always recommend visiting the manufacturer's website to download the latest printer driver and support software *before* you install your printer. That way, you know that you're up-to-date. (Don't forget to check the Read Me file that accompanies your new software to make sure that no new system requirements have come about!)

Save and close open files and applications before installing your printer. You might have to restart your iMac to complete the installation.

The physical connections for your printer are pretty simple:

✔ Make sure that your printer's USB cable is plugged in to both your iMac and the printer itself. (Naturally, you'll use one of the iMac's USB ports on the back of the computer, unless you've already added a USB hub to expand your external horizons.)

✔ After the USB connection is made, plug the printer into an AC wall socket and turn it on.

Don't forget to add the paper, check the ink or toner cartridge(s), and remove all the packing material from your printer!

Additional printer installation steps depend on whether you have the manufacturer's installation software for your printer.

Sure, I've got the install software

If your printer comes with its manufacturer's installation disc (and you have either an internal or external optical drive), follow these steps when everything is connected and powered on:

1. Insert the installation disc in the iMac's optical drive.

If you download the printer's installation software as a disk image file (ending with the extension .dmg), simply double-click that file. OS X will display it on your Desktop, just as if it were a DVD or an external hard drive. Now you can follow along with the rest of the steps in this procedure.

The disc contents usually appear in a Finder window. If they don't, double-click the installation disc icon on the Desktop to open the window.

2. **Double-click the installation application to start the ball rolling.**

3. **Follow the onscreen instructions.**

   Files get copied to your hard drive.

   You might have to restart your iMac.

You're ready to print!

Don't forget to visit your printer manufacturer's website to check for any driver updates for your particular model.

Whoops, I've got diddly-squat (Software-wise)

Didn't get an installation CD? Try installing the printer without software, or download the software from the manufacturer's website.

Installing without software

If you didn't get an installation CD with your printer (or you can't locate the installation software to download), you might be lucky enough that your printer's driver was included in your installation of OS X. First, press ⌘+P within an application to display the Print dialog, where you can check whether the printer you connected is already recognized.

If it's not displayed, here's how to check for that pesky driver after you connect the printer and switch it on:

1. **Open the System Preferences window.**

2. **Click the Printers & Scanners icon.**

3. **Click the Add button (which sports a plus sign).**

4. **Check the Printer list in the Add Printer window to see whether your printer has already been added automatically within Mavericks.**

   If your printer appears here, dance a celebratory jig. You can close System Preferences and choose that printer from the Print dialog in your applications. (You can even set it as the default from the System Preferences Printers & Scanners pane. Just click the Default Printer pop-up menu to select your new printer.)

Downloading software

If you don't have installation software and your iMac doesn't automatically match your USB printer with a driver, it's time to check the Internet to locate a Mavericks-compatible driver for your printer.

Check the manufacturer's website for your printer's software and any additional information for operating your printer under OS X Mavericks. Look for

✔ **Special software drivers that the printer might need:** Install any drivers you find *before* you run an installation application. Otherwise, the installation app might not be able to recognize or configure the printer if the driver hasn't been installed first.

✔ **Technical documents or FAQs covering your printer under Mavericks.**

✔ **Installation application:** If the manufacturer offers an installation application for your printer, download the application and run it.

Network printers

Your wired or wireless Ethernet network provides a quick and easy way to share any printer that's already connected to your iMac. Follow these steps to share your printers across the network with others:

1. **Click the System Preferences icon on the Dock.**
2. **Click the Sharing icon.**
3. **Select the On check box next to the Printer Sharing service entry.**
4. **Click Close to exit System Preferences.**

In most cases, a printer that you share appears automatically in the Print dialog on other computers connected to your network. Therefore, if you want to access a printer being shared by another Mac across your network, open the Print dialog within your application and click the Printer pop-up menu to select it.

If the remote printer isn't listed automatically, you can dig a little further. To add a printer that another Mac on your network is sharing to your list of printers, follow these steps:

1. **Click System Preferences on the Dock.**
2. **Click the Printers & Scanners icon.**
3. **Click the Add button (which carries a plus sign).**
4. **Click the Default button on the toolbar.**

   Mavericks displays all the available local shared printers.

5. **Click the desired printer and then click Add.**

   Depending on the built-in support within Mavericks for the printer you're accessing or sharing, you may have to install the driver on your Mac or the other Macs on your network as well.

Connecting Scanners

USB and FireWire scanners practically install themselves. As long as the model is listed as OS X–compatible and supports the TWAIN device standard (as just about all scanners do), things really *are* plug-and-play. (Not sure whether a scanner is OS X–compatible? Check the system requirements on the scanner's box or on the manufacturer's website.)

If you have the scanner manufacturer's installation disc, go ahead and use it. However, most scanners don't require specialized drivers, so even that orphan model that you picked up from Uncle Milton last year should work (if it's recognized by OS X). It doesn't hurt to check the manufacturer's website to see whether any of the software has been updated since the disc was produced.

If OS X doesn't support your older scanner, a third-party application might be able to help. Get thee hence to Hamrick Software at www.hamrick.com and download a copy of the latest version of VueScan. This great scanning application supports more than 2,000 scanner models, including a number that don't work with Mavericks otherwise. At $40, it's a world-class bargain, to boot.

Ready to go? Make sure that your scanner is powered on and connected to your iMac (and that you load a page or photograph to scan). If your scanner's installation disc provided you with a proprietary scanning application, I recommend that you use that application to test your scanner. In fact, it's Mark's Maxim time!

If your printer or scanner includes bundled applications, *try them!*

Sure, OS X has the Printers & Scanners pane within System Preferences for printers and the Image Capture application for scanners and digital cameras, but these are bare-bones tools compared with the print manager and image acquisition software that comes bundled with your hardware. I turn to the built-in hardware handling stuff that comes with Mavericks only when I don't have anything better.

Hey, I'm not saying that anything's wrong with Image Capture, which is in your Applications folder, in case you need to use it. However, don't expect Image Capture to support any specialized features offered by your scanner (like one-button e-mail or web publishing). You have to use the application especially designed for your manufacturer and model to take advantage of any extras that it offers. For alternatives, many image-editing applications (like Adobe Photoshop or Photoshop Elements) might offer more scanning features than Image Capture.

Using Photo Booth

Many Apple switchers and first-time owners quickly notice the tiny square lens and LED light at the top of the iMac's svelte frame. What gives?

Mystery solved, good reader: That's the lens of your iMac's built-in FaceTime HD camera, which allows you to capture video or snap a quick, fun series of photos via the Photo Booth application that comes with Mavericks.

What's that you say? You've never used a computer video camera? Well then, good reader, you've come to the right place!

The FaceTime HD camera's indicator light glows green whenever you're taking a snapshot or recording video . . . which, when you think about it, is A Good Thing (especially if you prefer chatting at home in Leisure Mode).

If you need a quick picture of yourself for use on your web page, or perhaps your iChat icon needs an update to show off your new haircut, use Photo Booth to capture images at 720p resolution and 32-bit color. Although today's digital cameras can produce a much higher-quality photo, you can't beat the built-in convenience of Photo Booth for that quick snapshot!

To snap an image in Photo Booth, follow these steps:

1. **Launch Photo Booth from the Dock or from Launchpad.**

   Photo Booth features a very different appearance in full-screen mode, complete with a fancy wooden stage and curtain! To try things out in full-screen mode, choose View⇨Enter Full Screen.

2. **Choose to take one image, four quick photos as a group, or digital video.**

   The three buttons at the lower-left side of the Photo Booth window allow you to switch among taking one photo, four photos in a row (arranged as a group, like an arcade photo booth), or a movie clip.

3. **(Optional) Click the Effects button to choose an effect you'd like to apply to your image.**

   Photo Booth displays a screen of thumbnail preview images so that you can see how each effect changes the photo (see Figure 12-1). To move through the thumbnail screens, click the Previous and Next arrow buttons that appear around the Effects button.

   You can produce some of the simple effects you might be familiar with from Photoshop, such as a black-and-white image or a fancy colored-pencil filter, but you can also play with some mind-blowing distortion effects and even very convincing "faux" thermal and X-ray cameras!

Of course, you can always launch your favorite image editor afterward to use a filter or effect on a photo — for example, the effects available in iPhoto — but Photo Booth can apply these effects automatically as soon as you take the picture.

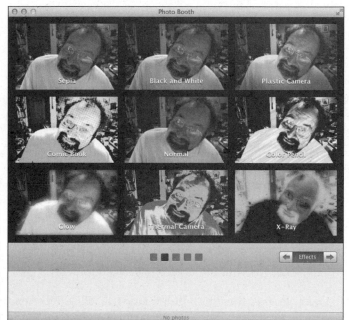

Figure 12-1: Photo Booth does one thing particularly well — candid photography.

4. **(Optional) Click a thumbnail to apply the desired effect.**

   When you choose an effect, Photo Booth automatically closes the Effects display.

   To return the display to normal, click the Normal thumbnail, which appears in the center. (Um, that would be Paul Lynde's spot, for those of you old enough to remember *Hollywood Squares.*)

5. **Click the red Camera button.**

The image (or video clip) appears in the filmstrip at the bottom of the window. Photo Booth keeps a copy of all the images and clips you take in the filmstrip so that you can use them later. After you click a photo or film clip in the filmstrip, the familiar Share button appears, inviting you take any one of a series of actions, including

---

Who needs a fancy green screen?

Ever admired the animated background behind your favorite TV weather prognosticator? Believe it or not, you don't need an expensive "green screen" backdrop (and time spent in a video-editing application) to create the same effect. Instead, use Photo Booth to create those outrageous images and video clips! Photo Booth provides a surprising array of visual effects you can use.

Within Photo Booth, click the Effects button to start the ball rolling and then click the right arrow next to the Effects button until you reach the series of thumbnails with names like Hologram, Pop Art, Fish, and Rollercoaster.

These are the animated backgrounds. Click a background, and Photo Booth asks you to step outside the frame for a second so that your iMac can detect the patterns behind you. When the background animation begins, step back into the frame and capture your image or video clip. (Just as you do with a real green screen backdrop, you get the best results if you shoot your images and video in front of a blank white wall.)

You're not limited to the Apple animated backgrounds, either: Use your own image or video clip by choosing one of the eight predefined User Backdrop thumbnails.

✔ Sending the photo in an e-mail or as a Messages attachment

✔ Saving the photo directly to iPhoto

✔ Sharing the photo or video on Twitter, Facebook, or Flickr

✔ Using the image as your Mavericks user account icon

To delete an image from the Photo Booth filmstrip, click the offending photo and then click the X button that appears in the upper-left corner.

Conversing with FaceTime

With Apple's FaceTime technology, you can video chat with owners of iOS devices and Macs — and if they can run FaceTime, they're guaranteed to have the right video hardware!

As of the time of this writing, FaceTime-compatible devices include

✔ **Macs running OS X Lion or later**

Mac owners running Snow Leopard 10.6.6 or later can also buy the FaceTime application from the App Store.

✔ **An iPhone 4/4s or 5/5s/5c running iOS 4.1 or higher**

> ✔ **A second-generation iPad (or later)**
> ✔ **A fourth-generation (or later) iPod touch running iOS 4.1 or higher**

If you're running a mobile device under iOS 6 or later, you can use either a Wi-Fi or cellular connection to use FaceTime, and your iMac requires either a wired or Wi-Fi connection.

To launch FaceTime, click the jaunty-looking video camera icon on the Dock. The first time you use the application, you have to enter your Apple ID and your e-mail address. The folks you chat with on the other end use that same e-mail address to call you via FaceTime. (iPhone 4-series and 5-series owners can be called using their telephone numbers.)

To change the e-mail address that other FaceTime users use to call you, choose FaceTime➪Preferences and then click the E-mail link under the heading You Can Be Reached for Calls At.

After you sign in, FaceTime displays your Contacts list by default. To initiate a call with any contact, click the name in the list. FaceTime displays the e-mail and telephone numbers for the contact (once again, taken from your Contacts database). Click the e-mail or telephone number that FaceTime should use, and the connection process begins. To return to the Contacts list and choose another person, click the All Contacts button at the top of the window.

Apple isn't satisfied with providing a mere contacts list, however! You can use a number of other methods for selecting someone to call:

- ✔ **Recent Calls:** Click the Recents button to choose a contact that you've called or attempted to call, or has called you within the recent past. Click the All or Missed buttons at the top of the window to further filter the Recents list.

- ✔ **Groups:** If you've set up one or more groups within your Contacts database, you can display them by clicking the Groups button. For example, if you've created a Contacts group containing all your fellow employees within your company, you can easily locate and call a specific person without wading through all your friends and family as well.

- ✔ **FaceTime Search:** Click within the familiar Search box, begin typing the contact's first or last name, and FaceTime displays the matching entries.

- ✔ **Favorites:** Sure, you have folks you like to chat with all the time, and it's easy to add them to the Favorites list. (Those who don't make the Favorites list don't have to know, right?) Click the desired contact and then click the Add to Favorites button. To display your favorite contacts at any time, click the Favorites button in the FaceTime window.

When the call is accepted, you see a large video window with a smaller "picture-in-picture" display. The video from the other person fills the large window, and the video that you're sending to that person appears in the small display, as shown in Figure 12-2. Click the End icon to end the FaceTime call.

Figure 12-2:
The
FaceTime
window in
action.

To switch FaceTime into Landscape mode and take advantage of your iMac's widescreen display, choose Video⇨Use Landscape or press ⌘+R. (Why let the iPhone 4/5 series, iPod touch, and iPad owners have all the landscape fun?)

Turning Your iMac into a TV — And More

Your iMac's beautiful LED screen would seem to be the perfect artist's canvas for watching cable or satellite TV broadcasts, but there's no coaxial (cable or satellite) input on the back of your computer (and no TV tuner nestled within). Therefore, unless you invest in some additional hardware, you're restricted to downloading movies.

Such an obvious need is going to be filled quickly, and a number of different hardware manufacturers have produced external devices that can merge your iMac and your TV signal. Most are USB peripherals, and many have all the features of today's TiVo and digital video recorders.

My favorite example is the EyeTV HD, from Elgato (`www.elgato.com`), which uses a USB connection. Check out what this superstar includes for your investment of $200:

- ✔ Basic cable and satellite-ready with a coaxial connector
- ✔ The ability to capture HD or SD video from a camcorder or VCR
- ✔ Capability to schedule recordings with an onscreen program guide
- ✔ Full-screen TV display or in a window anywhere on your Desktop
- ✔ No external power supply required

I really love the ability to fast-forward through commercials, and I can take anything that I record on my iMac and use it in iMovie. The addition of TV under your control sorta finalizes the whole digital hub thing, now doesn't it?

Part IV
Living the iLife

In this part . . .

- ✔ Build the digital media library of your dreams with iTunes
- ✔ Create slideshows and photo books with iPhoto
- ✔ Put your moviemaking talents to work with iMovie
- ✔ Use GarageBand to compose and record your own music

Chapter 13

The Multimedia Joy of iTunes

Sometimes, words just aren't enough. iTunes is that kind of perfection.

To envision how iTunes changes your iMac, you have to paint the picture with *music* — music that's easy to play, search, and transfer from device to device. Whether it be classical, alternative, jazz, rock, hip-hop, or folk, I can guarantee you that you won't find a better application than iTunes to fill your life with your music. And podcasts. And video. And TV shows. And online education. And Internet radio. (See how hard it is to pin down this wonderful application? Along with your iMac, iTunes really does form the hub of your digital lifestyle.)

In this chapter, I lead you through all the features of my absolute favorite member of the iLife suite . . . and it's going to be pretty doggone obvious how much I appreciate this one piece of software.

What Can I Play on iTunes?

Simply put, iTunes is a media player; it plays audio and video files. These files can be in any of many different formats. Some of the more common audio formats that iTunes supports are

✔ **MP3:** The small size of MP3 files has made them popular for file trading on the Internet. You can reduce MP3 files to a ridiculously small size (albeit at the expense of audio fidelity), but a typical CD-quality, three-minute pop song in MP3 format has a size of 3–5MB.

✔ **AAC:** *AAC* (short for Advanced Audio Coding) is an audio format that's very similar to MP3; in fact, AAC files offer better recording quality at the same file sizes. However, this format is less compatible with non-Apple MP3 players and software. (Luckily, you can still burn AAC tracks to an audio CD, just as you can MP3 tracks.) The tracks that you download from the iTunes Store are in AAC format.

The iTunes Store's *iTunes Plus* tracks are also in AAC format, and these tracks are also not copy-protected, and they're encoded at a higher-quality 256 Kbps rate — hence their higher price.

✔ **Apple Lossless:** Another format direct from Apple, *Apple Lossless* format provides the best compromise between file size and sound quality: These tracks are encoded without loss of quality. However, Apple Lossless tracks are somewhat larger than AAC, so this format is generally the favorite of the most discerning audiophiles.

✔ **AIFF:** The standard Macintosh audio format produces sound of the absolute highest quality. This high quality, however, also means that the files are pretty doggone huge. A typical pop song in AIFF format has a size of 30–50MB (about 10MB per minute of audio).

✔ **WAV:** Not to be outdone, Microsoft created its own audio file format (WAV) that works much like AIFF. It can reproduce sound at higher quality than MP3, but the file sizes are very large, virtually identical in size to AIFF files. (Think 10MB of hard drive space per minute of audio.)

✔ **CD audio:** iTunes can play audio CDs. Because you don't usually store CD audio anywhere but on an audio CD, file size is no big whoop (but once again, 10MB of hard drive space per minute of music is a good approximation).

✔ **MP2:** A close cousin of the far more popular MP3 format, MP2 is the preferred format in radio broadcasting and is a standard audio format for HDV camcorders. It produces file sizes similar to MP3 format.

✔ **Movies and video:** You can buy and download full-length movies, TV shows, music videos, and movie trailers from the iTunes Store . . . and, with an Apple TV unit connected to your home theater system, you can watch those movies and videos from the comfort of your sofa on the other side of your living room (or even from your bedroom on the other side of your house). The movies you buy and rent from the iTunes Store are copy protected and can be retrieved only with your Apple ID.

✔ **Podcasts:** These audio downloads are like public-access radio and TV programs for your iPod, but iTunes can play and organize them, too. Some podcasts also include video and photos to boot.

✔ **iTunes U:** iTunes offers educational materials (such as slideshows, presentations, and class recordings) from a wide variety of colleges and technical institutions — and virtually all are free for the download!

✔ **Ringtones:** iPhone owners, rejoice! iTunes automatically offers to create ringtones for your iPhone (and iPad and iPod touch) from the tracks you've bought on the iTunes Store. (You can also create ringtones with GarageBand, using songs you've added to your iTunes library or tunes you've composed yourself.) You can even use these ringtones on your iMac, with the FaceTime and Messages applications.

✔ **Audiobooks:** No longer do you need cassettes or audio CDs to enjoy your spoken books. iTunes can play them for you, or you can send them to your iPod, iPhone, or iPad for listening on the go.

✔ **Streaming Internet radio:** You can listen to a continuous broadcast of songs from one of tens of thousands of Internet radio stations, with quality levels ranging from what you'd expect from FM radio to the full quality of an audio CD. You can't save the music in iTunes, but streaming radio is still great fun. (In fact, I run my own station. . . . More on MLC Radio later in the chapter.)

Playing an Audio CD

If you have an external optical drive (or an older iMac with a built-in SuperDrive), playing an audio CD in iTunes is easy. Insert the CD in your drive's disc slot or tray, start iTunes by clicking its icon on the Dock, and click the Play button. (Note that your iMac might be set to automatically launch iTunes when you insert an audio CD.) The iTunes interface resembles that of a traditional cassette or CD player. The main playback controls of iTunes are Play, Previous Song, Next Song, and the volume slider, as shown in Figure 13-1.

Click the Play button to begin listening to a song. While a song is playing, the Play button toggles to a Pause button. Clicking that button again pauses the music. If you don't feel like messing around with the mouse or trackpad, you can always use the keyboard. The spacebar acts as the Play and Pause buttons. Press the spacebar to begin playback; press it again to pause.

Click the Next Song button to advance to the next song on the CD. The Previous Song button works like the Next Song button but with a slight twist: If a song is playing and you click the Previous Song button, iTunes first returns to the beginning of the current song (just like a CD player). To advance to the previous song, double-click the Previous Song button. To change the volume of your music, click and drag the volume slider.

As with other Macintosh applications, you can control much of iTunes with the keyboard. Table 13-1 lists some of the more common iTunes keyboard shortcuts.

Previous

Play/Pause

Next   Volume slider

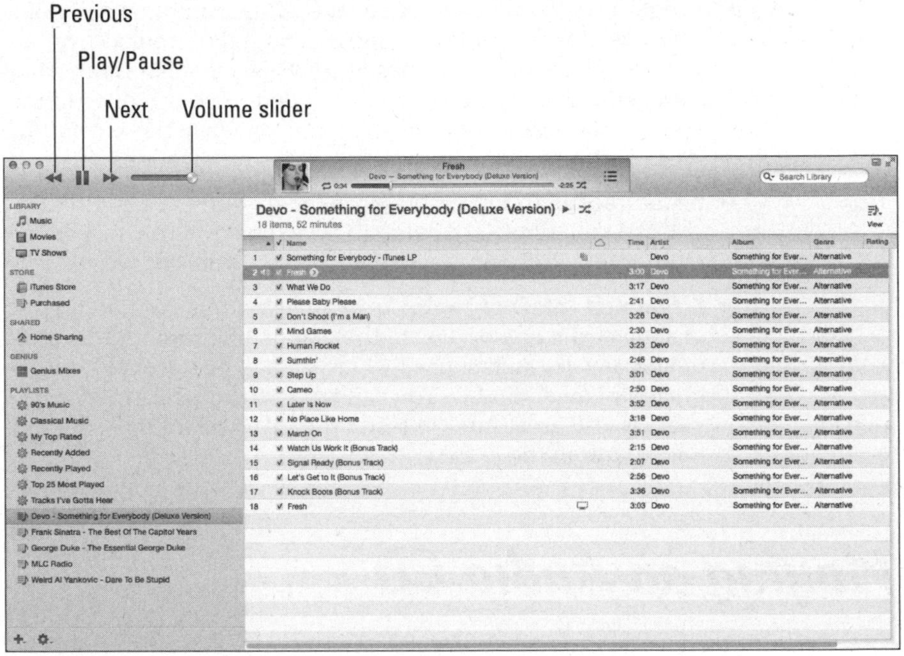

Figure 13-1:
The main playback controls: Play, Previous, and Next.

Table 13-1	Common iTunes Keyboard Shortcuts
Press This Key Combination	*To Do This*
Spacebar	Play the currently selected song if iTunes is idle.
Spacebar	Pause the music if a song is playing.
→	Advance to the next song.
←	Go back to the beginning of a song. Press a second time to return to the previous song.
⌘+↑	Increase the volume of the music.
⌘+↓	Decrease the volume of the music.
⌘+Option+↓	Mute the audio if any is playing. Press again to play the audio.

Playing Digital Audio and Video

In addition to playing audio CDs, iTunes can play the digital audio files that you download from the Internet or obtain from other sources in the WAV, AAC, Apple Lossless, AIFF, MP2, and MP3 file formats. (Read all about these different formats earlier in this chapter.)

Enjoying a digital audio file is just slightly more complicated than playing a CD. After downloading or saving your audio files to your iMac, open the Finder and navigate to the stored files. Then simply drag the music files (or an entire folder of music) from the Finder into the Music entry in the iTunes Source list. The added files appear in the Music section of your iTunes Library. Think of the Library as a master list of your digital media.

To view the Music Library, select the Music entry in the left column of the iTunes player, as shown in Figure 13-2. Heck, you can also drag a song file from a Finder window and drop it on the iTunes icon on the Dock, which adds it to your Music Library as well. (In a similar manner, you can view your movies and TV shows by clicking their entries in the Source list. Right now, however, the focus is on music, so I discuss playing video in more depth later in the chapter.)

If the Sidebar at the left side of the iTunes window isn't displayed as it is in Figures 13-1 and 13-2, choose View➪Show Sidebar, or press ⌘+Option+S.

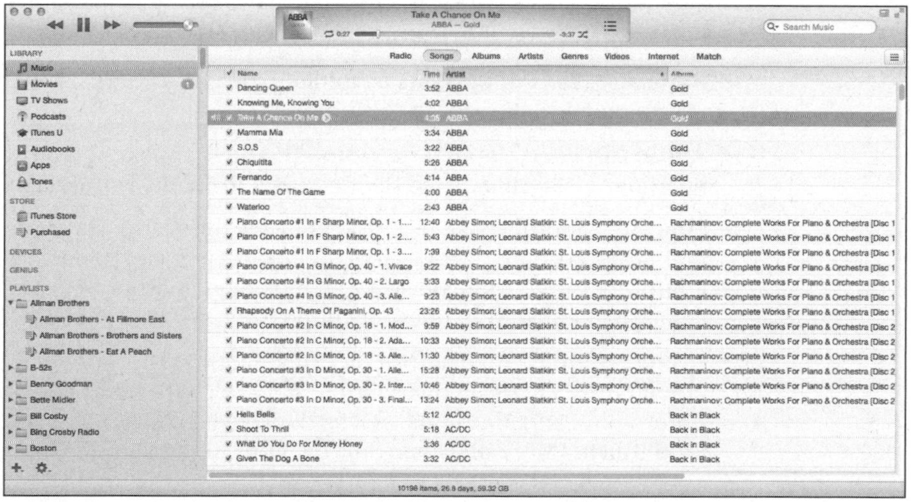

Figure 13-2: The Music Library keeps track of all your audio files.

If you drop the file on top of a playlist name in the Source list, iTunes adds it to that particular playlist as well as the main Library. (More about playlists in a bit.) If you drop a folder of songs on top of the Playlists header, iTunes creates a new playlist using the name of the folder and adds all the songs in the folder to the new playlist.

To play a song, just double-click it in the Music list. Alternatively, you can use the playback controls (Play, Previous Song, and Next Song) that I discuss earlier in this chapter (refer to Figure 13-1).

The Source list of iTunes can list up to eight possible sources for music:

- **Library:** This section contains Music, Movies, TV Shows, Podcasts, iTunes U, Apps (for iPhone, iPod touch, and iPad), Ringtones (for both mobile devices and your iMac), iPod Games, and Radio. (Think *Internet radio,* which I discuss further in the upcoming section, "Internet Radio.")

- **Store:** I discuss the iTunes Store in the later section, "Buying Digital Media the Apple Way."

- **Devices:** If an iPod is connected, it appears in the list. (And yes, Virginia, other models of MP3 players from other companies will also appear in the list if iTunes supports them.) If you connect an iPhone or iPad to your iMac, it shows up here as well.

- **Genius:** Click the Genus heading and click the Turn On Genius button to allow iTunes to automatically create playlists from songs in your iTunes music library. You can also allow Genius to recommend music, movies, and TV shows based on the titles you already have in your iTunes Library. (More on this feature later in the chapter.)

- **Playlists:** Think of playlists as folders you use to organize your music. (More on playlists later in this chapter.)

- **Audio CD:** Load a standard audio CD, and it appears under the Devices heading . . . anything from the Bee Gees to Justin Timberlake.

- **Shared:** If another Mac or PC on your local network is running iTunes and is set to share part or all of its library, you can connect to the other computer for your music. (Shared music on another Mac appears as a separate, named folder in the Source list.)

- **Home Sharing:** You can turn on Home Sharing to share your iMac's media library across your wireless network with up to five other computers (PCs and Macs), as well as devices like iPhones, iPads, and the iPod touch. (More on Home Sharing later in the chapter.)

If you've invested in an Apple TV, it appears in the list as well, allowing iTunes to share media with your Apple TV, which in turn sends it to your ED- (enhanced definition) or HD- (high definition) TV.

Notice also that the Library displays information for each song that you add to it, such as

- ✔ **Name:** The title of the song
- ✔ **Time:** The length of the song
- ✔ **Artist:** The artist who performs the song
- ✔ **Album:** The album on which the song appears

If some of the songs that you're adding don't display anything for the title, album, or artist information, don't panic; most MP3 files have embedded data that iTunes can read. If a song doesn't include any data, you can always add the information to these fields manually. I show you how later, in the section "Setting or changing song information manually."

Clicking any column heading in the Library list causes iTunes to reorder the Library according to that category. For example, clicking the Name column heading alphabetizes your Library by song title. I click the Time heading often to sort my Library according to the length of the songs. Oh, and you can drag column titles to reorder them any way you like (except for the checkbox column at the far left, which remains fixed).

You can browse your Music Library in a number of ways. First, click the Music entry (beneath Library, in the Source list) to select it. By default, the application uses *Songs* mode (active in Figure 13-2), where each song is one entry. Then click the

- ✔ Third mode button to sort your Library into tracks by *album*
- ✔ Fourth mode button to group tracks by *artist*
- ✔ Fifth mode button to browse by musical *genre*

You can also view your iTunes Radio and Internet Radio stations, or see your iTunes Match library in iCloud. All three modes require an Internet connection, and I cover them later in the chapter.

Browsing the Library

After you add a few dozen songs to iTunes, viewing the Library can become a task. Although viewing a master list is nice for some purposes, it becomes as cumbersome as an elephant in a subway tunnel if the list is very long. To help out, iTunes can display your Library in another format, too: namely, browsing mode. To display the Library in browsing mode, click the View menu, hover your cursor over the Column Browser item, and click the Show Browser item, or press the ⌘+B keyboard shortcut.

Will I trash my Count Basie?

Novice iTunes users, take note: iTunes watches your back when you trash tracks.

To illustrate: Suppose you delete a song from the Library that's located only in the iTunes music folder (which you didn't copy into iTunes from another location on your hard drive). That means you're about to delete the song entirely, and no copy will remain on your iMac at all. Rest assured, though, that iTunes prompts you to make sure that you really want to move the file to the Trash. (I get fearful e-mail messages all the time from readers who are loath to delete anything from iTunes because they're afraid they'll trash their digital music files completely.)

Remember: If you delete a song from the Library that *also* exists elsewhere on your hard drive (outside the reach of the iTunes Music folder), it isn't deleted from your hard drive. In fact, if you mistakenly remove a song that you meant to keep, just drag it back into iTunes from the Finder, or even from the Trash. 'Nuff said.

The Browse mode of iTunes displays your library in a compact fashion, organizing your tunes into these sections:

- ✔ Genres
- ✔ Artists
- ✔ Albums
- ✔ Composers
- ✔ Groupings

When you select an artist from the Artists list, iTunes displays that artist's albums in the Albums list. Select an album from the Albums list, and iTunes displays that album's songs in the bottom section of the Browse window. (Those Apple software designers . . . always thinking of you and me.) You can also specify which sections you want included in Browse mode from the View⇨Column Browser menu item. Click a section name to toggle the display of that section.

Finding songs in your Music Library

As your collection of audio files grows large, you might have trouble locating that Swedish remix version of "I'm Your Boogie Man." To help you out, iTunes has a built-in Search function. To find a song, type some text into the Search field of the main iTunes window. While you type, iTunes tries to find a selection that matches your search text. The search is quite thorough, showing any matching text from the artist, album, song title, and genre fields in the results.

For example, if you type **electronic** into the field, iTunes might return results for the band named *Electronic* or other tunes that you classified as *electronic* in the Genre field. (The section "Know Your Songs," later in this chapter, tells you how to classify your songs by genre, among other options.) Click the magnifying glass at the left side of the Search field to restrict the search by Artists, Albums, Composers, and Songs.

Removing old music from the Library

After you spend some time playing songs with iTunes, you might decide that you didn't *really* want to add 40 different versions of "Louie Louie" to your Library. (Personally, I prefer either the original or the cast from the movie *Animal House.*) To remove a song from the Library, click the song to select it and then press the Delete key on your keyboard.

You can also remove a song from the Library by dragging it to the Trash on your Dock.

Watching video

Watching video in iTunes is similar to listening to music. To view your video collection, click one of these entries in the Source list:

- ✔ Movies
- ✔ TV Shows

Whether you select Movies or TV Shows, iTunes displays your videos as thumbnails or in Cover Flow view. Music videos appear as a Smart Playlist, and they also appear in the Music library.

From your collection, you can

- ✔ **Double-click a video thumbnail or an entry in the list.**
- ✔ **Drag a QuickTime video clip from the Finder window to the iTunes window.** Video files that can be viewed using QuickTime typically have the file extensions .mov or .mp4.

iTunes plays video in the box below the Source list, within the iTunes window, in a separate window, or in full-screen mode, depending on the setting you choose from the View⇨Video Playback menu item. In full-screen mode, move your pointer to display a control strip at the bottom of the screen. The control strip sports a slider bar that you can drag to move through the video, a volume control, Play/Pause, and Fast Forward/Reverse buttons.

Keeping Slim Whitman and Slim Shady Apart: Organizing with Playlists

Your iTunes Music Library can contain thousands upon thousands of songs: If your Library grows anywhere near that large, finding all the songs in your lifelong collection of Paul Simon albums is *not* a fun task. Furthermore, with the Library, you're stuck playing songs in the order that iTunes lists them.

To help you organize your music into groups, use the iTunes playlist feature. A *playlist* is a collection of some of your favorite songs from the Library. You can create as many playlists as you want, and each playlist can contain any number of songs. Whereas the Library lists all available songs, a playlist displays only the songs that you add to it. Further, any changes that you make to a playlist affect only that playlist, leaving the Library untouched.

To create a playlist, you can do any of the following:

- **Choose File⇨New Playlist.**

- **Press ⌘+N.**

- **Choose File⇨New Playlist from Selection.** This creates a new playlist and automatically adds any tracks that are currently selected.

- **Right-click a song and choose Create Genius Playlist from the menu that appears.** iTunes builds a playlist of songs that are similar in some way (typically by matching the genre of the selection or the beats per minute, but also based on recommendations from other iTunes members).

    Your iMac needs an Internet connection to create a Genius playlist, and the larger your music library, the longer it will take iTunes to build your playlist. You'll also need to turn on the Genius feature (choose Store⇨Turn on Genius and enter your Apple ID).

    Genius playlists can sometimes mix tracks with explicit content with less-objectionable material — especially in the comedy and rap genres.

- **Drag a folder containing audio files from a Finder window onto the Playlists heading.**

- **Click the New Playlist button in the iTunes window (the plus sign button in the lower-left corner) and choose New Playlist.** You get a newly created empty playlist (the toe-tappin' *untitled playlist*).

All playlists appear in the Source list. To help organize your playlists, it's a good idea to, well, *name* them. (Aren't you glad now that you have this book?) For example, suppose you're planning a party for your polka-loving friends. Instead of running to your computer after each song to change the music, you could create a polka-only playlist. Select and start the playlist at the beginning of the party, and you won't have to worry about changing the music the whole night. (You can concentrate on the accordion.) To load a playlist, select it in the Source list; iTunes displays the songs for that playlist.

The same song can appear in any number of playlists because the songs in a playlist are simply pointers to songs in your Music Library — not the songs themselves. Add and remove them at will to or from any playlist, secure in the knowledge that the songs remain safe in the Library. Removing a playlist is simple: Select the playlist in the Source list and then press Delete. Bottom line: Removing a playlist doesn't actually delete any songs from your Library.

Some playlists are smarter than others

Open the File menu to see the New Smart Playlist menu command. You can also create a new Smart Playlist by clicking the Add button (a plus sign) at the bottom of the Source list.

The contents of a Smart Playlist are automatically created from a specific condition or set of conditions that you set via the Smart Playlist dialog. You can limit the track selection by mundane things, such as album, genre, or artist; or you can get funky and specify songs that were played last, or by the date you added tracks, or even by the sampling rate or total length of the song. For example, iTunes can create a playlist packed with songs that are shorter than three minutes, so you can fill your iPod Shuffle with more stuff! Ah, but wait, you're not limited to a single criterion. If you want to add another criterion, click the plus sign at the right side of the dialog and you get another condition field to refine your selection even further.

You can choose the maximum songs to add to the Smart Playlist, or limit the size of the playlist by the minutes or hours of play or the number of megabytes or gigabytes the playlist will occupy. (Again, great for automatically gathering as much from your KISS collection as will fit into a specific amount of space on a CD or your iPod.) Select the Live Updating check box for the ultimate in convenience. iTunes automatically maintains the contents of the Smart Playlist to keep it current with your conditions at all times in the future. (If you remove tracks manually from a Smart Playlist, iTunes adds other tracks that match your conditions.)

Now think about what all these settings mean when combined . . . *whoa.* Here's an example yanked directly from my own iTunes Library. I created a Smart Playlist that selects only those songs in the Rock genre. It's limited to 25 songs, selected by least often played, and live updating is turned on. The playlist is named Tracks I've Gotta Hear because it finds the 25 rock songs (from my collection of 6,782 songs) that I've heard least often! After I listen to a song from this smart playlist, iTunes automatically "freshens" it with another song, allowing me to catch up on the tracks I've been ignoring. Completely, unbelievably *sweet*— and another reason why iTunes is the best music player on Planet Earth!

Know Your Songs

Besides organizing your music into Elvis and non-Elvis playlists, iTunes gives you the option to track your music at the song level. Each song that you add to the Music Library has a complete set of information associated with it. (See upcoming Figure 13-3.) iTunes displays this information in the Info dialog, including

- **Name:** The name of the song

- **Artist:** The name of the artist who performed the song

- **Album Artist:** The name of the artist responsible for a compilation or tribute album

- **Album:** The album where the song appears

- **Grouping:** A group type that you assign

- **Composer:** The name of the astute individual who actually *wrote* the song

- **Comments:** A text field that can contain any comments on the song

- **Genre:** The classification of the song (such as rock, jazz, or pop)

- **Year:** The year the artist recorded the song

- **Track Number:** The position of the song on the original album

- **Disc Number:** The original disc number in a multi-CD set

- **BPM:** The beats per minute (indicates the song's tempo)

You can display this information by clicking a song name and pressing ⌘+I; the fields appear on the Info tab.

Setting the song information automatically

Each song that you add to the iTunes Music Library might have song information included with it. If you add music from a commercial audio CD, iTunes connects to a server on the Internet and attempts to find the information for each song on the CD. If you download a song from the Internet, it often comes with some information embedded in the file already; the amount of included information depends on what the creator supplied. (And believe me, it's often misspelled as well — think *Leenard Skeenard*.) If you don't have an Internet connection, iTunes can't access the information and displays generic titles instead.

Setting or changing song information manually

If iTunes can't find your CD in the online database or someone gives you an MP3 with incomplete or inaccurate information, you can change the information yourself — and believe me, you want at least the artist and song name! To view and change the information for a song, perform the following steps:

1. **Select the song in either the Music Library list or a playlist.**

2. **Press ⌘+I or choose File➪Get Info.**

3. **Edit the song's information under the Info tab, as shown in Figure 13-3.**

The more work you put into setting the information of the songs in your Music Library, the easier it is to browse and use iTunes. Incomplete song information can make it more difficult to find your songs in a hurry. If you prefer, you don't have to change all information about a song (it just makes life easier later if you do). Normally, you can get away with setting only a song's title, artist, album, and genre. The more information you put in, however, the faster you can locate songs and the easier they are to arrange. iTunes tries to help by automatically retrieving known song information, but sometimes you have to roll up your sleeves and do a little work. (Sorry, but some things just can't be automated.)

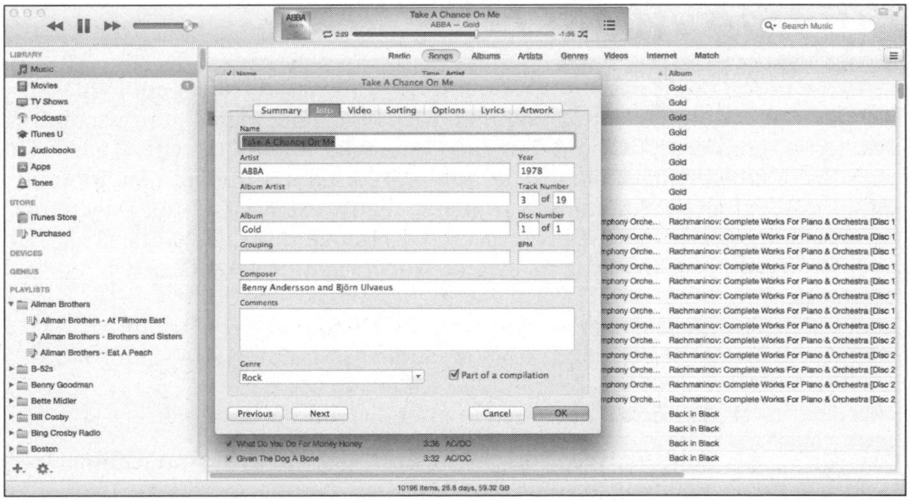

Figure 13-3: View and edit song information here.

"What about cover art, Mark?" Well, I'm overjoyed that you asked! iTunes can try to locate artwork automatically for the tracks you select. (Note that embedding large images can significantly increase the size of the song file.) Follow these steps:

1. **Select the desired songs from the track list.**

2. **Choose File⇨Library⇨Get Album Artwork.**

You can set iTunes to automatically attempt the addition of album artwork every time you rip tracks from an audio CD, or when you add songs without artwork to your Music Library. Choose iTunes⇨Preferences, click the Store button, and select the Automatically Download Album Artwork check box. (By the way, if you buy tracks or an album from the iTunes Store, Apple always includes album covers automatically. Thanks, Cupertino crowd!)

Want to manually add album covers to your song info? Select one (or all) of the songs from a single album in the track list, display the Info dialog, and click the Artwork tab. Now launch Safari, visit Amazon.com, and do a search on the same album (or search an online artwork library like AllCDCovers.com (www.allcdcovers.com). Drag the cover image from the web page right into the Info dialog and drop it on top of the "sunken square" image well. When you click OK, the image appears in the Summary pane, and you can display it while your music is playing by pressing ⌘+G or clicking the Show or Hide Song Artwork button at the lower left of the iTunes window.

Ripping Audio Files

You don't have to rely on Internet downloads to get audio files. If your iMac is equipped with an optical drive, you can create your own MP3, AAC, Apple Lossless, AIFF, and WAV files from your audio CDs with iTunes. The process of converting audio files to different formats is *ripping.* (Audiophiles with technical teeth also call this process "digital extraction," but they're usually ignored at parties by the popular crowd.) Depending on what hardware or software you use, each has its own unique format preferences.

The most common type of ripping is to convert CD audio to AAC or MP3 format. To rip MP3s from an audio CD, follow these simple steps:

1. **Launch iTunes by clicking its icon on the Dock.**

   Alternatively, you can locate iTunes in your Applications folder or from Launchpad.

2. **Choose iTunes⇨Preferences.**

3. **In the Preferences window that appears, click the General toolbar button.**

4. **Click the Import Settings button that appears at the bottom of the Preferences dialog.**

5. **Choose MP3 Encoder from the Import Using pop-up menu.**

6. **Choose High Quality (160 Kbps) from the Setting pop-up menu, click OK to return to the Preferences dialog, and then click OK again to return to iTunes.**

   This bit rate setting provides the best compromise between quality (better than CD quality, which is 128 Kbps) and file size (tracks will be significantly smaller than audiophile bit rates, such as 192 Kbps or higher).

7. **Load an audio CD into your iMac's optical drive.**

   The CD title shows up in the iTunes Source list (under the Devices heading, on the left side of the iTunes window). The CD track listing appears on the right side of the window.

   If iTunes asks you whether you want to import the contents of the CD into your Music Library, you can click Yes and skip the rest of the steps; however, if you've disabled this prompt, just continue with the remaining two steps.

8. **Clear the check box of any song that you don't want to import from the CD.**

   All songs on the CD have a check box next to their title by default. Unmarked songs aren't imported. The Browse button changes to Import CD.

9. **Click the Import CD button.**

Here's an additional form of ripping: If you have a USB turntable or cassette deck connected to your iMac, you can digitize your old analog recordings on albums and cassettes into shiny digital audio files. You might find just buying the same music from the iTunes Store simpler, but if your treasured music isn't available on the Store or on audio CD, it's the next best thing!

Tweaking the Audio for Your Ears

Besides the standard volume controls that I mention earlier in this chapter, iTunes offers a full equalizer. An *equalizer* permits you to alter the volume of various frequencies in your music, allowing you to boost low sounds, lower high sounds, or anything in between.

To open the Equalizer (shown in Figure 13-4), choose Window⇨Equalizer or press ⌘+Option+2. Use the leftmost slider (Preamp) to set the overall level of the Equalizer. The remaining sliders represent various frequencies that the human ear can perceive. Setting a slider to a position in the middle of its travel causes that frequency to play back with no change. Move the slider above the midpoint to boost that frequency; conversely, move the slider below the midpoint to reduce the volume of that frequency.

Continue adjusting the Equalizer sliders until your music sounds the way you like it. In case you prefer to leave frequencies to the experts, the iTunes Equalizer has several predefined settings to match most musical styles. Open the pop-up menu at the top of the Equalizer window to choose a genre. After you adjust the sound to your satisfaction, close the Equalizer window to return to the iTunes interface and relax with those funky custom notes from James Brown. iTunes remembers your settings until you change them again.

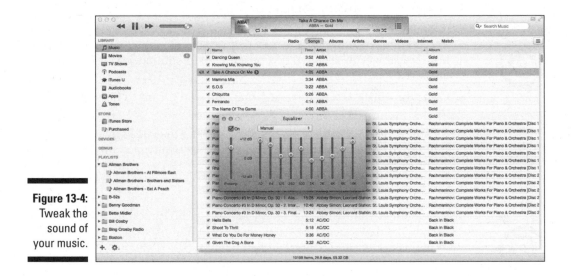

Figure 13-4: Tweak the sound of your music.

A New Kind of Radio Station

Besides playing back your favorite audio files, iTunes can also tune in Internet radio stations from around the globe. You can listen to any of a large number of preset stations, seek out lesser-known stations not recognized by iTunes, or even add your favorite stations to your playlists. You can also use the new iTunes Radio feature to create a custom station dedicated to just the genres and artists you prefer. This section shows you how to do it all.

Internet radio

Although it's not a radio tuner in the strictest sense, iTunes can locate virtual radio stations all over the world that send audio over the Internet — a process usually dubbed "streaming." iTunes can track down hundreds of Internet radio stations in a variety of styles with only a few mouse clicks.

To begin listening to Internet radio with iTunes, click the Internet button located at the top of the window. (If the Internet button doesn't appear, click the iTunes menu and click Preferences, then click the Internet Radio checkbox on the General pane to enable it.) The result is a list of more than 20 types of radio stations, organized by genre.

When you expand an Internet category by clicking its disclosure triangle, iTunes queries a tuning server and locates the name and address of dozens of radio stations for that category. Whether you like Elvis or not-Elvis (those passing fads, such as new wave, classical, or alternative), something's here for everyone. The Internet also offers news, sports, and talk radio.

After iTunes fetches the names and descriptions of radio stations, double-click one that you want to hear. iTunes immediately jumps into action, connects to the station, and begins to play it.

What's with the numbers next to the station names?

When choosing an Internet radio station, keep your Internet connection speed in mind. If you're using a broadband DSL or cable connection — or if you're listening at work over your company's high-speed network — you can listen to stations broadcasting at 128 Kbps (or even higher). The higher the bit rate, the better the music sounds. At 128 Kbps, for example, you're listening to sound that's almost as good as an audio CD.

However, if you're listening over a dialup modem connection, iTunes can't keep up with audio streaming at higher bit rates, so you're limited to stations broadcasting at 56 Kbps or lower.

Tuning in your own stations

Although iTunes offers you a large list of popular radio stations on the web, it's by no means comprehensive. Eventually, you might run across a radio station that you'd like to hear but don't find listed in iTunes. Luckily, iTunes permits you to listen to other stations, too. To listen to a radio station that iTunes doesn't list, you need the station's web address.

In iTunes, choose File⇨Open Stream (or press ⌘+U). In the Open Stream dialog that appears (as shown in Figure 13-5), enter the URL of your desired radio station and then click OK. Within seconds, iTunes tunes in your station.

Figure 13-5:
Tuning into MLC Radio, my Internet radio station.

"I have an itch to hear 'Kung Fu Fighting'!"

This particular technology author has a preference for a certain hot jam spot: *MLC Radio*, the Internet radio station I've been running for several years now. I call my station a '70s Time Machine because it includes hundreds of classic hits from 1970–1979, inclusive. You hear everything from "Rock and Roll Hoochie Koo" by Rick Derringer to "Moonlight Feels Right" by Starbuck. (Hey, I'm summing up a decade here, so be prepared for both Rush and the Captain and Tennille.) The station broadcasts at 128 Kbps (near audio CD quality), so you need a broadband connection to listen. For the radio's Internet address or help connecting to MLC Radio visit my website at www.mlcbooks.com, and then follow the steps in the next section to add MLC Radio to your playlists!

Radio stations in your playlists

If you find yourself visiting an online radio station more than once, you'll be glad to know that iTunes supports radio stations in its playlists. To add a radio station to a playlist from the Radio list, do the following:

1. **Open the category that contains the station you want to add to your playlist.**

2. **Locate the station that you want to add to your playlist and drag it from the Radio list to the desired playlist on the left.**

   If you haven't created any playlists yet, see the section "Keeping Slim Whitman and Slim Shady Apart: Organizing with Playlists," earlier in this chapter, to find out how.

Adding a radio station that doesn't appear in the Radio list is a bit trickier but possible nonetheless. Even though iTunes allows you to load a radio station URL manually by using the Open Stream command from the Advanced menu, it doesn't give you an easy way to add it to the playlist. Follow these steps to add a specific radio station to a playlist:

1. **Add any radio station from the Radio list to your desired playlist.**

   Any station in the list will do because you'll immediately change both the station's URL and name to create your new station entry in the playlist.

2. **Press ⌘+I or choose File➪Get Info to bring up the information dialog for that station.**

3. **Click the Summary section and change the URL by clicking the Edit URL button.**

4. **Enter the desired URL and click OK.**

5. **Click the Info tab, type the new station name, and then click OK.**

Creating a custom iTunes Radio station

The recent addition of iTunes Radio makes it possible for you to listen to the artists, songs, and genres that you prefer in iTunes, without selecting a specific Internet radio station! To use iTunes Radio, click the Radio button at the top of the iTunes window, and then type the artist name, song name, or genre you'd like to add to your station.

As you download new music from the iTunes Store (and add new artists and genres in iTunes Radio), the service learns more about your musical tastes and can automatically play and recommend new music, much like the Genius feature that I discuss earlier in this chapter.

Like Internet radio, the iTunes Store, and the Apple iTunes Match subscription service, iTunes Radio requires an Internet connection and an Apple ID.

Your iTunes Radio station is automatically shared among all your Macs running OS X Lion or later (as well as any devices you own running iOS 7 or later).

iTunes and iCloud Together

iTunes is connected closely with the Apple iCloud service, allowing you to share music betwixt all your Macs and iOS devices. But how do you pull your audio and video out of that floating nimbus? Try this: Sign in with your Apple ID, select your Music Library in the Source list, and then choose View⇨Show Music in the Cloud. Bam! All the audio and video that you've purchased from the iTunes Store appears in your Library. Note, however, that those items don't exist on your local drive — consider those entries as placeholders for the stuff you can download, allowing you to see (and search for) what's available through iCloud. (And, if you've purchased as much from the iTunes Store as I have, you'll save many, many gigabytes of storage space on your iMac's drive by just downloading certain songs.)

To download a local copy of any iCloud item, simply click the iCloud icon next to the item. After the local copy is saved to your iMac's drive, the iCloud icon disappears, and you're ready to listen or watch your purchase.

To hide the iCloud placeholder entries from your Library and display just the stuff on your Mac's drive, choose View⇨Hide Music in the Cloud.

Apple's iTunes Match subscription service builds on this same functionality, allowing you to store *all* your music in iCloud (including the songs you've ripped from audio CDs and downloaded from other sources) and listen to it on any of your Macs or iOS devices! When you join iTunes Match, all the songs that aren't available from the iTunes Store are automatically uploaded to iCloud.

At the time of this writing, the service is $25 per year and is limited to a maximum of 10 devices and 25,000 songs. *Note:* Purchases you make from the iTunes Store don't count toward that 25,000 song limit.

To subscribe to iTunes Match or manage your Match storage, click the Match button at the top of the iTunes window.

iSending iStuff to iPod, iPhone, and iPad

If you're cool enough to own an iPod, you'll be happy to know that iTunes has features for your personal audio and video jukebox as well. *iPods,* Apple's multimedia players, comprise an entire family of portable devices (ranging from $49 to about $249) that can hold anywhere from about several hundred to literally thousands of songs, as well as podcasts, photos, and video. This great gadget and those like it have become known worldwide as *the* preferred portable digital media player.

If you own an iPod touch, iPhone, or iPad, you probably already know that these devices can act as your music player as well. You can buy all sorts of applications for these devices on the iTunes Store, and iTunes even keeps track of these applications as part of your iTunes Library.

You connect your iPod to any Macintosh or Windows PC with USB 2.0 ports with the included cable. After the iPod is connected, you can synchronize the iPod with iTunes. By default, this process is automatic: The iPod and the iTunes software communicate with each other and figure out what items are in your iTunes Library (as compared with the iPod Library). If they discover songs, podcasts, and video in your iTunes Library that are missing from your iPod, the items automatically transfer to the iPod. Conversely, if the iPod contains stuff that's no longer in iTunes, the iPod automatically removes those files from its drive.

Go back and reread that last sentence above about the iPod **automatically removing** files from its drive. (I'll wait here.) Apple added this feature in an effort to be attentive to copyright concerns. The reasoning is that if you connect your iPod to your friend's computer, you can't transfer songs from the iPod to that computer. Of course, you could always look at it from the marketing perspective as a feature that makes sure your iMac and iPod are always in total sync. Whatever the case, pay close attention and read all warning dialogs when connecting to a computer other than your own, or you might wipe out your iPod's library.

You can change your settings so that iTunes auto-syncs only selected playlists. Or if you're really nervous, you can manually manage the contents of your iPod with iTunes.

Sharing Media across a Network

Ready to share music, podcasts, and video — *legally,* mind you — with other folks on your local network? You can offer your digital media to other iTunes users across your home or office. Follow these steps:

1. **Choose iTunes⇨Preferences to open the Preferences dialog.**

2. **Click Sharing.**

3. **Select the Share My Library on My Local Network check box.**

4. **Specify whether you want to share your entire library or only selected playlists and files.**

   Sharing selected playlists is a good idea for those Meatmen and Sex Pistols fans who work at a cubicle farm in a big corporation.

5. **If you want to restrict access to just a few people, select the Require Password check box; then type a password in the text box.**

6. **Click OK.**

Your shared folder appears within the Source list for all iTunes users who enabled the Look for Shared Libraries check box on the General pane of their iTunes Preferences dialog. Note that the music you share with others can't be imported or copied, so everything stays legal.

Want to change that frumpy default name for your shared media library to something more exotic, like "Dan's Techno Beat Palace"? No problem. Display the Preferences dialog again, but this time, click the General button, click in the Library Name text box, and edit your network entertainment persona to your heart's content.

You can also share your media library by using Home Sharing, which allows multiple devices to join in the fun. That includes both Mac computers and iOS devices (your iPad, iPhone, and iPod touch, running iOS 4.3 or later). Home Sharing requires a wireless network connection for all your devices, and you'll have to enter the same Apple ID information on each device. To turn on Home Sharing in iTunes, choose File from the iTunes menu, hover your cursor over the Home Sharing submenu, and choose Turn On Home Sharing. (Don't forget to repeat this setup on each computer.) After Home Sharing is enabled, shared libraries will appear in the Source list under the Shared heading.

Burning Music to Shiny Plastic Circles

Besides being a great audio player, iTunes is adept at creating CDs. iTunes makes recording songs to a CD as simple as a few clicks. Making the modern version of a compilation *(mix)* tape is easier than getting a kid to eat ice cream. iTunes lets you burn CDs in one of three formats:

- ✓ **Audio CD:** This is the typical kind of commercial music CD that you buy at a store. Most typical music audio CDs store up to 800MB of data, which translates into about 80 minutes of music.

- ✓ **Data CD or DVD:** A standard CD-ROM or DVD-ROM is recorded with the audio files. This kind of disc can't be played in any standard audio CD player (even if it supports MP3 CDs, which I discuss next). Therefore, you can listen to these songs only by using iTunes (or another media player) on an iMac or a PC.

- ✓ **MP3 CD:** As does the ordinary computer CD-ROM that I describe, an MP3 CD holds MP3 files in data format. However, the files are arranged in such a way that they can be recognized by audio CD players that support the MP3 CD format (especially boom boxes, DVD players, personal CD players, and car stereos). Because MP3 files are so much smaller than the digital audio tracks found on traditional audio CDs, you can fit as many as 160 typical four-minute songs on one disc. These discs can also be played on your iMac via iTunes.

Keep in mind that MP3 CDs aren't the same as the standard audio CDs that you buy at the store, and you can't play them in older audio CD players that don't support the MP3 CD format. Rather, this is the kind of archival disc that you burn at home for your own collection, or for use in a CD/DVD player or car audio system that supports MP3 discs.

To begin the process, build a playlist (or select an existing playlist that you want to record). If necessary, create a new playlist and add to it whatever songs you would like to have on the CD. (See the earlier section "Keeping Slim Whitman and Slim Shady Apart: Organizing with Playlists," if you need a refresher.) With the songs in the correct order, right-click the playlist and choose Burn Playlist to Disc to commence the disc burning process. Click the desired recording format (again, usually Audio CD) in the Burn Settings dialog that appears.

To save yourself from sonic shock, I always recommend that you enable the Sound Check check box before you burn. iTunes will adjust the volume on all the songs on your audio CD so that they'll play at the same volume level.

Ready to go? Click Burn and load the blank disc, and iTunes lets you know when the recording is complete.

Feasting on iTunes Visuals

Sure, iTunes is a feast for the ears, but did you know that it can provide you with eye candy as well? With just a click or two, you can view mind-bending graphics that stretch, move, and pulse with your music, as shown in Figure 13-6.

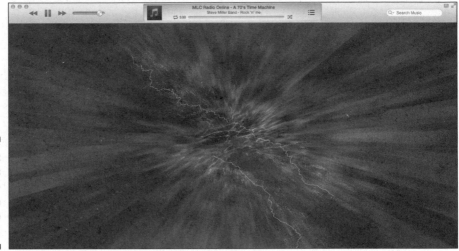

Figure 13-6: iTunes can display some awesome patterns!

To begin viewing iTunes visuals, choose View➪Show Visualizer (or press ⌘+T). Immediately, most of your iTunes interface disappears and begins displaying groovy lava lamp–style animations (like, *sassy,* man). To stop the visuals, choose View➪Hide Visualizer (or press ⌘+T again). The usual sunny aluminum face of iTunes returns.

You can also change the viewing size of the iTunes visuals. From the View menu item, choose Full Screen (or press ⌘+Control+F). To escape from Full Screen mode, click or press Esc.

You can still control iTunes with the keyboard while the visuals are zooming around your screen. See Table 13-1 earlier in this chapter for a rundown on common keyboard shortcuts.

Exercising Parental Authority

Do young children use your iMac? I'll be honest here: A large amount of content within the iTunes Store, including audio, movies, and even apps, is stuff that I don't consider suitable for kids. And what about the media that others in the family may decide to share? Such is the world we live in today, and the good folks at Apple recognize that you may not want to inadvertently allow your kids to have access to explicit content.

Luckily, you can use the Parental Control preferences settings within iTunes to build a secure fence around content that's for "grown-ups only." Heck, you can even banish items from the Source list entirely. Figure 13-7 illustrates the Parental pane within the iTunes Preferences dialog.

You must log in with an Administrator account to change these settings, just as you do for the Parental Controls within the Mavericks System Preferences dialog. If the settings are *locked* — the padlock icon at the bottom of the dialog is closed — click it and supply your administrator password to unlock them.

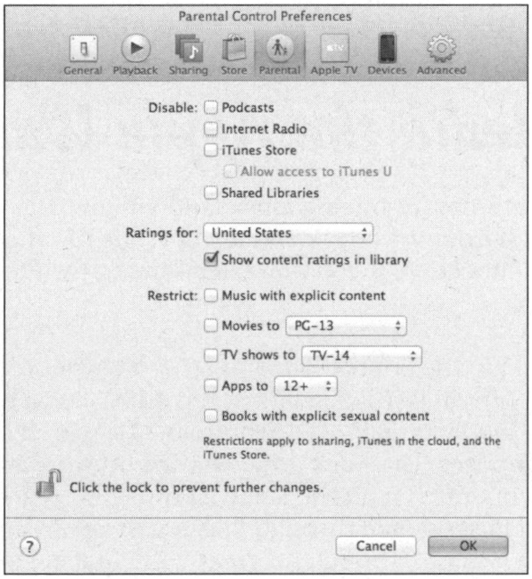

Figure 13-7:
Protect
your kids
from explicit
content
using the
Parental
settings.

To enable Parental Controls, follow these steps:

1. **Choose iTunes⇨Preferences.**

2. **Click the Parental tab.**

3. **Select any of the Disable check boxes to prevent access to those features.**

   Disabling features inside iTunes applies to *all* user accounts — no matter who is logged in! You'll notice that any features you disable disappear completely from the Source list at the left side of the iTunes window after you click OK at the end of these steps.

4. **Open the Ratings For pop-up menu and choose your country.**

   Because Apple maintains separate iTunes Stores for different nations, you can choose which country's iTunes Store to monitor. If you like, you can disable the display of content ratings within your iTunes Library by deselecting the Show Content Ratings in Library check box.

5. **To restrict specific content within the iTunes Store, select the check box next to the source; then open the corresponding pop-up menu to choose the restriction level.**

   Note that these restrictions apply only to content on the iTunes Store and media shared with your Mac. Content within your iTunes Library is never restricted.

6. **Click the padlock icon at the bottom of the dialog to close it and prevent any changes.**

7. **Click OK.**

Buying Digital Media the Apple Way

The hottest spot on the Internet for buying music and video is the iTunes Store, which you can reach from the cozy confines of iTunes — that is, as long as you have an Internet connection. If you don't, it's time to turn the page to a different chapter.

Click the iTunes Store item in the Source list, and after a few moments, you're presented with the latest offerings. Click a link in the store list to browse according to media type, or click the Power Search link to search by song title, artist, album, or composer. The Back and Forward buttons at the top of the iTunes Store window operate much the same as those in Safari, moving you forward or backward in sequence through pages you've already seen. Clicking the Home button (which, through no great coincidence, looks like a miniature house) takes you back to the Store's main page.

To display the details on a specific album, track, video, podcast, or audio-book (whew), just click it. If you're interested in buying just certain tracks (for that perfect road warrior mix), you get to listen to 90 seconds of any track — for free, no less, and at full sound quality. To add an item to your iTunes Store shopping cart, click the Add Song/Movie/Album/Video/Podcast/Audiobook button (sheesh!). When you're ready to buy, click the Shopping Cart item in the Source list and then click the Buy Now button. (At the time of this writing, tracks are usually 99 cents a pop, and an entire album is typically $9.99. What a bargain!)

The iTunes Store creates an account for you based on your e-mail address, and it keeps secure track of your payment information for future purchases. After you use the iTunes Store once, you rarely have to log in or retype your credit card information again.

The tracks and files that you download are saved to a separate playlist called Purchased. After the download is finished, you can play them, copy them to other playlists, burn them to CD or DVD, share 'em over your network, or ship them to your iOS devices using iCloud, just as you can any other item in your iTunes Library.

 iTunes can automatically download the media you purchase on another iCloud device (including another Mac and your iPhone, iPad, or iPod touch). To set up automatic downloading, choose iTunes⇨Preferences to open the Preferences dialog, and then click the Store tab. After you sign in at the iTunes Store, you can choose to download music or app purchases, and you have the option to check for new downloads automatically. Click OK to save your changes.

Remember all those skeptics who claimed that buying digital audio and video could never work over the Internet because of piracy issues and high costs? Well, bunkie, hats off to Apple: Once again, our favorite technology leader has done something the *right* way!

Chapter 14

The Masterpiece That Is iPhoto

Do you still own a camera that uses real film? (Heck, have you ever *seen* a film camera?) The digital camera has reached the pinnacle that those funny (strange) marketing people refer to as *saturation* (virtually everyone owns one or a smartphone that sports a built-in camera), and iPhoto was written to address the needs of every person with a digital camera and an iMac!

With iPhoto, you organize, edit, and even publish your photographs. (It sports more features than a handful of Swiss Army knives.) After you shoot your photos with a digital camera (or even scan images from original film prints or negatives), you can import them into iPhoto, edit them, and publish them. You're not limited to photos that you take yourself, either; you can edit, share, and organize all kinds of digital image files. You can even create a photo album and use the iPhoto interface to order a handsome hardbound copy shipped to you, or create a slideshow that you copy to a USB flash drive.

To sum it all up, I'm willing to bet that iPhoto is either the first or the second iLife application that you fall in love with (running neck and neck with iTunes). In this chapter, I show you how you can work digital image magic with true Apple panache!

Delving into iPhoto

In Figure 14-1, you can see most of the major controls offered in iPhoto. (Other controls automatically appear when you enter different modes; I cover them in upcoming sections of this chapter.)

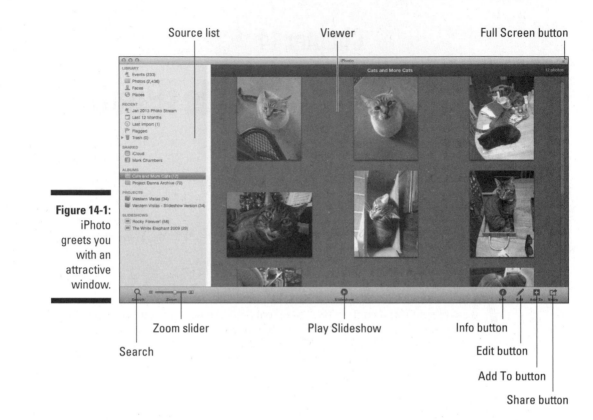

Source list   Viewer   Full Screen button

Figure 14-1:
iPhoto
greets you
with an
attractive
window.

Zoom slider   Play Slideshow   Info button

Search

Edit button

Add To button

Share button

Although these controls and sections of the window are covered in more detail in the following sections, here's a quick rundown of what you're looking at when you first launch iPhoto:

- **Source list:** This list of image locations determines which photos iPhoto displays.

  - You can choose to display either your entire image library or just the last set of digital images that you downloaded from your camera.

  - You can create new albums of your own that appear in the Source list, which make it much easier to organize your photos.

  - Photos can be grouped by *Event* (when they were taken), *Faces* (who appears in the photos), and *Places* (where photos were taken).

  - You can view the photos you've shared online using Facebook, Twitter, and Flickr (and those from your other Macs and iOS devices via Photo Stream, if you're using the Apple iCloud feature).

  - You can create books, calendars, cards, and slideshows.

Right-click in any empty part of the Source list to add a new blank album, book, or slideshow to your Source list.

✔ **Viewer:** This pane displays the images from the currently selected photo source.

You can drag or click to select photos in the Viewer for further tricks, such as assigning keywords and image editing.

✔ **Full Screen:** Click this button in the upper-right corner of the window to switch to a full-screen display of your photos. In full-screen mode, the Source list disappears, and both images and events appear as thumbnails. You can double-click a thumbnail to view the image (or the contents, if it's an event) using your iMac's entire screen real estate. You can also use the same controls that I discuss later in this chapter for chores such as sharing and editing images; the toolbar is still available at the bottom of the screen.

✔ **Search:** Click the button with the magnifying glass icon to display the Search text box, where you can locate photos by specific criteria. Just click in the box and start typing to search by description and title, or even Faces and Places (which I cover later in the chapter).

✔ **Zoom:** Drag this slider to the left to reduce the size of the thumbnails in the Viewer. This allows you to see more thumbnails at one time, which is a great boon for quick, visual searches. Drag the slider to the right to expand the size of the thumbnails, thereby making it easier to differentiate details between similar photos in the Viewer.

✔ **Play Slideshow:** Select an event, album, book, or slideshow in the Source list (or multiple images you've selected in the Viewer) and then click this button to start a full-screen slideshow using those images.

✔ **Info:** Click this button to display information on the currently selected photos (or the item selected in the Source list).

✔ **Edit:** Click this button to edit the currently selected photos. (I cover editing in depth later in the chapter.)

✔ **Add To:** Click this button to add the currently selected photos to an existing album, slideshow, book, card, or calendar.

✔ **Share:** Click this button to share the currently selected photos on Flickr, Twitter, or Facebook. Choose Photo Stream to send the selected photos to your iPhone, iPad, or iPod touch using iCloud. You can also order prints, attach the photos to a text message, or e-mail them. (Heck, if you've got a printer connected to your iMac, you can even produce your own glossies.)

Working with Images in iPhoto

Even a superbly designed image display and editing application such as iPhoto would look overwhelming if everything were jammed into one window. Thus, Apple's developers provide different operational modes (such as editing and book creation) that you can use in the one iPhoto window. Each mode allows you to perform different tasks, and you can switch modes at just about any time by clicking the corresponding toolbar button.

In this section, I discuss three of these modes — import, organize, and edit — and what you can do when you're in them. Then I conclude the chapter with sections on publishing and sharing your images.

Import Images 101

In *import* mode, you're ready to download images directly from your digital camera — as long as your specific camera model is supported in iPhoto. To find many of the cameras that are supported in iPhoto, visit the Apple iPhoto support page:

```
www.apple.com/macosx/upgrade/cameras.html
```

And you're not limited to cameras, of course: You can also import photos from a memory card reader (such as the SDXC card slot sported by your iMac) or even a Kodak PhotoCD.

Follow these steps to import images:

1. **Connect your digital camera to your iMac.**

   Plug one end of a USB cable into your camera and the other end into your iMac's USB port.

2. **Prepare your camera to download images.**

   The procedure for downloading images varies by camera, but the process usually involves turning the camera on and choosing a "Download" or "PC" mode. Check your camera's user guide for more details.

3. **Launch iPhoto.**

   Your iMac will probably launch iPhoto automatically when your camera is detected, but you can always launch iPhoto manually by clicking its icon on the Dock (or double-clicking it in your Applications folder).

4. **Type an event name for the imported photos, such as** 21st Birthday Party **or** Godzilla Ravages Tokyo.

   Depending on your birthday parties, this could be the same event.

5. **(Optional) To have iPhoto automatically separate images into separate events based on the date they were taken, select the Split Events check box.**

6. **Click the Import All button to import your photographs from the camera.**

   The images are added to your Photo Library, where you can organize them as you want.

   To select specific images to import, hold down the ⌘ key and click each desired photo; then click Import Selected instead of Import All.

   Depending on the camera, iPhoto may also import video clips.

7. **Specify whether the images you're importing should be deleted from the camera afterward.**

   If you don't expect to download these images again to another computer or another device, you can choose to delete the photos from your camera automatically. This saves you a step, frees space for new photos, and helps eliminate the guilt that can crop up when you nix your pix. (Sorry, I couldn't resist.)

"What's that about an Event, Mark?" After you download the contents of your digital camera, those contents count as a virtual *Event* in iPhoto — based on either the date that you imported them or the date they were taken. For example, you can always display the last images you imported by clicking Last Import. If you want to see photos from your son's graduation, they appear as a separate Event. (Events and Last Import will both appear in the Source list.) Think about that. . . . It's pretty tough to arrange old-fashioned film prints by the moment in time that they document, but iPhoto makes it easy for you to see just which photos are part of the same group! I explain more about Events in the next section.

Importing images from your hard drive

Adding images stored on your hard drive, a CD, a DVD, an external drive, or a USB flash drive is easy. If images are in a folder, just drag that folder from a Finder window and drop it into the Source list in the iPhoto window. iPhoto automatically creates a new album using the folder name, and you can sit back while the images are imported into that new album. iPhoto recognizes images in several formats: JPEG, GIF, RAW, PNG, PICT, PSD, PDF, and TIFF.

If you have individual images, you can drag them as well. Select the images in a Finder window and drag them into the desired album in the Source list. To add them to the album currently displayed in the Viewer, drag the selected photos and drop them in the Viewer instead. (If you don't want to add them to any specific album at this time, drag the images to the Photos entry in the Source list instead.)

If you'd rather import images by using a standard Mac Open dialog, choose File➪Import to Library. Simplicity strikes again!

Organize mode: Organizing and sorting your images

In the days of film prints, you could always stuff another shoebox with your latest photos or buy another sticky album to expand your library. Your digital camera, though, stores images as files instead, and many folks don't print their digital photographs. Instead, you can keep your entire collection of digital photographs and scanned images well ordered and easily retrieved by using iPhoto's *organize* mode. Then you can display them in a slideshow, e-mail them, print them, use them as Desktop backgrounds, or burn them to an archive disc.

A new kind of photo album

The most familiar method of organizing images in iPhoto is the *album*. Each album can represent any designation you like, be it a year, a vacation, your daughter, or your daughter's ex-boyfriends. Follow these steps:

1. **Create a new album.**

   You can choose File⇨New Album, press ⌘+N, or right-click in the Source list and choose New Album. (You can see right-click menu in Figure 14-2.) If you've selected any image thumbnails in the Viewer, they'll be automatically added to the new album. If you don't have any photos selected, you get a funky dialog asking whether you're sure you want to create an empty album, and then you have to click Continue.

   iPhoto creates the new album entry in the Source list as an editing text box.

2. **Type the name for your new photo album into the text box.**

3. **Press Return.**

Figure 14-2:
Add a new album in iPhoto.

iPhoto also offers a special type of album called a Smart Album, which you can create from the File menu. (For even faster action, press Option+⌘+N.) If you're familiar with the Smart Folders you can use within the Finder and the Smart Playlists within iTunes (see Chapter 13), you've figured this one out already. A *Smart Album* contains only photos that match certain criteria that you choose, including the keywords and rating that you assign your images. Other criteria include text in the photo filenames, dates the images were added to iPhoto, and any comments you might have added (as well as camera-specific data, such as ISO and shutter speed). Now here's the really nifty angle: iPhoto *automatically* builds and maintains Smart Albums for you, adding new photos that match the criteria and deleting those that you remove from your Photo Library (as well as removing the photos that no longer match the Smart Album's criteria)! Smart Album icons carry a gear symbol in the Source list.

You can display information about the currently selected item in the information pane at the far right of the window. Just click the Info button at the bottom of the iPhoto window, which sports the familiar "*i*-in-a-circle" logo. You can also type a short note or description in the Add a Description box that appears in the Info pane, or add keywords to help you organize your photos.

You can also change the existing information for an image by selecting it in the Viewer and clicking the Info button. Click the Name heading or the Add a Description heading in the pane to display a text edit box, and you can simply type a new value.

You can drag images from the Viewer into any album you choose. For example, you can copy an image to another album by dragging it from the Viewer to the desired album in the Source list.

To remove a photo that has fallen out of favor, follow these steps:

1. **In the Source list, select the desired album.**

2. **In the Viewer, select the photo (click it) that you want to remove.**

3. **Press Delete.**

When you remove a photo from an album, you *don't* remove the photo from your collection (represented by the Photos entry under the Library heading in the Source list) because an album is just a group of links to the images in your collection, just like how a playlist in iTunes is a group of links to songs in your Music Library. If you want to completely remove an offending photo from iPhoto, click the Photos entry under the Library heading to display your entire collection of images and delete the picture there. The photo disappears from all albums with which it is associated.

To remove an entire album from the Source list, just click it in the Source list to select it — in the Viewer, you can see the images that it contains — and then press Delete. (Alternatively, right-click the offending album and choose Delete Album.)

To rename an album, click the entry under the Albums heading in the Source list to select it and then click again to display a text box. Type the new album name and then press Return.

Change your mind? iPhoto comes complete with a handy-dandy Undo feature. Just press ⌘+Z, and it's as though your last action never happened. (A great trick for those moments when you realize you just deleted your only image of your first car from your Library.) For an extra level of backup protection, you can invest in an external hard drive and use the awesome Mavericks Time Machine backup feature (more on that in Chapter 24).

Arranging stuff by Events

As I mention earlier, an *Event* is a group of images that you shot or downloaded at the same time. iPhoto assumes that those images belong together (which is usually a pretty safe assumption). Figure 14-3 illustrates some of the Events I've created in my iPhoto collection.

An Event can be renamed, just as an album can — you just use a different procedure. Click the Events entry under the Library heading in the Source list to display your Events in the Viewer; then click the existing Event name in the caption underneath the thumbnail. A text box appears in which you can type a new name; click Return to update the Event.

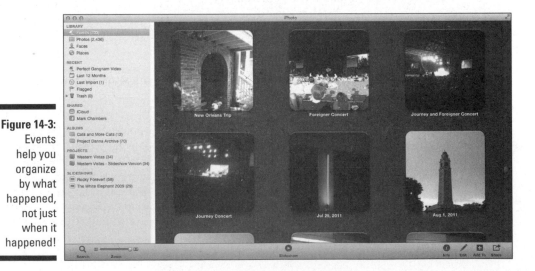

Figure 14-3: Events help you organize by what happened, not just when it happened!

Although a photo can appear in multiple albums, it can appear in only one Event.

Try moving your cursor over an Event thumbnail in the Viewer, and you'll see that iPhoto displays the date range when the images were taken, as well as the total number of images in the Event. Ah, but things get *really* cool when you move your cursor back and forth over an Event with many images: The thumbnail animates and displays all the images in the Event! (Why can't I think of this stuff? This is the future, dear readers.)

To display the contents of an Event in the Viewer, just double-click the Event thumbnail. To return to the Events thumbnails, click the All Events button at the top of the Viewer.

Decided to merge those Prom Event pictures with your daughter's Graduation Event? No problem! You can simply drag one Event thumbnail on top of another. Alternatively, click the Events entry under the Library heading in the Source list to display your Events and then hold down ⌘ while you click the Events that you want to merge. Heck, if the Events you want to merge are selected, right-click one of them and choose Merge Events from the menu that appears. Click Merge in the confirmation dialog that appears.

Whilst organizing, you can create a brand-new empty Event by choosing Events⇨Create Event. ***Hint:*** Make sure that no events are selected first. Feel free to drag photos from albums, other Events, or your Photo library into your new Event.

Working with Faces and Places

iPhoto includes two organizational tools: Faces and Places. These two categories appear in the Library section of the Source list.

First, tackle Faces. (Ouch. Don't literally tackle anyone's face, dear reader.) Faces is a sophisticated recognition system that automatically recognizes human faces within the photos that you add to your Library. (I don't know whether it works well with pets — but you can try, anyway.) Naturally, you have to identify — *tag* — faces before iPhoto can recognize them.

To tag a face, follow these steps:

1. **In the Source list, click the Photos item to display your image library.**

2. **In the Viewer, click the photo with a person you want to tag.**

   The photo is selected, as indicated by the yellow border.

3. **Click the Info button on the iPhoto toolbar at the bottom of the window.**

   iPhoto displays the Info pane you see in Figure 14-4.

Figure 14-4:
Adding
another
mug to my
collection of
Faces. (That
still doesn't
sound right.)

4. **In the Faces section of the Info pane, click the Add a Face link.**

   Note that iPhoto has indicated each person's face in the photo with a label. If a face has already been tagged, the label will match the person's face.

5. **Choose a name option, depending on whether the face is recognized, unrecognized, or incorrectly identified:**

   • *If iPhoto recognizes the face correctly and the name matches the person,* click the check mark to confirm the tag.

   • *If the face is unrecognized (labeled as Click to Name),* click the label to open a text box and type the person's name.

   • *If the face is incorrectly identified,* click the X at the right of the text box, and then you can enter a new name.

   If the name appears on a Contacts contact card — or is recognized as one of your Facebook friends — you can click the matching entry that appears to confirm the identity. Wowzers!

   To delete a Face recognition box that isn't necessary, hover your cursor over the box and click the X button that appears at the top-left corner of the box.

   If iPhoto doesn't recognize the face at all in the photo (which can happen if the person's face is turned at an angle to the camera, or is in a darker area of the photo), click the box border and drag the box over the person's face. If necessary, you can resize the box using the four handles at the corner of the box. Now you can click the label and type the person's name.

6. **After you finish identifying faces in the photo, click the Info button to hide the Info pane.**

After you tag an image, it appears in your Faces collection, which you can view by clicking the Faces entry in the Source list. You can double-click a portrait in your Faces collection to see all the images that contain that person.

Notice the Confirm Additional Faces button that appears next to the person's name? Click it, and iPhoto displays other photos that may contain this person's face, allowing you to tag the person there as well. If a face is a match, click the thumbnail to confirm it.

As you might expect, the more photos you add for a specific person, the better iPhoto gets at recognizing that person!

Places makes it easy to track the location where photos were taken, but it requires a digital camera that includes GPS tracking information in the image metadata for iPhoto to do so without your help. (This is a relatively new feature for digital cameras, so older models aren't likely to support GPS tracking. Naturally, both the iPhone and the 3G/4G iPad support this feature.) Places also requires an Internet connection because it uses Google Maps.

Click the Places entry in the Source list to display a global map, with pushpins indicating where your photos were taken. You can switch the Places map between terrain and satellite modes, or choose a hybrid display. If you're familiar with Google Maps, these settings are old friends of yours.

If you click a specific photo (that includes location information) to select it and then click the Info button, you'll see a close-up map of the location where the photo was taken.

Alternatively, click the text Location buttons at the top of the map to display a character-based browser, where you can click country, state, city, and place names.

No matter which view mode you choose, clicking a pushpin or location displays the images taken in that area.

Organizing with keywords

"Okay, Mark, albums, Events, Faces, and Places are great ideas, but there has to be a way to search my collection by category!" Never fear, good iMac owner. You can also assign descriptive *keywords* to images to help you organize your collection and locate certain pictures fast. iPhoto comes with a number of standard keywords, and you can create your own as well.

To illustrate, suppose you'd like to identify your images according to special events in your family. Birthday photos should have their own keyword, and anniversaries deserve another. By assigning keywords, you can search for Elsie's sixth birthday or your silver wedding anniversary (no matter what Event or album they're in), and all related photos with those keywords appear like magic! (Well, *almost* like magic. You need to choose View⇨Keywords, which toggles the Keyword display in the Viewer.)

iPhoto includes a number of keywords that are already available:

- ✔ Favorite
- ✔ Family
- ✔ Kids
- ✔ Vacation
- ✔ Birthday
- ✔ RAW
- ✔ Photo Booth
- ✔ Photo Stream
- ✔ Movie
- ✔ Checkmark

What's the Checkmark all about, you ask? It's a special case: Adding this keyword displays a tiny check mark icon in the bottom-right corner of the image. The checkmark keyword comes in handy for temporarily identifying specific images because you can search for just your check-marked photos.

To assign keywords to images (or remove keywords that have already been assigned), select one or more photos in the Viewer. Choose Window➪Manage My Keywords or press ⌘+K to display the Keywords window, as shown in Figure 14-5.

You're gonna need your own keywords

I'll bet you take photos of things other than just kids and vacations, and that's why iPhoto allows you to create your own keywords. Display the iPhoto Keywords window by pressing ⌘+K, click the Edit Keywords button, and then click Add (the button with the plus sign). iPhoto adds a new unnamed keyword to the list as an edit box, ready for you to type its name.

You can rename an existing keyword from this same window, too. Click a keyword to select it and then click Rename. Remember, however, that renaming a keyword affects *all the images* *that were tagged with that keyword.* That might be confusing when, for example, photos originally tagged as Family suddenly appear with the keyword Foodstuffs. (I recommend applying a new keyword and deleting the old one if this problem crops up.)

To change the keyboard shortcut assigned to a keyword, click the Shortcut button. To remove an existing keyword from the list, click the keyword to select it and then click the Delete button, which bears a minus sign.

Figure 14-5:
Add
keywords
to these
selected
images.

Drag the keyword buttons that you use the most to the Quick Group section of the Keywords window, and iPhoto automatically creates a keyboard shortcut for each keyword in the Quick Group. Now you don't even need to display the Keywords window to get business done!

Click the buttons for the keywords that you want to attach to the selected images to mark them. Or click the highlighted keyword buttons that you want to remove from the selected images to disable them.

Digging through your library with keywords

Behold the power of keywords! To sift through your entire collection of images by using keywords, click the Search button on the toolbar at the bottom of the iPhoto window, click the magnifying glass icon at the left side of the Search box, and choose Keyword from the pop-up menu. iPhoto displays a pop-up Keywords panel, and you can click one or more keyword buttons to display just the photos that carry those keywords.

The images that remain in the Viewer after a search must have *all* the keywords that you specified. If an image is identified, for example, by only three of four keywords you chose, it isn't a match and won't appear in the Viewer. (You can create a Smart Album with specific keywords to get around this limitation.)

To search for a photo by words in its description, just click in the Search box and start typing. You can click that same magnifying glass by the Search box to search through your images by date and rating as well.

Speaking of ratings . . .

Playing favorites by assigning ratings

Be your own critic! iPhoto allows you to assign any photo a rating of anywhere from zero to five stars. I use this system to help me keep track of the images that I feel are the best in my library. Select one (or more) image and then assign a rating using one of the following methods:

- ✔ Choose Photos⇨My Rating and then choose the desired rating from the pop-up submenu.

- ✔ Hover your cursor over the photo and click the More button in the lower-right corner of the thumbnail; then click the desired star rating in the menu that appears.

- ✔ Use the ⌘+0 through ⌘+5 shortcuts.

Sorting your images just so

The View menu provides an easy way to arrange your images in the Viewer by a number of different criteria. Choose View⇨Sort Photos and then click the desired sort criteria from the pop-up submenu. You can arrange the display by date, keyword, title, or rating. If you select an album in the Source list, you can also choose to arrange photos manually, which means that you can drag and drop thumbnails in the Viewer to place them in the precise order you want them.

Naturally, iPhoto allows you to print selected images, but you can also send photos via e-mail or text message or by using Facebook, Twitter, Flickr, or Photo Stream. Click Share and then choose the desired destination from the submenu.

Edit mode: Removing and fixing stuff the right way

Not every digital image is perfect — just look at my collection if you need proof. For those shots that need a pixel massage, iPhoto includes a number of editing tools that you can use to correct common problems.

The first step in any editing job is to select the image you want to fix in the Viewer. Then click the Edit button on the iPhoto toolbar to display the Edit mode controls at the right side of the window, as shown in Figure 14-6. Now you're ready to fix problems, using the tools that I discuss in the rest of this section. (If you're editing a photo that's part of an Event, album, Faces, or Places, note the spiffy scrolling photo strip at the bottom, which allows you to switch to another image to edit from the same grouping.) Note that iPhoto always displays the Quick Fixes tab when you first enter Edit mode.

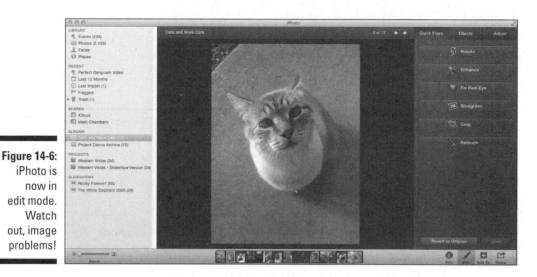

Figure 14-6:
iPhoto is
now in
edit mode.
Watch
out, image
problems!

While you're editing, you can use the Next and Previous buttons at the left of the tab button to move to the next image in the current group (or back to the previous image).

TIP
If you'd prefer to edit images while using more of your screen real estate, click the Full Screen button at the upper-right corner of the iPhoto window. To switch back to the standard window arrangement, click the Full Screen button again or simply press the Esc key.

TIP
Need more features than iPhoto provides when editing a prized photograph? iPhoto even allows you to specify another image-editing application like Photoshop Elements (instead of the built-in editing controls I cover in this section). First, click iPhoto, choose Preferences, and then click the Advanced tab. From the Edit Photos pop-up menu, click Choose App; then navigate to the image editor you want to use, select it, and click Open. Now close the Preferences dialog, and iPhoto will automatically open the application you selected when you click the Edit button! If you decide to return to iPhoto's built-in editing controls, just open the Advanced pane again, open the Edit Photos pop-up menu again, and choose In iPhoto.

When you're done with Edit mode, click the (wait for it . . .) Edit button again to return to the Viewer!

Rotating tipped-over shots

If an image is in the wrong orientation and needs to be turned to display correctly, click the Rotate button to turn it once in a counterclockwise direction. Hold down the Option key while you click the Rotate button to rotate in a clockwise direction.

Find yourself using that Option key often when rotating? Consider reversing the default direction! Choose iPhoto➪Preferences and click the General tab; then select the Rotate radio button to change the default direction (a great idea if your camera's shots typically need rotating in the opposite direction).

Crop 'til you drop

Does that photo have an intruder hovering around the edges of the subject? You can remove some of the border by *cropping* an image, just as folks once did with film prints and a pair of scissors. (We've come a long way.) With iPhoto, you can remove unwanted portions from the edges of an image; it's a great way to get Uncle Milton's stray head (complete with toupee) out of an otherwise perfect holiday snapshot.

Follow these steps to crop an image:

1. **From the Quick Fixes tab, click the Crop button.**

2. **Select the portion of the image that you want to keep.**

   In the Viewer, click and drag the handles on the rectangle to outline the part of the image that you want. Remember that whatever is outside this rectangle disappears after the crop is completed.

   When you drag a corner or edge of the outline, a semi-opaque grid (familiar to amateur and professional photographers as the nine rectangles from the Rule of Thirds) appears to help you visualize what you're claiming. (Check it out in Figure 14-7.)

   You can expand the outline to the full dimensions of the image at any time by just clicking the Reset button.

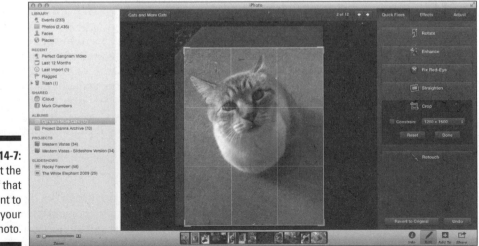

Figure 14-7: Select the stuff that you want to keep in your photo.

3. **(Optional) Choose a preset aspect ratio.**

   If you want to force your cropped selection to a specific aspect ratio — say, 4 x 3 or 16 x 9 for a widescreen desktop background, or 4 x 6 or 5 x 7 to match the dimensions of photo paper — click select the Constrain check box and then select that ratio from the Constrain pop-up menu.

4. **Click the Done button.**

   Oh, and don't forget that you can use iPhoto's Undo feature if you mess up and need to try again. Just press ⌘+Z.

iPhoto features multiple Undo levels, so you can press ⌘+Z several times to travel back through your last several changes. Alternatively, you can always return the image to its original form (before you did any editing at all) by clicking the Revert to Original button.

Straightening what's crooked

Was your camera slightly tilted when you took the perfect shot? Never fear! Click the Straighten button and then drag the Angle slider to tilt the image in the desired direction. Click the Done button to return to Edit mode.

Enhancing images to add pizzazz

If a photo looks washed out, click the Enhance button to increase (or decrease) the color saturation and improve the contrast. Enhance is automatic, so you don't have to set anything — but be prepared to use Undo if you're not satisfied with the changes.

Removing rampant red-eye

Unfortunately, today's digital cameras can still produce the same "zombies with red eyeballs" as traditional film cameras. *Red-eye* is caused by a camera's flash reflecting off the retinas of a subject's eyes, and it can occur with both humans and animals. (I'm told pets get *green-eye* or *blue-eye,* but iPhoto can handle them, too!)

iPhoto can remove that red-eye and green-eye and turn frightening zombies back into your family and friends! Click the Fix Red-Eye button and then select a demonized eyeball by clicking in the center of it. (If the Red-Eye circular cursor is too small or too large, drag the Size slider to adjust the dimensions.) To complete the process, click the Done button.

Retouching like the stars

The iPhoto Retouch feature is perfect for removing minor flecks or lines in an image (especially those you've scanned from prints). Click Retouch, and notice that the cursor turns into a circle; as with the Red-Eye tool, you can drag the Size slider to change the size of the Retouch cursor. Just drag the cursor across the imperfection and click Done when you're finished touching things up. Don't forget to take a moment and marvel at your editing skill!

As I mention earlier in the chapter, when you first enter Editing mode, the Quick Fixes tab is selected, providing you with the tools I've already covered. (These are the changes you'll make most often, so having Quick Fixes as the default selection makes sense.) However, you can also choose to apply an effect from the Effects tab or make specific changes to the appearance of an image from the Adjust tab.

Effects tab: Switching to black-and-white or sepia

Ever wonder whether a particular photo in your library would look better as a black-and-white *(grayscale)* print? Or perhaps an old-fashioned sepia tone in shades of copper and brown? Just click the Effects tab, which offers nine different effects that you can apply to the photo. You can also make "one-click" changes to your photo from the Effects tab, including lightening and darkening an image or enhancing the contrast.

Adjust tab: Tweaking photo properties manually

Click the Adjust tab to perform very precise manual adjustments to brightness and contrast (the light levels in your image) as well as attributes such as sharpness, shadow, and highlight levels. To adjust a value, make sure that nothing's selected in the image and then drag the corresponding slider until the image looks the way you want. Click the Close button to return to Edit mode.

Producing Your Own Coffee-Table Masterpiece

Book mode unleashes what I think is probably the coolest feature of iPhoto: the chance to design and print a high-quality bound photo book! After you complete an album — all the images have been edited just the way you want, and the album contains all the photos you want to include in your book — iPhoto can send your images as data over the Internet to a company that prints and binds your finished book for you. (No, they don't publish *For Dummies* titles, but then again, I don't get high-resolution color plates in most of my books, either.)

At the time of this writing, you can order many different sizes and bindings. The largest size is a 13" x 10" hardcover book with 20 double-sided pages for about $50 (extra pages cost $1.50 each). Smaller sizes include an 8.5" x 11" softcover book with 20 double-sided pages for about $20 and a hardcover 8.5" x 11" album with 20 double-sided pages for about $30 (shipping included for both). Extra pages can be added at $0.70 and $1.00 a pop, respectively.

iPhoto can also produce and automatically order calendars and cards (both the postal and greeting varieties), using a process similar to the one I describe in this section for producing a book. Who needs that stationery store in the mall anymore? (You can even order old-fashioned prints from the Share toolbar menu.)

If you're going to create a photo book, make sure that the images have the highest quality and highest resolution. The higher the resolution, the better the photos look in the finished book. I personally always try to use images of more than 1200 pixels in the shortest dimension. You should also make sure that you've added enough images to the album or event you'll be using because you need to populate the entire book. (Although you can add extra pages later, each book requires a minimum number of pages.) Don't forget to include a good mix of landscape and portrait shots!

To create a photo book, follow these steps:

1. **Click the desired album or event in the Source list to select it.**

   Make sure that no individual photos are selected in the Viewer. This way, iPhoto uses all the images in the chosen location.

2. **Click the Add To toolbar button and choose Create Book from the pop-up menu.**

3. **Select the type of book using the Binding buttons (Hardcover, Softcover, and Wire-bound) at the top of the window; for book size, use the Size buttons (Small, Large, and Extra-Large) at the left side of the window.**

   Your choices determine the number of pages and the size of the book.

4. **Choose a theme.**

   Use the left- and right-arrow keys to cycle through the theme selections. The theme you choose determines both the layout scheme and the background graphics for each page. To change the color scheme for a theme, click one of the color swatches at the right side of the window.

5. **Click Create.**

   iPhoto adds your new book project under the Projects heading in the Source list (using the name of the album or event where the photos were located), and you see the controls shown in Figure 14-8.

   In Book mode, the Viewer displays a collection of thumbnail images, each of which represents a portion of your book — the front cover, internal pages, or back cover. To display the photos you selected, click the Photos button on the toolbar at the bottom right of the window. You can drag any image thumbnail into one of the photo placeholders to add it to the page.

   It's easy to switch to another theme at any time by clicking the Change Theme button at the top right of the window.

Figure 14-8:
Preparing
to publish
my own
coffee-table
masterpiece.

6. **(Optional) Rearrange the page order to suit you by dragging the thumbnail of any page from one location to another.**

   If you'd prefer a book without page numbers, right-click any page and choose Show Page Numbers to toggle it off. (The Show Page Numbers menu item turns gray to indicate that it's disabled.)

7. **(Optional) To change the look of the cover or a single page, click the cover or a page to select it; then click the Layout button on the toolbar to change the color and design layout for that element.**

   Clicking a design thumbnail automatically updates the page display.

8. **Double-click a page to edit captions and short descriptions.**

   Click any one of the text boxes in the page display and begin typing to add text to that page. *Note:* Some themes don't have caption or description text boxes.

   After you're done editing, click the All Pages button at the top of the window to return to your full spread.

9. **(Optional) To add pages to your book, click the Add Page button on the toolbar.**

   As I mention earlier, the price for additional pages varies according to the size and type of binding you choose.

10. **To view the book at any time, right-click any page and choose Preview Book.**

    After a short wait, the OS X Preview application opens, and you can scroll through the contents of your book (or even print a quick copy). To close the Preview window, choose Preview⇨Quit Preview.

11. **When you're ready to publish your book, click the Buy Book button at the bottom center of the window.**

12. **In a series of dialogs that appears, iPhoto guides you through the final steps to order a bound book.**

    Note that you'll be asked for credit card information, so have that plastic ready.

 Why limit yourself to just paper copies of your publishing success? You can also right-click any page and choose Save Book as PDF to create a snazzy electronic version of your book.

I really need a slideshow

You can use iPhoto to create slideshows! Click the album or Event you want to display in the Source list; then click the Add To button and choose Slideshow. Click New Slideshow, and iPhoto adds an unnamed entry under Slideshows in the Source list. Just like creating a new album, type the name for the slideshow in the text box and press Return. A scrolling thumbnail strip appears at the top of the Viewer, displaying the images in the album or Event. Click and drag the thumbnails to appear in the desired order.

Click the Themes button on the Slideshow toolbar to choose the theme for your slideshow. The theme you choose controls the animation, transition type, and screen layout that iPhoto will use — everything from the classic Ken Burns "moving photo" animation to a really nifty Sliding Panels layout.

To choose background music for your slideshow, click the Music button on the Slideshow toolbar to display Apple's theme music as well as the tracks from your iTunes Library. To choose a standard theme, open the Source pop-up menu and choose Theme Music; select that perfect song and click Choose. To choose an iTunes song or playlist, open the Source pop-up menu and choose a playlist — or throw caution completely to the wind and choose one of your GarageBand compositions. (I cover GarageBand

in Chapter 16.) You can also create a custom playlist by selecting the Custom Playlist for Slideshow check box. Then drag the individual songs you want to the song list at the bottom of the dialog. (You can drag them to rearrange their order in the list as well.) Click Choose to accept your song list.

To configure your slideshow, click the Settings button on the Slideshow toolbar and click the All Slides tab. In the dialog that appears, you can specify the amount of time that each slide remains on the screen, as well as an optional title slide. Widescreen Mac owners appreciate the Aspect Ratio pop-up menu, which allows you to choose a 16:9 widescreen display for your slideshow.

Click the This Slide tab to set the selected photo to display in black and white, sepia, or antique coloring. You can also set the display time and transition type for each photo from this tab.

To display a quick preview of your slideshow without leaving the iPhoto window, click Preview; this is a handy way of determining whether the theme and music you've selected are really what you want. When you're ready to play your slideshow, click the Play button, and iPhoto switches to full-screen mode. To create a movie file from your completed slideshow, click Export on the Slideshow toolbar.

Putting Photo Stream to Work

iPhoto includes the *Photo Stream* feature that automatically shares the photos you take among your iMac, your PC, and any Apple device running iOS 5.0 or later (which includes your iPhone 4 or later, your second or later-generation iPad, and your iPod touch). Click Share and choose Photo Stream, and iPhoto automatically sends the selected images to all compatible devices over your Wi-Fi connection. (Note that all devices using Photo Stream must be configured using the same Apple ID.)

To turn on Photo Stream, choose iPhoto⇨Preferences and click the iCloud toolbar button. Then select the My Photo Stream check box.

Optionally, you can also specify whether iPhoto should automatically import Photo Stream photos to you library and also whether iPhoto should automatically upload the most recent 1,000 photos to Photo Stream for sharing with your other devices.

You can also choose to share specific photos by using shared photo streams, which can be turned on from the iPhoto Preferences dialog. Choose iPhoto⇨ Preferences, click the iCloud tab on the toolbar, and select the Photo Sharing check box.

To subscribe to a shared photo stream invitation from another person, click the iCloud entry in the Source list, click the desired shared stream entry, and then click Accept.

To create your own shared photo stream, select the images you want to share, click the Share button on the toolbar, click the iCloud button, and then click the New Photo Stream menu item that appears. iPhoto prompts you for the e-mail addresses of the folks you want to invite to your shared photo stream. After each e-mail address has been entered, click the Share button in the dialog to start the ball rolling.

When creating a shared photo stream, don't forget to select the Public Website check box if you want to share images with friends and family who don't own a Mac or an iOS device.

Is that Facebook, Twitter, and Flickr I spy?

Indeed it is! iPhoto includes direct connections to both your Facebook and Twitter social networking accounts (www.facebook.com and www.twitter.com) and your Flickr online gallery account (www.flickr.com), allowing you to simply select one or more photos and send them automatically to any of these services! Click the Share button on the toolbar to select the type of account.

The first time you select photos in Viewer (or an album or Event in the Source list) and choose either option, iPhoto prompts you for permission to set up your connection. (Of course, this will require you to enter your Facebook, Twitter, and Flickr account information — hence the confirmation request.) Click Set Up and provide the data that each site requires.

After you set up your accounts, simply select your photos, albums, or Events, click the Share toolbar button, and then choose the menu item for the desired service. Apple, you absolutely *rock!*

E-Mailing Photos to Aunt Mildred

iPhoto can help you send your images through e-mail by automating the process. The application can prepare your image and embed it automatically in a new message. (In fact, you don't even have to open Apple Mail because everything is done within iPhoto.)

To send an image through e-mail, select it and click the Share button on the toolbar; then click the Mail menu item. (You can select up to ten images if you hold down the ⌘ key while clicking.) The layout shown in Figure 14-9 appears, allowing you to choose a theme for your message (complete with a background image and matching font selection). You can also specify the size of the images from the Photo Size pop-up menu, which can save considerable downloading time for those recipients who are still using a dialup connection. To add the images as attachments to the message, select the Attach Photos to Message check box.

Most ISP (Internet service provider) e-mail servers don't accept an e-mail message larger than 5MB or 6MB, so watch that Message Size display at the bottom of the window. (In fact, the encoding necessary to send images as attachments can *double* the size of each image!) If you're trying to send a number of images and the size goes over 5MB, you might have to open the Photo Size pop-up menu and choose a smaller size (reducing the image resolution) to get them all in a single message.

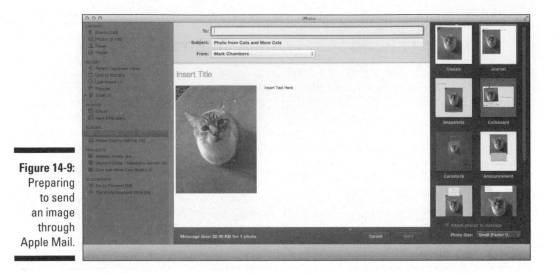

Figure 14-9:
Preparing
to send
an image
through
Apple Mail.

When you're satisfied with the total file size and the theme, click within the To field and enter the recipient's e-mail address. Then click the Subject field and enter a title for the message. To add your own text to the message, double-click the theme's default text and begin typing.

When everything is perfect, click Send. iPhoto takes care of the rest!

Chapter 15

Making Film History with iMovie

- ▶ Taking stock of the iMovie window
- ▶ Importing and adding media content
- ▶ Using transitions in your movie
- ▶ Putting text titles to work
- ▶ Adding animated maps
- ▶ Creating a movie trailer
- ▶ Sharing your movie with others

Remember those home movies that you used to make in high school? They were entertaining and fun to create, and your friends were impressed. In fact, some kids are so downright inspired that you're not surprised when you discover at your high school reunion that they turned out to be graphic artists, or got involved in video or TV production.

iMovie, part of the iLife suite, makes movie-making as easy as those home-made movies. Apple simplifies all the technical stuff, such as importing video and adding audio, leaving you free to concentrate on your creative ideas. In fact, you won't find techy terms such as *codecs* or *keyframes* in this chapter at all. I guarantee that you'll understand what's going on at all times. (How often do you get a promise like that with video-editing software?)

With iMovie, your digital video (DV) camcorder, and the other parts of the iLife suite, you can soon produce and share professional-looking movies, with some of the same creative transitions and titles used by Those Hollywood Types every single day. All on your iMac, all by yourself.

If you turn out to be a world-famous Hollywood Type Director in a decade or so, don't forget the little people — like computer book authors — along the way!

Shaking Hands with the iMovie Window

If you've ever tried using a professional-level video-editing application, you probably felt as though you were suddenly dropped into the cockpit of a jumbo jet. In iMovie, though, all the controls you need are easy to use and logically placed.

To launch iMovie, click the iMovie icon on the Dock or within Launchpad. (It looks like a star from the Hollywood Walk of Fame.) You can also click the Applications folder in any Finder window Sidebar and then double-click the iMovie icon.

To follow the examples I show you here, take these strenuous steps and create a new movie project:

1. **Choose File⇨New Movie (or press ⌘+N).**

   iMovie displays the dialog you see in Figure 15-1.

Figure 15-1:
Creating a
new movie
project
within
iMovie.

You can also create movie *trailers* (a short preview or teaser) within iMovie, as I demonstrate later in this chapter. Generally, however, you create your trailer project *after* your movie is completed (unless, of course, you're specifically creating just a trailer). Why? For the same reason that studios create trailers after the filming is finished: After you complete your movie, you'll have all the clips imported already, and you'll have a better idea of what you want to include while "teasing" your audience!

2. **Click a Theme thumbnail to select a theme to apply to your finished movie.**

   iMovie automatically adds the transitions and titles that correspond to that theme.

   Normally, this is what you want to do. However, you can add transitions and titles manually, as I'll show you later in this chapter. So if you decide not to use a theme out of the gate, click the No Theme thumbnail.

3. **Click the Create button.**

4. **Type a name for your project.**

5. **Click OK.**

   iMovie adds the new project to the thumbnail list in the Project Library pane, and you're on your way! Check out Figure 15-2: This is the whole enchilada, in one window.

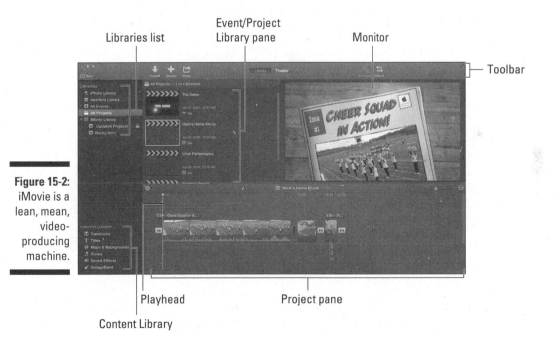

Libraries list

Event/Project Library pane

Monitor

Toolbar

Figure 15-2: iMovie is a lean, mean, video-producing machine.

Playhead

Project pane

Content Library

The controls and displays that you'll use most often are

✔ **Monitor:** Think of this as being just like your TV or computer monitor. Your video clips, still images, and finished movie play here. You'll also crop and rotate your video within the monitor.

✔ **Content Library:** This row of buttons allows you to add effects such as transitions, titles, music, and sound effects.

✔ **Libraries list:** This list allows you to display your photos (from your iPhoto and Aperture libraries) as well as all the video clips you can add to your project from events you've imported. You can also select an existing iMovie project from the iMovie Library. To hide the Libraries list and make more room for the Event/Project Library pane, click the Hide button that appears near the top-left corner of the iMovie window. (To display the Libraries list again, click the same button, which now reads Show.)

✔ **Event/Project Library pane:** If you select an event from the All Events entry in the Libraries list, iMovie displays a thumbnail of that event's content in the *Event* pane. (Move your mouse over the Event thumbnail to see previews of the clips.) If you decide you want to include a clip, double-click the Event to display the clips and add the desired clip to your project. This pane also acts as the *Project Library* pane, where you can display your iMovie projects; click the All Projects entry in the Libraries list to display your projects as thumbnails. To load a project, just double-click the thumbnail, and it appears in the Project pane.

The Event/Project Library pane displays different content, depending on the entry you select in the Library list.

✔ **Project pane:** This pane is where most of your work gets done within iPhoto, displaying the elements you added to that specific project (such as video clips, still photos, and audio clips). Your movie appears as a linear "strip" of thumbnails, making it easy to select, insert, and delete elements.

✔ **Playhead:** The red vertical line that you see in the Event and Project panes is the *playhead,* which indicates the current editing point while you're browsing your clips or creating your movie. When you're playing your movie, the playhead moves to follow your progress through the movie.

✔ **Toolbar:** This strip of buttons allows you to import video, share your completed movies, enhance and adjust video clips, and switch between the iMovie Library and iMovie Theater. (More on iMovie Theater later in the chapter.)

Those are the major highlights of the iMovie window. A director's chair and megaphone are optional, of course, but they do add to the mood.

A Bird's-Eye View of Moviemaking

I don't want to box in your creative skills here — after all, you can attack the moviemaking process from a number of angles. (Pun, unfortunately, intended.) However, I've found that my movies turn out the best when I follow a linear process, so before I dive into specifics, allow me to provide you with an overview of moviemaking with iMovie.

Here's my take on the process, reduced to seven basic steps:

1. Import your video clips from your DV camcorder, FaceTime HD camera, iPhoto Library, or your hard drive.

2. Drag your new selection of clips from the Event pane to the Project pane and arrange them in the desired order.

3. Import or record audio clips (from iTunes, GarageBand, or external sources, such as audio CDs or audio files that you've recorded yourself) and add them to your movie.

4. Import your photos (directly from iPhoto, Aperture, or your hard drive) and place them where needed in your movie.

5. Add professional niceties, such as voiceovers, transitions, effects, and text to the project.

6. Preview your film and edit it further if necessary.

7. Share your finished film with others through the web, e-mail, your Apple TV, an iOS device (an iPhone, iPad, or iPod touch), or within iMovie Theater. If your iMac has an optical drive, you can also use a DVD recording application to create a DVD movie disc using your exported movie. I use (and recommend) Toast 11 Titanium from Roxio, at www.roxio.com.

 Wondering how you save your project in iMovie — especially when there's no Save item on the File menu? iMovie automatically saves your project as you work, leaving you free to concentrate on your moviemaking art!

Importing the Building Blocks

Sure, you need video clips to create a movie of your own, but don't panic if you have but a short supply. You can certainly turn to the other iLife applications for additional raw material. (See, I told you that whole "integration thing" would come in handy.)

Along with video clips you import from your DV camcorder, your iMac's built-in FaceTime HD camera, and your hard drive, you can call on iPhoto and Aperture for still images (think credits) and iTunes and GarageBand for background audio and effects. In this section, I show you how.

Pulling in video clips

Your iMac is equipped already with the extras that come in handy for video editing — namely, a large hard drive and ports to connect stuff. Depending on the iMac model you're using and your external devices, you may use a USB or

FireWire connection. Today's mass-storage camcorders, tablets, and smart-phones use a USB connection to transfer clips. I cover both FireWire mini-DV camcorders and USB mass-storage devices in this section.

Oh, and don't forget that your iMac has a FaceTime HD camera on board, ready to record clips — heck, you're a self-contained movie studio!

Here's the drill if your clips are on your FireWire mini-DV camcorder or mass-storage USB video device:

1. **Plug the proper cable into your iMac.**

2. **Set the camcorder to VTR (or VCR) mode.**

   Some camcorders and digital cameras call this *Play mode.*

3. **Click the Import button on the toolbar (refer to Figure 15-2).**

   iMovie opens the Import window.

4. **Open the Import To pop-up menu at the top of the Import window and choose the destination for your new video clips.**

   To create a new event for the imported clips, choose New Event. Alternatively, you can import into an existing Event or an existing iMovie project. Heck, if your family reunion spanned more than one day, you can create a new Event for each day. (How do they think up these things?)

5. **Click the desired video source in the Source list at the right of the Import window.**

   If you're using a tape-based camcorder, playback controls appear under the Camera Import window, mirroring the controls on your FireWire DV camcorder. This allows you to control the unit from iMovie. *Keen!* If you're using a mass-storage camcorder connected by USB, you instead get an Import All button beneath the thumbnails of available clips. (Note that this button changes to Import Selected if you select one or more of the clips.)

   If you choose your FaceTime HD camera from the list, you'll see a real-time preview and a Big Red Record button. Click the Record button to start and stop recording. (You can skip the rest of the steps in this section, which deal only with USB and FireWire camcorders.)

6. **To import selected clips from your FireWire DV camcorder, advance the video to a couple of seconds before the point where you want to start your capture; then click Import.**

7. **Click OK and admire your handiwork.**

   iMovie begins transferring the footage to your iMac and automatically adds the imported clips to the specified destination.

If your clips are already on your hard drive, rest assured that iMovie can import them, including those in high-definition video (HDV) format. iMovie also recognizes a number of other video formats, as shown in Table 15-1.

Table 15-1	Video Formats Supported by iMovie
File Type	*Description*
DV	Standard 4:3 digital video
DV Widescreen	Widescreen 16:9 digital video
MOV	QuickTime movies
HDV and AVCHD	High-definition (popularly called *widescreen*) digital video, in 720p and 1080i
MPEG-2	Digital video format used for DVD movies
MPEG-4	A popular format for streaming Internet and wireless digital video, as well as handheld iOS devices such as the iPad, iPhone, and iPod touch

To import a movie file, follow this bouncing ball:

1. **Click the Import button on the toolbar.**

2. **Click the drive that stores your clips in the Sidebar and navigate to their location.**

3. **Select the desired clips in the list.**

4. **From the Import To pop-up menu at the top of the Import window, choose the destination within iMovie.**

5. **Click Import.**

   Alternatively, you can also drag a video clip from a Finder window and drop it in the Project pane.

Making use of still images

Still images come in handy as impressive-looking titles or as ending credits to your movie. (To be truly professional, make sure you list a gaffer and a best boy.) However, you can use still images also to introduce scenes, close scenes, or separate clips according to your whim. For example, I use stills when delineating the days of a vacation within a movie or different Christmas celebrations over time.

Here are two methods of adding stills to your movie:

- ✔ **Adding images and video clips from iPhoto or Aperture:** Click the iPhoto Library entry in the Libraries list to experience the thrill that is your iPhoto Library, right from iMovie (as shown in Figure 15-3). You can elect to display your entire iPhoto Library or more selective picks, such as specific albums, Faces, Places, or Events. (Even your Facebook images are within reach.) When you find the image you want to add, just drag it to the right spot in the Project pane.

  If you've installed Apple's Aperture photo application, you can also access images from Aperture by clicking the Aperture Library item in the Libraries list.

- ✔ **Importing images from your hard drive:** If you're a member of the International Drag-and-Drop Society, you can drag TIFF, JPEG, GIF, PICT, PNG, and PSD images directly from a Finder window and drop them into the Project pane as well.

Figure 15-3:
Pulling still images from iPhoto is child's play.

Importing and adding audio from all sorts of places

You can pull in everything from Wagner to Weezer as both background music and sound effects for your movie. In this section, I focus on how to get those notes into iMovie and then how to add them to your movie by dragging them to the Project pane.

You can add audio from a number of sources:

- **Adding songs from iTunes and GarageBand:** Click the iTunes button in the Content Library (or press ⌘+4) to display the contents of your iTunes Library. Click the desired song in the scrolling list (which displays all your music). To display a playlist or Smart Playlist, click the Music drop-down list box above the waveform display. Figure 15-4 illustrates the dynamite ABBA playlist I selected for this project. You can add a track to your movie by dragging any song entry from the list to the desired spot in the Project pane.

  You're not limited to iTunes for ear candy, however. If you exported any original music you've composed in GarageBand to your iTunes Library, you can use those songs in your own movie! Click the GarageBand button in the Content Library to view your GarageBand music, and then drag and drop to your heart's content.

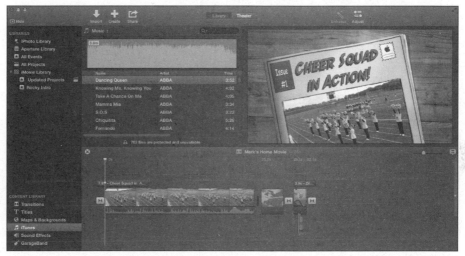

Figure 15-4: Calling on my iTunes Library to add ABBA to my iMovie.

- **Adding sound effects:** If you need the sound of a horse galloping for your Rocky Mountain vacation clips, click Sound Effects in the Content Library. iMovie includes a number of top-shelf audio effects that you can use in the sound effects audio track in the Project pane. This way, you can add sound effects even when you've already added a background song. Again, to add a sound effect, drag it to the perfect spot in the Project pane.

  If you have several gigabytes of music in your iTunes Library, it might be more of a challenge to locate Janis Joplin's rendition of "Me and Bobby McGee," especially if she's included in a compilation. Let your iMac do the digging for you! Click in the Search box above the track list and begin typing a song name. iMovie narrows down the song titles displayed to those that match the characters you type. To reset the search box and display all your songs in the Library or selected playlist, click the X icon that appears to the right of the box.

✔ **Recording directly from a microphone:** Yep, if you're thinking voiceover narration, you've hit the nail on the head. Check out the sidebar "Narration the easy way" for the scoop.

You can fine-tune both the audio within a video clip or an audio clip that you add to your project. With the desired audio or video selected in the Event pane, click the Adjust button at the top of the window, and then click one of the buttons that appear above the Viewer. These buttons provide audio controls that allow you to change the volume of the selected clip. You can even add effects to your audio, such as Shortwave Radio or Cathedral, and you can use iMovie's built-in Equalizer to fine-tune the audio. When you're done tweaking, click the Adjust toolbar button again. (Oh, and don't forget that you can always return the clip to its original settings; just click the Reset Clip button at the right side of the Viewer.)

Narration the easy way

Ready to create that award-winning nature documentary? You can add voiceover narration to your iMovie project that would make Jacques Cousteau proud. In fact, you can record your voice while you watch your movie playing, allowing perfect synchronization with the action! To add narration, follow these steps:

1. **Press V to display the Voiceover controls under the Viewer.**

2. **Click the Voiceover Options button and select the input device.**

   iMacs sport a decent internal microphone, but you can always add a USB or digital Toslink microphone to your system.

3. **Drag the input volume slider to a comfortable level.**

4. **To mute the audio from your movie (which may make it easier to concentrate on your narration), select the Mute Project check box.**

5. **Click in the desired spot within your movie in the Project pane where the narration should begin.**

6. **Click the Start Recording button.**

   iMovie prompts you with three tones before the playhead reaches your selected spot in your movie, so make sure you begin speaking after the third tone.

7. **Watch the video while you narrate so that you can coordinate your narration track with the action.**

8. **Click the red Stop Recording button to stop recording.**

   iMovie adds an icon to the Project pane underneath the video with the voiceover.

9. **Click the Close button in the Voiceover controls.**

Building the Cinematic Basics

Time to dive in and add the building blocks to create your movie. Along with the video clips, audio tracks, and still images that you've imported, you can add Hollywood-quality transitions, optical effects, and animated text titles. In this section, I demonstrate how to elevate your collection of video clips into a real-life, honest-to-goodness movie.

Adding clips to your movie

You can add clips to your movie via the Project pane and the Event pane. The Dynamic Duo works like this:

- ✔ **Project pane:** This displays the media you've added to your project so far, allowing you to rearrange the clips, titles, transitions, and still images in your movie.

- ✔ **Event/Project Library pane:** This pane acts as the source repository for all your clips, displaying them arranged by Event (the date they were shot or the date they were imported) or by Project (media you've added to existing iMovie projects).

Typically, you'll add a clip to your movie from an Event. Follow these steps:

1. **Click the All Events entry in the Libraries list.**

2. **Move your cursor across clips in the Event pane to watch a preview of the video.**

3. **When you have decided what to add to your project, you can either add the entire clip or a selection.**

    - *To select an entire clip:* Right-click the clip's thumbnail and choose Select Entire Clip from the menu that appears.

    - *To select a portion of a clip:* Click and hold, and then drag your cursor across the thumbnail. A yellow frame appears around your selection. To change the length of the selected video, hover your cursor over either end of the clip and drag the handle that appears on either side. If you make a mistake while selecting video, just click any empty space within the Event pane to remove the selection frame and try again.

4. **Drag the selection from the Event pane to the spot where it belongs in the Project pane.**

    Alternatively, you can press the E key.

Preview your work — and do it often.

iMovie includes a Play Full Screen button, which appears when you move your cursor to the Viewer. (Alternatively, press ⌘+Shift+F or choose View⇨ Play Full Screen to watch the selection.) Press the spacebar to pause, and press Esc to return to iMovie. Of course, you can also move your cursor across the filmstrip in the Edit pane to quickly browse your project.

To play a selection from the beginning, press \ (the slash that leans to the left). If you've ever watched directors at work on today's movie sets, you may have noticed that they're constantly watching a monitor to see what things will look like for the audience. You have the same option in iMovie!

Marking clips

While you're watching video in the Event/Project Library pane, you may decide that a certain clip has a favorite scene or that another clip has material you don't want, such as Uncle Ed's shadow puppets. (Shudder.) iMovie features *Favorite* and *Rejected* frames, allowing you to view and use your best camera work (and ignore the worst stuff).

To mark a great video clip as a Favorite, select and right-click a range of frames or the entire clip in the Event/Project Library pane, and then click the Favorite menu item (or press F). To mark clips that are sub-par, select the offending clip in the Event/Project Library pane and press Delete (or right-click and choose Reject). Clips marked as Favorites have a green line on top of the clip, and clips marked as Rejected have a red line.

You can use the Search Filter option to specify which type of marked clips are shown: Click the pop-up menu next to the Search field at the top of the Event/ Project Library pane. Your options include displaying all clips, displaying just Favorite clips, hiding Rejected clips, or displaying just Rejected clips.

If you decide that a Rejected clip isn't so bad after all, or that a Favorite really isn't your best work, no problem. Unmark any selected Favorite or Rejected scene in the Event/Project Library pane by choosing Mark⇨Unrate (or just press U).

Removing clips from your movie

Don't like a clip? Bah. To banish a clip from your movie, follow these steps:

1. **Click the offending clip in the Project pane to select it.**

   Alternatively, you can select a portion of a clip by holding the button down and then dragging the selection box that appears.

2. **Press Delete.**

This deletes the clip from the Project pane, but the clip is still available if you choose All Events or the iMovie Library from the Libraries list.

If you remove the wrong clip, don't panic. Instead, use iMovie's Undo feature (press ⌘+Z) to restore it.

Reordering clips in your movie

If Day One of your vacation appears after Day Two, you can easily reorder your clips and stills by dragging them to the proper space in the Project pane. When you take your finger off the mouse (or trackpad), iMovie automatically moves the rest of your movie aside with a minimum of fuss and bother.

Editing clips in iMovie

If a clip has extra seconds of footage at the beginning or end (as it should, to ensure you get all the action), you don't want that superfluous stuff in your masterpiece. Our favorite video editor gives you the following functions:

- ✔ **Crop:** Removes unwanted material from a video clip or still image
- ✔ **Rotate:** Rotates a clip or image on its center axis
- ✔ **Trim:** Trims frames from a video clip

Before you can edit, however, you have to select a section of a clip:

1. **Click a clip or an image in either the Project pane (where changes you make are specific to this project) or the Event pane (where edits you make are reflected in any project using that footage).**

   iMovie displays the clip or image in the monitor.

2. **To select the entire clip or image, simply click it.**

3. **Drag your cursor across the thumbnail to select the section of the media you want to edit.**

   Some editing functions, such as Crop and Rotate, will automatically apply to the entire clip.

   The selected region is surrounded by a yellow frame. You're ready to edit that selected part of the clip.

Move your cursor to the beginning or ending of the selection, and handles will appear. You can make fine changes to the selected section by dragging them.

- ✔ **To crop:** Click the Adjust button at the top of the screen to display the editing controls in the Viewer, and then click the Crop button. Drag the edges of the frame using the handles to select the section you want to keep. To preview your selection, click the Play button that appears when you move your cursor into the Viewer pane. When you're ready, click the Done button (which bears a check mark), and everything but the selected region is removed.

- ✔ **To rotate:** Click the Adjust button and then click the Crop button. Now you can click one of the two rotation buttons that appear at the right side of the Viewer (both of which carry a box and curved arrow icon). Each click rotates the media 90 degrees in the indicated direction. Click the Done button (with the check mark) when the clip or image is properly oriented.

- ✔ **To trim:** Right-click the selection and choose Trim to Playhead from the contextual menu. iMovie removes the frames up to the playhead position from the selected video.

Edits that you make to one clip or still image can actually be copied to multiple items! Select the edited clip and choose Edit⇨Copy from the iMovie menu. Now you can select one or more clips and choose Edit⇨Paste Adjustments to apply Video, Audio, or Crop edits. (To apply all three types of edits, just choose All.)

Transitions for the masses

Many iMovie owners approach transitions as *visual bookends:* They merely act as placeholders that appear between video clips. Nothing could be farther from the truth, though, because judicious use of transitions can make or break a scene. For example, which would you prefer after a wedding ceremony — an abrupt, jarring cut to the reception, or a gradual fadeout to the reception?

Today's audiences are sensitive to transitions between scenes. Try not to overuse the same transition. Pick two or three that match the mood of your film and the scenes between which you're transitioning. Also weigh the visual impact of a transition carefully. You might even decide that having no transition is the most effective (directors call this deliberate lack of a transition a *jump cut*).

iMovie includes a surprising array of transitions, including old favorites (such as Fade In and Dissolve) and some nifty stuff that you might not be familiar with (such as Cube and Page Curl). To display your transition collection (see Figure 15-5), click the Transitions entry in the Content Library (or press ⌘+1).

To see what a particular transition looks like, move your cursor over the thumbnail to display the transition in miniature.

Adding a transition couldn't be easier: Drag the transition from the thumbnail list and drop it between clips or between a clip and a still image in the Project pane. In iMovie, transitions are applied in real time.

Figure 15-5: Add transitions for flow between clips in iMovie.

Even Gone with the Wind had titles

The next stop on our iMovie Hollywood Features Tour is the Titles list, shown in Figure 15-6. You'll find it by clicking the Titles entry in the Content Library or by pressing ⌘+2. You can add a title with a still image, but iMovie also includes everything you need to add basic animated text to your movie.

Most of the controls you can adjust are the same for each animation style. You can change the font, the size of the text, and the color of the text. To add a title manually, follow these steps:

1. **Select a Title animation thumbnail from the Titles list and drag it to the desired spot in the Project pane.**

    Note that the title is displayed in the Viewer as well as the Project pane.

2. **Select the Title and click the Adjust button at the top of the window.**

3. **Click the Title Settings button (which bears a capital T symbol) to make any changes to the fonts or text attributes.**

4. **Click in the text box within the Viewer to delete the default text and type your own titles.**

5. **Click the Done button to save your changes.**

6. **Click the Play button in the Viewer to preview your title.**

   iMovie displays a preview of the effect in the monitor with the settings that you choose.

Figure 15-6:
Add titles
for your next
silent film.

Adding maps and backgrounds

iMovie includes easy-to-use animated maps — think Indiana Jones traveling by airplane from place to place — and static backgrounds that can be used with your titles. To display them, click the Maps & Backgrounds entry in the Content Library (or press ⌘+3).

To use an animated map, drag one of the globe or map thumbnails to the Project pane. After the globe or map is created, select it and click the Adjust button to display the controls above the Viewer. Click the Map Settings button (which bears a globe icon) and then click the Start Location button (and, optionally, the End Location button) to enter the start and stop points for the animation. Type a city or place name to see your choices. (Heck, you can even type in an airport code or decimal coordinates to specify the spot.) Click Done and watch as iMovie animates your location (or your trip) in seconds!

To add a static background from the browser, drag it to the desired spot within the Project pane.

Have a seat in the iMovie Theater

After you produce a great movie, what's the easiest way to watch it? Or, instead, quickly and easily share that movie with your other iOS devices and your Apple TV? The answer is iMovie *Theater mode,* where you can add completed movies, trailers, and individual video clips — and everything is automatically shared using iCloud! (Any Mac or iOS device with iMovie installed also includes its own iMovie Theater, and the stuff you add appears there.)

If you just want to present your content on your own iMac, one click of the Theater mode button at the top of the iMovie window displays thumbnails of the content that you've shared to the Theater (without having to load a finished movie project in Library mode). Double-click any thumbnail to view that item. To switch back to Library mode and work on your current iMovie project, click the Library button at the top of the window.

To add a movie, trailer, or video clip in the Event/ Project Library pane, just click the item to select it, click the Share button on the toolbar at the top of the iMovie window, and click the Theater button.

Creating an Honest-to-Goodness Movie Trailer

Yes, friends, you read that correctly! As I mention at the beginning of the chapter, iMovie includes a Trailer feature that can actually turn your film clips into a Hollywood-class preview, complete with genre transitions and background music.

To create a trailer project, follow these steps:

1. **Choose File⇨New Trailer (or press ⌘+Shift+N).**

2. **Click a Movie Trailer thumbnail to select it.**

   If you hover your cursor over the thumbnail and click the Play icon that appears, iMovie displays a nifty preview of the trailer style that you selected. You can click different thumbnails to preview their look before you make your decision. Naturally, you'll want to choose a trailer style that most closely matches the mood you want to project with your movie.

   Note that each trailer has a suggested number of cast members. This number reflects the number of people that will appear in the clip "place-holders" during the editing process. (More on this in a page or two.)

3. **Click Create.**

4. **Type a name for your project and click OK.**

iMovie replaces the Project pane with the Trailer pane, as shown in Figure 15-7. On the Outline tab, you can edit the titles used in the trailer, as well as pop-up lists for information, such as the gender of the star(s) and the logo style you want for your "studio" at the beginning of the trailer. To change a text field, click in it and type the new text. You'll see the changes you make in the Trailer display appear in the monitor in real time.

After you complete your edits to the titles, click the Storyboard tab. Now you can edit the text for each transition: Simply click the text to display the edit box and type. You can also drag clips from your Event pane (or from a Finder window) to fill the storyboard's placeholders for video clips. To delete a clip from the storyboard, click it to select it and then press Delete.

To preserve the "look and feel" of the trailer storyboard, try to match your clips with the description and suggested activity indicated by the placeholder. (In other words, don't stick a wide-angle video clip of the family dog cavorting in the yard in a placeholder marked "Closeup." You get the idea.)

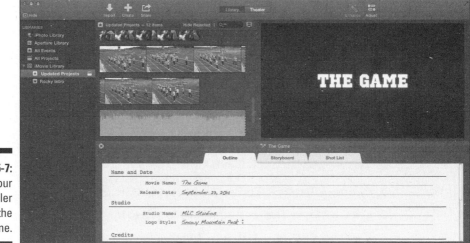

Figure 15-7: Build your movie trailer from the Trailer pane.

The Storyboard tab might not look like an editing timeline, but you can move the cursor anywhere within the storyboard to preview your trailer! The play-head indicator appears wherever the cursor appears, allowing you to watch the clip or transition that it's resting upon. You'll soon be sweeping your mouse to the left or right to move through each section of your trailer.

For an overall listing of each clip required for the full trailer, click the Shot List tab. On this tab, clips are organized by type. For example, all the action clips appear in one section, and all the landscape and closeup clips are grouped together as well. If necessary, you can also add, delete, or swap video clips from the Shot List.

To preview your trailer in its entirety, move your cursor inside the Viewer and click the Play button (or the Play Full-Screen button at the far right of the Viewer controls). Naturally, any storyboard placeholder that you haven't filled with a clip will display just the placeholder.

Note that iMovie displays your trailer when you click the Updated Projects entry in the Libraries list, and it now appears in the Event/Project Library pane.

I bet all those hard-working Hollywood video editors are fuming at how easy it is to create a trailer in iMovie!

Sharing Your Finished Classic with Others

Your movie is complete, iMovie has saved it automatically to your drive, and now you're wondering where to go from here. Select your movie in the Event/Project Library pane and click Share on the toolbar at the top of the window. iMovie can unleash your movie upon your unsuspecting family and friends (and even the entire world) in a number of ways:

- ✔ **iTunes:** Send your movie to your iTunes Library as a movie.
- ✔ **Theater:** Add your movie to the iMovie Theater on your iMac.
- ✔ **YouTube/Facebook/Vimeo/CNN iReport:** Why, certainly you can send your iMovie directly to any of these websites! Can it get more convenient than that? (I think not.)
- ✔ **File:** Create a copy of your movie on your hard drive in one of four different resolutions (from Standard Definition to High Definition).
- ✔ **Email:** Send your movie as an e-mail message attachment.

When you choose a sharing option, iMovie displays the video quality for the option and makes automatic changes to the movie attributes. (For example, choosing Email reduces the finished movie as far as possible in file size.)

If you're worried about permanently reducing the quality of your project by sharing it in a smaller size, fear not! When you choose a sharing option to export your movie, your original project remains on your hard drive, unchanged, so you can share a better-quality version at any time in the future.

Chapter 16

Recording Your Hits with GarageBand

Do you dream of making music? I've always wanted to join a band, but I never devoted the time nor learned to play the guitar. You know the drill: Those rock stars struggled for years to gain the upper hand over an instrument, practicing for untold hours, memorizing chords, and. . . . Wait a second. I almost forgot. You don't need to do *any* of that now!

Apple's GarageBand lets a musical wanna-be (like yours truly) make music with an iMac — complete with a driving bass line, funky horns, and perfect drums that never miss a beat. In fact, the thousands of prerecorded loops on tap in this awesome application allow you to design your music to match that melody running through your head, from techno to jazz to alternative rock.

This chapter explains everything you need to know to create your first song. I also show you how to import your hit recording into iTunes so that you can listen to it on your iPod with a big silly grin on your face (as I do) or add it to your next iMovie project or iPhoto slideshow.

Shaking Hands with Your Band

As you can see in Figure 16-1, the GarageBand window isn't complex at all, and that's good design. In this section, I list the most important controls so that you know your Play button from your Loop Browser button.

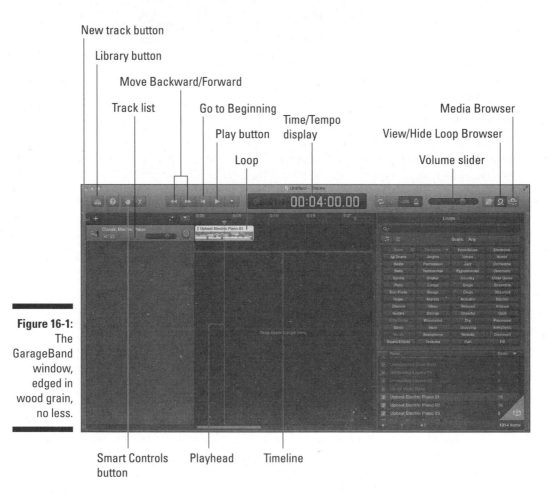

Figure 16-1: The GarageBand window, edged in wood grain, no less.

Your music-making machine includes

✔ **Track list:** In GarageBand, a *track* is a discrete instrument that you set up to play one part of your song. For example, a classical piece for string quartet would have four tracks — one each for violin, viola, cello, and bass. The Track list contains all the tracks in your song arranged so that you can easily see and modify them, like the rows in a spreadsheet.

A track begins in the list, stretching out to the right all the way to the end of the song. As you can see in the upper left of Figure 16-1, I already have one track defined — a Classic Electric Piano.

✔ **Timeline:** This scrolling area holds the loops (see the following bullet) that you add, compose, or record, allowing you to move and edit them easily. When a song plays, the Timeline scrolls to give you a visual look at your music. (Bear with me; you'll understand that cryptic statement in a page or two.)

✔ **Loop:** *Loops* — prerecorded clips of an instrument being played in a specific style and tempo — are the building blocks of your song. Most are five seconds in length, and others are even shorter. You can drag loops from the Loop Browser to a track and literally build a bass line or a guitar solo. (It's a little like adding video clips in iMovie to build a film.) Loops can also be repeated within a track, which I'll discuss further in a page or two.

✔ **Playhead:** This vertical line is a moving indicator that shows you the current position in your song while it scrolls by in the Timeline. You can drag the playhead to a new location at any time. The playhead also acts like the insertion cursor in a word processing application: If you insert a section of a song or a loop from the Clipboard, it appears at the current location of the playhead. (More on copying and inserting loops later, so don't panic.)

✔ **New Track button:** Click this button to add a new track to your song.

✔ **View/Hide Loop Browser button:** Click the button with the loop icon to display the Loop Browser at the right side of the window; click it again to close it. You can see more of your tracks' contents at a time without scrolling by closing the Loop Browser.

✔ **View/Hide Media Browser button:** Click this button (which bears icons of a filmstrip, camera, and musical note) to display the Media Browser at the right side of the window; click it again to close it (and see more of your tracks). Use the Media Browser to add media (in this case, digital song files or movies) to your GarageBand project for use as ringtones.

✔ **Go to Beginning button:** Clicking this button immediately moves the playhead back to the beginning of the Timeline. (Note this button appears only when you're not playing a song.)

✔ **Move Back/Forward One Measure buttons:** To move quickly through your song by jumping to the previous or next measure, click the corresponding button.

✔ **Play button:** Hey, old friend! At last, a control that you've probably used countless times before — and it works just like the same control within iTunes or on your audio CD player. Click Play, and GarageBand begins playing your entire song. Notice that the Play button turns green. To pause the music, click Play again; the button loses that sexy green sheen, and the playhead stops immediately.

✔ **Time/Tempo display:** This cool-looking LCD display shows you the current playhead position in seconds.

You can click the clock icon at the left of the display to choose Beats & Project mode, which includes

- *Measures:* Display the current measure and mark the beat
- *Chord:* Display note and chord names
- *Project:* Show or change the key, tempo, and signature for the song

✔ **Volume slider:** Here's another familiar face. Just drag the slider to raise or lower the volume.

Of course, more controls are scattered around the GarageBand window, but these are the main controls used to compose a song . . . which is the next stop!

Composing Made Easy

In this section, I cover the basics of composition in GarageBand, working from the very beginning. Follow along with this running example:

1. **Click the GarageBand icon in the Dock — it looks like an electric guitar.**

2. **If GarageBand opens a window for a previous project, close it by clicking the Close button in each window.**

   GarageBand displays the top-level New Project dialog, as shown in Figure 16-2.

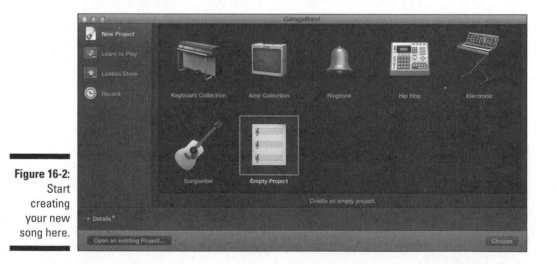

Figure 16-2: Start creating your new song here.

3. **Click New Project from the list at the left.**

4. **Click the Empty Project icon and click the Choose button.**

   GarageBand displays the Source dialog.

5. **Click the Software Instrument icon.**

   In this chapter, I focus on using software instrument tracks, which are the easiest for a nonmusician to use.

6. **Click the Create button.**

   You see the window shown in Figure 16-1. Now you're ready to add tracks.

Adding tracks

Although I'm not a musician, I am a music lover, and I know that many classical composers approached a new work in the same way you approach a new song in GarageBand: by envisioning the instruments that they wanted to hear. (I imagine Mozart and Beethoven would've been thrilled to use GarageBand, but I think they did a decent job with pen and paper, too.)

If you've followed along to this point, you've noticed

✔ **A Musical Typing keyboard in your GarageBand window:** You can record the contents of a software instrument track by playing the Musical Typing keyboard layout. (As you might imagine, this isn't the best solution.) If you're a musician, the best method of recording your own notes is with a MIDI instrument, which I discuss later in the chapter. You can display the Musical Typing keyboard window at any time by pressing ⌘+K. If the Musical Typing keyboard window is on the screen and you don't need it, banish the window by pressing ⌘+K, or by clicking the Close button in the keyboard window.

✔ **The example song with only one empty track:** If you want to write the next classical masterpiece for Classic Electric Piano, that's fine. (I'm a big fan of this instrument, so I use this track later in the example.) Note that you can always delete a track completely, however — click the offending track to select it and then choose Track⇨Delete Track from the GarageBand menu bar.

These are the five kinds of tracks you can use in GarageBand:

✔ **Software instrument tracks:** These tracks aren't audio recordings. Rather, they're mathematically precise algorithms that your Mac *renders* (builds) to fit your needs. If you have a MIDI instrument connected to your Mac, you can create your own software instrument tracks. (More on MIDI instruments later in this chapter.)

✔ **Real instrument tracks:** These tracks are actual audio recordings, such as your voice or a physical instrument without a MIDI connection. (Think microphone.)

✔ **Electric Guitar and Bass tracks:** GarageBand includes a real instrument track especially made for either an electric guitar or bass, which allows you to use a number of different amplifiers and *stompboxes* (those effect pedals that electric guitarists are always poking with their foot to change the sound of their instruments).

✔ **Drum track:** I call this feature "Ringo in a Box" — a drum track that's automatic, yet *very* configurable and easy to customize. There are presets galore, so you can quickly jump into different drum sets and playing styles!

✔ **Video tracks:** The video sound track appears if you're *scoring* (adding music) to an iMovie movie. Along with the video sound track, you get a cool companion video track that shows the clips in your movie. (More on this in the "Look, I'm John Williams!" sidebar, later in this chapter.)

Time to add a software instrument track of your very own. Follow these steps:

1. **Press ⌘+Option+N (or click the New Track button).**

   GarageBand displays the New Track sheet.

2. **Click the Software Instrument icon and then click Create.**

3. **From the Library pane on the far left, choose the general instrument category you want.**

   I chose Guitar, which prompts a second list of choices to the right, still in the Library pane.

4. **From the second list, choose your specific style of weapon, such as Classic Clean for a simple playing style.**

   Figure 16-3 illustrates the new track that appears in your list when you follow these steps. Now you're ready to rock with both the original electric piano and an electric guitar! If you like, you can hide the Library by clicking the Show/Hide Library button at the upper-left corner of the window.

GarageBand includes a Songwriter project (also available from the top-level New Project dialog; refer to Figure 16-2). When you choose a Songwriter project, GarageBand presents you with a full set of instrument tracks, plus a real instrument track for your voice. You're instantly ready to start adding loops and recording your own voice!

Figure 16-3:
The new track appears, ready to rock.

Choosing loops

After you have a new, empty track, you can add loops to build your song from the Loop Browser. Apple provides you with thousands of loops to choose from, in a mind-boggling variety. Click the Loop Browser button (which bears the loop symbol, somewhat like a roller coaster; refer to Figure 16-1) to display your collection, as shown in Figure 16-4.

Figure 16-4:
The Loop Browser is a great hangout for any musician.

Looking for just the right loop

The running project already includes two tracks but no loops yet. (Refer to Figure 16-3.) Just for grins, add a Classic Electric Piano loop. Follow these steps to search through your loop library for just the right rhythm:

1. **In the Loop Browser, click the button that corresponds to the instrument you're using.**

   I chose the Elec Piano button.

   A list of different beats appears in the pane at the bottom of the Loop Browser window. (Check out Figure 16-4 for a sneak peek.)

2. **Click one of the loops with a green musical-note icon.**

   Go ahead; this is where things get fun! GarageBand begins playing the loop nonstop, allowing you to get a feel for how that particular loop sounds.

   The examples I chose for this chapter are software instruments, which are identified by a green musical-note icon. (If you've got a band at home, have at it with live instruments.)

3. **Click another entry in the list, and the application switches immediately to that loop.**

   Now you're beginning to understand why GarageBand is so cool for both musicians and the note-impaired. It's like having your own band, with members who never get tired, never miss a beat, and play whatever you want while you're composing. (Mozart would've *loved* this.)

   If you want to search for a particular instrument, click in the Search box at the top of the Loop Browser and type the text you want to match. GarageBand returns the search results in the list.

4. **Scroll down the list and continue to sample the different loops until you find one that fits like a glove.**

   For this reporter, it's Upbeat Electric Piano 01; see Figure 16-4.

5. **Drag the entry to your Classic Electric Piano track and drop it at the very beginning of the Timeline (as indicated by the playhead).**

   Your window will look like Figure 16-5.

If you want that same beat throughout the song, you don't need to add any more loops to that track. (More on extending that beat in the next section.) However, if you want the piano's beat to change later in the song, you add a second loop after the first one in the *same* track. For now, leave this track as is.

Figure 16-5:
A track
with a loop
added.

Whoops! Did you do something that you regret? Don't forget that you can undo most actions in GarageBand by pressing the old standby ⌘+Z immediately afterward.

Second verse, same as the first

When you compose, you can add tracks for each instrument that you want in your song:

- ✔ Each track can have more than one loop.
- ✔ Loops *don't* have to start at the beginning; you can drop a loop anywhere in the Timeline.

For example, you might prefer to start a song with just your drum kit, with your bass line beginning some time later (for a funkier opening).

You put loops on separate tracks so that they can play simultaneously on different instruments. If all your loops in a song are added on the same track, you hear only one loop at any one time, and all the loops use the same software instrument. By creating multiple tracks, you give yourself the elbow room to bring in the entire band at the same time. It's über-convenient to compose your song when you can see each instrument's loops and where they fall in the song.

Click the Reset button in the Loop Browser to choose another instrument or genre category.

Look, I'm John Williams!

You, too, can be a famous composer of soundtracks . . . well, perhaps not quite as famous as Mr. Williams, but even he had to start somewhere. To add a GarageBand score to an iMovie, choose Track➪Show Movie Track from the GarageBand menu bar to display the Movie track. Now choose File➪Open Movie, select the movie, and click Open.

At this point, you add and modify instrument tracks and loops just as you would any other GarageBand project. The existing sound for the iMovie project appears in the Movie Sound track. A Video Preview thumbnail appears within the Movie track. When you click the Play button, the video is shown as well so that you can check your work and tweak settings (as described later in the chapter).

After you finish composing, choose File➪Movie➪Export Audio to Movie. You'll be able to select the quality of the movie file. Note that you won't be able to edit your finished movie file using iMovie again, so scoring should always be the last step in your filmmaking process!

Resizing, repeating, and moving loops

If you haven't already tried listening to your entire song, try it now. You can click Play at any time without wreaking havoc on your carefully created tracks. Sounds pretty good, doesn't it?

But wait: I bet the song stopped after about five seconds, right? (You can watch the passing seconds using either the Time/Tempo display or the second rule that appears at the very top of the Timeline.) I'm sure that you want your song to last more than five seconds! After the playhead moves past the end of the last loop, your song is over. Click Play again to pause the playback; then click the Go to Beginning button (labeled in Figure 16-1) to move the playhead back to the beginning of the song.

The music stops so soon because your loops are only so long. As I mention earlier, most loops are five seconds in length, and others are even shorter. To keep the groove going, you have to do one of three things:

✔ **Resize the loop.** Hover your cursor over either the left or right edge of most loops, and an interesting thing happens: Your cursor changes to icon representing the left or right edge of the loop with an arrow pointing away from the loop. That's your cue to click and drag — and as you drag, some loops expand to fill the space you're making, repeating the beats in perfect time. By resizing a loop, you can literally drag the loop's edge as long as you like.

✔ **Repeat the loop.** Depending on the loop that you chose, you might find that resizing it doesn't repeat the measure. Instead, the new part of the loop is simply dead air. In fact, the length of many loops is limited to anywhere from one to five seconds. However, if you move your cursor over the *corner* of a loop that you want to extend, it turns into a vertical line with a circular arrow, which tells you that you can click and *repeat* the loop. GarageBand actually adds multiple copies of the same loop automatically, for as far as you drag the loop. In Figure 16-6, you can see how I repeated the Upbeat Electric Piano 01 loop.

✔ **Add a new loop.** You can switch to a different loop to change the flow of the music. Naturally, the instrument stays the same, but there's no reason you can't use a horn-riff loop in your violin track (as long as it sounds good played by a violin)! To GarageBand, a software instrument track is compatible with *any* software instrument loop that you add from the Loop Browser as long as that loop is marked with your old friend, the green musical note.

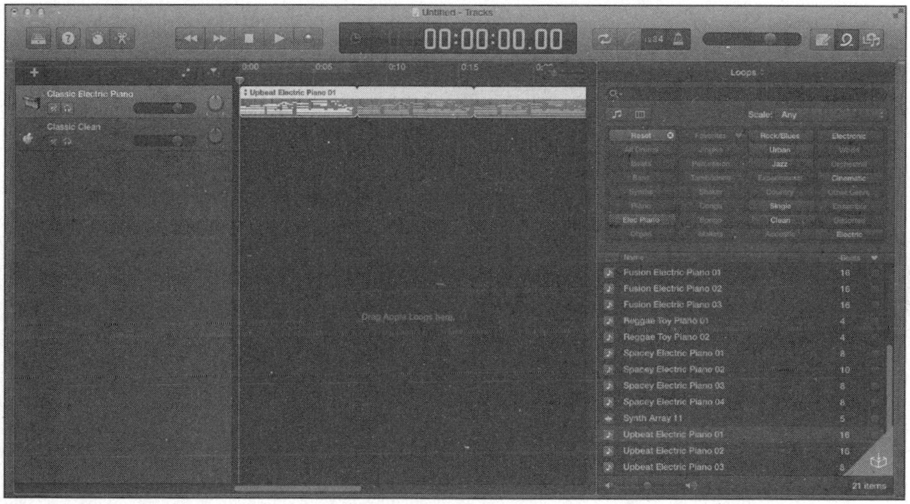

Figure 16-6: By repeating a loop, you can keep the notes flowing.

You can also use the familiar Cut (⌘+X), Copy (⌘+C), and Paste (⌘+V) editing keyboard shortcuts to cut, copy, and paste loops both on the Timeline and from track to track. And you can click a loop and drag it anywhere.

A track doesn't have to be filled for every second with one loop or another. Most of my songs have a number of repeating loops with empty space between them as different instruments perform solo.

Each track can be adjusted so that you can listen to the interplay between two or more tracks or hear how your song sounds without a specific track:

- ✔ Click the tiny speaker button under the track name in the list, and the button turns blue to indicate that the track is muted. To turn off the mute, click the speaker icon again.

- ✔ You can change the volume or balance of each individual track by using the mixer that appears next to the track name. This comes in handy if you want an instrument to sound louder or confine that instrument to the left or right speaker.

Using the Arrangement track

GarageBand includes another method you can use to monkey with your music: Use the *Arrangement track* to define (or *mark*) specific sections of a song, allowing you to reorganize things by selecting, moving, and copying entire sections. For example, you're probably familiar with the chorus (or refrain) of a song and how often it appears during the course of the tune. With the Arrangement track, you can reposition the entire chorus within your song, carrying all the loops and settings within the chorus along with it! If you need another chorus, just copy that arrangement.

To use the Arrangement track, display it by choosing Track➪Show Arrangement Track from the GarageBand menu bar. The Arrangement track then appears as a thin strip at the top of the Track list. Click the Add Marker button (the circular button bearing a plus sign) at the right side of the Arrangement track, and you'll see a new marker appear (as shown in Figure 16-7). You can drag the right side of the Arrangement marker to the left or right to resize it, or drag it to move it anywhere in the song.

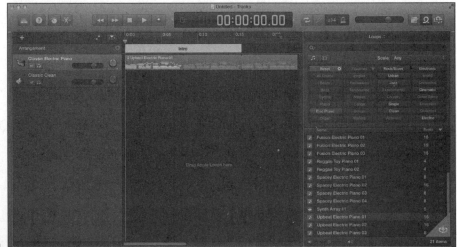

Figure 16-7: I just added a new marker in my song's Arrangement track.

To rename an Arrangement marker, click the current name to display the menu of existing marker names, click Rename, type a new name for the marker in the text box, and press Return. In Figure 16-7, you can see that the first marker is named *Intro*.

Now, here's where Arrangement markers get *cool*:

- ✔ **To move an entire Arrangement marker:** Click anywhere in the marker's title bar (except the title itself) and then drag it anywhere you like in the song. (You can hold down Shift while clicking multiple contiguous markers to select more than one.)

- ✔ **To copy an Arrangement marker:** Hold down the Option key and drag the desired marker's title to the spot where you want the copy to appear.

- ✔ **To empty the regions in an Arrangement marker:** Select it and press Delete. To completely delete the marker, press Delete a second time.

Tweaking the settings for a track

You don't think that bands like Rush or U2 just "play and walk away," do you? No, they spend hours after the recording session is over, tweaking their music in the studio and on the mixing board until every note sounds just as it should. You can adjust the settings for a track, too. The tweaks that you can perform include adding effects (pull a Hendrix, and add echo and reverb to your electric guitar track) and kicking in an equalizer (for fine-tuning the sound of your background horns).

To make adjustments to a track, follow these steps:

1. **Click the desired track in the track list to select it.**

2. **Click the Smart Controls button at the top left of the GarageBand window (labeled in Figure 16-1).**

   You can also press B to hide or display the Smart Controls pane.

3. **Click the Controls tab to show the settings shown in Figure 16-8.**

4. **Click the knob control or slider for a specific effect to change the sound.**

   GarageBand offers a Visual Equalizer window that you can use to create a custom equalizer setting for each track. From the Smart Controls pane, click the EQ button. To change the Bass, Low Mid, High Mid, or Treble setting for a track, click and drag the equalizer waveform in the desired direction. And yep, you can do this while your song is playing, so you can use both your eyes *and* ears to define the perfect settings!

5. **Click the Smart Controls button (or press B) to return to GarageBand.**

Figure 16-8:
Finesse
your tune
by tweaking
the sound
of a specific
track.

Join in and jam . . . or talk!

GarageBand is even more fun if you happen to play an instrument! (And yes, I'm envious, no matter how much I enjoy the techno and jazz music that I create. After all, take away my iMac and I'm back to playing the kazoo . . . at least until I absorb all the Learn to Play lessons for the guitar. More on Learn to Play in a later sidebar.)

Most musicians use MIDI instruments to play music on the computer. That pleasant-sounding acronym stands for *Musical Instrument Digital Interface*. A wide variety of MIDI instruments is available these days, from traditional MIDI keyboards to more exotic fun, such as MIDI saxophones. For example, Apple sells a 49-key MIDI keyboard from Line 6 for around $150. Alternatively, the highly recommended Casio CTX-3000 offers 61 keys, and it's available online for about $130. (Both keyboards connect to your iMac using a USB cable.)

If you have an older instrument with traditional round MIDI ports — you'll never confuse them with USB connectors — you need a USB-to-MIDI converter. You can find this type of converter for around $50 on websites catering to musicians.

After your instrument is connected, you can record tracks using any software instrument. Create a new software instrument track as I demonstrate in this chapter, select it, and then play a few notes. Suddenly you're playing the instrument you chose! If nothing happens, check the MIDI status light — which appears in the Time display (refer to Figure 16-1) — to see whether it blinks with each note you play. If not, check the installation of your MIDI connection and make sure you've loaded any required drivers, as well as your MIDI settings within QuickTime and the input settings in the System Preferences Sound pane.

Drag the playhead to a beat or two before the spot in the Timeline where you want your recording to start. This gives you time to match the beat. Then click the big red Record button and start jamming! When you're finished, click the Play button to stop recording.

Time for a Mark's Maxim:

Save your work often in GarageBand, just as you do in the other iLife applications. One power blackout, and you'll never forgive yourself. When you're pleased with the progress you've made in your project, press ⌘+S and enjoy the peace of mind (and use Time Machine with an external backup drive for good measure).

Sharing Your Songs

After you finish your song, you can play it whenever you like through GarageBand. But then again, that isn't really what you want, is it? You want to share your music with others with an audio CD or download it to your iPod so that you can enjoy it yourself while walking through the mall!

iTunes to the rescue! As with the other iLife applications that I cover in this book, GarageBand can share the music you make through the digital hub that is your Mac.

Hey, GarageBand, teach me how to play!

In the early days of GarageBand, you were limited to creating music — and if you were a nonmusician like yours truly, GarageBand had no practical use as a tool for teaching yourself how to actually *play* an instrument.

Ah, but Apple's addition of Learn to Play actually turns GarageBand into your private video tutor for basic piano and guitar! From the New Project dialog (see Figure 16-2), click the Learn to Play entry in the list on your left to display your guitar and piano lessons. Right out of the box, you have a solid Introduction to both instruments. You can also download more lessons — which cover more advanced topics such as fingering and chords — for each instrument from the Lesson Store (available from the New Project dialog). Your onscreen instructor can even record what you play.

In fact, GarageBand includes the How Did I Play feature, which can pinpoint the portions of a lesson that you played correctly and which

spots in the song you need to work on. (I'm told musicians call such trouble spots *flubs.* Having no musical talent whatsoever, anything I attempted to play would be one giant flub.) To try How Did I Play, open your favorite lesson, click the Record button (with the red dot in the center) and begin playing. To stop recording, click the Play button. Now you can see the portions of the song that you played correctly (where the notation area is green) and those spots where you (um) flubbed (the notation area turns red). Oh, and make sure that your instrument is in tune, because even correct notes played on an instrument that's out of tune produce errors for How Did I Play!

If you find the free Learn to Play lessons valuable, you can move up to the Artist lessons, which are taught by famous musicians (including favorites of mine such as Alex Lifeson, John Fogerty, and Sting, who actually teaches you how to play "Roxanne")!

Creating song files and ringtones in iTunes

You can create an AAC song file (or even a ringtone) from any project in just a few simple steps:

1. **Open the project that you want to share.**

2. **Choose Share⇨Song to iTunes from the GarageBand menu bar.**

   GarageBand displays the settings you see in Figure 16-9.

   To create a ringtone and send it to iTunes, choose Share⇨Ringtones to iTunes from the GarageBand menu bar.

3. **Click in each of the text boxes to type the title, artist name, composer name, album name, and iTunes playlist for the tracks you create.**

   You can leave the defaults as they are, if you prefer. Each track that you export is named after the song's name in GarageBand.

4. **From the Quality pop-up menu, choose the proper audio quality for the finished file.**

   The higher the quality, the larger the file.

5. **Click the Share button.**

   After a second or two of hard work, your Mac opens the iTunes window and highlights the new (or existing) playlist that contains your new audio, whether it be a song or a ringtone.

Figure 16-9:
Tweaking settings for iTunes audio files.

Exporting a project

Sometimes you'd like to create an audio file from a GarageBand project, but you'd rather not automatically add that song or ringtone to your iTunes Music Library. (Perhaps you now have the audio proof that a family member does indeed snore.) In that case, you can always export a song straight to your hard drive by following these steps:

1. **Open the project that you want to export.**

2. **Choose Share⇨Export Song to Disk.**

3. **Type a name for the audio file.**

   Click the button next to the Save As text box to select a specific location where the file should be created, or choose a preset from the Where pop-up menu.

4. **From the Quality pop-up menu, choose the desired audio quality.**

   As with sharing a song to iTunes, the higher the quality, the larger the file.

5. **Click Export.**

Burning an audio CD

Ready to create a demo CD with your latest GarageBand creation? If your iMac has an internal or external optical drive, follow these steps to burn an audio disc from within GarageBand:

1. **Open the song that you want to record to disc.**

2. **Load a blank disc into your optical drive.**

   If you see a dialog requesting that you choose an action, click the Ignore button.

3. **Choose Share⇨Burn Song to CD.**

Note that the CD you create has only one track. To include more tracks on the CD, share the song to your iTunes Library (as described earlier), create a playlist containing the desired songs, and burn that playlist within iTunes.

Part V

Getting Productive with iWork and Other Tools

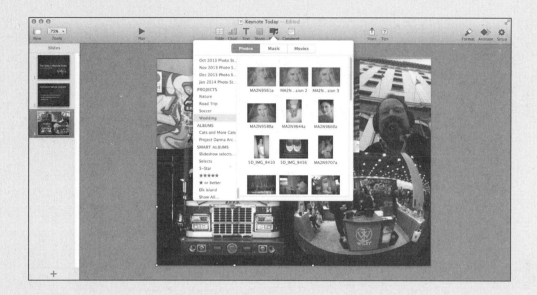

Learn about network troubleshooting using *ping* online at www.dummies.com/extras/imac.

In this part . . .

- ✔ Use Pages to produce professional posters, flyers and letters
- ✔ Build spreadsheets quickly and easily using Numbers
- ✔ Create superb-looking presentations for business or school with Keynote
- ✔ Share your iMac with others with user accounts
- ✔ Join or create a wired or wireless Ethernet network

Chapter 17

Desktop Publishing with Pages

. . . .

. . . .

*W*hat's the difference between word processing and desktop publishing? In a nutshell, it's in how you *design* your document. Most folks use a word processor like an old-fashioned typewriter. . . much the way I'm using Microsoft Word right now. (Yawn.)

A *desktop publishing application* allows far more creativity in choosing where to place text, how to align graphics, and how to edit formats. In this chapter, I show you how to set your inner designer free from the tedious constraints of word processing! Whether you need a simple letter, a stunning brochure, or a multipage newsletter, Pages can handle the job with ease — and you'll be surprised at how simple it is to use.

Creating a New Pages Document

To create a new Pages document, follow these steps:

1. **Click the Pages icon on the Dock.**

   If the Pages icon doesn't appear on your Dock, click the Launchpad icon and then click the Pages icon (which looks like a document and pen). If you haven't installed the three iWork applications yet — Pages, Numbers, and Keynote — click the App Store icon in your Dock and download them directly!

2. Click the New Document button in the lower-left corner of the Open dialog.

Pages displays the Template Chooser window shown in Figure 17-1.

You can also create a new Pages document at any time from the File menu. Just click New to display the Template Chooser window.

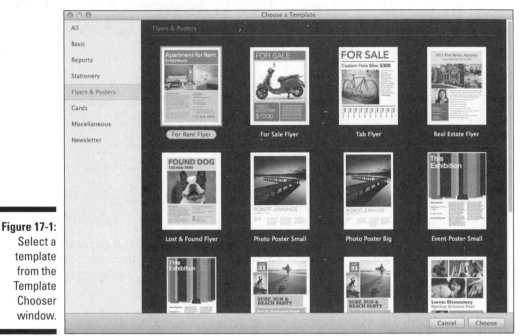

Figure 17-1:
Select a
template
from the
Template
Chooser
window.

3. In the list to the left, click the type of document you want to create.

The thumbnails on the right are updated with templates that match your choice.

4. Click the template that most closely matches your needs.

5. Click the Choose button to open a new document in the template you selected.

Open an Existing Pages Document

Of course, you can always open a Pages document from a Finder window. Just double-click the document icon. (The All My Files location in the Finder window Sidebar makes it easy to track down a document.) You can also open a Pages document from within the program. Follow these steps:

1. Launch Pages as I describe in the previous section.

2. **Press ⌘+O to display the Open dialog.**

   The Open dialog operates much the same as a Finder window in Icon, List, or Column view mode. To open a document that you've already saved in your iCloud folder, click the iCloud button in the top-left corner of the Open dialog. To open a document on your hard drive or network, click the On My Mac button.

3. **Click the desired drive in the Devices list at the left of the dialog and then click folders and subfolders until you locate the Pages document.**

   You can also click in the Search box at the top of the Open dialog and type in a portion of the document name or its contents.

   If you're using Icon view mode (or you're displaying the Preview column in Column view mode), you can hover your cursor over a document thumbnail and quickly flip through the different pages by clicking on the left and right arrows that appear. This "find" feature can help you iden-tify a particular Pages document without even opening it

4. **Double-click the thumbnail (or filename) to load it.**

   If you want to open a Pages document that you've edited in the recent past, things get even easier! Just choose File⇨Open Recent, and you can open the document with a single click from the submenu that appears.

Saving Your Work

Pages fully supports the Mavericks Auto-Save feature, but you may feel the need to manually save your work after you finish a significant edit (or if you need to take a break while designing). If you're editing a document that has already been saved at least once, a new version of the document is saved to its current location — and you can immediately continue your work.

If, however, you're working on a *new* document that hasn't previously been saved, follow these steps to save it:

1. **With the Pages document open, press ⌘+S.**

2. **Type a filename for your new document.**

3. **Open the Where pop-up menu and choose a location to save the document.**

   Note that Pages defaults to your iCloud folder as the target location — this way, you can open and edit your Pages document on any Mac or iOS device that shares the same Apple ID. Alternatively, click the button sporting the down arrow to expand the Save As sheet. This allows you to navigate to a different location on your hard drive or network, or to create a new folder to store this Pages project.

4. **Click Save.**

You can create a version of a Pages document by choosing File⇨Save. To revert the current document to an older version, choose File⇨Revert To. Pages gives you the option of reverting to the last saved version, or you can click Browse All Versions to choose from multiple versions of the document.

Touring the Pages Window

Before you dive into any real work, let me show you around the Pages window! You'll find the following major components and controls, as shown in Figure 17-2:

✔ **Pages list:** This thumbnail list displays all the pages you've created within your document. (For a single-page document, of course, the Page list will contain only a single thumbnail.) You can switch instantly between different pages in your document by clicking the desired thumbnail in the list. If the list isn't visible, click the View button at the left side of the Pages toolbar and click Show Page Thumbnails.

✔ **Layout pane:** This section takes up most of the Pages window — it's where you design and edit each page in your document.

✔ **Toolbar:** Yep, Pages has its own toolbar. The toolbar keeps all the most common application controls within easy, one-click reach.

✔ **Format Drawer:** This window extension allows you to quickly switch the appearance of selected paragraphs, characters, and lists. You can hide and display the Format Drawer by clicking the Format button on the toolbar.

Toolbar

Figure 17-2: The major points of interest in the Pages window.

Pages list

Layout pane

Format Drawer

Entering and Editing Text

If you've used a modern word processing program, you'll feel right at home typing within Pages. The bar-shaped text cursor, which looks like a capital letter *I*, indicates where the text you enter will appear in a Pages document. To enter text, simply begin typing. To edit existing text in your Pages document, select and highlight the text. As you type, Pages replaces the existing text. You can delete text by clicking and dragging across the characters to highlight them; then press Delete.

Using Text and Graphics Boxes

Within Pages, text and graphics appear in *boxes,* which can be resized by clicking and dragging one of the handles that appear around the edges of the box. (Click the box to select it and then hover your cursor over one of the square handles, and you'll see that it changes to a double-sided arrow, indicating that Pages is ready to resize the box.)

You can also move a box, including all the stuff it contains, to another location within the Layout pane. Click in the center of the box and drag the box to the desired spot. Note that Pages displays yellow alignment lines to help you align the box with other elements around it (or with regular divisions of the page, such as the vertical center of a poster or flyer). Figure 17-3 illustrates a box containing text that I'm moving; note the vertical and horizontal alignment lines that automatically appear.

Figure 17-3: Move a text box within the Layout pane.

To select text or graphics within a box, you must first click the box to select it and then double-click the line of text or the graphic that you want to change.

The Three Amigos: Cut, Copy, and Paste

"Hang on, Mark, you've covered moving stuff, but what if you want to *copy* a block of text or a photo to a second location? Or how about cutting something from a document open in another application?" Good questions, dear reader! That's when you can call on the power of the cut, copy, and paste features within Pages. The next few sections explain how you do these actions.

Cutting stuff

Cutting selected text or graphics removes it from your Pages document and places that material on your Clipboard. (Think of the *Clipboard* as a holding area for snippets of text and graphics that you want to manipulate.) To cut text or graphics, select some material and choose Edit⇨Cut or press ⌘+X.

Copying text and images

When you copy text or graphics, the original selection remains untouched, but a copy of the selection is placed on the Clipboard. Select some text or graphics and choose Edit⇨Copy or press ⌘+C. To copy selected items by dragging, hold down the Option key while you drag the items to their destination.

If you cut or copy a new selection on to the Clipboard, it erases what was there. In other words, the Clipboard holds only the latest material you cut or copied.

Pasting from the Clipboard

Are you wondering what you can do with the stuff that's stored in your Clipboard? Pasting the contents of the Clipboard places the material at the current location of the insertion cursor.

WARNING!

You must paste the contents before you cut or copy again to avoid losing what's on the Clipboard.

To paste the Clipboard contents, click the insertion cursor at the location you want and choose Edit⇨Paste or press ⌘+V.

Formatting Text the Easy Way

If you feel that some (or all) of the text in your Pages document needs a face-lift, you can format that text any way you like. Formatting lets you change the color, font family, character size, and attributes as necessary.

After the text is selected, you can apply basic formatting in two ways:

✔ **Use the Format Drawer.** The Format Drawer appears at the right side of the Pages window, as shown in Figure 17-2, and the controls it displays will vary according to the selection you've made. (Click the Format button on the toolbar, which looks like a tiny blue paintbrush, to display and hide the drawer.) Click to select a font control to display a pop-up menu and then click your choice. For example, open the Font Family pop-up menu to change the font family from vanilla Arial to a more daring font. You can also select characteristics, such as the text's paragraph style, or choose italicizing or bolding. The Format Drawer also provides buttons for both vertical and horizontal text alignment.

✔ **Use the Format menu.** Most controls displayed within the Format Drawer are also available from the Format menu. Click Format and hover the mouse cursor over the Font menu item, and you can then apply bolding, italicizing, and underlining to the selected text. You can also make the text bigger or smaller. To change the alignment from the Format menu, click Format and hover the mouse cursor over the Text menu item.

Adding a Spiffy Table

In the world of word processing, a *table* is a grid that holds text and graphics for easy comparison. You can create a custom table layout within Pages with a few simple clicks.

Follow these steps:

1. **Click the insertion cursor at the location where you want the table to appear.**

2. Click the Table button on the Pages toolbar.

Pages displays thumbnail images of different table styles. You have a selection of colors, and some tables also include highlighted rows and columns, as shown in Figure 17-4. Use the left and right buttons to display different style thumbnails until you find the one that's closest to the table you need.

Don't worry if the style isn't exactly right. You can always change the layout by selecting the table and displaying the Format Drawer, where you can fine-tune all sorts of font, color, grid, and border options.

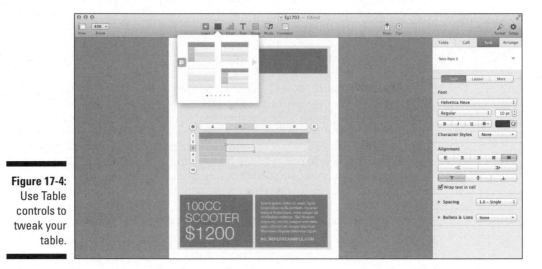

Figure 17-4: Use Table controls to tweak your table.

3. Click the style thumbnail to insert the table.

If you need to change the number of rows or columns in your table, Pages makes it easy! To add or delete rows or columns directly from the table, select it and then click the row and column buttons that appear (each of which bears an equal sign, as shown in Figure 17-4).

4. Click within a cell in the table to enter text.

The table cell automatically resizes and "wraps" the text you enter to fit.

You can paste material from the Clipboard into a table. See the earlier section "Pasting from the Clipboard" for details on pasting.

Here are a few pointers on how to dress up your table and make its data more attractive or readable:

✔ **Change the borders on a selected cell.** Open the Format Drawer, click the Cell tab, and then click the Border section.

Select a range of multiple cells in a table by holding down Shift as you click. Hold down ⌘ and click to select multiple cells that aren't contiguous.

✔ **Add a background color to selected cells or fill them with an image for a background.** Click the Cell tab and then click the Fill section in the Format Drawer and choose a type of background.

Adding Alluring Photos

You can choose between two methods of adding a picture within your Pages document:

✔ **As a floating object:** You place the image in a particular spot, and it doesn't move even if you make changes to the text.

✔ **As an inline object:** The image flows with the surrounding text as you make layout changes.

To add a floating object, drag an image file from a Finder window and place it at the spot you want within your document. Alternatively, you can click the Media button on the toolbar, click Photos, navigate to the location where the file is saved, and click the image thumbnail. Figure 17-5 illustrates the Media Browser in action.

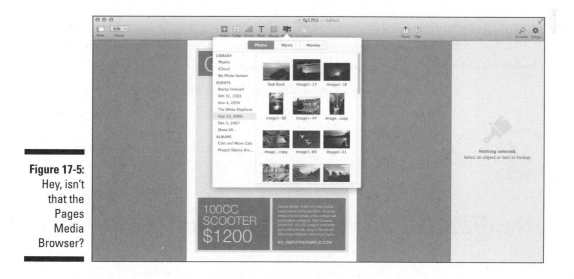

Figure 17-5:
Hey, isn't that the Pages Media Browser?

Note that a floating object (such as a shape or an image) can be sent to the *background,* where text will not wrap around it. To bring a background object back as a regular floating object, click the object to select it and choose Arrange➪Bring to Front. (More about background objects later in this chapter.)

To add an inline object, hold down the ⌘ key as you drag an image file from a Finder window and place it where you want within your document. You can also click the Media toolbar button and click Photos to display the Media Browser. Navigate to the location where the file is saved, hold down the ⌘ key, and drag the image thumbnail to the spot where you want it in the document.

To resize an image object, click the image to select it and then drag one of the selection handles that appear along the border of the image. (The handles look like tiny squares.) The side-selection handles drag only that edge of the frame. The corner-selection handles resize both adjoining edges of the selection frame. Hold down the Shift key so that the vertical and horizontal proportions remain fixed.

Adding a Background Shape

To add a shape (such as a rectangle or circle) as a background for your text, follow these steps:

1. **Click the insertion cursor in the location you want.**

2. **Click the Shape button on the Pages toolbar and choose a shape.**

   The shape appears in your document.

3. **Click the center of the shape and drag it to a new spot.**

   Shapes can be resized or moved in the same manner as image boxes. See the preceding section.

You can type over a shape set as a background. Before you do, though, select the shape and choose Arrange➪Send to Back.

Are You Sure about That Spelling?

Pages can check spelling as you type (the default setting) or check it after you complete your document. If you find automatic spell-checking distracting, you should definitely pick the latter method.

As my technical editor reminds us, spell-checking confirms only that a word is correctly spelled, *not* that it's the right word for the job! If you've ever "red" a document that someone else "rote," you "no" what he means.

To check spelling as you type, follow these steps:

1. **Click the Edit menu and hover the cursor over the Spelling and Grammar menu item.**

2. **Choose Check Spelling While Typing from the submenu that appears.**

   If a possible misspelling is found, Pages underlines the word with a red, dashed line.

3. **Right-click the word to choose a possible correct spelling from the list or choose Ignore Spelling if it's spelled correctly.**

To turn off automatic spell-checking, click the Check Spelling While Typing menu item again to deselect it.

To check spelling manually, follow these steps:

1. **Click within the document to place the text insertion cursor where the spell check should begin.**

2. **Click Edit and hover the cursor over the Spelling and Grammar menu item; then choose Check Document Now from the submenu that appears.**

3. **Right-click any possible misspellings and choose the correct spelling, or choose Ignore Spelling if the word is spelled correctly.**

Printing Your Pages Documents

Ready to start the presses? You can print your Pages document on real paper, of course, but don't forget that you can also save a tree by creating an electronic, PDF-format document instead of a printout. You'll find the PDF button within the standard Mavericks Print dialog.

To print your Pages document on old-fashioned paper, follow these steps:

1. **Within Pages, choose File➪Print.**

   Pages displays the Print sheet.

2. **Click in the Copies field and enter the number of copies you need.**

3. **Select the pages to print.**

   - *To print the entire document,* select All.

   - *To print a range of selected pages,* select the From radio button and then enter the starting and ending pages.

4. **Click the Print button to send the document to your printer.**

Sharing That Poster with Others

Besides printing — which is, after all, so *very* passé these days — you can choose to share your Pages document electronically in a number of ways:

- ✔ **Sharing on iCloud:** If you stored your new masterpiece in your iCloud folder, you can send a link to the finished document in a number of different ways. Click the Share button on the Pages toolbar, and then hover your cursor over the Share Link via iCloud item to send the link through Mail, Messages, Twitter, or Facebook. The recipient of the link can easily view your document with a single click!

- ✔ **Sending a Copy:** If you'd prefer to send a copy of the actual document — which the recipient can open using Pages on their own Mac or iOS device — click Share on the toolbar, and then hover your cursor over the Send a Copy item. You can send the document via Mail or Messages, or make it available through AirDrop (if the recipient is within the range of your iMac's Wi-Fi signal). If you decide to send your Pages document as an e-mail attachment, don't forget that most ISPs have a maximum message size. If your document is too large, it will likely be rejected by your mail server.

- ✔ **Exporting:** You're not limited to sharing over that Internet thing! Pages can also export your work directly to your drive in one of five different formats: a PDF document, a Word document, an ePub file (for use with electronic book apps like iBooks), a document compatible with the previous version of Pages, or even plain text. (Remember when everything was in plain text?) Choose File⇨Export To and pick your format, and Pages displays any options you can set for that format. When you're ready, click Next and then select the location where Pages should save the file. Click Export and sit back while your favorite desktop publishing application does all the work.

If the recipient of your document doesn't need to edit your work, I recommend PDF format, which will keep your document as close to how it appears in Pages as possible.

Chapter 18

Creating Spreadsheets with Numbers

*A*re you downright afraid of spreadsheets? Does the idea of building a budget with charts and all sorts of fancy graphics send you running for the safety of the hall closet? Well, good iMac owner, Apple has once again taken something that everyone else considers super-complex and turned it into something that normal human beings can use! (Much as Apple did with video editing and songwriting — heck, is there *any* type of software that Apple designers can't make intuitive and easy to use?)

In this chapter, I get to demonstrate how the Numbers spreadsheet program can help you organize data, analyze important financial decisions — and yes, even maintain a household budget! You'll soon see why Numbers is specifically designed with the home Mac owner in mind.

Before You Launch Numbers . . .

Just in case you're not familiar with applications like Numbers and Microsoft Excel — and the documents they create — let me provide you with a little background information.

A *spreadsheet* organizes and calculates numbers by using a grid system of rows and columns. The intersection of each row and column is a *cell,* which can hold either text or numeric values (along with calculations called *formulas* and *functions* that are usually linked to the contents of surrounding cells).

Spreadsheets are wonderful tools for making decisions and comparisons because they let you "plug in" different numbers — such as interest rates or your monthly insurance premium — and instantly see the results. Some of my favorite spreadsheets that I use regularly are

✔ Car and mortgage loan comparisons

✔ A college planner

✔ My household budget (not that we pay any attention to it)

Creating a New Numbers Document

Like Pages (the Apple desktop publishing application; see Chapter 17), Numbers ships with a selection of templates that you can modify quickly to create a new spreadsheet. For example, after a few modifications, you can easily use the Budget, Loan Comparison, and Mortgage templates to create your own spreadsheets.

To create a spreadsheet project file, follow these steps:

1. **Click the Launchpad icon on the Dock.**

2. **Click the Numbers icon.**

3. **Click the New Document button in the lower-left corner of the Open dialog that appears.**

   Numbers displays the Template Chooser window, as shown in Figure 18-1. (To display the Template Chooser window and start a new Numbers project at any time, just choose File➪New.)

4. **From the list to the left, click the type of document you want to create.**

   The document thumbnails on the right are updated with templates that match your choice.

5. **Click the template that most closely matches your needs.**

6. **Click the Choose button to open a new document using the template you selected.**

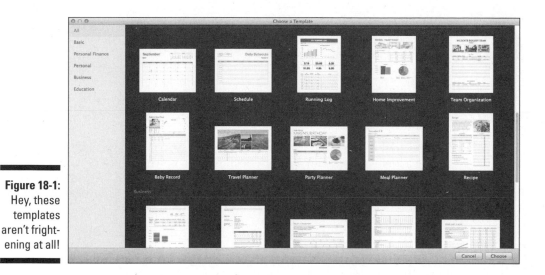

Figure 18-1:
Hey, these templates aren't frightening at all!

Opening an Existing Spreadsheet File

If you see an existing Numbers document in a Finder window (or you locate it using Spotlight or the All My Files location), just double-click the Document icon to open it; Numbers automatically loads and displays the spreadsheet. However, it's equally easy to open a Numbers document from within the program. Follow these steps:

1. **From Launchpad, click the Numbers icon to run the program.**

2. **Press ⌘+O to display the Open dialog.**

As an iMac power user running OS X Mavericks, you can save and load Numbers documents directly to and from your iCloud folder. All three iWork applications — Pages, Numbers, and Keynote — feature an Open dialog that can display the contents of your iCloud folder as well as your iMac's internal drive. Click the iCloud or On My Mac button to switch locations.

3. **Click the On My Mac button and then click the desired drive in the Devices list at the left of the dialog. Drill down through folders and subfolders until you locate the desired Numbers document.**

If you're unsure where the document is, click in the Search box at the top of the Open dialog and type in a portion of the document name, or even a word or two of text it contains. Note that you can choose to search your drive, your iCloud folder, or both.

4. **Double-click the spreadsheet to load it.**

If you want to open a spreadsheet you've been working on over the last few days, choose File ⇨ Open Recent to display Numbers documents that you've worked with recently.

Save Those Spreadsheets!

Thanks to the Auto-Save feature in Mavericks, you no longer have to fear losing a significant chunk of work because of a power failure or a coworker's mistake. However, if you're not a huge fan of retyping data, *period,* you can always save your spreadsheets manually after making a major change. Follow these steps to save your spreadsheet to your hard drive:

1. **Press ⌘+S.**

   If you're saving a document that hasn't yet been saved, the Save As sheet appears.

2. **Type a filename for your new spreadsheet.**

3. **Open the Where pop-up menu and choose a location to save the file.**

   Common locations are your Desktop, Documents folder, or Home folder.

   If the location you want isn't listed in the Where pop-up menu, click the down-arrow button next to the Save As text box to display the full Save As dialog. Click the desired drive in the Devices list at the left of the dialog and then click folders and subfolders until you reach the desired location. Alternatively, type the folder name in the Spotlight search box at the top right and double-click the desired folder in the list of matching names. (As an extra bonus, you can also create a new folder in the full Save As dialog.)

4. **Click Save.**

After you save a Numbers document for the first time, you can create a version of that document by choosing File ⇨ Save. To revert the current document to an older version, choose File ⇨ Revert To. You can choose to revert to the last saved version, or you can click Browse All Versions to browse multiple versions of the document and choose one of those to revert to.

Exploring the Numbers Window

Apple has done a great job of minimizing the complexity of the Numbers window. Figure 18-2 illustrates these major points of interest:

- ✔ **Sheets tabs:** Because a Numbers project can contain multiple spreadsheets, they're displayed in the Sheets tabbed bar at the top of the window. To switch among spreadsheets in a project, click the desired tab.

- ✔ **Sheet canvas:** Numbers displays the rows and columns of your spreadsheet in this section of the window; you enter and edit cell values within the sheet canvas.

- ✔ **Toolbar:** The Numbers toolbar keeps the most common commands you'll use within easy reach.

- ✔ **Format Drawer:** Located at the right side of the Numbers window, the Format Drawer displays editing controls for the object that's currently selected regardless of whether it's a selection of text, a table, or a single cell. (If you enter an equal sign into a cell to enter a formula, the Format Drawer changes into the Function Drawer, where you can specify a calculation that Numbers should perform.)

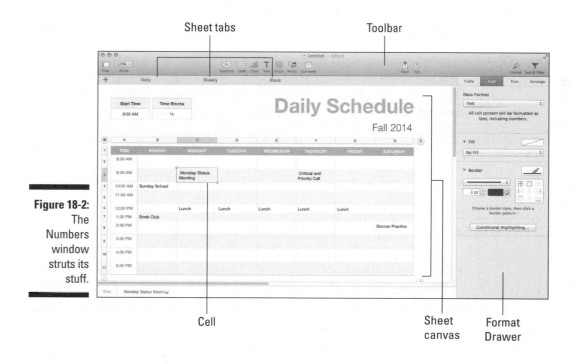

Figure 18-2: The Numbers window struts its stuff.

Navigating and Selecting Cells in a Spreadsheet

You can use the scroll bars to move around in your spreadsheet, but when you enter data into cells, moving your fingers from the keyboard is a hassle. Numbers has various handy navigation shortcut keys that you can employ, and I list them in Table 18-1. After you commit these keys to memory, your productivity level shoots straight to the top.

Table 18-1	Movement Shortcut Keys in Numbers
Key or Key Combination	*Where the Cursor Moves*
Left arrow (←)	One cell to the left
Right arrow (→)	One cell to the right
Up arrow (↑)	One cell up
Down arrow (↓)	One cell down
Home	To the beginning of the active worksheet
End	To the end of the active worksheet
Page Down	Down one screen
Page Up	Up one screen
Return	One cell down (also works within a selection)
Tab	One cell to the right (also works within a selection)
Shift+Return	One cell up (also works within a selection)
Shift+Tab	One cell to the left (also works within a selection)

You can also use the mouse or trackpad to select cells in a spreadsheet:

- To select a *single* cell, click it.
- To select a *range* of multiple adjacent cells, click a cell at any corner of the range you want and then drag in the direction you want.
- To select a *column* of cells, click the alphabetic heading button at the top of the column.
- To select a *row* of cells, click the numeric heading button on the far left of the row.

Entering and Editing Data in a Spreadsheet

After you navigate to the cell in which you want to enter data, you're ready to type your data. Follow these steps to enter That Important Stuff:

1. **Either click the cell or press the spacebar.**

   A cursor appears, indicating that the cell is ready to hold any data you type.

2. **Enter your data.**

   Spreadsheets can use both numbers and alphabetic characters within a cell; either type of information is considered data in the Spreadsheet World.

3. **When you're ready to move on, press Return (to save the data and move one cell down) or press Tab (to save the data and move one cell to the right).**

Make a mistake? No big deal:

- ✔ **To edit data:** Click within the cell that contains the data error (to select the cell) and then click the cell again to display the insertion cursor. Drag the insertion cursor across the characters to highlight them and then type the replacement data.

- ✔ **To delete characters:** Select the cell and then highlight the characters and press Delete.

Selecting the Correct Number Format

After you enter your data (in a cell, row, or column), you might need to format it so that it appears correctly. For example, say you want certain cells to display a specific type of number, such as a dollar amount, percentage, or date. Numbers gives you a healthy selection of number-formatting possibilities.

Characters and formatting rules — such as decimal places, commas, and dollar and percentage notation — are part of number formatting. If your spreadsheet contains units of currency, such as dollars, format it as such. Then all you need to do is type the numbers, and the currency formatting is applied automatically.

To specify a number format, follow these steps:

1. **Select the cells, rows, or columns you want to format.**

2. **Click the Format toolbar button.**

3. **Click the Cell tab in the Format Drawer.**

4. **From the Data Format pop-up menu, choose the type of formatting you want to apply (as shown in Figure 18-3).**

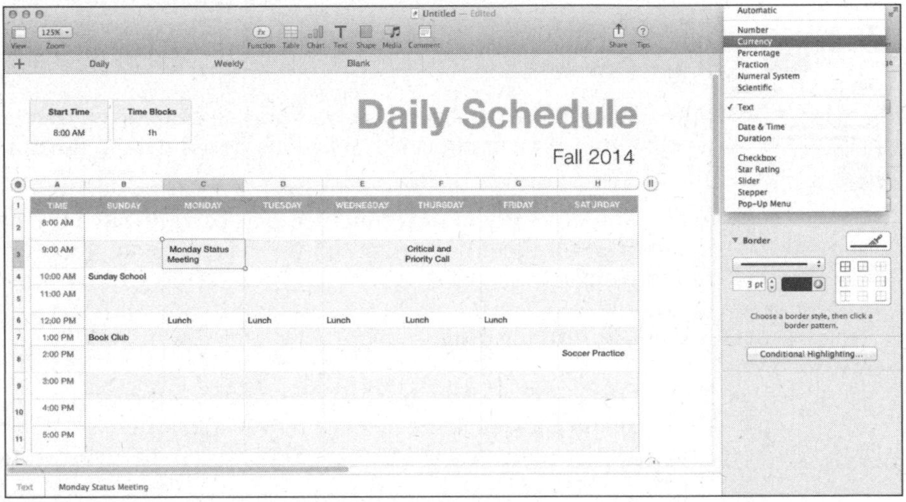

Figure 18-3:
From the Format Drawer, you can format the data you've entered.

Aligning Cell Text Just So

You can also change the alignment of text in the selected cells. The default alignment is flush left *for text* and flush right *for numeric data.* Follow these steps:

1. **Select the cells, rows, or columns you want to format.**

   See "Navigating and Selecting Cells in a Spreadsheet," earlier in this chapter, for tips on selecting stuff.

2. **Click the Format toolbar button.**

3. **Click the Text tab of the Format Drawer to display the settings you see in Figure 18-4.**

4. **Click the corresponding Alignment button to choose the type of formatting you want to apply.**

   You can choose left, right, center, justified, and text left and numbers right. Text can also be aligned at the top, center, or bottom of a cell.

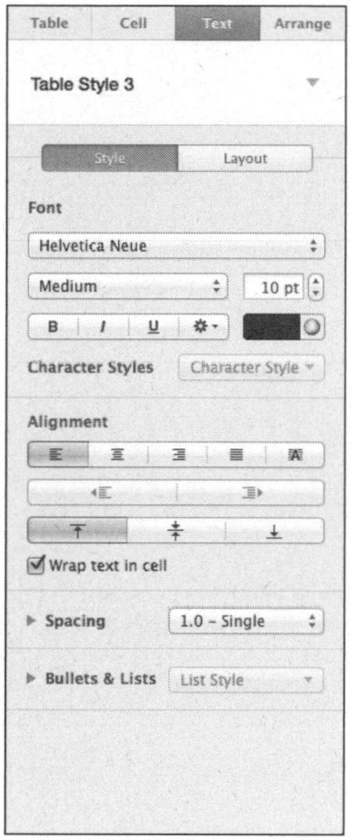

Figure 18-4:
Set text
alignment
within a cell.

Do you need to set apart the contents of some cells? For example, you might need to create text headings for some columns and rows or to highlight the totals in a spreadsheet. To change such formatting, select the cells, rows, or columns you want to format and then open the Font Family, Font Size, or Font Color buttons on the Text tab.

Formatting with Shading

Shading the contents of a cell, row, or column is helpful when your spreadsheet contains subtotals or logical divisions. Follow these steps to shade cells, rows, or columns:

1. **Select the cells, rows, or columns you want to format.**

2. **Click the Format toolbar button.**

3. **Click the Cell tab of the Format Drawer.**

4. **Click the triangle next to the Fill heading and choose a shading option from the Fill pop-up menu.**

   Figure 18-5 illustrates the controls for a gradient fill.

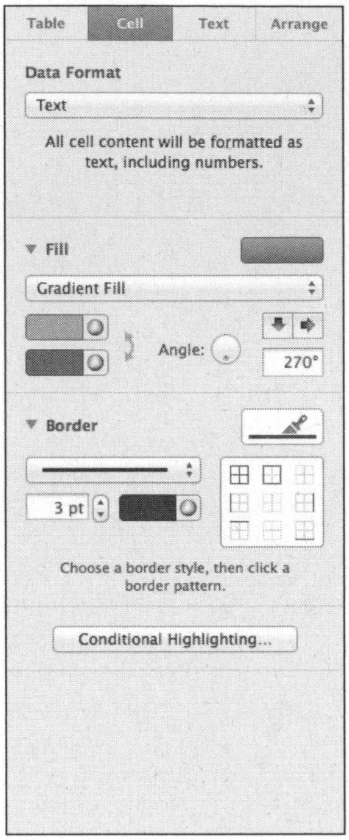

Figure 18-5:
Adding
shading
and colors
to cells,
rows, and
columns
is easy in
Numbers.

5. **Click the color box to select a color for your shading.**

   Numbers displays a color picker (also shown in Figure 18-5).

6. **Click to select a color.**

7. **After you achieve the effect you want, click the color box again to close the color picker.**

You can also add a custom border to selected cells, rows, and columns from the Cell tab. Click the triangle next to the Border heading to select just the right border.

Inserting and Deleting Rows and Columns

What's that? You forgot to add a row, and now you're three pages into your data entry? No problem. You can easily add — or delete — rows and columns. First, select the row or column adjacent to where you want to insert a row or column (or the one that you want to delete) and do one of the following:

- ✔ **For a row:** Right-click and choose Add Row Above, Add Row Below, or Delete Row from the shortcut menu that appears.

- ✔ **For a column:** Right-click and choose Add Columns Before, Add Columns After, or Delete Column from the shortcut menu that appears.

If you select multiple rows or columns, right-click and choose Add. Numbers inserts the same number of new rows or columns as what you originally selected.

You can also insert rows and columns via the Table menu at the top of the Numbers window.

The Formula Is Your Friend

It's time to talk about *formulas,* which are equations that calculate values based on the contents of cells you specify in your spreadsheet. For example, if you designate cell A1 (the cell in column A at row 1) to hold your yearly salary and cell B1 to hold the number 12, you can divide the contents of cell A1 by cell B1 (to calculate your monthly salary) by typing this formula into any other cell:

```
=A1/B1
```

Formulas in Numbers always start with an equal sign (=), and may include one or more functions as well. A *function* is a preset mathematical, statistical, or engineering calculation that will be performed, such as the sum (or average) of a series of cells.

"So what's the big deal, Mark? Why not use a calculator?" Sure, you could. But maybe you want to calculate your weekly salary. Rather than grab a pencil and paper, you can simply change the contents of cell B1 to 52, and boom! The spreadsheet is updated to display your weekly salary.

That's a simple example, of course, but it demonstrates the basis of using formulas (and the reason why spreadsheets are often used to predict trends and forecast budgets). It's the "what if?" tool of choice for everyone who works with numeric data.

To add a simple formula within a spreadsheet, follow these steps:

1. **Select the cell that will hold the result of your calculation.**

2. **Type = (the equal sign).**

   The Formula Box appears within the confines of the cell.

3. **Click the Format button on the Numbers toolbar to display the available functions in the Functions Drawer (as shown in Figure 18-6).**

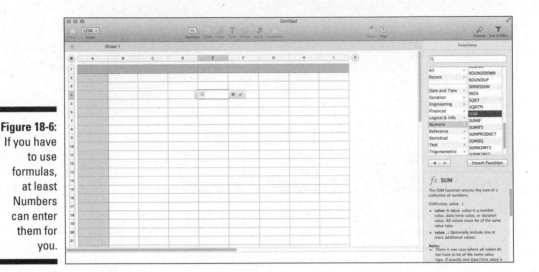

Figure 18-6:
If you have to use formulas, at least Numbers can enter them for you.

4. **Click the category of calculation you want from the left column of the Functions Drawer.**

   Instead of scrolling through the entire function library, it's easier to choose a category — such as *Financial* for your budget spreadsheet — to filter the selection. (Alternatively, you can click in the Search box and type a function name or keyword.)

   To display more information about a specific function, click it in the right column of the Functions Drawer. In Figure 18-6, choosing the SUM function brings up a description at the bottom of the Functions Drawer.

5. **After you select the perfect function in the right column, click the Insert Function button.**

   The function appears in the Formula box, along with any arguments it requires.

   In case you're not familiar with the term *argument,* it refers to a value specified in a cell that's used by a formula. For example, the SUM formula adds the contents of each cell you specify to produce a total; each of those cell values is an argument.

6. **Click an argument button in the formula and click the cell that contains the corresponding data.**

   Numbers automatically adds the cell you indicated to the formula. Repeat this for each argument in the formula.

7. **After you finish, click the Accept button — the green check mark — to add the formula to the cell.**

That's it! Your formula is now ready to work behind the scenes, doing math for you so that the correct numbers appear in the cell you specified.

Adding Visual Punch with a Chart

Sometimes you just have to see something to believe it — hence using the data you add to a spreadsheet to generate a professional-looking chart! After you've entered the data you want to chart, follow these steps:

1. **Select the adjacent cells you want to chart by dragging the mouse.**

   To choose individual cells that aren't adjacent, you can hold down the ⌘ key as you click.

2. **Click the Chart button on the Numbers toolbar.**

   The Chart button bears the symbol of a bar graph.

   Numbers displays the thumbnail menu you see in Figure 18-7. Note that you can display different categories of charts by clicking one of the three tabs at the top (2D/3D/Interactive), and the menu can be scrolled to reveal additional thumbnails by using the left- and right-arrow buttons.

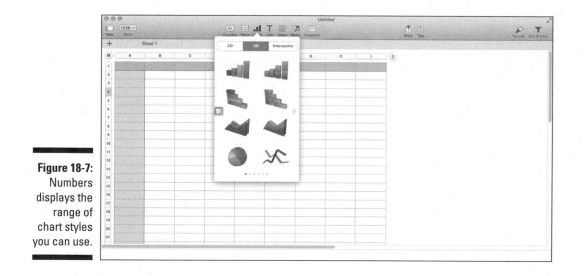

Figure 18-7: Numbers displays the range of chart styles you can use.

3. **Click the thumbnail for the chart type you want.**

   Numbers inserts the chart as an object within your spreadsheet so that you can move the chart. You can drag using the handles that appear on the outside of the object box to resize your chart.

   With your chart selected, click the Format toolbar button to display our old friend the Format Drawer, complete with the controls you can use to customize the appearance of your chart. For example, you can change the colors and add (or remove) the title and legend.

4. **To change the default title, click the title box once to select it; click it again to edit the text.**

Chapter 19

Building Presentations with Keynote

*I*t seems like only yesterday that I was giving business presentations with a clunky overhead projector and black-and-white acetate transparencies. Fancy color gradients and animation were unheard of, and the only sound my presentations made was the droning of the projector's fan. I might as well have been using tree bark and chalk.

Thank goodness those "cave painting" days are gone forever because cutting-edge presentation software like Keynote makes slide creation easy and — believe it or not — *fun!* This is the application that Steve Jobs once used for his Macworld keynotes every year, and there's so much visual candy available that you'll never need to shout to wake your audience again.

In this chapter, I first demonstrate how simple it is to build a stunning Keynote presentation. Then you can see how to start and control your slide display from your keyboard (or even your iPhone, iPad, or iPod touch). And don't forget that you can print your slides and notes so your audience can keep a copy of your brilliant work.

Creating a New Keynote Project

As do the other applications in the iWork suite, Keynote begins the document creation process with a Theme Chooser window. To create a new presentation project, follow these steps:

1. **Click the Launchpad icon on the Dock.**

2. **Click the Keynote icon (which looks like a speaker's lectern).**

3. **Click the New Document button in the lower-left corner of the Open dialog.**

   The Theme Chooser window shown in Figure 19-1 appears. (I have to say that these are probably the most stunning visual building blocks I've ever seen in a presentation application.)

4. **Choose the aspect ratio, using the Standard or Wide buttons at the top of the window.**

   Although you don't necessarily need to select an exact match for the screen resolution of your iMac, it's a good idea to select the closest value to the maximum resolution of your projector. (If someone else is providing the projector, the Standard size is the more compatible choice.) If you'll present on a typical high-resolution computer monitor, widescreen will provide a better display.

Figure 19-1:
Select a template from the Theme Chooser window.

5. **Click the theme thumbnail that most closely matches your needs.**

6. **Click the Choose button to open a new document that uses the theme you selected.**

Opening a Keynote Presentation

If an existing Keynote presentation file is visible in a Finder window, you can double-click the document icon to open the project. If Keynote is already running, however, follow these steps to load a project from within the application:

1. **Press ⌘+O to display the Open dialog.**

2. **Click the desired drive in the Devices list at the left of the dialog; then click folders and subfolders until you've located the Keynote project. If the project is stored in your iCloud folder, click the iCloud button at the top left of the dialog and then double-click the desired project thumbnail.**

   If the project is stored on your hard drive, the All My Files location can quickly display all your documents, or you can use the Search box at the top of the Open dialog to locate the document by name or by some of the text it contains.

3. **Double-click the filename to load it.**

If you want to open a Keynote document that you've edited in the recent past, things get even easier! Just choose File➪Open Recent, and you can open the document with a single click from the submenu that appears.

Saving Your Presentation

Because Keynote provides full support for the OS X Auto-Save feature, saving your work often isn't as critical as it used to be. To safeguard your work in a world of power failures, though, follow these steps:

1. **Press ⌘+S.**

   If you're saving a document that hasn't yet been saved, the familiar Save As sheet appears.

2. **Type a filename for your new document.**

3. **From the Where pop-up menu, choose a location to save the document.**

   By default, Keynote saves the project directly to your iCloud folder (iCloud appears in the Where pop-up menu), making it available to other Macs and iOS devices using the same Apple ID. To select a location not available from the Where pop-up menu, click the button with the down-arrow symbol to expand the sheet. You can also create a new folder from the expanded sheet.

4. **Click Save.**

You can create a version of a Keynote presentation by choosing File⇨Save. To revert the current presentation to an older version, choose File⇨Revert To. Keynote gives you the option of reverting to the last saved version, or you can click Browse All Versions to browse multiple versions of the presentation and revert to any saved version.

Putting Keynote to Work

Ready for the 5-cent tour of the Keynote window? Launch the application and create or load a project, and you'll see the tourist attractions shown in Figure 19-2:

- ✓ **Slides list:** Use this thumbnail list of all the slides in your project to help you navigate quickly. Click a thumbnail to switch instantly to that slide.

   The Slides list can also display your project in outline format, allowing you to check all your discussion points. (This is a great way to ferret out any "holes" in your presentation's flow.) While in outline mode, you can still jump directly to any slide by clicking the slide's title in the outline. To display the outline, choose View⇨Outline. You can switch back to the default Navigator Slides list by choosing View⇨Navigator.

- ✓ **Layout pane:** Your slide appears in its entirety in this pane. You can add elements to and edit the content of the slide from the Layout pane.

- ✓ **Toolbar:** As does the toolbar in Pages and Numbers, the Keynote toolbar makes it easy to find the most common controls you'll use while designing and editing your slides. Clicking an icon on the toolbar performs an action, just as selecting a menu item does.

- ✓ **Presenter Notes pane:** If you decide to add notes to one or more slides (either for your own use or to print as additional information for your audience), click the View icon on the toolbar and select Show Presenter Notes (or choose View⇨Show Presenter Notes) to open the Notes pane. This text box appears under the Layout pane.

- ✓ **Format Drawer:** Keynote displays this pane on the right side of the window when you click the Format button, allowing you to format selected text and images on the fly.

Slides list

Play presentation

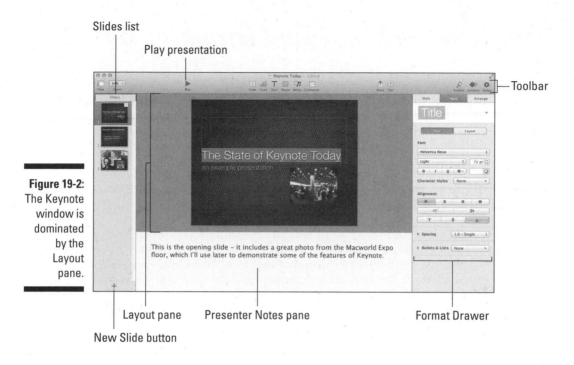

Toolbar

Figure 19-2:
The Keynote
window is
dominated
by the
Layout
pane.

Layout pane   Presenter Notes pane   Format Drawer

New Slide button

Adding Slides

Keynote creates a single Title slide when you first create a project. However,
not many presentations are complete with just a single slide! To add more
slides to your project, use one of these methods:

- ✔ Click the New Slide button at the bottom of the Slides list (which bears a
plus sign).
- ✔ Choose New Slide from the Slide menu.
- ✔ Press ⌘+Shift+N.
- ✔ Right-click an existing slide in the Slides list and choose New Slide from
the menu that appears.

Keynote adds the new slide to your Slides list and automatically switches to
the new slide in the Layout pane.

Need a slide that's very similar to an existing slide you've already designed?
Right-click the existing slide and choose Duplicate to create a new slide just
like it. (Consider it cloning without the science.)

To move slides to different positions in the Slides list (that is, change the
order in your Keynote presentation), drag each slide thumbnail to the
desired spot in the list.

Working with Text and Graphics Boxes

All the text and graphics placeholders on your first Title slide appear within boxes. Keynote uses these boxes to manipulate text and graphics. You can resize a box (and its contents) by clicking the box and dragging one of the handles that appear around the edges of the box. (Your cursor will change into a double-sided arrow when you're "in the zone.") A side selection handle drags only its edge of the frame, whereas corner selection handles resize both adjoining edges of the selection frame.

To keep the proportions of a box constrained, hold down Shift while dragging its corner handles.

Boxes make it easy to move text and graphics together (as a single unit) to another location within the Layout pane. Click in the center of the box and drag the box to the desired spot; Keynote displays alignment lines to help you align the box with other elements around it (or with regular divisions of the slide, like horizontal center). As you can see in Figure 19-3, I'm moving a box on the slide to a new location, and Keynote has supplied an alignment line to help me place it correctly.

To select a box, click it once. To select text or graphics within a box (see the following section), double-click the box.

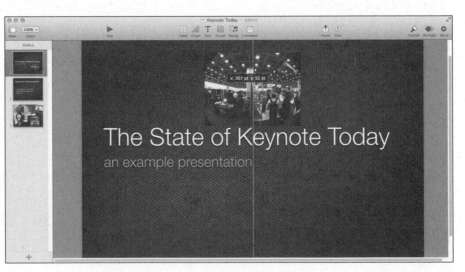

Figure 19-3:
Alignment
lines are
provided by
Keynote as
you move
boxes.

When you're resizing a photo in a box, hold down the Shift key while you drag the frame. This will tell Keynote to preserve the aspect ratio of the image so that the vertical and horizontal proportions remain fixed. You can also flip images horizontally or vertically from the Arrange menu.

To delete an image, just click it to select it and press the Delete key.

Adding and Editing Slide Text

As with Pages, which also uses boxes for text layout, you can add or edit text in Keynote with ease. For example, say you have a box with the placeholder text `Double-click to edit`. Just double-click in that box, and the placeholder text disappears, leaving the field ready to accept new text. Any new text you type appears at the blinking cursor within the box.

You can easily add a new text box at any time. Just click the Text button in the Keynote toolbar and click one of the sample styles that appear. Your new text box appears in the middle of the slide.

To edit existing text in your Keynote document, click — using the bar-shaped cursor to select just the right spot in the text — and drag the insertion cursor across the characters to highlight them. Type the replacement text, and Keynote obligingly replaces the old text with the new text you type.

To delete text, click and drag across the characters to highlight them; then press Delete. You can also delete an entire box and all its contents: Right-click the offending box and choose Delete from the menu that appears.

When the contents of a box are just right and you're finished entering or editing text, click anywhere outside the box to hide it from view. You can always click the text again to display the box later.

Formatting Slide Text for the Perfect Look

Keynote doesn't restrict you to the default fonts for the theme you chose. It's easy to format the text in your slides: a different font family, font color, text alignment, and text attributes (such as bolding and italicizing) on the fly.

Select the desired text by double-clicking a box and then dragging the text cursor to highlight the characters. Now apply your formatting using one of these two methods:

- ✔ **The Format Drawer:** The font controls in the Format Drawer work in one of two ways: Either click a font control to display a pop-up menu or click a button to immediately perform an action. Opening the Font Size pop-up menu, for example, displays a range of sizes for the selected text. With a single click of the B (bold) button, add the bold attribute to the highlighted characters. To create bullets and lists, click the Text tab at the top of the Format Drawer.

- ✔ **The Format menu:** The controls on the Keynote Format menu generally mirror those in the Format Drawer. To change the alignment from the Format menu, click Format and hover the cursor over the Text menu item. To change text attributes, click Format and hover your mouse over the Font menu.

Using Presenter's Notes in Your Project

As I mention earlier, you can type presenter's text notes in the Notes pane. I use them for displaying related topic points while presenting my slideshow. However, you can also print the notes for a project along with the slides, so presenter's notes are also great for including reminders and To Do points for your audience in handouts.

To type your notes, just click within the Notes pane; if that pane is hidden, choose View➪Show Presenter Notes, or click the View button at the far left of the Keynote toolbar and choose Show Presenter Notes. When you're done adding notes, click in the Slides list or the Layout pane to return to editing mode.

To display your notes while practicing, use the Keynote Rehearsal feature. Click the Play menu at the top of the Keynote window, choose Rehearse Slideshow, click the Tools icon at the top right, and select the Presenter Notes check box to enable it. Now you can scroll through the notes while the slideshow runs! (More on slideshows in a second.)

Every Good Presentation Needs Media

Adding audio, photos, and movies to a slide is drag-and-drop easy in Keynote! Simply drag an image, an audio, or a movie file from a Finder window and place it at the spot you want within your document.

You can also use the Media Browser. To do so, click the Media button on the toolbar and then click the Photos, Music, or Movies tab to select the desired type. Keynote displays the contents of your various media collections (such as your iPhoto and iTunes libraries). When you find the file you want to add, drag it to the spot you want in the document. Figure 19-4 illustrates the Media Browser in action.

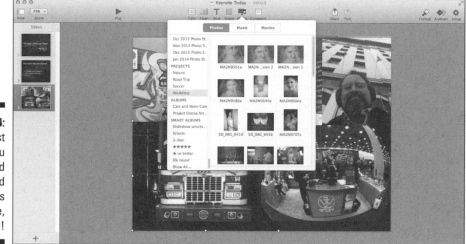

Figure 19-4: It's not just photos. You can add audio and movie clips to a slide, too!

Adding a Background Shape

Text often stands out on a slide when it sits on top of a background shape. To add a shape (such as a rectangle or circle) as a background for your text, follow these steps:

1. **Click the insertion cursor in the location you want.**

2. **Click the Shape button on the Keynote toolbar and choose a shape.**

   The shape appears in your document.

3. **Click the center of the shape and drag it to a new spot.**

   As with image boxes, you can resize or move shapes. Earlier in this chapter, read about how to do just that.

4. **When the shape is properly positioned and sized, select it and choose Arrange⇨Send to Back.**

   You want to "send the shape to the back" so that any text you enter sits in front of the shape — not hidden behind it.

Of course, you're not limited to creating shapes and graphics within Keynote; consider using applications like Adobe Photoshop or Illustrator to create graphics that you can import into your slides! As I mention earlier, you can easily drag and drop your new graphic into a slide from a Finder window.

Creating Your Keynote Slideshow

The heart of a Keynote presentation is the slideshow that you build from the slides you've created. A Keynote slideshow is typically presented as a full-screen presentation, with slides appearing in linear order as they are sorted in the Slides list.

You run a Keynote slideshow simply by clicking the Play button on the toolbar or by choosing Play⇨Play Slideshow from the menu. You can advance to the next slide by clicking, or by pressing the right bracket key, which looks like this:].

Of course, other controls are available besides just the ones that advance to the next slide! Table 19-1 illustrates the key shortcuts you'll use most often during a slideshow.

Table 19-1	Keynote Slideshow Shortcut Keys
Key	*Action*
] (right bracket)	Next slide
[(left bracket)	Previous slide
Home	Jump to first slide
End	Jump to last slide
C	Show or hide the pointer
(*number*)	Jump to the corresponding slide in the Slides list
U	Scroll notes up
D	Scroll notes down
N	Show current slide number
H	Hide slideshow and display last application used (the presentation appears as a minimized icon on the Dock)
B	Pause slideshow and display a black screen (press any key to resume the slideshow)
Esc	Quit

Keynote offers a number of settings that you can tweak to fine-tune your slide-show. To display these settings, choose Keynote➪Preferences and click the Slideshow button in the Preferences window.

If you have an iPhone, iPad, or iPod touch handy and you've installed the iOS version of Keynote on your device, display the Preferences window and click the Remote tab to link your device to your iMac and Keynote. Now you can use your handheld device as a remote and use it during your slideshow!

Printing Your Slides and Notes

Okay, I'll be honest: I don't always print handouts for every presentation I give. However, if you're presenting a lengthy slideshow with plenty of information that you'd like your audience to remember or refer to later, nothing beats handouts that include scaled-down images of your slides (and, optionally, your presenter's notes).

You're not limited to just paper, though! You can also use Keynote to create an electronic PDF (portable document format) file instead of a printed hand-out, which your audience members can download from your website. Or, if you're an educator with access to an interactive whiteboard (such as a SMART Board), you can use this new technology with Keynote.

To print your slides and notes, follow these steps:

1. **Within Keynote, choose File➪Print or press ⌘+P.**

   Keynote displays the Print sheet that you see in Figure 19-5. (Note that some printer-specific features may be different on your screen.)

2. **Click the desired format; each format displays a different set of Layout options.**

   - *Slide:* Print each slide on a separate page at full size. You can option-ally choose to print the presenter notes for each slide as well.

   - *Grid:* Print multiple slides on a page at a reduced size. From the Slides per Page pop-up menu, specify the number of slides that Keynote should print on each page.

   - *Handout:* Print a handout with multiple slides per page (and, option-ally, with presenter's notes). Again, you can choose how many slides will appear on each page.

   - *Outline:* Print the contents of your Slides list in Outline view.

3. **Select the pages to print.**

   • *To print the entire document,* select the All radio button.

   • *To print a range of selected slides,* select the From radio button and then enter the starting and ending pages.

4. **Select or deselect additional options from the Options section.**

5. **Click the Print button to send the job to your printer.**

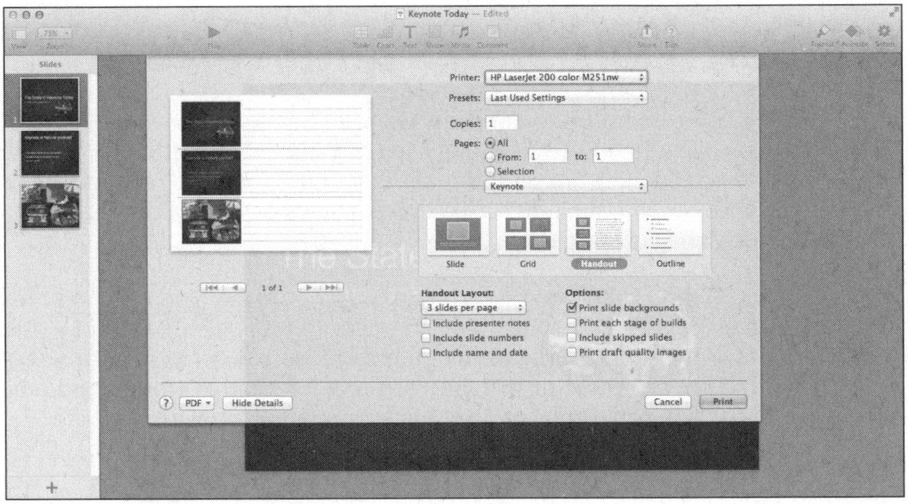

Figure 19-5:
Keynote
offers a
wide range
of printing
options for
your slides
and notes.

You can also send a copy of your finished presentation as an attachment within Mail or Messages — or, if the presentation is saved to your iCloud folder, you can provide others with a web link through Twitter or Facebook. I invite you to click the Share button on the toolbar to explore your sharing options. Note that sharing a link for viewing a presentation is different from sending an actual copy of the Keynote document. For example, if your recipient will need to edit your presentation, you should send a copy rather than a link.

Chapter 20

Creating a Multiuser iMac

- -

In This Chapter

▶ Enjoying the advantages of a multiuser iMac

▶ Understanding access levels

▶ Adding, editing, and deleting user accounts

▶ Restricting access for managed accounts

▶ Configuring your login window

▶ Sharing files with other users

▶ Securing your stuff with FileVault

- -

*E*verybody wants a piece. (Of your iMac, that is.)

Perhaps you live in a busy household with kids, significant others, grandparents, and a wide selection of friends — all of them clamoring for a chance to spend time on the Internet, take care of homework, or enjoy a good game.

On the other hand, your iMac might occupy a classroom or a break room at your office — someplace public, yet everyone wants his own Private iDaho on the iMac, complete with a reserved spot on the hard drive and his own hand-picked attractive Desktop background.

Before you throw your hands up in the air in defeat, read this chapter and take heart! Here you find all the step-by-step procedures, explanations, and tips to help you build a *safe* multiuser iMac that's accessible to all.

(Oh, and you still get to use it, too. That's not being selfish.)

Once Upon a Time (An Access Fairy Tale)

Okay, so you don't have Cinderella, Snow White, or that porridge-loving kid with the trespassing problem. Instead, you have your brother, Bob.

Every time Bob visits your place, it seems he needs to do "something" on the Internet, or he needs a moment with your iMac to bang out a quick message, using his web-based e-mail application. Unfortunately, Bob's forays onto your iMac always result in stuff getting changed, like your Desktop settings, Contacts database, and Safari bookmarks.

What you need, good reader, is a visit from the Account Fairy. Your problem is that you have but a single user account on your system, and Mavericks thinks that Bob is *you*. By turning your iMac into a multiuser system and giving Bob his own account, though, Mavericks can tell the difference between the two of you — keeping your druthers separate!

With a unique user account, Mavericks can track all sorts of things for Bob, leaving *your* computing environment blissfully pristine. A user account keeps track of stuff such as

- ✔ Contacts entries
- ✔ Safari bookmarks and settings (sigh)
- ✔ Desktop settings, including background images, screen resolutions, and Finder tweaks
- ✔ iTunes libraries, just in case Bob brings his own music (resigned sigh)

Plus, Bob gets his own reserved Home folder on your iMac's hard drive, so he'll quit complaining about how he can't find his files. Oh, and did I mention how user accounts keep others from accessing *your* stuff? And how you can lock Bob out of where-he-should-not-be, such as certain applications, Messages, Mail, and websites (including that offshore Internet-casino site that he's hooked on)?

Naturally, this is only the tip of the iceberg. User accounts affect just about everything you can do in Mavericks and on your iMac. The moral of my little tale? A Mark's Maxim to the rescue:

Assign others their own user accounts, and let Mavericks keep track of everything. Then you can share your iMac with others and still live happily ever after!

Big-Shot Administrator Stuff

Get one thing straight right off the bat: *You* are the administrator of your iMac. In network-speak, an *administrator* (or *admin* for short) is the one with the power to Do Unto Others — creating new accounts, deciding who gets access to what, and generally running the multiuser show. In other words, think of yourself as the Monarch of OS X (the ruler, not the butterfly).

I always recommend that you have only one (or perhaps two) accounts with administrator-level access on any computer. This makes good sense because you can be assured that no one can monkey with your iMac while you're away from the keyboard. So why might you want a second admin account? Well, if you're often away on business, you might need to assign a second administrator account to a *trusted* individual who knows as much about your iMac as you do. (Tell 'em to buy a copy of this book.) That way, if something breaks or an account needs to be tweaked in some way, the other person can take care of it whilst you're gone (but without giving that person access to your personal data).

In this section, I explain the typical duties of a first-class iMac administrator.

Deciding who needs what access

The three most common levels of individual user accounts offered by Mavericks are

- ✔ **Admin (administrator):** See the beginning of this section.
- ✔ **Standard level:** Perfect for most users, these accounts allow access to just about everything but don't let the user make drastic changes to Mavericks or create new accounts.
- ✔ **Managed with Parental Controls level:** These are standard accounts with specific limits that are assigned either by you or by another admin account.

Another Mark's Maxim is in order:

Assign other folks standard-level accounts and then decide whether each new account needs to be modified to restrict access as a managed account. *Never assign an account admin-level access unless you deem it truly necessary.*

Standard accounts are quick and easy to set up, and I think they provide the perfect compromise between access and security. You'll find that standard access allows your users to do just about anything they need to do, with a minimum of hassle.

Managed accounts (with Parental Controls) are highly configurable, so you can make sure that your kids don't end up trashing the hard drive, sending junk mail, or engaging in unmonitored chatting. (*Note:* Parents, teachers, and those folks designing a single public access account for a library or organization — this means *you.*)

Mavericks also provides Group and Sharing Only accounts, but I generally recommend that you shy away from these highly specialized levels. Stick with the Big Three levels to ensure that everyone has the proper access to your iMac.

Working with the Guest account

The *Guest* account is a convenient method of granting someone temporary access to your Mac — in fact, your guest doesn't even need a password to log in! Your Guest account has all the attributes of a standard account, so the visitor has little chance of accidentally (or purposefully) damaging your system. However, after the guest user logs out, the Guest account is "flushed," and the data and files that person created using the account are deleted automatically. This feature allows the next guest to start with a clean slate. (Note that files saved to an external drive and files saved to the Shared folder by the Guest account will remain after the user logs out.)

By default, the Guest account is disabled. To turn on this feature, open System Preferences, click Users & Groups, and then click the Guest User entry in the list. (You may have to click the Lock icon in the lower-left corner of the Users & Groups pane and provide your admin password before you can continue.) Select the Allow Guests to Log In to This Computer check box.

Oh, and don't forget that you can enable specific Parental Controls for the Guest account, just as you can for any other account. That should come in handy if your daughter has a slumber party coming up this weekend. . . .

Adding users

All right, Mark, enough pregame jabbering — show this good reader how to set up new accounts! Your iMac already has one admin-level account set up for you (created during the initial Mavericks setup process), and you need to be logged in with that account to add a user. To add a new account, follow these steps:

1. **Click the System Preferences icon on the Dock and then click the Users & Groups icon to display the pane that you see in Figure 20-1.**

2. **Click the New User button — the one with the plus sign at the bottom of the accounts list, under the Login Options button — to display the New User sheet shown in Figure 20-2.**

If your New User button is grayed out, your Users & Groups pane is locked. Remember that you can toggle the padlock icon at the lower-left corner of most of the panes in System Preferences to lock or allow changes. To gain access, do the following:

   a. *Click the padlock icon to make changes to the Users & Groups pane.*

   b. *When Mavericks prompts you for your admin account password (the account you're currently using), enter it.*

   c. *Click Unlock.*

   Now you can click the New User button.

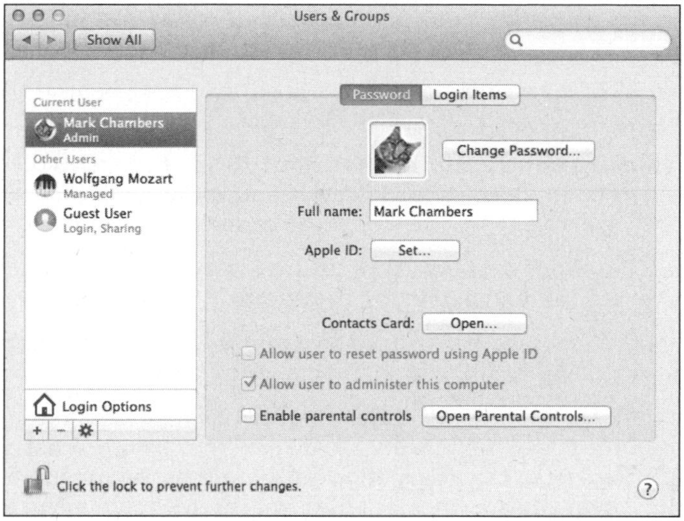

Figure 20-1: Add new user accounts here.

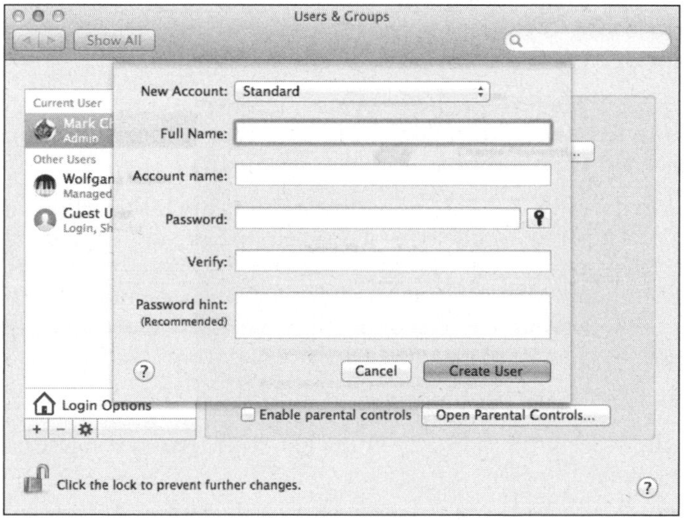

Figure 20-2: Fill out those fields, and you have a new user.

3. **From the New Account pop-up menu, specify the account level status.**

   Choose Administrator, Standard, or Managed with Parental Controls.

   WARNING!

   You should have only one or two administrator-level users, and your account is already an admin account.

4. **Type the name that you want to display for this account in the Full Name text box and then press Tab to move to the next field.**

Mavericks displays this name on the Login screen, so behave! (For example, "Bob" has only one "o" the last time I checked.)

5. **(Optional) Although Mavericks automatically generates the user's *account name* (for use in Messages, and for naming the user's Home folder), you can type a new one. (No spaces, please.) Press Tab again.**

6. **In the Password text box, type the password for the new account and then press Tab to move to the next field.**

Generally, I recommend using a password of at least six characters, using a mixture of alphabetic and numeric characters.

Run out of password ideas? No problem! Click the key button (to the right of the Password text box) to display the Password Assistant, from which Mavericks can automatically generate password suggestions of the length you specify. Click the Suggestion pop-up menu or type directly into the field, and Mavericks automatically adds the password you generated into the Password field.

7. **In the Verify text box, retype the password you chose and press Tab again to continue your quest.**

8. **(Optional) Mavericks can provide a password hint after three unsuccessful login attempts. To offer a hint, type a short question in the Password Hint text box.**

From a security standpoint, password hints are taboo. (Personally, I **never** use 'em. If someone is having a problem logging in to a computer I administer, you better believe I want to know *why.*) Therefore, despite the recommendation Mavericks shows here, I strongly recommend that you skip this field. But and if you *do* offer a hint, **keep it vague!** Avoid hints like "Your password is the name of the Wookie in *Star Wars.*" *Geez.*

9. **Click the Create User button.**

The new account shows up in the list at the left of the Users & Groups pane.

Each user's Home folder has the same default subfolders, including Movies, Music, Pictures, Sites, and such. A user can create new subfolders within his Home folder at any time.

Here's one more neat fact about a user's Home folder: No matter what the account level, most of the contents of a Home folder can't be viewed by other users. (Yes, that includes admin-level users. This way, everyone using your iMac gets her own little area of privacy.) Within the Home folder, only the Sites and Public folders can be accessed by other users from within a Finder window — and only in a limited fashion. More on the Sites and Public folders later in this chapter.

Modifying user accounts

Next, consider the basic modifications that you can make to a user account, such as changing existing information or selecting a new picture to represent that user's unique personality.

To edit an existing account, log in with your admin account, display the System Preferences window, and click Users & Groups to display the account list. Then follow these steps:

1. **Click the account that you want to change.**

   Don't forget to unlock the Users & Groups pane if necessary. See the earlier section "Adding users" to read how.

2. **Edit the settings that you need to change.**

   For example, you can reset the user's password, or (if absolutely necessary) upgrade the account to admin level.

3. **Click the Picture well and then click a thumbnail image to represent this user (as shown in Figure 20-3).**

   An easy way to get an image is to use one from your hard drive by simply dragging a new image from a Finder window into the Picture well. Click iCloud to choose an image from your Photo Stream, or click Faces to pick one of the faces that you've tagged within iPhoto. Alternatively, you can click Camera and then click the Snapshot button — which bears a tiny camera — to grab a picture from your iMac's FaceTime HD video camera. After you capture the essence of your subject as a photo, click Done to return to the Users & Groups pane.

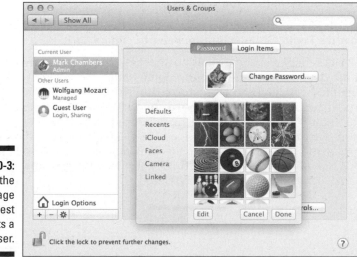

Figure 20-3: Pick the image that best represents a user.

Using the default login settings, Mavericks displays this image in the Login list next to the account name.

4. **When everything is correct, press ⌘+Q to close the System Preferences dialog.**

You don't need to save your changes (as a separate step) within System Preferences. Mavericks does that automatically when you close the System Preferences window.

Standard-level users have some control over their accounts — they're not helpless, ya know. Standard users can log in, open System Preferences, and click Users & Groups to change the account password or picture, as well as the Contacts Card assigned to them in the Mavericks Contacts application and the Apple ID associated with their account. All standard users can also set up Login Items, which I cover later in this chapter. Note, however, that managed users might not have access to System Preferences at all, so they can't make changes. (Read about this in the upcoming section "Managing access settings for an account.")

I banish thee, Mischievous User!

Not all user accounts last forever. Students graduate, co-workers quit, kids move out of the house (at last!), and Bob might even find a significant other who has a faster cable modem. We can only hope.

Anyway, no matter what the reason, you can delete a user account at any time. Log in with your admin account, display the Users & Groups pane in System Preferences, and then follow these steps to eradicate an account:

1. **Click the account that you want to delete.**

2. **Click the Delete User button (which bears the Minus Sign of Doom, below the Login Options button; refer to Figure 20-1).**

Mavericks displays a confirmation sheet, as shown in Figure 20-4. By default, the contents of the user's Home folder are saved in a disk image file — which you can restore with Disk Utility — in the Deleted Users folder. This safety option is a good idea if the user might return in the future, allowing you to retrieve her old stuff. However, this option is available only if you have enough space on your hard drive to create the Home folder image file. You can also choose to leave the user's Home folder as-is (but naturally you won't regain any space, even though the user account is deleted).

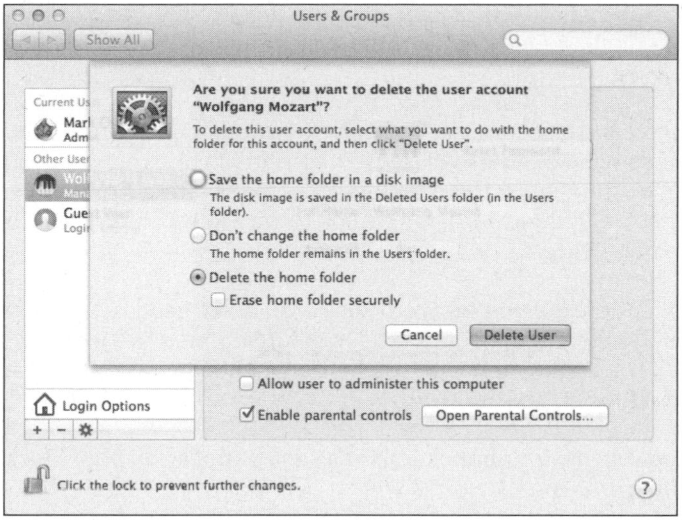

Figure 20-4:
This is your
last chance
to save the
stuff from a
deleted user
account.

3. **To clean up completely (and reclaim the hard drive space that the user's Home folder is taking up), select the Delete the Home Folder radio button and then click the Delete User button.**

   Mavericks wipes everything connected with the user account off your hard drive.

4. **Press ⌘+Q to close the System Preferences dialog.**

Time once again for a Mark's Maxim:

Always **delete unnecessary user accounts. Otherwise, you're leaving holes in your iMac's security — and eating up disk space.**

Setting up Login Items and Parental Controls

Every account on your iMac can be customized. Understandably, some settings are accessible only to admin-level accounts, and others can be adjusted by standard-level accounts. In this section, I introduce you to the things that can be enabled (or disabled) within a user account.

Automating with Login Items

Login Items are applications or documents that can be set to launch or load automatically as soon as a specific user logs in — for example, Apple

Mail or Contacts. In fact, a user must be logged in to add or remove Login Items. Even an admin-level account can't change the Login Items for another user.

A user must have access to the Users & Groups pane within the System Preferences window in order to use Login Items. As you can read in the following section, a user can be locked out of System Preferences, which makes it more difficult for Login Items to be added or deleted for that account. (Go figure.)

If an application appears on your Dock, you don't need to follow the upcoming steps to add that application to your Login Items list; instead, simply right-click the application icon on the Dock, choose the Options submenu, and then choose Open at Login.

To set Login Items for applications that *don't* appear on your Dock, follow these steps:

1. **Click the System Preferences icon on the Dock and then click the Users & Groups icon.**

2. **Click the Login Items tab to display the settings that you see in Figure 20-5.**

   It bears repeating: You can change the Login Items for only the account that's currently logged in, so make sure to select the Current User account in the list at the left.

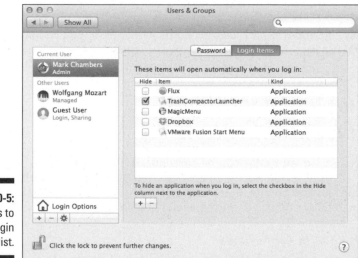

Figure 20-5: Add apps to your Login Items list.

3. **Click the Add button (with the plus sign) to display a file selection sheet.**

4. **Navigate to the application you want to launch each time you log in, click it to select it, and then click Add.**

   If you're in the mood to drag and drop, just drag the applications you want to add from a Finder window and drop them directly into the list.

5. **Press ⌘+Q to quit System Preferences and save your changes.**

Login Items are launched in the order that they appear in the list, so feel free to drag the items into any order you like.

Managing access settings for an account

A standard-level account with restrictions is called a *managed* account. (You can read about these accounts earlier in this chapter.) With these accounts, you can restrict access to many different places within Mavericks and your iMac's applications via Parental Controls. (Naturally, admin-level accounts don't need Parental Controls because an admin account has no restrictions.)

In short, Parental Controls come in handy in preventing users — family members, students, co-workers, friends, or the public at large — from damaging your computer, your software, or Mavericks itself and also from accessing inappropriate material on the Internet (or even just using your iMac after bedtime). If an account has been restricted with Parental Controls, the account description changes from Standard to Managed in the Accounts list.

To display the Parental Controls for a standard account, start here:

1. **Log in with an admin-level account.**

2. **Open System Preferences and then click Users & Groups.**

3. **Click the Standard account in the list and then select the Enable Parental Controls check box.**

Now click the Open Parental Controls button to display the specific category tabs that you see in Figure 20-6:

✔ **Apps:** These settings (which I discuss in more detail in a second) affect what the user can do within Mavericks as well as what the Finder itself looks like to that user.

Mavericks keeps a number of different types of *text log files* (which track where the user goes on the Internet, which applications are launched by the account, and the contents of any Messages conversations in which the user was a participant). To view these logs from any of the tabs, click the Logs button at the bottom of the pane. From this single sheet, you can monitor all the logs for a particular account and track Internet activity for any managed user.

✔ **Web:** These settings control the Safari application. Mavericks offers three levels of control for websites:

- *Allow Unrestricted Access to Websites:* Select this radio button to allow unfettered access for this user.

- *Try to Limit Access to Adult Websites Automatically:* You can allow Safari to automatically block websites that it deems "adult." To specify particular sites that Safari should allow or deny, click the Customize button.

- *Allow Access to Only These Websites:* Select this radio button to specify which websites the user can view. To add a website, click the Add button (which bears a plus sign); Mavericks then prompts you for a title and the website address.

✔ **People:** Select the Limit Mail and the Limit Messages check boxes to specify the e-mail and instant messaging (IM) addresses that this user can communicate with. To add an address that the user can e-mail or chat with, click the Add button. You can also specify whether the user can join multiplayer games or add friends in Game Center.

Figure 20-6:
You don't have to be a parent to assign Parental Controls!

If you want a notification if the user is attempting to send an e-mail to someone not in the list, select the Send Requests To check box to enable it and then type your e-mail address in the text box.

✔ **Time Limits:** Parents, click the Time Limits tab, and you'll shout with pure joy! You can limit an account to a certain number of hours of usage per weekday (Weekday Time Limits), limit to a specified number of hours of usage per weekend day (Weekend Time Limits), and set a bedtime computer curfew time for both school nights (Sunday through Thursday) and weekend days.

✔ **Other:** As you might expect from the name, this tab offers a number of important restrictions that don't fall into one of the other four categories.

- *Disable Built-in Camera:* Specify whether the account has access to your iMac's built-in camera. (Note that an external USB Web camera isn't affected by this setting.)

- *Disable Dictation:* Enable this check box to turn off the Dictation feature in Mavericks.

- *Hide Profanity in Dictionary:* If you prefer that profane terms be hidden within the Dictionary for this user, select the Hide Profanity in Dictionary check box.

- *Limit Printer Administration:* With this check box enabled, the user can print to the default printer and switch to other assigned printers, but can't change printer settings, add a printer, or delete a printer.

- *Disable Changing the Password:* Enable this check box to prevent the user from changing her account password.

- *Limit CD and DVD Burning:* Enable this check box to prevent the user from recording CDs or DVDs via the built-in disc recording features in OS X. (Note, however, that if you load a third-party recording program, such as Roxio Toast, the user can still record discs with it, so you probably want to disallow Toast access for the user in question from the App category.)

If you're creating a single standard-level account for an entire group of people to use — for example, if you want to leave the machine in kiosk mode in one corner of the office, or if everyone in a classroom will use the same account on the machine — I recommend disabling the ability to change the account password. (Oh, and please do me a favor and promise me you *won't* create a system with just one admin-level account that everyone is supposed to use! Instead, keep your one admin-level account close to your bosom and create a standard-level account for the Unwashed Horde.)

You can always tell whether an account has been assigned Parental Controls because the account description changes from Standard to Managed in the Accounts list.

Of particular importance are the Apps controls. Click the Apps tab to modify these settings:

✔ **Use Simple Finder:** The Simple Finder is a great idea for families and classrooms with smaller children. For the ultimate in restrictive Mavericks environments — think public access or kiosk mode — you can assign the Simple Finder to an account. Even the Dock itself is restricted, sporting only the Finder icon, Trash, the Dashboard, and those folders that allow users to access their documents and applications.

✔ **Limit Applications:** When this option is enabled, you can select the specific applications that appear to the user. These restrictions are in effect whether the user has access to the full Finder or just the Simple Finder. You can also choose whether to allow access to apps downloaded from the App Store by age group; open the Allow App Store Apps pop-up menu to specify a maximum age.

  • *To allow access to all the applications of a specific type:* Select the check box next to the desired group heading to enable it. This includes App Store applications, Other Apps, Widgets, and Utilities.

  • *To restrict access to all applications within a group:* If a group heading check box is enabled and you want to deny access to all the applications in that group, click the check box next to the heading to disable it.

  • *To toggle restriction on and off for specific applications within these groups:* Click the triangle icon next to each group heading to expand its list and then either select or deselect the check box next to the desired applications. Mavericks denotes partial access within a group — a mixture of full and restricted applications — with a dash mark in the group heading check box.

  To locate a specific application, click in the Search box and type the application name.

  • *To add a new application to the Allowed Apps list:* Drag its icon from the Finder and drop it in the list within the Other Apps group. After you add an application, it appears in the Other Apps group, and you can toggle access to it on and off as you can with the applications in the named groups.

✔ **Prevent the Dock from Being Modified:** If you select this check box, the user can't add or remove applications, documents, and folders from the Dock in the full Finder.

Multiuser Rules for Everyone

After you're hip on user accounts and the changes you can make to them, turn to a number of topics that affect all users of your iMac — things like how they log in, how a user can share information with everyone else on the computer, and how each user account can be protected from unscrupulous outsiders with state-of-the-art encryption. (Suddenly you're James Bond! I told you Mavericks would open new doors for you.)

Logging on and off in Mavericks For Dummies

Hey, how about the login screen itself? How do your users identify themselves? Time for another of my "Shortest books in the *For Dummies* series" special editions. (The title's practically longer than the entire book.)

Mavericks offers four methods of logging folks in to your multiuser iMac:

- **The username and password login:** This is the most secure type of login screen you'll see in Mavericks because you have to actually type your account username and your password. (A typical hacker isn't going to know all the usernames on your iMac.) Press Return or click the Log In button to compete the process.

  When you enter your username and password, you see bullets instead of your password because Mavericks displays bullet characters to ensure security. Otherwise, someone could simply look over your shoulder as you type and see your password.

- **The list login:** This login screen offers a good midpoint between security and convenience. Click your account username in the list and type your password when the login screen displays the password prompt. Press Return or click the Log In button to continue.

- **Fast User Switching:** This feature, as shown in Figure 20-7, allows another user to sit down and log in while the previous user's applications are still running in the background. This is perfect for a fast e-mail check or a scan of your eBay bids without forcing someone else completely off the iMac. By default, when you turn on Fast User Switching, Mavericks displays the currently active user's name at the right side of the Finder menu bar.

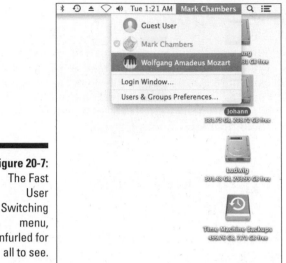

Figure 20-7:
The Fast
User
Switching
menu,
unfurled for
all to see.

To switch to another account, follow these steps:

a. *Click the current user's name in the Finder menu (see Figure 20-7) to display the Fast User Switching menu.*

b. *Click the name of the user who wants to log in.*

Mavericks displays the login window, just as if the iMac had been rebooted.

The previous user's stuff is still running, so you definitely shouldn't reboot or shut down the iMac!

To switch back to the previous user, follow these steps:

a. *Click the username again in the Finder menu.*

b. *Click the previous user's name from the Fast User Switching menu.*

For security, Mavericks prompts you for that account's login password.

✔ **Auto login:** This is the most convenient method of logging in but offers no security whatsoever. Mavericks automatically logs in the specified account when you start or reboot your iMac.

I *strongly* recommend that you use auto login only if

• Your iMac is in a secure location.

• You are the only one using your iMac.

• You're setting up a public-access iMac, in which case you want your iMac to immediately log in with the public account you've set up.

Working in a public environment? ***Never*** set an admin-level account as the auto login account. This is the very definition of ASDI, or *A Supremely Dumb Idea*.

To set up a username/password or list login, open System Preferences, click the Users & Groups icon, and then display the Login Options settings (see Figure 20-8). Select the List of Users radio button for a list login screen, or select the Name and Password radio button to require your users to type their full username and password.

To enable Fast User Switching, mark the Show Fast User Switching Menu As check box (as shown in Figure 20-8). You can specify whether the menu displays a user's full name (the default), a short name, or an account icon in the Finder menu bar.

To set Auto Login, choose the account that Mavericks should use from the Automatic Login pop-up menu (as shown by the now-legendary Figure 20-8).

Figure 20-8: Configure your login settings from the Login Options pane.

Logging out of Mavericks all the way (without Fast User Switching) is a cinch. Just click the Apple menu (🍎) and then choose Log Out. (From the keyboard, press ⌘+Shift+Q.) A confirmation dialog appears that will automatically log you off in one minute — but don't forget that if someone walks up and clicks Cancel, he'll be using your iMac with your account! You can bypass the confirmation dialog by pressing Option while choosing Log Out (or combining it with the keyboard shortcut). Your iMac returns to the login screen, ready for its next victim. Heed this Mark's Maxim:

Always **click the Log Out button on the logout confirmation dialog before you leave your iMac (or hold down the Option key while choosing Log Out from the menu or pressing the Logout keyboard shortcut).**

Interesting stuff about sharing stuff

You might wonder where shared documents and files reside on your iMac. That's a good question. Like just about everything in Mavericks, there's a simple answer. The Users folder on your iMac has a *Shared* folder within it. To share a file or folder, you should place it in the Shared folder.

You don't have to turn on File Sharing in the Sharing pane of System Preferences to use Shared folders on your iMac. Personal File Sharing affects only network access to your machine by users of other computers.

Each user account on your iMac also has a *Public* folder within that user's Home folder. This is a read-only folder that other users on your iMac (and across the network) can access: They can only open and copy the files that it contains. (Sorry, no changes to existing documents from other users, or new documents from other users.) Every user's Public folder contains a *Drop Box* folder, where other users can copy or save files but can't view the contents. Think of the Drop Box as a mailbox where you drop off stuff for the other user.

Encrypting your hard drive can be fun

Storing sensitive information and documents on your iMac always incurs a risk. Although your login password should ensure that your data is off limits to everyone else, consider an extra level of security to prevent even a dedicated hacker from accessing your stuff — *especially* if you're sharing your iMac computer in a multiuser environment. (In other words, consider a little more protection than just user permissions for those all-important Fantasy Football formations that you'll unleash next season.)

To offer that extra level of security, Mavericks includes *FileVault,* which provides disk encryption that prevents just about anyone except the CIA or FBI from gaining access to the files on your hard drive. (You'll notice that things slow down just a bit when you're logging in and out or working with files that are several gigabytes in size, but for those of us who need the peace of mind, this minimal performance hit is worth it.) You can enable the FileVault feature from the Security & Privacy pane in System Preferences.

Two passwords control access to your hard drive when FileVault is active, and without them, the data contained on your hard drive is impossible for just about anyone to read:

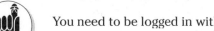

✔ **Your login password:** The nice thing about FileVault is that it's completely invisible to you and your users. In other words, when you log in, Mavericks automatically takes care of decrypting and encrypting the stuff on your drive for you. You literally won't know that FileVault is working for you — which is how computers are *supposed* to work.

✔ **The Recovery Key:** This code can be used by an admin-level user to unlock your drive if you forget your login password. Mavericks provides you with this key when you turn on the FileVault feature. **I highly recommend that you write down this key and store your copy in a safe place, away from your Mac**.

You need to be logged in with an admin-level account to turn on FileVault.

To turn on FileVault protection within Mavericks, follow these steps:

1. **Click the System Preferences icon on the Dock and then click the Security & Privacy icon.**

2. **Click the FileVault button.**

3. **Click the Turn on FileVault button.**

   Mavericks displays a sheet that lists all the user accounts on your iMac. Naturally, given that you're logged in, Mavericks has already confirmed your account. However, in order for *other* users to access your hard drive after FileVault is running, each user account must be separately enabled. (If an account is not enabled, that person can no longer access anything on the hard drive after it has been encrypted.)

4. **Click the Enable User button for each account on your system and enter that user's account password.**

   Mavericks displays a sheet prompting you to type the user's account password. After a user is enabled, she gets a cheery green check mark in the list.

5. **When all users have been enabled, click Continue.**

6. **Write down the Recovery Key and store the copy in a safe location; then click Continue.**

   You can also take a snapshot of your screen while the Recovery Key is displayed and then print that image separately. Doing so is A Good Idea because it helps prevent errors while copying that excruciatingly long Recovery Key by hand. To take a snapshot image of the screen, press ⌘+Shift+3. (The image file appears on your Desktop.)

7. **After Mavericks encrypts your hard drive and logs you out, log in again normally.**

   You're done — and far more secure!

Again, do not forget your account login password, and make doggone sure that your admin user never forgets the Recovery Key! If you forget these passwords, you can't read anything on your hard drive, and even the smartest Apple support technician will tell you that nothing can be done.

Chapter 21

Building (Or Joining) a Network

*I*n my book, network access ranks right up there with air conditioning and the microwave oven. As with other "I can't imagine life without them" kinds of technologies, it's hard to imagine sharing data from your iMac with others around you without a network. Sure, I guess you could still create a *sneakernet* (the old-fashioned term for running back and forth between computers with a floppy disk), but these days, Apple computers don't even *have* floppy drives. (Even with a USB flash drive, a sneakernet is still a hassle.)

Whether you use your network to share an Internet connection, challenge your friends to a nice relaxing game of World War II battlefield action, or stream your MP3 collection to other computers that use iTunes, you'll wonder how you ever got along without one. In this chapter, I fill you in on all the details you need to know to get your iMac hooked up to a new (or an existing) network.

What, Exactly, Is the Network Advantage?

If you have other family members with computers or if your iMac is in an office with other computers (including those rascally PCs), here's just a sample of what you can do with a network connection:

✔ **Share an Internet connection.** This is *the* major reason that many families and most small businesses install a network. Everyone can simultaneously use the same digital subscriber line (DSL) or cable Internet connection on every computer on the network, while easily communicating and sharing files with each other at the same time.

✔ **Share a printer.** You say your fellow employee — or even worse, your big sister — has a great printer connected to her computer? Luckily, that printer can be shared with anyone across your network.

✔ **Copy and move files of all sizes.** Need to get a large iMovie project from one Mac to another? With a network connection, you can accomplish this task in just seconds. Otherwise, you'd have to burn that file to a DVD-R or use a flash drive. A network connection makes copying as simple as dragging the project folder from one Finder window to another.

✔ **Share documents across your network.** Talk about a wonderful collaboration tool. For example, you can drop a Microsoft Word document or Keynote presentation file into your Public folder and ask for comments and edits from others in your office.

✔ **Stream music and video.** With iTunes, you can share your audio and video media collection on your iMac with other Macs and PCs on your network. Your eyes and ears can't tell the difference!

✔ **Play multiplayer games.** Invite your friends over and tell 'em that you're hosting a *LAN party* — that's the techno-nerd term for a large gathering of game players, connected through the same network, all playing the same multiplayer game. (Suddenly you'll see firsthand just how devious a human opponent can be.) Each participant needs to buy a copy of the same game, naturally, but the fun you'll have is worth every cent you spend. Don't forget the chips!

If your iMac isn't within shouting distance of an existing network or you don't plan on buying any additional computers, stop right here — a lone iMac hanging out in your home with no other computers around probably won't need a network.

If you have just your iMac and an Internet connection and you have no plans to add another computer or a shared printer, a network isn't necessary.

The Great Debate: Wired versus Wireless

After you decide that you indeed need a network for your home or office, you have another decision to make: Should you install a *wired* network (running cables between your computers) or a *wireless* network? Heck, should you throw caution completely to the wind and build a combination network with both wireless and wired hardware?

Your first instinct is probably to choose a wireless network for convenience. After all, this option allows you to eliminate running cables behind furniture (or in the ceiling of your office building). Ah, but I must show you the advantages to a wired network as well. Table 21-1 shows the lowdown to help you make up your mind.

Table 21-1	Network Decision Making	
Factor	*Wireless Networks*	*Wired Networks*
Speed	Moderate	Much faster
Security	Moderate	Better
Convenience	Better	Worse
Compatibility	Confusing standards	Easier to understand
Cables	Few (or none)	Required

As I call it, here are the advantages of choosing a wired or a wireless network setup:

✔ **Wired:** Using a wired network offers two significant perks over a wireless network:

   • *Faster speeds:* In general, wired networks that are compatible with your iMac are many times faster than the fastest 802.11n or 802.11ac wireless connections.

   The performance of a wireless connection can be compromised by interference (from impeding structures, such as concrete walls; and from household appliances, such as some wireless phones and microwave ovens) and by distance.

• *Better security:* A wired network doesn't broadcast a signal that can be picked up outside your home or office, so it's more secure.

Hackers can attack through your Internet connection. Always use a firewall. I subtly emphasize this point in the section "USE YOUR FIREWALL!" later in this chapter.

✔ **Wireless:** A wireless connection really has only one advantage, but it's a big one: *convenience* (which, in this case, is another word for *mobility* for all your networked devices).

Accessing your network anywhere within your home or office — without expensive cables — is so easy. You can also easily connect a wireless printer. And when you're using an AirPort Express mobile Base Station, even your home stereo can get connected to your MP3 collection on your iMac. Read more about Base Stations later on.

Sharing Internet Access

It's time to see what's necessary to share an Internet connection. In this section, I cover two methods of connecting your network to the Internet. (And before you open your wallet, keep in mind that you might be able to use your iMac to share your broadband connection across your network!)

Using your iMac as a sharing device

Figure 21-1 illustrates how you can use your iMac to provide a shared Internet connection across a simple wireless network, using either

✔ **A broadband DSL or cable connection**

✔ **A Mavericks-compatible external USB dialup modem**

I recommend sharing a dialup modem Internet connection *only* if you have no other option. A dialup modem connection really can't handle the data transfer speeds for more than one computer to access the Internet comfortably at one time. (In plain English, an external USB modem that you add to your iMac isn't fast enough for both you and your significant other to surf the web at the same time.) Sharing a dialup connection just isn't practical — and for many folks, even a single computer accessing the Internet over a dialup modem connection is far too slow.

In either configuration, your iMac uses the OS X Mavericks built-in Internet connection sharing feature to get the job done, *but your iMac must remain turned on to allow Internet sharing.* I show you how to do this in "Network Internet connections," later in this chapter.

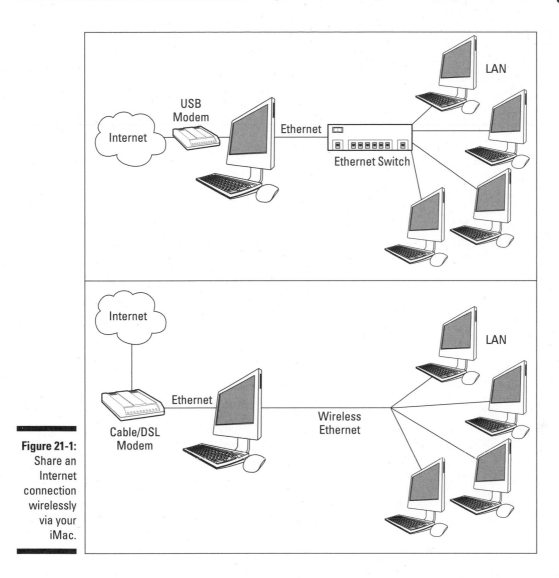

Figure 21-1:
Share an
Internet
connection
wirelessly
via your
iMac.

Using a dedicated Internet sharing device

Figure 21-2 illustrates how a broadband connection works if you use a dedicated Internet sharing device (often called an *Internet router*) to connect to your cable or DSL modem. You have to buy this additional hardware, but your iMac doesn't have to remain turned on just so that everyone can get on the Internet.

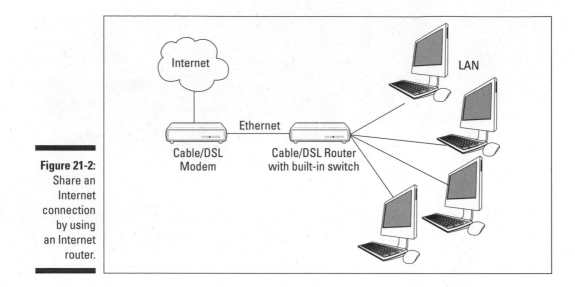

Figure 21-2:
Share an
Internet
connection
by using
an Internet
router.

Internet routers usually include either wired or wireless network connections — and many include both.

Setting up an Internet router is usually a pretty simple matter, but the configuration depends on the device manufacturer and usually involves a number of different settings in System Preferences that vary according to the model of router you're installing. Grab a diet cola, sit down with the router's manual, and follow the installation instructions you'll find there. (In some cases, you may need to set up your cable or DSL modem as a *bridge* between your ISP and your router, which should be covered in your modem and router manuals as well.)

Most Internet routers offer a DHCP (Dynamic Host Configuration Protocol) server, which automatically assigns Internet protocol (IP) addresses, and I *strongly* recommend that you turn on this feature!

What Do You Need to Connect?

Most *normal* folks — whom I define as those who have never met a network system administrator, and couldn't care less — think that connecting to a network probably involves all sorts of arcane chants and a mystical symbol or two. In this section, I provide you with the shopping list that you need to set up a network, or connect to a network that's already running.

Wireless connections

Today's iMacs come complete with built-in AirPort Extreme wireless hardware, so if you already have an AirPort Extreme or Express Base Station, you're set to go. Otherwise, hold on tight while I lead you through the hardware requirements for wireless networking. (Kinda ironic, don't you think?)

The maximum signal range — and effectiveness — of any wireless network can be impeded by intervening walls or by electrical devices, such as microwave ovens and some wireless phones, all of which can generate interference.

Connecting an iMac to an existing wireless network

Connecting an Intel iMac to an existing wireless network requires no extra hardware because your hardware is already built in. (Whew. That was easy!)

Using a base station to go wireless

If you decide that you want to build your own wireless network, you eschew cables, or you want to add wireless support to your existing wired network, you need a *base station*. The base station can act as a bridge between computers using wireless and your existing wired network. Such a wireless base station will have either

- ✔ A port that can connect to your existing wired network's switch

- ✔ A full built-in switch for wired connectivity (which means you can sell your old wired Ethernet switch to your sister in Tucson)

And, of course, a base station can simply act as a central switch for your wireless network (with no support for a wired network at all).

You can use either a cool Apple Base Station or a boring 802.11n or 802.11ac generic wireless base station; however, the Apple hardware requires less configuration and tweaking. (Sounds like a Mark's Maxim!)

If you don't want the hassle of tweaking PC hardware to accommodate your iMac, buy Apple hardware and software.

Apple Base Station models

As listed in Table 21-2, your iMac can work with three different Apple Base Station models for wireless networking:

- ✔ **AirPort Extreme**

   I recommend using AirPort Extreme if your network needs an enhanced antenna, which provides greater range. You can read about connectivity ranges in the upcoming Table 21-2. The Extreme is also a good pick if you need wired connectivity on your network.

✔ **AirPort Express**

I recommend using AirPort Express if you want to

- *Carry your wireless base station with you.* Express is much smaller than the other Apple Base Station models. (Think "party on the patio" or a LAN gaming get-together at a friend's house.)

- *Extend the range of an existing network.* Add an Express at the limit of your existing wireless network, and you can benefit from the additional range it provides.

- *Connect your home stereo for wireless music streaming.* You can use the AirPlay sharing feature in iTunes.

✔ **AirPort Time Capsule**

Apple's AirPort Time Capsule unit isn't just a wireless remote hard drive for use with the Time Machine backup feature that's built-in to Mavericks: It can also act as a full AirPort Extreme Base Station. In fact, the wireless specifications for an AirPort Time Capsule unit and an AirPort Extreme Base Station are almost identical.

The latest 802.11ac standard used by the AirPort Extreme and AirPort Time Capsule delivers a connection that's several times faster than the old AirPort Base Station's 802.11b/802.11g/802.11n standards. 802.11ac is also compatible with *all* the older standards — 802.11b/a/g/n — so I highly recommend that you stick with 802.11ac in the future. It plays well with others, and at warp speed, to boot!

Table 21-2	Apple Wireless Network Base Stations	
Feature	*AirPort Extreme/AirPort Time Capsule*	*AirPort Express*
Price	$199/$299	$99
Users (maximum)	50	50
802.11ac support	Yes	No
802.11n support	Yes	Yes
802.11g support	Yes	Yes
802.11b support	Yes	Yes
LAN Ethernet jack (high-speed Internet connection)	Yes	Yes
WAN Ethernet jack (wired computer network)	Yes	No
Stereo mini-jack	No	Yes
USB printer port	Yes	Yes

The names of the Apple Base Stations are irritatingly similar; Apple usually does a better job differentiating their product names. Jot down the name of your model on a sticky note and stick it on your iMac's Desktop just so that you don't get confused.

Installing an Apple Base Station is simple:

1. **If you have a DSL or cable modem, connect it to the Ethernet LAN port on the Base Station with an Ethernet cable.**

2. **If you have an existing wired Ethernet computer network using a switch or router, connect it to the WAN (wide area network) port on the Base Station with an Ethernet cable.**

   Only the AirPort Extreme and AirPort Time Capsule stations have a WAN port.

3. **If you have a USB printer, connect it to the USB port on the Base Station.**

   I cover the steps to share a printer in the upcoming section "Sharing a network printer."

4. **Connect the power cable.**

5. **Switch on your Base Station.**

6. **Run the installation software provided by Apple on your iMac.**

Using non-Apple base stations

If any company other than Apple manufactured your wireless base station, the installation procedure is almost certainly the same. (Naturally, you should take a gander at the manufacturer's installation guide just to make sure, but I have added many different brands of these devices in the past using essentially the same steps for each one.)

However, I should note that Apple wireless hardware uses a slightly different security encryption standard than most PC wireless hardware, which results in an extra hurdle when connecting to a non-Apple base station with your iMac. (More on this in the next section. For now, just remember that I recommend using Apple wireless hardware with your iMac whenever possible. It's just a little easier!)

Joining a wireless network

As far as I'm concerned, the only two types of base stations on the planet are Apple and non-Apple (which includes all 802.11ac, 802.11n, and 802.11g Base Stations and access points). In these two sections, I relate what you need to know to get onboard, using either type of hardware.

Apple AirPort Base Stations

To join a wireless network that's served by any flavor of Apple Base Station, follow these steps on each Mac with wireless support:

1. **Click the System Preferences icon on the Dock.**

2. **Click the Network tab.**

3. **From the Connection list on the left, click Wi-Fi.**

   Note that Wi-Fi may appear labeled as *Ethernet 2* instead. Whatever name it's assigned on your iMac, however, you'll still see the familiar "Wi-Fi fan" icon next to the port name.

4. **Mark the Show Wi-Fi Status in Menu Bar check box.**

5. **Click the Apply button.**

6. **Press ⌘+Q to quit System Preferences and save your settings.**

7. **Click the Wi-Fi status icon (which once again looks like a fan) on the Finder menu bar.**

8. **From the Wi-Fi menu, choose an existing network connection that you'd like to join.**

   The network name is the same as the network name you chose when you set up your AirPort Base Station.

9. **If you set up a secure network, enter the password you assigned to the network during setup.**

By the way, security is always A Good Thing, and I strongly recommend that you enable the password encryption features of your Apple Base Station while installing it. (Luckily, the Apple Base Station setup application leads you through this very process.) In the words of an important Mark's Maxim:

Keep uninvited guests out of your network! Use your base station's security features and encrypt your data!

Some wireless networks might not appear in your Wi-Fi menu list. These are *closed networks,* which can be specified when you set up your AirPort Base Station. You can't join a closed network unless you know the exact network name (which is far more secure than simply broadcasting the network name). To join a closed network, follow these steps:

1. **Select Join Other Network from the Wi-Fi menu.**

   To open the menu, click the AirPort status icon (which looks like a fan) on the Finder menu bar.

2. **Type the name of the network.**

3. **If the network is secured with *WEP* or *WPA2* encryption — the two most popular security standards for protecting your data through encryption — click the Security pop-up menu and select which type of encryption is being used.**

WPA2 is a far superior standard, so choose it over WEP whenever possible.

4. **Enter the network password, if required.**

To disconnect from a Wi-Fi network, click the Wi-Fi menu and either

✔ **Choose Turn Wi-Fi Off.**

✔ **Connect to another Wi-Fi network.**

In other words, if you choose another available Wi-Fi network from the Wi-Fi menu, your iMac will automatically drop the previous connection. (You can be connected to only one wireless network at a time, which makes Good Sense.)

Sending files the easy AirDrop way

AirDrop is the local Mac-to-Mac file transfer feature built in to OS X Mavericks. It couldn't be much easier to use because literally no setup and no passwords are involved! However, I have three caveats (don't I always?):

✔ AirDrop works only with Macs running OS X Lion and later, and only with specific models. On the desktop side, it works with iMac (early 2009 or newer), Mac mini (mid-2010 or newer), and Mac Pro (early 2009 or newer). On the laptop side, AirDrop works with MacBook Pro (late 2008 or newer), MacBook Air (late 2010 or newer), and MacBook (late 2010 and newer).

✔ AirDrop uses the Wi-Fi hardware built in to today's Macs, so don't forget to turn Wi-Fi on first. (If you're displaying the Wi-Fi status icon in your Finder menu bar, click the icon and choose Turn Wi-Fi On.)

✔ You'll have to be within Wi-Fi signal range of another Mac to use AirDrop. Note, however, that the two computers *don't* have to be using the same Wi-Fi network. (For example, my iMac uses a wired connection to my network, but because the iMac has internal Wi-Fi hardware, I can use AirDrop to send files to my MacBook Pro.)

To use AirDrop to transfer files to another Mac, both users should click the AirDrop icon in any Finder window sidebar to join the AirDrop group. After a short delay, you'll see the account pictures for all the Macs within signal range that have AirDrop open. Drag the files you want to transfer to the person's picture. Both you and the recipient are prompted for confirmation before the transfer begins. When the transfer is completed, the files you sent are saved in the recipient's Downloads folder.

After you're done using AirDrop, just close the Finder window displaying the account pictures and you'll exit from the AirDrop group. (Don't forget that you have to open AirDrop again if someone wants to send you files, so I personally leave my AirDrop Finder window open and minimized to the Dock!)

Using non-Apple Base Stations

If you're using your iMac to connect to a non-Apple base station, you might need to follow a specific procedure that takes care of the slightly different password functionality used by standard 802.11b/g/n/ac hardware.

Mavericks can take care of many potential wireless "language barriers" caused by security encryption (the two most common forms are WEP and WPA2), so whether you need to massage your password to connect to your non-Apple base station depends on the specific hardware and encryption system that it uses.

To read or print the latest version of this procedure, fire up Safari and visit `http://kbase.info.apple.com/index.html`, searching on the number HT1126. (This is the Apple Knowledge Base article number, which you can type in the first search field.) This article provides the details on how to convert a standard wireless encrypted password to a format that your AirPort Extreme hardware can understand.

Wired connections

If you're installing a wired network, your iMac already comes with most of what you need for joining your new cabled world. You just connect the hardware and configure the connection. Don't forget that you also need cables and an inexpensive Ethernet switch. (If you're using an Internet router or other hardware sharing device, it almost certainly has a built-in four- or eight-port switch.)

Connecting iMac hardware to a wired network

Your Ethernet 10/100/1000 port (which looks like a slightly oversized telephone/modem port) is located in the line of ports on the back of your iMac, ready to accept a standard Ethernet Cat5/Cat5E/Cat6 cable with RJ-45 connectors. If you're connecting to an existing wired network, you need a standard Cat5/Cat5E/Cat6 Ethernet cable of the necessary length. I recommend a length of no more than 25 feet because cables longer than 25 feet are often subject to line interference (which can slow down or even cripple your connection). You also need a live Ethernet port from the network near your iMac. Plug the cable into your iMac and then plug the other end into the network port.

Wired network hardware

If you don't know your switch from your NIC, don't worry. Here, I provide you with a description of the hardware that you need for your wired network.

Wired network components

If you're building your own wired network, you need

- ✔ **A switch:** This gizmo's job is to provide more network ports for the other computers in your network. They typically come in four- and eight-port configurations.

  As I mention earlier in this chapter, most Internet routers (sometimes called *Internet sharing devices*) include a built-in switch. If you've already invested in an Internet router, before you go shopping for a switch, make doggone sure that the router doesn't already come equipped with the ports you need!

- ✔ **A number of Ethernet cables:** Exactly how many cables you need is determined by how many computers and networked devices (like network printers) you're connecting. If you're working with a Gigabit Ethernet system, you need Cat5E or Cat6 cables. Cat6 cables provide better performance, but they are more expensive.

Naturally, if you're using a broadband Internet connection on your home network, you also have a DSL or cable modem. These boxes always include a port for connecting to your wired Ethernet network. (If you have one of the new breed of *wireless* cable or DSL modems — which acts as a wireless base station — don't panic, because it should also have a wired port for connecting to your existing switch.)

Wired network connections

After you assemble your cables and your router or switch, connect the Ethernet cables from each of your computers to the router or switch and then turn on the device. (Most need AC power to work.) Check the manual that comes with your device to make sure that the lights you're seeing on the front indicate normal operation. (Colors vary by manufacturer, but green is usually A Good Color.)

Next, connect your cable or DSL modem's Ethernet port to the WAN port on your switch with an Ethernet cable. If your modem isn't already on, turn it on now and check for normal operation.

When your router or switch is powered on and operating normally, you're ready to configure OS X for network operation. Just hop to the upcoming section "Connecting to the Network." (How about that? Now you can add network technician to your rapidly growing computer résumé!)

Joining a wired Ethernet network

After all the cables are connected and your central connection gizmo is plugged in and turned on, you've essentially created the hardware portion of your network. Congratulations! (Now you need a beard and suspenders.)

With the hardware in place, it's time to configure Mavericks. In this section, I assume that you're connecting to a network with an Internet router or switch that includes a DHCP server.

Follow these steps on each Mac running OS X that you want to connect to the network:

1. **Click the System Preferences icon on the Dock.**

2. **Click the Network icon (under Internet & Network).**

3. **From the Connection list on the left, click Ethernet.**

4. **Open the Configure IPv4 pop-up menu (see Figure 21-3) and choose Using DHCP.**

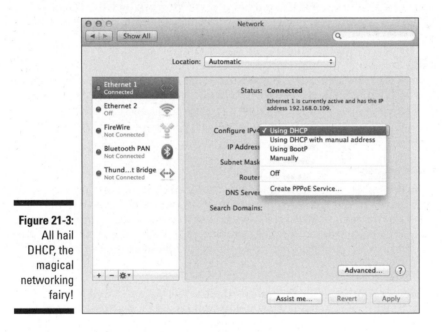

Figure 21-3:
All hail DHCP, the magical networking fairy!

5. **Click the Apply button.**

The Apply button is grayed out in the figure because my status (in this dialog) is Connected.

Enjoy the automatic goodness as OS X connects to the DHCP server to obtain an IP address, a subnet mask, a gateway router IP address, and a Domain Name System (DNS) address. (Without a DHCP server, you'd have to add all this stuff manually. Ugh.)

A few seconds after clicking the Apply button, you should see the information come up. You might also notice that the DNS Server field is empty, but fear not: OS X is really using DNS Server information provided by the DHCP server.

6. **Press ⌘+Q to quit System Preferences and save your settings.**

   You're on!

Connecting to the Network

All right! The hardware is powered up, the cables (if any) are installed and connected, and you configured Mavericks. You're ready to start (or join) the party. In this section, I show you how to share data and devices with others on your network.

Sharing stuff nicely with others

It works . . . by golly, it works! Okay, now what do you *do* with your all-new shining chrome network connection? Ah, my friend, let me be the first to congratulate you, and the first to show you around! In this section, I cover the most popular network perks. (And the good news is that these perks work with both wired and wireless connections.)

Network Internet connections

If your DSL or cable modem plugs directly into your iMac (rather than a dedicated Internet sharing device or Internet router), you might ponder just how the other computers on your network can share that spiffy high-speed broadband connection. If you're running a wireless network, it comes to the rescue!

Follow these steps to share your connection wirelessly:

1. **Click the System Preferences icon on the Dock.**

2. **Click the Sharing icon.**

3. **Click the Internet Sharing entry in the Services list to the left of the pane.**

4. **From the Share Your Connection From pop-up menu, choose Ethernet.**

5. **Mark the Wi-Fi check box (in the To Computers Using list).**

6. **Select the On check box next to the Internet Sharing entry in the Services list.**

   Mavericks displays a warning dialog stating that connection sharing could affect other computers on your network. If you intend to share the Internet connection provided on an existing network at your home or office that you didn't set up, contact your network administrator first! (Best to avoid sowing chaos and disorder.)

7. **Click Start in the warning dialog to continue.**

8. **Click the Close button to exit System Preferences.**

Sharing an Internet connection (without an Internet router or a dedicated hardware device) through OS X requires your iMac to remain on continuously. This is no big deal if you're using your iMac as a web server — and your iMac has absolutely no problem remaining on ad infinitum — but tell others on your network that the svelte iMac must remain on, or they'll lose their Internet connection! Sharing your Internet using your iMac also requires that you enable the Wake for Network Access check box within the Energy Saver pane in System Preferences.

Don't forget that you won't need to configure Internet sharing if your DSL or cable modem connects to a dedicated sharing device or router. That snazzy equipment automatically connects your entire network to the Internet.

Network file sharing

You can swap all sorts of interesting files with other Macintosh computers on your network. When you turn on File Sharing, Mavericks lets all Macs on the network connect to your iMac and share the files in your Public folder. (**Note:** Sharing across a network is different from sharing a single computer betwixt several people. I cover that environment in Chapter 20.)

Follow these steps to start sharing files and folders with others across your network:

1. **Click the System Preferences icon on the Dock.**

2. **Click the Sharing icon.**

3. **Select the On check box next to the File Sharing service entry to enable the connections for Mac and Windows sharing.**

   Other Mac users can connect to your computer by clicking Go in the Finder menu and choosing the Network menu item. The Network window appears, and your iMac is among the choices. If the other Macs are running Mavericks, your iMac's shared files and folders appear in a Finder window, and they're listed under the Shared heading in the Sidebar.

Windows XP users should be able to connect to your Mac from their My Network Places window, and Vista/Windows 7 users can use the Network window. (Windows 8 users should head to the Network panel instead.) Those lucky Windows folks also get to print to any shared printers you've set up. (The following section covers shared printers.)

4. **Click the Close button to exit System Preferences.**

Mavericks conveniently reminds you of the network name for your iMac at the top of the Sharing pane.

Sharing a network printer

Boy, howdy, do I love describing easy procedures, and sharing a printer on a Mac network ranks high on the list! You can share a printer that's connected to your iMac (or your AirPort Extreme, AirPort Time Capsule, or AirPort Express Base Station) by following these very simple steps:

1. **Click the System Preferences icon on the Dock.**

2. **Click the Sharing icon.**

3. **Select the On check box next to the Printer Sharing service entry.**

4. **From the list at the right of the System Preferences window, select the printer you want to share by clicking the check box.**

5. **Click the Close button to exit System Preferences.**

A printer that you share automatically appears in the Print dialog on other Macs connected to your network.

USE YOUR FIREWALL!

Yep. That's the only heading in this entire book that's all uppercase. It's that important.

The following Mark's Maxim, good reader, isn't a request, a strong recommendation, or even a regular Maxim; consider it an absolute commandment (right up there with *Get an antivirus application now*).

Turn on your firewall *now*.

When you connect a network to the Internet, you open a door to the outside world. As a consultant to several businesses and organizations in my hometown, I can tell you that the outside world is chock-full of malicious individuals who would *dearly love* to inflict damage on your data or take control of your iMac for their own purposes. Call 'em hackers, call 'em delinquents, or call 'em something I can't repeat, but *don't let them in!*

Mavericks comes to the rescue again with the built-in firewall within OS X. When you use this, you essentially build a virtual brick wall between you and the hackers out there (both on the Internet and even within your local network). Follow these steps:

1. **Click the System Preferences icon on the Dock.**

2. **Click the Security & Privacy icon.**

3. **Click the Firewall tab.**

4. **Click the Turn On Firewall button to activate your firewall.**

5. **Click the Firewall Options button.**

6. **Select the Automatically Allow Signed Software to Receive Incoming Connections check box.**

7. **Select the Enable Stealth Mode check box.**

   This is an important feature that prevents hackers from *trolling* for your iMac on the Internet — or, in normal-speak, searching for an unprotected computer — so it's much harder for them to attack you.

8. **Click OK.**

9. **Click the Close button to exit System Preferences.**

Mavericks even keeps track of the Internet traffic that you *do* want to reach your iMac, such as web page requests and file sharing. When you activate one of the network features that I demonstrate in the preceding section, Mavericks automatically opens a tiny "hole" (called a *port* by network types) in your firewall to allow just that type of communication to your iMac. For example, if you decide to turn on File Sharing (as I demonstrate earlier), Mavericks automatically allows incoming file access.

You can also add ports for applications that aren't on the firewall's Allow list. These applications include third-party instant messaging (IM) clients, multiplayer game servers, and the like. Depending on the type of connection, Mavericks will often automatically display a dialog prompting you for confirmation before allowing certain traffic, so most folks won't need to do anything manually.

However, you *can* add a program manually to your list of allowed (or blocked) Firewall ports. Follow these steps:

1. **Click the System Preferences icon on the Dock.**

2. **Click the Security & Privacy icon.**

3. **Click the Firewall tab.**

4. **Click the Firewall Options button.**

5. **Click the Add button (which bears a plus sign).**

   Mavericks displays a standard File browsing sheet.

6. **Browse to the application that requires access to the outside world — or the application that you want to block from outside communication — and click it to select it.**

7. **Click the Add button in the File sheet.**

   The application appears in the Firewall list. By default, it's set to Allow Incoming Connections.

8. **If you want to block any incoming communication to the application, click the Allow Incoming Connections pop-up menu and choose Block Incoming Connections instead.**

9. **Click the Close button to exit System Preferences.**

Part VI
The Necessary Evils: Troubleshooting, Upgrading, Maintaining

In this part . . .

- ✔ Troubleshoot and fix problems with your iMac
- ✔ Expand your iMac with additional RAM, external drives, and more
- ✔ Maintain your iMac properly for peak performance
- ✔ Back up your iMac using Time Machine

Chapter 22

It Just . . . Sits . . . There

I wish you weren't reading this chapter.

Because you are, though, I can only surmise that you're having trouble with your iMac and that it needs fixing. (The other possibility — that you just like reading about solving computer problems — is more attractive, but much more problematic.)

Consider this chapter a crash course in the logical puzzle that is computer *troubleshooting:* namely, the art of finding out What Needs Fixing. You also see what you can do when you just plain can't fix the problem by yourself.

Oh, and you're going to encounter a lot of Tips and Mark's Maxims in this chapter — all of them learned the hard way, so I recommend committing them to memory on the spot!

Can You Troubleshoot? Yes, You Can!

Anyone can troubleshoot. Put these common troubleshooting myths to rest:

✔ **It takes a college degree in computers to troubleshoot.** Tell that to my troubleshooting kids. They'll think it's a hoot because they have Apple computers of their own at home and at school. You can follow all the steps in this chapter without any special training.

✔ **I'm to blame.** Ever heard of viruses? Failing hardware? Buggy software? Any of those things can be causing the problem. Heck, even if you *did* do something by accident, I'm willing to bet it wasn't on purpose. It's Mark's Maxim time:

Don't beat yourself up. Your iMac can be fixed.

✔ **I need to buy expensive utility software.** Nope. You can certainly invest in a commercial testing and repair utility if you like. My favorites are Techtool Pro from Micromat (www.micromat.com) and Drive Genius 3 from Prosoft Engineering (www.prosofteng.com), but a third-party utility isn't a requirement for troubleshooting. (I would, however, consider an antivirus application as a must-have, and you should have one already. Hint, hint.)

✔ **There's no hope if I can't fix it.** Sure, parts fail, and computers crash, but your Apple Service Center can repair just about any problem. And (ahem) if you backed up your iMac (as I preach throughout this book), you'll keep that important data (even if a new hard drive is in your future).

✔ **It takes forever.** Wait until you read the Number One Rule in the next section; the first step takes but 15 seconds and often solves the problem. Naturally, not all problems can be fixed so quickly, but if you follow the procedures in this chapter, you should fix your iMac (or at least know that the problem requires outside help) in a single afternoon.

With those myths banished for good, you can get down to business and start feeling better soon.

Basic Troubleshooting 101

In this section, I walk you through my Should-Be-Patented Troubleshooting Tree as well as the Mavericks built-in troubleshooting application, Disk Utility. I also introduce you to a number of keystrokes that can make your iMac jump through hoops.

The Number One Rule: Reboot!

Yep, it sounds silly, but the fact is that rebooting your iMac can often solve a number of problems. If you're encountering these types of strange behavior with your iMac, a reboot might be all you need to heal

✔ Intermittent problems communicating over a network

✔ A garbled screen, strange colors, or screwed-up fonts

✔ The Swirling Beach Ball of Doom that won't go away after several minutes

✔ An application that locks up

✔ An external device that seems to disappear or can't be opened

To put it succinctly, here's a modest Mark's Maxim:

Always try a reboot before beginning to worry. *Always.*

Try to save all your open documents before you reboot. That might not be possible, but try to save what you can.

If you need to force a *locked* application (one that's not responding) to quit so that you can reboot, follow these steps to squash that locked application:

1. **Click the Apple (⌘) menu and choose Force Quit, or press the ⌘+Option+Escape keyboard shortcut.**

   The dialog that you see in Figure 22-1 appears on your screen.

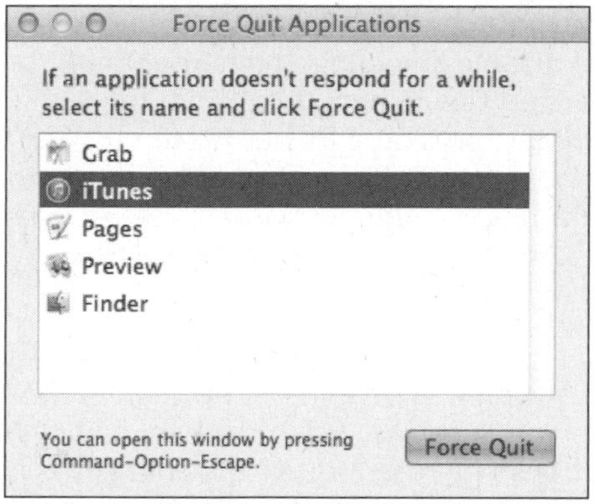

Figure 22-1:
Force a
recalcitrant
application
to take off.

2. **Click the offending application and then click the Force Quit button.**

   If you can get everything to quit, you should be able to click the Apple menu and choose Shut Down (not Restart) without a problem.

If your iMac simply won't shut down (or you can't get the offending application to quit), do what must be done:

1. **Press and hold your iMac Power button until it shuts itself off.**

   You have to wait about four seconds for your iMac to turn itself off.

2. **Wait about ten seconds.**

3. **Press the Power button again to restart the computer.**

Note that you should not simply pull your iMac's power cord out of the AC socket (or turn off your power strip) to turn it off.Pressing and holding the power switch on your iMac is a less destructive path to the same end.

After everything is back up, check whether the problem is still apparent. If you use your iMac for an hour or two and the problem doesn't reoccur, you likely fixed it!

Rebooting fixes problems because it resets *everything* — even your network connection. Rebooting also fixes problems due to brownouts or those notorious AC power flickerings that we all notice from time to time.

Special keys that can come in handy

A number of keys have special powers over your iMac. No, I'm not kidding! These keys affect how your iMac starts up, and they can really come in handy whilst troubleshooting.

Using Safe Boot mode

You can use Safe Boot mode to force OS X Mavericks to run a directory check of your boot hard drive and disable any Login Items that might be interfering with Mavericks. Use the Shut Down menu item from the Apple (🍎) menu to completely turn off your iMac; press the Power button to start the computer. Then press and hold down the Shift key immediately after you hear the startup tone. After Mavericks has completely booted, restart your iMac again (this time without the Shift key) to return to normal operation.

Startup keys

Table 22-1 provides the lowdown on startup keys. Hold the indicated key down either *when you push your iMac Power button* or *immediately after the screen blanks during a restart*. (As I just mentioned, the Shift key is the exception; it should be pressed and held down after you hear the startup tone.)

Table 22-1	Startup Keys and Their Tricks
Key	*Effect on Your iMac*
C	Boots from the CD or DVD that's loaded in your optical drive (if you have one)
Media Eject	Ejects the CD or DVD in your optical drive (if you have one)
Option	Displays a system boot menu, allowing you to choose the operating system and startup volume
Shift	Prevents your Login Items from running; runs a directory check
T	Starts your iMac in FireWire or Thunderbolt Target Disk mode
⌘+R	Boots from the Mavericks Recovery HD
⌘+V	Show OS X Console messages
⌘+S	Starts your iMac in Single User mode
⌘+Option+P+R	Resets Parameter RAM (PRAM) and NVRAM

Some of the keys/combinations in Table 22-1 might never be necessary for your machine, but you might be instructed to use them by an Apple technician. I'll warrant that you'll use at least the ⌘+R startup key fairly often.

All hail Disk Utility, the troubleshooter's friend

The Mavericks *Disk Utility* is a handy tool for troubleshooting and repairing your hard drive. You can find it in the Utilities folder within your Applications folder.

Fire up Disk Utility, click the volume that's giving you a headache from the list at the left side of the window, and click the First Aid tab to bring up the rather powerful-looking window shown in Figure 22-2.

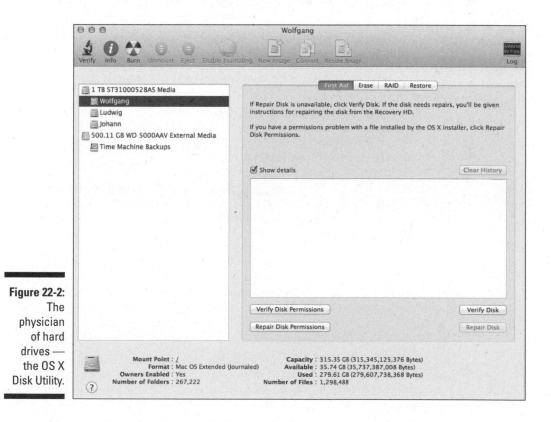

Figure 22-2: The physician of hard drives — the OS X Disk Utility.

Danger, Will Robinson!

Many Disk Utility functions can actually **wipe your hard drives clean of data** instead of repairing them! These advanced functions aren't likely to help you with troubleshooting a problem with your existing volumes, anyway.

Remember: *Don't* use these Disk Utility functions unless an Apple technician *tells* you to use them:

✔ Partitioning and erasing drives

✔ Setting up RAID arrays

✔ Restoring files from disk images

In the left column of the Disk Utility window, you can see

✔ **The *physical* hard drives in your system (the actual hardware)**

✔ **The *volumes* (the data stored on the hard drives)**

You can always tell a volume because it's indented underneath the physical drive entry.

✔ **Any CD or DVD loaded on your iMac**

✔ **Disk images you've mounted**

✔ **USB, Thunderbolt, or FireWire flash drives**

For example, Figure 22-2 shows that I have one 1TB internal hard drive and one 500.11GB external hard drive. The internal hard drive has three volumes (Wolfgang, Johann, and Ludwig), and the external drive has one volume (Time Machine Backups).

The information at the bottom of the Disk Utility window contains the specifications of the selected drive or volume . . . things like capacity, free space, and the number of files and folders for a volume, or connection type and total capacity for a drive.

Repairing disk permissions

Because Mavericks is built on a Unix base, lots of permissions can apply to the files on your drive — that is, who can open (or read or change) every application, folder, and document on your hard drive. Unfortunately, these permissions are often messed up by wayward applications or power glitches or application installers that do a subpar job of cleaning up after themselves. And if the permissions on a file are changed, often applications lock up or refuse to run altogether.

I recommend repairing your disk permissions with Disk Utility once weekly. Although repairing your permissions may not fix every application you've installed, it still covers all Apple software (and stuff you've downloaded from the App Store). Figure 22-3 shows a permissions repair sweep on my internal hard drive's volume.

Use these steps to repair permissions on your iMac's hard drive:

1. **Make sure that you're logged in with an admin account.**

   Chapter 20 shows you how to log in as an admin user.

2. **Save and close any open documents.**

3. **Click the Launchpad icon in the Dock; then click the Utilities (or Other) folder and click the Disk Utility icon.**

   Alternatively, click Go⇨Utilities.

4. **Click the volume that you want to check.**

   You can repair permissions only on a boot drive.

5. **Click the Repair Disk Permissions button.**

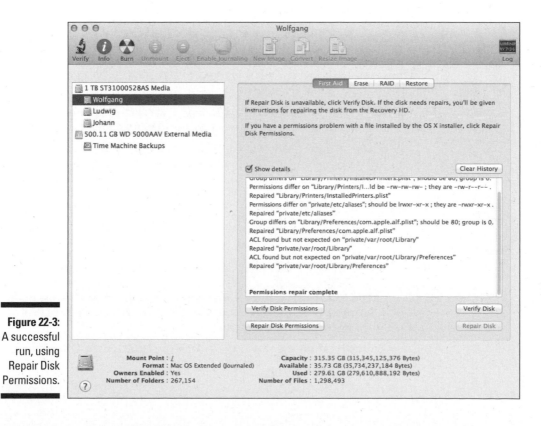

Figure 22-3:
A successful run, using Repair Disk Permissions.

I don't worry about verifying. If something's wrong, you end up clicking Repair Disk Permissions, anyway. Just click Repair Disk Permissions; if nothing pops up, that's fine.

6. **To finish the process, always reboot after repairing permissions.**

   This last step allows you to see whether a problem has been corrected!

Repairing disks

Disk Utility can check the format and health of both hard drives and volumes with Verify Disk — and, if the problem can be corrected, fix any error with Repair Disk.

Using Disk Utility to repair your hard drive carries a couple of caveats:

✔ **You can't verify or repair the boot disk or the boot volume.** This actually makes sense because you're using that disk and volume right now.

If you have an external drive connected to your iMac that has a Mavericks boot volume, you can boot from the OS X installed on the external drive to check your current startup disk. Or you can boot your system from the Recovery HD partition and run Disk Utility from the menu. (To choose the startup volume, open System Preferences and click the Startup Disk icon, or restart your iMac and hold down the ⌘+R startup key shortcut to boot directly to the Recovery HD partition.)

Using one of these methods, you should be able to run Disk Utility and select your boot hard drive or volume, and the Verify Disk and Repair Disk buttons should be enabled.

✔ **You can't repair CDs and DVDs.** CDs and DVDs are read-only media and thus can't be repaired at all (at least by Disk Utility).

If your iMac is having trouble reading a CD or DVD, wipe the disc with a soft cloth to remove dust, oil, and fingerprints. Should that fail, invest in a disc-cleaning contrivance of some sort.

I generally check my disks once every two or three days. If your iMac is caught by a power failure or OS X locks up, however, check disks immediately after you restart your iMac.

If you need to verify and repair a disk or volume, follow these steps:

1. **If you need to repair your *boot drive and volume,* save all your open documents and reboot from either *an external drive* or *your OS X Mavericks Recovery HD partition.***

2. **Click Launchpad on the Dock; then click the Utilities (or Other) icon.**

3. **Click the Disk Utility icon.**

4. **In the list at the left side of the Disk Utility window, click the disk or volume that you want to check.**

5. **Click the Repair Disk button.**

6. **If changes were made (or if you had to boot from a disc or external drive), reboot after repairing the disk or volume.**

Mark's iMac Troubleshooting Tree

As the hip-hop artists say, "All right, kick it." And that's just what my iMac Troubleshooting Tree is here for. If rebooting your iMac hasn't solved the problem, follow these steps in order (either until the solution is found or you run out of steps — more on that in the next section).

Step 1: Investigate recent changes

This is a simple step that many novice Mac owners forget. Simply retrace your steps and consider what changes you made recently to your system. Here are the most common culprits:

- **Did you just finish installing a new application?** Try uninstalling it by removing the application directory and any support files that it might have added to your system (or by running the uninstall program, if one is available), and then reinstalling it from scratch.

- **Did you just apply an update or a patch to an application?** Keeping your applications current with the most recent patches and updates from the developer's website is always a good idea, but an update can go awry. Uninstall the application and reinstall it without applying the patch. If your iMac suddenly works again, check the developer's website or contact its technical support department to report the problem.

- **Did you just update Mavericks by using Software Update?** Updating Mavericks can introduce problems within your applications that depend on specific routines and system files. Contact the developer of the application and look for updated patches that bring your software in line with the Mavericks updates. (And use the Automatically Check for Updates setting in the App Store System Preference pane to ensure that OS X is updated regularly.)

- **Did you just make a change within System Preferences?** Return the options that you changed back to their original settings; then consult Chapter 6 for information on what might have gone wrong. (If the setting in question isn't in Chapter 6, consider searching the Mavericks online Help system or the Apple support website for more clues.)

✔ **Did you just connect (or reconnect) an external device?** Try unplugging the device and then rebooting to see whether the problem disappears. Remember that many peripherals need software drivers to run — and without those drivers installed, they won't work correctly. (Not to mention that updated drivers may be available.) Check the device's manual or visit the company's website to search for software that you might need.

If you didn't make any significant changes to your system before you encountered the problem, proceed to the next step.

Step 2: Run Disk Utility

The preceding section shows how to repair disk permissions on your Mavericks boot drive.

If you're experiencing hard drive problems, consider booting from your OS X Recovery HD partition to run a full-blown Repair Disk checkup on your boot volume. (If the drive turns out to be faulty and you've been backing up with the Time Machine feature built in to Mavericks, you can also completely restore your system after the new drive is installed!)

Step 3: Check your cables

Cables work themselves loose, and they fail from time to time. Check all your cables to your external devices — make sure that they're snug — and verify that everything's plugged in and turned on. (Oh, and don't forget to check for crimps or even Fluffy's teeth marks in your cables.)

If a FireWire, Thunderbolt, or USB device acts up, swap cables around to find whether you have a bad one. A faulty cable can leave you pulling your hair out in no time.

Step 4: Check your Trash

Check the contents of your Trash to see whether you recently deleted files or folders by accident. Click the Trash icon on the Dock once to display the contents. If something's been deleted by mistake, drag it back to its original folder and try running the application again.

I know this one from personal experience. A slight miscalculation while selecting files to delete made an application freeze every time I launched it.

Step 5: Check your Internet and network connections

Now that always-on DSL and cable modem connections to the Internet are common, don't forget an obvious problem: Your iMac can't reach the Internet because your ISP is down, or your network is no longer working!

A quick visual check of your DSL or cable modem will usually indicate whether there's a connection problem between your modem and your ISP. For example, my modem has a very informative activity light that I always glance at first. However, if your iMac is connected to the Internet through a larger home or office network and you can't check the modem visually, you can check your Internet connection by pinging www.apple.com, as follows (see Figure 22-4):

1. **Click the Launchpad icon on the Dock and then click the Utilities (or Other) icon.**

2. **Click the Network Utility icon.**

3. **Click the Ping button.**

4. **Enter www.apple.com in the Address box.**

5. **Click the Ping button.**

   You should see successful ping messages similar to those in Figure 22-4. If you don't get a successful ping *and* you can still reach other computers on your network, your ISP is likely experiencing problems. If you can't reach your network at all, the problem lies in your network hardware or configuration.

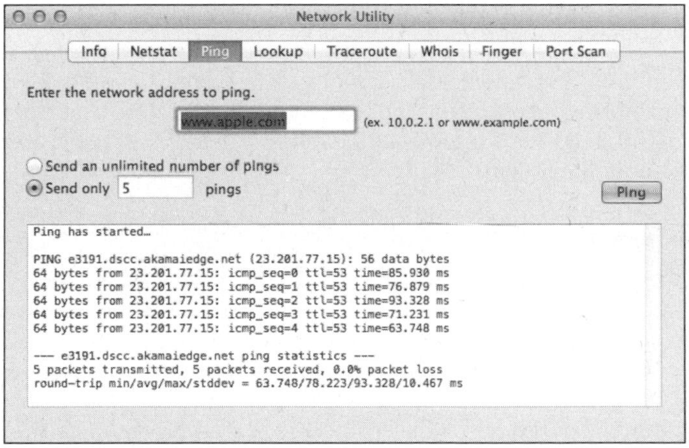

Figure 22-4: Ping www.apple.com to check your Internet connection.

Step 6: Think virus

If you made it to this point, it's time to run a full virus and malware scan — and make sure that your antivirus application has the latest updated data files, too. My antivirus application of choice is Virus Barrier 2013 from Intego (www.intego.com). (If a virus is detected and your antivirus application can't remove it, try *quarantining* it instead, which basically disables the virus-ridden application and prevents it from infecting other files.) I can also recommend ClamXav 2, the antivirus application from www.clamxav.com. (If you like ClamXav 2, you can send a donation to the author.)

Step 7: Disable your Login Items

OS X might encounter problems with applications that you've marked as Login Items within System Preferences. In this step, I show you how to identify login problems and how to fix 'em.

Checking for problems

It's time to use another nifty startup key (refer to Table 22-1). This time, hold down Shift after you hear the startup tone.

This trick disables your account's Login Items, which are run automatically every time you log in to your iMac. If one of these Login Items is to blame, your iMac will simply encounter trouble every time you log in.

Finding the Login Item that's causing trouble

If your iMac works fine with your Login Items disabled, follow this procedure for each item in the Login Items list:

1. **Open System Preferences, click Users & Groups, and then click the Login Items button.**

2. **Delete the item from the list; then reboot normally.**

   You can delete the selected item by clicking the Delete button, which bears a minus sign.

   When your iMac starts up normally with Login Items enabled, you discovered the perpetrator. You'll likely need to delete that application and reinstall it. (Don't forget to add each of the *working* Login Items back to the Login Items list!)

Step 8: Turn off your screen saver

This is a long shot, but it isn't unheard of to discover that a faulty, bug-ridden screen saver has locked up your iMac. (If you aren't running one of the Apple-supplied screen savers and your computer never wakes up from Sleep mode or hangs while displaying the screen saver, you found your prime suspect.)

Open System Preferences, click Desktop & Screen Saver, click the Screen Saver button, and then either switch to an Apple screen saver or drag the Start slider to Never.

If this fixes the problem, you can probably remove the screen saver by deleting the application in the Screen Savers folder inside your OS X Library folder. (If the application resides in the Library folder within your Home folder instead, hold down the Option key while clicking the Go menu, and then click the Library menu item that appears to jump there directly. Now you can open the Screen Savers folder you find there.) If you can't find the screen saver application at all, use Spotlight to search for it.

Step 9: Run System Information

Ouch. You reached Step 9, and you still haven't uncovered the culprit. At this point, you've narrowed the possibilities to a serious problem, like bad hardware or corrupted files in your OS X System folder. Fortunately, Mavericks provides System Information, which displays real-time information on the hardware in your system. Click the Apple menu and choose About This Mac, click More Info, and then click System Report. Figure 22-5 illustrates a typical healthy result from one of the Hardware categories, Graphics/Displays. Click each one of the Hardware categories in turn, double-checking to make sure that everything looks okay.

Figure 22-5: Check your iMac hardware from System Information.

You don't have to understand all the technical hieroglyphics. If a Hardware category doesn't return what you expect (like an attached external drive) or displays an error message, though, that's suspicious.

Okay, I Kicked It, and It Still Won't Work

Don't worry, friendly reader. Just because you've reached the end of my iMac tree doesn't mean you're out of luck. In this section, I discuss the online help available on the Apple website as well as local help in your own town.

Apple Help Online

If you haven't visited the Apple iMac Support site yet, run — don't walk — to www.apple.com/support/imac/intel, where you can find

- ✔ **iMac Troubleshooting Tips,** which identifies symptoms being displayed by your iMac and offers possible solutions
- ✔ **The latest patches, updates, and how-to tutorials** for the iMac
- ✔ **iMac and OS X discussion boards,** moderated by Apple
- ✔ **Tools** for ordering spare parts, checking on your remaining warranty coverage, and searching the Apple Knowledge Base
- ✔ **Do-it-yourself instructions** (PDF files) that you can follow to repair or upgrade your iMac

Local service, at your service

In case you need to take in your iMac for service, an Apple Store or Apple Authorized Service Provider is probably in your area. To find the closest service, launch Safari and visit

```
https://locate.apple.com/
```

Click the reassuring-looking Service button and choose Mac from the Select a Product pop-up list box to search by your current location, city and state, or zip code. The results are complete with the provider's mailing address, telephone number, and even a map of the location!

Always call your Apple service provider before you lug your (albeit lightweight) iMac all the way to the shop. Make sure that you know *your iMac's serial number* (which you can display in System Profiler) and *which version of OS X you're using.*

Chapter 23

I Want to Add Stuff

"No iMac is an island." Somebody famous wrote that, I'm sure.

Without getting too philosophical — or invoking the all-powerful Internet yet again — the old saying really does make sense. All computer owners usually add at least one *peripheral* (external device), such as a printer, backup drive, joystick, iPod, or scanner. I talk about the ports on your iMac in Chapter 1. Those holes aren't there to just add visual interest to the back end of your treasured iMac. Therefore, I cover your USB, Thunderbolt, and FireWire ports (and what you can plug in to them) in detail in this chapter.

Ah, but what about the stuff *inside* your supercomputer? That's where things get both interesting and scary at the same time. In this chapter, I also describe what you can add to the innards of some iMac models as well as how to get inside there if you work up the courage to go exploring. (Don't tell your family or your friends, but adding memory to a late-model 27" iMac is as simple as pressing a button and pulling on a couple of plastic levers. There's actually nothing to fear whatsoever.)

Here's the trick: Just make it sound like an adventure from *Mission: Impossible,* and folks will crown you their new resident techno-wizard!

More Memory Will Help

Hey, wait a second. No *however* stuck on the end? You mean that, for once, there isn't an exception? Aren't all computers different? Hard as it is to believe, just keep in mind this Mark's Maxim:

More memory helps.

Period. End of statement. No matter what type of computer you own, how old it is, or what operating system you use, adding more memory to your system (to the maximum it supports, of course) significantly improves the performance of your operating system (and practically every application that you run).

Memory maximizes the power of your computer: The more memory you have, the less data your iMac has to temporarily store on its hard drive. Without getting into virtual memory and other techno-gunk, just consider that extra memory as extra elbow room for your applications and your documents. Believe me, both OS X and Windows efficiently make use of every kilobyte of memory that you can provide.

Figuring out how much memory you have

To see how much memory you have on your computer, click the Apple menu ( ) and choose About This Mac. Figure 23-1 shows the dialog that appears.

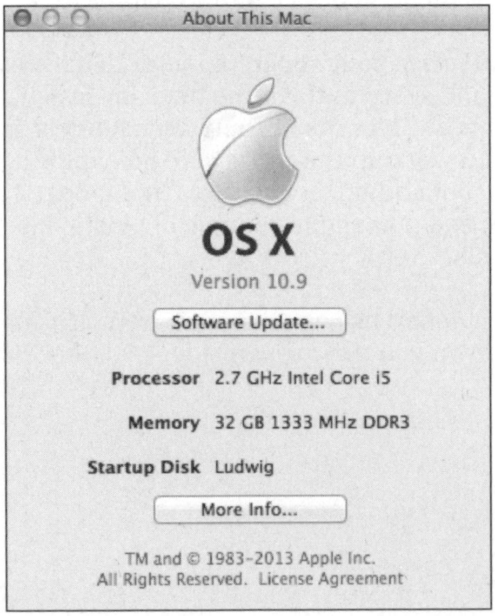

Figure 23-1:
Find out
how much
memory
your iMac
has.

About This Mac

OS X

Version 10.9

Software Update...

Processor 2.7 GHz Intel Core i5

Memory 32 GB 1333 MHz DDR3

Startup Disk Ludwig

More Info...

TM and © 1983–2013 Apple Inc.
All Rights Reserved. License Agreement

TIP

The 8GB of standard memory supplied by Apple is enough for running applications from the iLife and iWork suites as well as any of the applications bundled with Mavericks. If your primary applications include video editing, playing the latest crop of immersive 3D games, or image editing, though, you can use all the memory your iMac can hold — as you can see from Figure 23-1, my 27" iMac is stuffed with 32GB of RAM for just such applications.

Ah, but there's a caveat. (Go figure.) At the time of this writing, only the current crop of 27" iMacs has memory sockets that you — a Regular Human Being — can access. These models provide slots for four 1600 MHz PC3-12800 DDR3 SDRAM memory modules at up to 8GB each. (Don't fret over what those abbreviations mean. Rest assured that this memory type is fast.)

Unfortunately, the memory in a late-model (2012 and later) 21.5" iMac can't be replaced by anyone except an authorized Apple Service Center technician. So if you're using a 21.5" iMac, you can skip the rest of this section, except for the rest of this paragraph. If you're ready to order a *new* 21.5" iMac from Apple, I strongly recommend that you opt for as much additional memory as you can afford while configuring your dream machine. In the past, Apple's prices for RAM were . . . well . . . *outrageous* (as in, "Boy, howdy, I can't afford that!"). Recently, however, Apple's memory prices have become far more competitive, so I now recommend that you add memory while configuring and ordering either model of iMac.

How you plan memory upgrades depends on how much memory you want. If your 27" iMac uses the two default 4GB modules (8GB total) supplied by Apple, you can add RAM by inserting memory modules in the empty slots. At the time of this writing, a 4GB memory module should set you back about $40 or so.

If your iMac already has all four memory slots filled and you'd still like to add more system RAM, it's time to remove one or all of the existing modules and replace them with full 8GB modules. (Current prices for an 8GB module hover around $100.) With all four slots filled with 8GB modules, you'll have the coveted 32GB 27" iMac that marks you as one of the "In People."

If you've already bought your 27" iMac and you'd like to shop around for the best memory prices, I can heartily recommend any one of these online sources that cater to Mac owners:

- MacMall (www.macmall.com)
- CDW (www.cdw.com/content/brands/apple/default.aspx)
- Crucial (www.crucial.com)
- Small Dog Electronics (www.smalldog.com)
- Newegg (www.newegg.com)

Installing memory modules

I'm happy to report that adding extra memory to a 27" iMac is one of the easiest internal upgrades that you can perform. Therefore, I recommend that you add memory yourself unless you simply don't want to mess with your iMac's internal organs. Of course, your local Macintosh service specialist will be happy to install new RAM modules for you (for a price).

As you've concluded by this point in this book, Apple has designed the world's best all-in-one computer. That even includes making it EZ-Open. (Forgive me if your treasured work of art now reminds you of a longneck beer bottle. Come to think of it, the level of technical knowledge required to gain access to either one is about the same.)

Unlike earlier "picture frame" iMac models, however, you can't remove the back completely. In fact, Apple allows the owner of a 27" iMac to perform only one kind of upgrade, and there's only one opening you need to worry about. Naturally, an Apple repair technician can get deeper into the machine, but I hope that you never need aid from those folks.

You'll void your warranty by tinkering with anything other than your memory slots, so don't even *think* about it.

To add memory modules to a late-model 27" iMac, follow these steps:

1. **Get ready to operate.**

    a. *Spread a clean towel on a stable work surface, like your kitchen table.* The towel helps protect your screen from scratches.

    b. *Shut down your iMac.*

    c. *Unplug all cables from the computer.*

2. **Tilt the computer over and lay the screen flat (face-down) on top of the towel.**

3. **Press the button directly above the power cord socket.**

    The memory access door pops open.

4. **Remove the memory access door.**

5. **Stow the memory access door safely out of reach of kids and cats.**

    Tah-dah! That wasn't much of a challenge, was it? Take a moment to gaze with rapt fascination at a small portion of the bare innards of your favorite computer.

WARNING!

Let's get grounded!

Follow one cardinal rule when the unguarded insides of any computer are in easy reach: *Always ground yourself before you touch anything!* Your body can carry enough static electricity to damage the RAM you're installing or removing, and touching those modules without grounding yourself is an invitation for disaster.

Grounding yourself is easy to do: Just touch any metal surface around your work table, such as a chair leg or your local metal sink. After you

ground yourself, you can then safely handle RAM modules that you remove (if any) as well as the new ones that you're installing.

If you walk anywhere in the room — say, taking a sip of liquid reinforcement that you stashed a comfortable and safe distance away — you *must* ground yourself again before you get back to work. ***Remember:*** You can actually pick up a static charge by simply walking. Go figure.

6. ***Ground thyself!***

   Check out the "Let's get grounded!" sidebar.

7. **Gently pull outward on the two plastic securing levers and then pull them toward the bottom of the access door (as shown in Figure 23-2).**

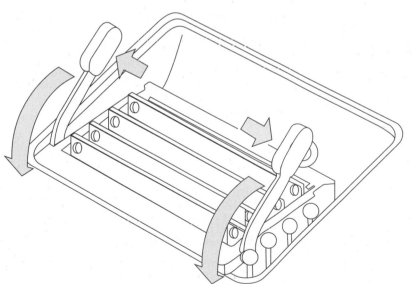

Figure 23-2:
Remove
a memory
module like
a pro.

8. **Remove a module by gripping it by the corners and gently pulling it straight upward.**

   Save the old module in the static-free packaging that held the new module. Your old RAM (which you can now sell on eBay) will be protected from static electricity.

9. **Position the new module in the socket.**

   a. *Line up the module's copper connectors toward the socket.*

   b. *Line up the notch in the module aligned with the matching spacer in the socket.* See what I mean in Figure 23-3, which shows the correct orientation for a late 2013 27" iMac.

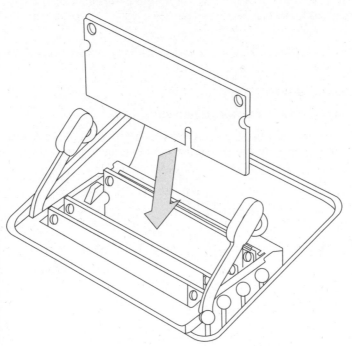

Figure 23-3:
Installing the new module is a snap (pun intended)!

10. **Press gently (but firmly) on both ends of the module until the module clicks into place.**

11. **Repeat Steps 8–10 for each module you're replacing.**

12. **Push the two securing levers back into their original position (you should hear a click when they're seated).**

13. Replace the memory access door.

14. Return your iMac to its natural upright stance and plug any cables you removed back into the back of the computer.

    Waxing nostalgic: This is rather like changing the oil on my Dad's 1970 Ford pickup truck.

Congratulations! You've done it — and you're now an iMac memory guru! To verify that all is well with your iMac, boot the computer, click the Apple menu (), and choose About This Mac. Your iMac should report the additional memory.

Can I Upgrade My Hard Drive?

Asking whether you can upgrade your hard drive is a trick question. Yes, you certainly *can* upgrade your hard drive. But before you start cruisin' the Internet for a 2TB monster, I have two suggestions:

✔ **Be sure you really *need* a hard drive upgrade.**

Apple is pretty generous when configuring hard drive storage for its base systems. (Current models run with anywhere from a 1TB to a whopping 3TB drive — yep, that's 3 *terabytes,* or 3,000GB! Something tells me that your prized walnut brownie recipe will have plenty of elbow room on a 3TB drive, as will as a huge amount of digital video.)

I'll be honest here: Most folks simply don't need more than 1TB of hard drive space. You're likely to find that you still have plenty of wide-open spaces for a typical family's needs on your hard drive unless you're heavily into

- Digital video (DV)

- Cutting-edge video games

- Tons of high-quality digital audio

- Four generations of high-resolution digital photos of your family (hey, it's possible!)

✔ **If you decide that you do need to upgrade, don't install your internal hard drive yourself.**

Read more about dealing with the installation of an internal hard drive in the upcoming section "Gotta have internal."

If you're short on hard drive space, first clean up your existing hard drive by deleting all the crud you don't need, such as game and application demos, duplicate or "work" copies of images and documents, archived files you downloaded from the Internet, and the contents of your Trash. You can read how in Chapter 24.

Consider your external options

If you *do* need additional hard drive space, I recommend using an external drive. Use a high-speed Thunderbolt or USB 3.0 port to connect a second hard drive the quick and easy way. (Owners of slightly older iMac models can use FireWire 800 as well.)

Most of today's Thunderbolt and USB peripherals don't even require the driver software that Mac old-timers remember with such hatred. You simply plug a device into one of these ports, and it works. And you can move your external drive between different Macs with a minimum of fuss and bother.

An external hard drive can do virtually anything that your internal hard drive can do. You can boot from it, for example, or install (and boot from) a different version of OS X (great for beta testers like me).

Apple's Time Capsule unit is an external hard drive with a difference: It stores the huge Time Machine backup files created by the Macs running OS X Lion (or later) on your network, and it uses a wireless connection to transfer data! (In fact, if you're thinking of adding a wireless base station to your wired network, your Time Capsule actually acts as a full AirPort Extreme Base Station, complete with USB port for connecting a USB printer.) At the time of this writing, Time Capsule is available with either a 2TB ($299) or 3TB ($399) drive.

Here's one problem with external drives, though. Even USB 3.0 and FireWire 800 transfer data more slowly this way than via an internal drive (only the newer Thunderbolt connections rival the speed of an internal drive). That's why most Mac owners use their external drives for storing backups, digital media, and little-used documents and applications. Their favorite applications and often-used documents are housed on the internal drive.

Putting a port to work

Current iMac models carry two kinds of high-speed ports, either of which is a good match for connecting any external device.

USB 3.0

The USB standard is popular because it's just as common in the PC world as in the Mac world. (Most PCs don't have a Thunderbolt port.) Your iMac carries its USB 3.0 ports on the back of the case, which are fully compatible with older USB 2.0 devices. Hardware manufacturers make one USB device that works on both Macs and PCs.

If you're using an older iMac with USB 2.0 ports, there's no need to spend extra money on USB 3.0 devices, since you won't get the performance boost. 'Nuff said.

FireWire 800

Current iMac models no longer carry a FireWire 800 port, but if you're using an older iMac (without a USB 3.0 port), you'll find that a FireWire 800 drive offers much better performance than either a FireWire 400 or a USB 2.0 drive.

The physical FireWire 800 connector is shaped differently than an older FireWire 400 port, so don't try to force the wrong connector into the wrong port!

Thunderbolt

Talk about raw speed. A Thunderbolt connection provides a blazing 10Gbps, which is an unbelievable 12 times faster than FireWire 800, and twice as fast as USB 3.0! You can use a Thunderbolt port to connect an external hard drive or even a high-resolution monitor or HD-TV. Luckily, the price for Thunderbolt external drives has dropped significantly since the port first appeared on the Mac, so you no longer have to pay a premium price for Thunderbolt devices.

Connecting an external drive

With Thunderbolt, or USB, you can install an external hard drive without opening your iMac's case. With your iMac turned on and the external drive disconnected from the AC outlet, follow these steps:

1. **Connect the FireWire, Thunderbolt, or USB cable betwixt the drive and your computer.**

2. **Plug the external drive into a convenient surge protector or UPS (uninterruptible power supply).**

3. **Switch on the external drive.**

4. **If the drive is unformatted (or formatted for use under Windows), partition and format the external drive.**

   The drive comes with instructions or software to help you do this. (Don't worry, external drives typically come from the factory completely empty, and you won't damage anything by formatting it. To be sure, check the drive's manual.) *Partitioning* divides the new drive into one (or more) volumes, each of which is displayed as a separate hard drive under Mavericks.

   If the drive comes preformatted for use with a Windows PC, I strongly suggest reformatting it for use with OS X. Doing so results in faster performance and more efficient use of space.

After the drive is formatted and partitioned, it immediately appears on the Desktop. *Shazam!*

Gotta have internal

If you decide that you have to upgrade your existing internal hard drive — or if your internal drive fails and needs to be replaced — you *must take your iMac to an authorized Apple Service Center* and allow the techs there to sell you a drive and make the swap. Here are four darned good reasons why:

- ✔ **Warranty:** As I mention earlier, you'll void your iMac's warranty by attempting a drive upgrade yourself.

- ✔ **Selection:** If you're worried about picking the proper drive, an Apple technician can order the right drive type and size for you . . . no worries.

- ✔ **Difficulty:** Swapping a hard drive in your iMac is nothing like adding RAM modules. It's complex and involves breaking into your iMac — not A Good Thing, even for the knowledgeable Mac guru.

- ✔ **Backup:** That very same Apple service technician can back up all the data on your existing drive and move it to the new drive, saving you from losing a single document. That will save you time and possible angst.

To those who *truly* won't be satisfied with their lives until they upgrade an internal drive in an iMac: Yes, I'm sure you can find a magazine article that purports to show you how. Even better, I've seen many how-to articles on the web that will lead you down a rosy path to a hard drive upgrade. Here's my take on those savvy instructions: You're walking into a field of land mines with someone else's map, so you had better have *complete* faith in your tech skills. (And a darn good backup.)

Weighing Attractive Add-Ons

The external toys I cover in this section might add a cord or two to your collection at the back of your iMac, but they're well worth the investment. And they can really revolutionize how you look at technologies such as television, digital audio, and computer gaming.

Game controllers

If you're ready to take a shot at the enemy — whether they be Nazi soldiers, chittering aliens, or the latest jet fighters — you'll likely find your keyboard and mouse somewhat lacking. (And if that enemy happens to be a friend of yours playing across the Internet, you'll be ruthlessly mocked while you're fumbling for the right key combination.) Instead, either pick up a USB joystick (for flying games) or a gamepad (for arcade and first-person shooting games)!

Hard drive arrays

In case you're not familiar with a hard drive array (typically called a *RAID array*), it's just a fancy moniker for an enclosure that holds multiple hard drives. "Grouping" hard drives like this provides a boost in speed, or you can use an array to make a self-maintaining redundant backup of all your data. Your Thunderbolt port is perfect for this high-tech magic.

Video controllers

For armchair directors, specialized USB digital video controllers make editing easier. The ShuttlePRO V2 from Contour Design (`www.contourdesign.com`) provides a 15-button jog control that can be configured to match any DV editor. For around $110, you'll have the same type of editing controller as do those dedicated video-editing stations that cost several thousand dollars.

Audio hardware

Ready to put GarageBand to the test with your favorite version of *Chopsticks?* You need a USB piano keyboard, and I recommend the Keystation 88es from M-Audio (`www.m-audio.com`), which retails for a mere $200. It provides 88 keys and uses a USB connection.

Chapter 24

Tackling the Housekeeping

*N*othing runs better than a well-oiled machine, and your iMac is no exception. (But please, don't *ever* oil your iMac — that's just a figure of speech.) In this chapter, I demonstrate how you can make good use of every byte of storage space provided by your hard drive.

With a little Mavericks maintenance, such as Time Machine (for backing up and restoring your hard drive) and frequent scans of your hard drive for permissions errors, you can ensure that your iMac is performing as efficiently as possible. Automator allows your iMac to perform tasks automatically that used to require your attention. In addition, configuring Software Update to run automatically can allow you to live life free and easy, watching your favorite reality TV and eating ice cream (or yogurt — your pick).

Cleaning Unseemly Data Deposits

Criminy! Where does all this stuff *come* from? Suddenly that spacious 1TB hard drive has 19GB left, and you start feeling pinched.

Before you consider buying a new internal or external hard drive (which you can read about in Chapter 23), take the smart step: "Sweep" your hard drive clean of unnecessary and space-hogging software.

Getting dirty (or, cleaning things the manual way)

If you're willing to dig into your data a little, there's no reason to buy additional software to help you clean up your hard drive. All you really need is the willpower to announce, "I simply don't need this particular item any longer." (Sometimes that's tougher than it might seem.)

Unnecessary files and unneeded folders

Consider all the stuff that you probably don't really need:

- Game demos and shareware that you no longer play (or even remember)
- Movie trailers and other QuickTime video files that have long since passed into obscurity
- Temporary files that you created and promptly forgot
- Log files that chronicle application installations and errors
- StuffIt and Zip archives that you downloaded and no longer covet
- iTunes music, video, and movies that no longer appeal

How hard is it to clean this stuff off your drive? Easier than you might think!

- You can quickly delete files.
- You can remove items from your iTunes Library.
- You can get rid of most of the space taken by any application (often the whole application) by deleting its application folder that was created during the installation process.

Removing an application or file from your hard drive usually takes two simple steps:

1. **Display the file or application folder in a Finder window.**

2. **Delete the file or folder with one of these steps:**

   - Drag the icon to the Trash.

   - Select the icon and press ⌘+Delete.

   - Right-click the icon and choose Move to Trash.

   - Select the icon and click the Delete button on the Finder toolbar (if you added one).

Truly, no big whoop.

Mac owners like you and me can once again feel superior to the Windows folks because most OS X applications don't need a separate, silly "uninstall" program (although some larger applications include one for convenience).

Don't forget to actually *empty* the Trash, or you'll wonder why you aren't regaining any hard drive space. (Mavericks works hard to store the contents of the Trash until you manually delete it, just in case you want to undelete something.) To get rid of that stuff permanently and reclaim the space, do the following:

1. **Click the Trash icon on the Dock and hold down the button — or right-click — until the pop-up menu appears.**

2. **Choose Empty Trash.**

Associated files in other folders

Some applications install files in different locations across your hard drive. (Applications in this category include the Microsoft Office suite and Adobe Creative Suite and Creative Cloud applications like Photoshop.) How can you clear out these "orphan" files after you delete the application folder?

The process is a little more involved than deleting a single folder, but it's still no big whoop. Here's the procedure:

1. **Click the Search text box in a Finder window.**

   You can read more about Search and Finder windows in Chapter 7.

2. **Type the name of the application in the Search text box.**

   Figure 24-1 shows this search. I want to remove Toast Titanium, so I search for every file with the word *toast* in its name.

3. **Decide which of these files belong to the to-be-deleted application.**

   Be sure that the files you choose to delete are part of the deleted application. For example, a text file with the name *Instructions on Making a Perfect Piece of Toast* might not be part of Toast Titanium.

   Many associated files either

   • Have the same icon as the parent application

   • Are in the Preferences, Caches, or Application Support folders

4. **In the Search Results window, click the associated file(s) that you want to delete and just drag them to the Trash.**

   Don't empty the Trash immediately after you delete these files. Wait a few hours or a day. That way, if you realize that you deleted a file that you truly need, you can easily restore it from the Trash.

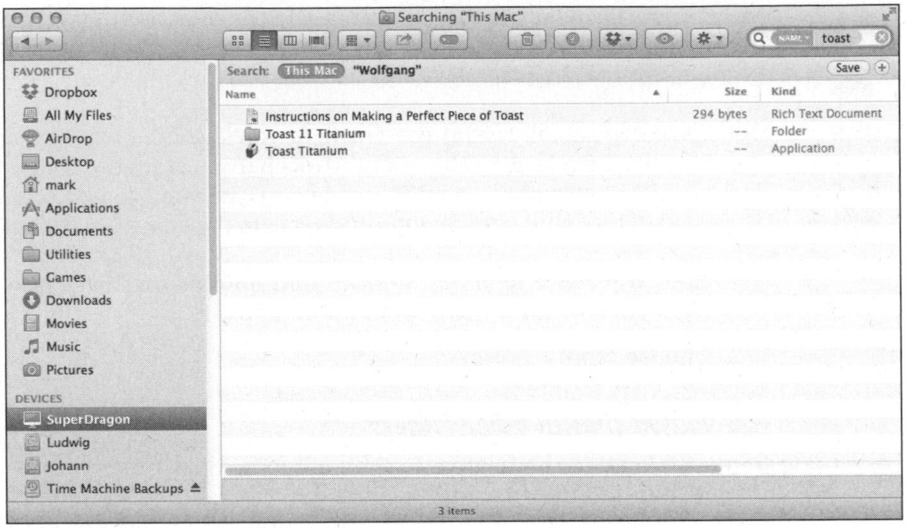

Figure 24-1:
Mine your hard drive for additional files to delete.

Using a commercial cleanup tool

If you'd rather use a commercial application to help you clean up your hard drive, a number of them are available, but most are shareware applications that perform only one task. For example, Tidy Up 3 from Hyperbolic Software (www.hyperbolicsoftware.com) does one thing, but it does it well. It finds duplicate files on your hard drive, matching by criteria such as filename, size, content, and extension. It's a good tool at $30.

For a truly comprehensive cleanup utility, I recommend CleanMyMac 2, from MacPaw (macpaw.com). Not much crud squeaks by all those search routines, including duplicates, orphan preference files, and log files. You can even remove unneeded language files to free space on your drive! CleanMyMac 2 sells for about $40.

Backing Up Your Treasure

Do it.

I'm not going to lecture you about backing up your hard drive . . . well, perhaps just for a moment. Imagine what it feels like to lose *everything* — names, numbers, letters, reports, presentations, saved games, photographs, and music. Then ask yourself, "Self, isn't all that irreplaceable stuff worth just a couple of hours every month?"

Time for a Mark's Maxim:

***Back up.* On a regular basis.**

Take my word for it — you will thank me some day!

You can back up your files either by saving them to external media or by using the awesome Time Machine feature included with Mavericks.

Saving Files

The simplest method of backing up files is simply to copy the files and folders to an external hard drive or a CD or DVD. Nothing fancy — in fact, I call this procedure the "quick-and-dirty backup" — but it works.

Backing up to an external hard drive

If you have an external hard drive on your iMac, you can easily drag backup files to it from your internal hard drive (I cover external hard drives in Chapter 23):

1. **Open separate Finder windows for**

   • The external hard drive

   • The internal hard drive

2. **Select the desired files that you want to back up from your internal drive.**

3. **Drag the selected files to the external drive window.**

Backing up to CD and DVD

You can burn backup files to a recordable CD or DVD, if you have an internal or external optical drive.

Burning backups from the Finder

To use the Finder's Burn feature to create a backup CD or DVD, follow these steps:

1. **Load a blank disc into your iMac's optical drive.**

   If you're using the default settings in the CDs & DVDs pane in System Preferences, a dialog appears, asking you to choose an action.

2. **From the Action pop-up menu, choose Open Finder and then click OK.**

   An icon named Untitled DVD appears on your Desktop. Double-click the icon to open a Finder window.

3. **Drag the files and folders that you want to back up into the disc's Finder window.**

   They can be organized any way you like. Don't forget that the total amount of data shouldn't exceed 4GB or so (on a standard recordable DVD) or 8GB (on a dual-layer recordable DVD). You can see how much free space remains on the disc at the bottom of the disc's Finder window.

4. **When you're ready to record, click File and then choose Burn Disc from the Finder menu.**

   You can also click the Burn button on the Recordable DVD bar, which appears at the top of the disc's Finder window.

5. **Choose the fastest recording speed possible.**

6. **Click Burn.**

Burning backups from other recording applications

If you've invested in Toast Titanium from Roxio (www.roxio.com) or another CD/DVD recording application, you can create a new disc layout to burn your backup disc. (Think of a layout as a "road map" indicating which files and folders Toast should store on the backup.)

You can save that disc layout and use it again. This simplifies the process of backing up the same files in the future (if you don't move folders or files from their current spot).

If you do decide to back up to CD/DVD or to an external backup drive without using Time Machine, it's a good idea to store that backup media somewhere safe, away from calamities. On the other hand, if you back up with Time Machine — as I'm about to demonstrate — you should instead leave your external drive plugged in to your iMac.

Putting Things Right with Time Machine

If you enable backups via the OS X Time Machine feature, you can literally move backward through the contents of your iMac's hard drive, selecting and restoring all sorts of data. Files and folders are ridiculously easy to restore — and I mean easier than *any* restore you've ever performed, no matter what the operating system or backup program. Time Machine can even handle such deleted items as Contracts entries! To sum it up, Time Machine should be an important and integral part of every Mac owner's existence.

Apple's AirPort Time Capsule device is designed as a wireless storage drive for your Time Machine backup files. If you're interested in a single Time Machine backup location for multiple Macs across your wireless network, an AirPort Time Capsule is a great addition to your home or office.

Before you can use Time Machine, you must have it enabled within the Time Machine pane in System Preferences. I cover the Time Machine configuration settings (and how to turn the feature on) in more detail in Chapter 6. You'll also need an external hard drive that provides considerably more storage capacity than the drive you're backing up. I recommend that your external Time Machine backup drive be at least twice the capacity of the drive you're backing up. (To check on the size of a drive displayed on your desktop, right-click the drive and choose Get Info.)

Here's how you can turn back time, step by step, to restore a file that you deleted or replaced in a folder:

1. **Open a Finder window and navigate to the folder that contained the file you want to restore.**

2. **Click the Time Machine icon on the Finder menu bar (which bears a clock with a counterclockwise arrow) and then click Enter Time Machine.**

   The oh-so-ultra-cool Time Machine background appears behind your folder, complete with its own set of buttons at the bottom of the screen (as shown in Figure 24-2). On the right, you see a timeline that corresponds to the different days and months included in the backups that Mavericks has made.

3. **Click within the timeline to jump directly to a date (displaying the folder's contents on that date).**

   Alternatively, use the Forward and Back arrows at the right to move through the folder's contents through time. (You should see the faces of Windows users when you "riffle" through your folders to locate something you deleted several weeks ago!)

   The backup date of the items you're viewing appears in the button bar at the bottom of the screen.

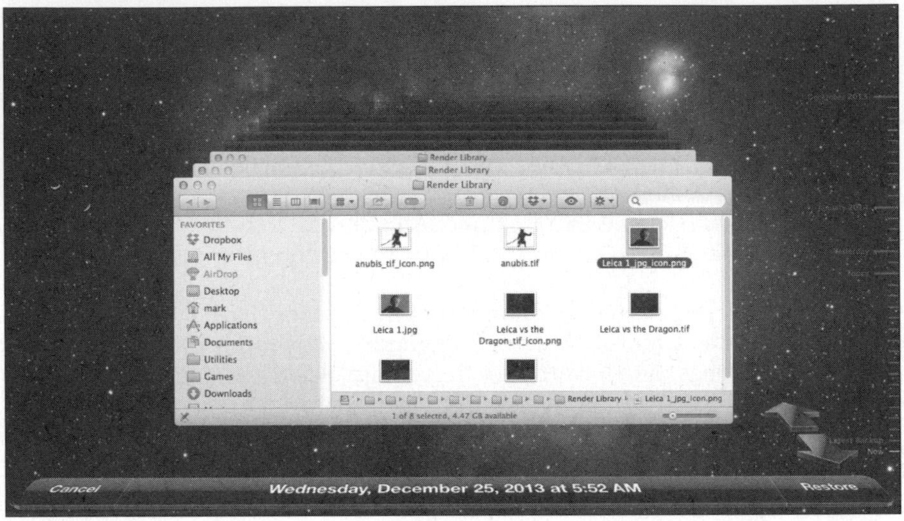

Figure 24-2:
Yes, Time
Machine
really *does*
look like
this!

4. **After you locate the file you want to restore, click it to select it.**

5. **Click the Restore button at the right side of the Time Machine button bar.**

   Time Machine returns you to the Finder, with the newly restored file now appearing in the folder. Out-*standing!*

To restore specific data from your Contacts database, launch the desired application first and then launch Time Machine. Instead of riffling through a Finder window, you can move through time within the application window.

For simple backup and restore protection, Time Machine is all that a typical Mac owner at home is likely to ever need. Therefore, a very easy Mark's Maxim to predict:

Get an external hard drive, connect it, and turn on Time Machine. *Do it now*. Don't make a humongous mistake.

Maintaining Hard Drive Health

Shifty-eyed, sneaky, irritating little problems can bother your hard drive: *permissions errors*. Incorrect disk and file permissions can

- ✔ Make your iMac lock up
- ✔ Make applications act screwy (or refuse to run at all)
- ✔ Cause weird behavior within a Finder window or System Preferences

To keep Mavericks running at its best, I recommend that you fix permissions errors at least once per week. Follow these steps:

1. **Click the Launchpad icon on the Dock and then click the Utilities icon.**

   From the keyboard, press ⌘+Shift+U to open the Utilities folder directly in a new Finder window.

2. **Double-click the Disk Utility icon.**

3. **Click the volume at the left that you want to check.**

   Volume is just computer-speak for a named partition, like Macintosh HD, which appears under your physical hard drive.

4. **Click the Repair Disk Permissions button.**

   Disk Utility does the rest and then displays a message about whatever it has to fix. (When will someone invent a *car* with a Repair Me button?)

Automating Those Mundane Chores

Mavericks's Automator application is a big hit among iMac power users. You use Automator (as shown in Figure 24-3) to create customized tools that automate repetitive tasks.

Figure 24-3: Automator is a dream come true for those who hate repetitive tasks.

You can also create *workflows,* which are sequential (and repeatable) operations that are performed on the same files or data, and then your Automator application can automatically launch whatever applications are necessary to get the job done.

Here's a great example: You work with a service bureau that sends you a CD every week with new product shots for your company's marketing department. Unfortunately, these images are flat-out *huge* — taken with a 16-megapixel camera — and they're always in the wrong orientation. Before you move them to the Marketing folder on your server, you have to use Preview to laboriously resize each image and rotate it, and then use the Finder window to save the smaller version.

With help from Automator, you can build a custom application that automatically reads each image in the folder, resizes it, rotates it, generates a thumbnail image, prints the image, and then moves the massaged images to the proper folder. Of course, you can run Automator from Launchpad. Currently, Automator can handle specific tasks within more than 80 applications (including the Finder), but both Apple and third-party developers are busy adding new Automator task support to all sorts of new and existing applications.

Creating an application in Automator

To create a simple application with Automator, launch the application and follow these steps:

1. **Select Application and click Choose.**

2. **Click the desired item in the Library list.**

   Automator displays the actions available for the item you've selected. Some of these items are media files, whereas others include Contacts cards, files and folders in the Finder, PDF documents, and even Apple Mail messages.

3. **Drag the desired action from the Library pane to the workflow pane.**

4. **Modify any specific settings provided for the action you chose.**

5. **Repeat Steps 1–3 to complete the workflow.**

6. **Click Run (upper right) to test your application.**

   Use sample files while you're fine-tuning your application, lest you accidentally do something deleterious to an original (and irreplaceable) file!

Figure 24-4 illustrates a workflow that will take care of the earlier example — resizing and rotating a folder full of images and then moving them to the Pictures folder.

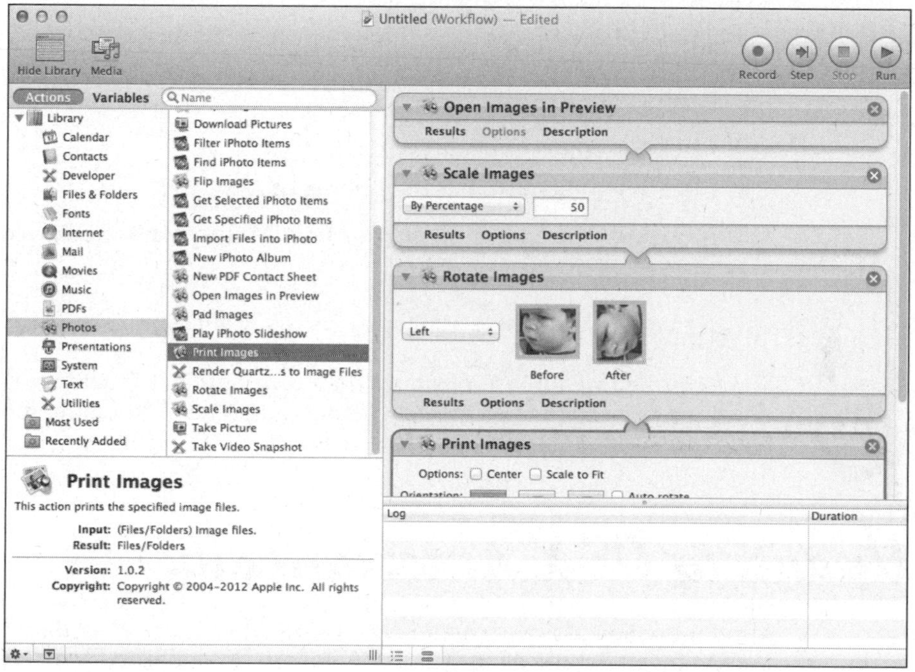

Figure 24-4:
Now you can handle 10 or 1,000 images in a folder. Your application does the work!

7. **When the application is working as you like, press ⌘+Shift+S to save it.**

8. **In the Save As dialog that appears, type a name for your new workflow.**

9. **Open the Where pop-up menu and specify a location where the file should be saved.**

10. **Open the File Format pop-up menu and choose Application.**

11. **Click Save.**

    Your new Automator application icon appears, sporting an Automator robot standing on a document.

    If you expect to use your new Automator application often, you can drag the application icon to your Dock or your Desktop.

TIP

To find all the actions of a certain type within the Library list, click in the Search box at the bottom of the Library pane and type in a keyword, such as **save** or **burn**. You don't even need to press Return!

Running applications at startup

If your Automator application should run every time you log in, follow these steps to set it up as a Login Item:

1. **Open System Preferences.**

2. **Display the Users & Groups pane.**

3. **Click the Login Items button.**

4. **Click the plus button at the bottom of the list.**

5. **Navigate to the location of your new Automator application.**

6. **Click Add.**

   Now your Automator application is *really* automatic.

Some third-party applications have their own Automator actions. Check the developer's website often to see whether additional Automator applications have been added that you can download.

Updating OS X Automatically

I prefer my iMac to take care of cleaning up after itself, so updating Mavericks should be automatic as well. In OS X Mavericks, operating system updates are performed by the Update feature built-in to the App Store application.

Update uses the Internet, so you need an Internet connection to shake hands with the Apple server and download any updates.

Software Update can be found in three convenient spots:

- ✔ **The Apple menu:** Click the Apple menu (🍎) and then click Software Update, which displays the Update window and alerts you to anything new that's available.

- ✔ **The App Store:** Click the Updates pane to display available updates.

- ✔ **System Preferences:** Click the App Store icon to display the pane that you see in Figure 24-5.

  If you take the System Preferences route, you can set Mavericks to check for updates automatically:

  a. *Select the Automatically Check for Updates check box.*

  b. *Make sure the Install App Updates and Install System Data Files and Security Updates check boxes are selected.*

Update covers every Apple application, so I usually check once daily just to make sure that I don't miss anything.

If something needs to be updated, the program alerts you, either automatically downloading the update(s) or displaying a notification letting you know what you can update (depending on the settings you choose in the System Preferences App Store pane).

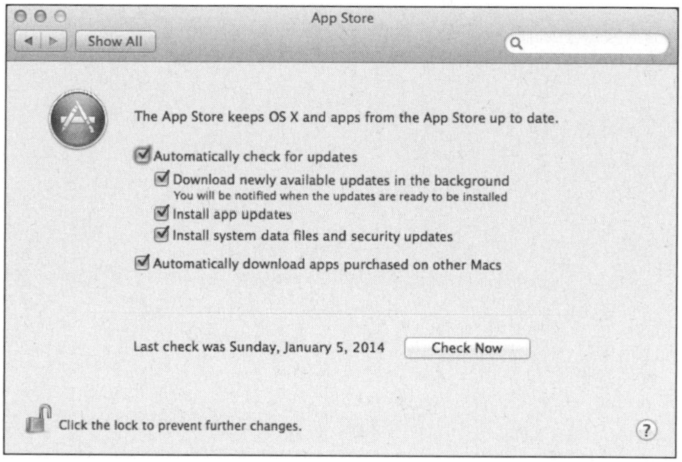

Figure 24-5:
Setting up
Software
Update
to launch
itself, all by
itself.

> ○ ○ ○   App Store
> ◄ ► | Show All | Q
>
> Ⓐ The App Store keeps OS X and apps from the App Store up to date.
>
>   ☑ Automatically check for updates
>   ☑ Download newly available updates in the background
>   You will be notified when the updates are ready to be installed
>   ☑ Install app updates
>   ☑ Install system data files and security updates
>
>   ☑ Automatically download apps purchased on other Macs
>
>   Last check was Sunday, January 5, 2014 | Check Now |
>
> 🔓 Click the lock to prevent further changes.   ⑦

You can even check for updates immediately from the App Store System Preferences pane — click the Check Now button. That, dear reader, is just plain thoughtful design.

If you've installed applications from the App Store, you'll be notified that updates are available for those applications by a tiny red circle next to the App Store icon in the Dock. (The number inside the circle indicates how many updates are available, much like the Mail icon on the Dock displays how many unread messages you have waiting for you.) Click the App Store icon to launch the Store and then click the Updates icon in the title bar.

Part VII
The Part of Tens

Enjoy an additional iMac Part of Tens chapter online at www.dummies.com/
extras/imac.

In this part . . .

- Take simple steps to speed up your computing
- Learn about computing pitfalls you should avoid at all costs

Chapter 25

Ten Ways to Speed Up Your iMac

*E*ven an iMac with an Intel Quad Core i7 processor can always go just a bit faster . . . or *can* it? There's actually a pretty short list of tweaks that you can apply to your iMac's hardware to speed it up, and these suggestions are covered in this chapter.

You can also work considerably faster within Mavericks by customizing your Desktop and your Finder windows, which makes it easier to spot and use your files, folders, and applications. That's in this Part of Tens chapter, too.

Finally, you can enhance your efficiency and make yourself a power user by tweaking yourself. (Sounds a bit tawdry or even painful, but bear with me, and you'll understand.)

Nothing Works Like a Shot of Memory

Okay, maybe *shot* is the wrong word, but adding additional memory to your iMac (by either replacing or adding a memory module) is the single surefire way to speed up the performance of your entire system. That includes every application as well as Mavericks itself.

With more memory, your iMac can hold more of your documents and data in memory, and thus has to store less data temporarily on your hard drive. It takes your iMac much less time to store, retrieve, and work with data when that data is in RAM (short for *random access memory*) rather than on your hard drive. That's why your system runs faster when you can fit an entire image in Adobe Photoshop in your iMac's system memory.

At the time of this writing, you can cram up to 32GB of memory in a 27" iMac model, and 21.5" models can be configured with extra memory as well when you order from the Apple online store.

Only 27" iMacs can be upgraded with additional memory *after* purchase.

Hold a Conversation with Your iMac

Many Mac owners will attest that you *can* significantly increase your own efficiency by using the Speakable Items feature, which allows you to speak common commands within applications and Finder windows. Your voice is indeed faster than either your mouse or your fingers! Common commands in the Speakable Items folder include "Log me out" and "Get my mail."

To enable Speakable Items, choose System Preferences⇨Accessibility, click the Speakable Items entry in the list at the left, and then select the On radio button next to Speakable Items. Remember that, by default, the speech recognition system is active only when you press and hold the Esc key.

Vamoose, Unwanted Fragments!

Apple would probably prefer that I not mention disk fragmentation because Mavericks doesn't come with a built-in defragmenting application. (Go figure.) A disk-defragmenting application reads all the files on your drive and rewrites them as continuous, contiguous files, which your machine can read significantly faster.

To keep your hard drive running as speedily as possible, I recommend defragmenting at least once monthly. You can use third-party applications like Prosoft Engineering's Drive Genius 3 (http://www.prosofteng.com) to defragment your drive.

Keep Your Desktop Background Simple

It's funny that I still include this tip in a chapter dedicated to improving performance. After all, I recommended using a solid color background in my first books on Mac OS 8 and Windows 98! Just goes to show you that some things never change.

If you're interested in running your system as fast as it will go, choose a solid-color background from the Desktop & Screen Saver pane in System Preferences. (In fact, there's even a separate category that you can pick called Solid Colors.)

Column Mode Is for Power Users

One of my favorite features of OS X is the ability to display files and folders in column view mode. Just click the Column button in the standard Finder window toolbar, and the contents of the window automatically align in well-ordered columns.

Other file display options require you to drill through several layers of folders to get to a specific location on your hard drive — for example, Users/mark/Music/iTunes/iTunes Music, which I visit on a regular basis. In column mode, however, a single click drills a level deeper, and often you won't even have to use the Finder window's scroll bars to see what you're looking for. Files and folders appear in a logical order. Plus, it's much easier to move a file (by dragging it from one location on your hard drive to another) in column mode.

Make the Dock Do Your Bidding

Just about every Mac owner considers the OS X Dock a good friend. But when's the last time you customized it — or have you ever made a change to it at all?

You can drag files and folders to the Dock, as well as web URLs, applications, and network servers. You can also remove applications and web URLs just as easily by dragging the icon from the Dock and releasing it on your Desktop.

I find that I make a significant change to my Dock icons at least once every week. I find nothing more convenient than placing a folder for each of my current projects in the Dock or adding applications to the Dock that I might be researching for a book or demonstrating in a chapter.

You can position the Dock at either side of the Desktop or even hide the Dock from sight entirely to give yourself an extra strip of space on your Desktop for application windows. Click the Apple menu (🍎) at the left side of the Finder menu bar and then hover your pointer over the Dock item to display these commands.

It All Started with Keyboard Shortcuts

Heck, keyboard shortcuts have been around since the days of WordStar and VisiCalc, back when a mouse was still just a living rodent. If you add up all those seconds of mouse-handling that you save by using keyboard shortcuts, you'll see that you can save hours of productive time every year.

You're likely already using some keyboard shortcuts, like the common editing shortcuts ⌘+C (Copy) and ⌘+V (Paste). When I'm learning a new application, I often search through the application's online help to find a keyboard shortcut table and then print that table as a quick reference. Naturally, you can also view keyboard shortcuts by clicking each of the major menu groups within an application. Shortcuts are usually displayed alongside the corresponding menu items.

Hey, You Tweaked Your Finder!

Here's another speed enhancer along the same lines as my earlier tip about customizing your Dock: You can also reconfigure your Finder windows to present you with just the tools and locations that you actually use (rather than what Apple *figures* you'll use).

For example, you can right-click the toolbar in any Finder window and choose Customize Toolbar. By default, the OS X Finder toolbar includes only the default icon set that you see at the bottom of the sheet, but you can drag and drop all sorts of useful command icons onto the toolbar. You can save space by displaying small icons, too.

With the introduction of Mavericks, Apple debuted Finder tabs, which I wax enthusiastic about in Chapter 4. Opening multiple tabs makes a Finder window just about as efficient as it can possibly be for operations such as moving files, quickly navigating between locations, and comparing items in different locations.

The Sidebar — which hangs out at the left side of the Finder window — is a healthy, no-nonsense repository for those locations that you constantly visit throughout a computing session. For example, I have both a Games folder and a Book Chapters folder that I use countless times every day (it's important to balance work with pleasure, you know) and I've dragged both of those folders to the Sidebar.

Keep in Touch with Your Recent Past

Click that Apple menu () and use that Recent Items menu! I know that sounds a little *too* simple, but I meet many new Apple computer owners every year who either don't know that the Recent Items menu exists or forget to use it. You can access both applications and documents that you've used within the last few days. Consider the Dock and Finder Sidebar as permanent or semipermanent solutions, and the Recent Items menu as more of a temporary solution to finding the stuff that you're working on Right Now.

Go Where the Going Is Good

To round out this Part of Tens chapter, I recommend another little-known (and underappreciated) Finder menu feature (at least among Macintosh novices): the Go menu, which is located on the Finder menu bar.

The Go menu is really a catch-all, combining the most important locations on your system (like your Home folder) with folders that you've used recently. Plus, the Go menu is the place where you can connect to servers or shared folders across your local network or across the Internet.

Pull down the Go menu today — and don't forget to try out those spiffy keyboard shortcuts you see listed next to the command names. (For example, press ⌘+Shift+H to immediately go to your Home folder.) And if a Finder window isn't open at the moment, a new window opens automatically. Such convenience is hard to resist!

Hold down the Option key when you click the Go menu and you'll be able to choose your personal Library folder (which is normally hidden) from the menu. This comes in handy when you have to troubleshoot problems with applications that save files or store configuration data in your Library folder.

Chapter 26

Ten Things to Avoid Like the Plague

*I*f you've read other books that I've written in the *For Dummies* series, you might recognize the title of this chapter: It's a favorite Part of Tens subject of mine that appears often in my work. I don't like to see any computer owner fall prey to pitfalls. Some of these pitfalls are minor — like being less than diligent about keeping your iMac clean — but others are downright catastrophic, like providing valuable information over the Internet to persons unknown.

All these potential mistakes, however, have one thing in common: They're *easily prevented* with a little common sense — as long as you're aware of them. That's my job. In this chapter, I fill in what you need to know. Consider these pages as experience gained easily (for you, that is!).

Keep Things Cool

I've met a number of iMac owners over the years who've parked their super-computers next to a heat source, "shoehorned" an iMac under a shelf, or draped something over the top of the screen. (That last one happens more often than you think, just because such a cover helps prevent dust from accumulating on the top of any computer.)

What, dear reader, do these three mistakes have in common? In a word, *heat*, which is something you must avoid. Don't forget that your iMac has the same heat-generating CPU, video card, and internal devices that any other computer has these days, but only a single pathway for air to flow. Trust me: Your motherboard and internal devices will suffer if you don't allow your iMac's internal fan to perform its job!

As I discuss in Chapter 1, the fan exhaust on your iMac is the slot at the top back of the case, so *don't ever cover that slot* with anything, and locate your iMac in a spot where there's plenty of ventilation directly above the computer. Also, avoid major heat sources anywhere around your iMac that could significantly raise its temperature.

Phishing Is No Phun

Phishing refers to an attempt by criminals to illegally obtain your personal information. If that sounds like an invitation to identity theft, it is — and thousands of sites have defrauded individuals like you and me (along with banks and credit card companies) out of billions of dollars.

A phishing scam works like this: You get an e-mail purporting to be from a major company or business (think eBay), government agency, social networking site, or major credit card company. The message warns you that you have to "update" your login or financial information to keep it current, or that you have to "validate" your information every so often — and the message ever-so-conveniently even provides you with a link to an official-looking web page (although sometimes full of spelling errors, and always with a bogus address). After you enter information on that bogus page, it's piped directly to the bad guys, and they're off to the races.

Here's a Mark's Maxim that every Internet user should take to heart:

No *legitimate* company or agency will ever solicit your personal information through an e-mail message!

Never respond to these messages. Don't use the link provided in the phishing e-mail! If you smell something phishy, open your web browser and visit the company's site (the *real* one) by typing in the address directly; then contact the company's customer support department to report the scam.

In fact, sending any valuable financial information through unencrypted e-mail — even to those whom you know and trust — is a bad idea. E-mail messages can be intercepted or can be read from any e-mail server that stores your message.

Don't Rely on a Single Password

Okay, confess: Are you using a single password for *everything* you do on your Mac? Is your Apple ID password the same as your user account password — and also the same as your password on every website you visit? Even your online banking? (Oh, my!)

If so, you're taking a big risk with both your personal data and your online reputation. All it takes is a single moment of weakness (perhaps when your friend or co-worker asks to use your Mac, or you use that "oh-so-convenient" universal password on a phishing website). No matter how your password gets out, you and your Mac are suddenly wide open to malicious attacks.

I recommend the same security measure that I recommend to my clients, family, and friends: Use a different password for each of the important websites you visit often, and keep a completely separate password reserved for your user account. I know it's a hassle to remember multiple passwords, but the alternative is no security at all.

Do You Really Want a Submerged Keyboard?

Your answer should be an unequivocal "No!" — and that's why everyone should make it a rule to park all beverages well out of range of keyboards, speakers, mice, backup drives, and any other piece of external hardware. Especially when kids or cats are in close proximity to your iMac.

Cleaning up a hazardous soda spill is hard enough in the clear, but if that liquid comes in contact with your hardware, you're likely to be visited with intermittent keyboard problems (or, in the worst-case scenario, a short in an external peripheral or your iMac's motherboard).

Suffice it to say that 12 inches of open space can make the difference between a simple cleanup and an expensive replacement!

Don't Use Antiquated Utility Software

If you're using OS X Mavericks, you should upgrade your older utility programs. These older disk utility applications can actually do more damage than good to a hard drive under OS X Mavericks. A number of things always change when Apple makes the leap to a new version of OS X, including subtle changes to disk formats and memory management within applications. With an out-of-date utility, you could find yourself with corrupted data.

Make sure that you diagnose and repair disk and file errors by using only a utility application that's specifically designed to run in Mavericks, like Drive Genius 3 from Prosoft Engineering (www.prosofteng.com). Your iMac's hard drive will definitely thank you.

(Oh, and while you're at it, don't forget to check the manufacturer's website for any updates to drivers or application software for your third-party external hardware! 'Nuff said.)

Don't Endorse Software Piracy

This one's a real no-brainer. Bear in mind that Apple's overall market share among worldwide computer users currently weighs in at little more than 17 percent. Software developers know this, and they have to expect (and *receive*) a return on their investment or they're going to find something more lucrative to do with their time. As a shareware author, I can attest to this fact firsthand.

An iMac is a great machine, and Mavericks is a great operating system, but even the best hardware and the sexiest desktop won't make up for an absence of good applications. Pay for what you use, and everyone benefits.

Call It the Forbidden Account

You might never have encountered the *root,* or *System Administrator,* account within OS X — and that's always A Good Thing. Note that I'm not talking about a standard administrator (or admin) account here. Every iMac needs at least one admin account (in fact, it might be the only visible account on your computer), and any standard user account can be toggled between standard and admin status with no trouble at all (by another admin account).

The root account, though, is a different beast altogether, and that's why it's disabled by default. All Unix systems have a root account; because Mavericks is based on a Unix foundation, it has one, too. Anyone logging in with the root account can do *anything* on your system, including deleting or modifying files in the System folder (which no other account can access). Believe me: Deliberately formatting your hard drive is about the only thing worse than screwing up the files in your System folder.

Luckily, no one can accidentally access the root/System Administrator account. In fact, you can't assign the root account with System Preferences; you must use the Terminal application in Utilities (within your Applications folder). Unless an Apple support technician tells you to enable and use it, you should promptly forget that the root account even exists.

Don't Settle for a Surge Suppressor

Technically, nothing is wrong with using a surge suppressor to feed power to your iMac and all your external peripherals, but it doesn't do the *entire* job. Your system is still wide open to problems caused by momentary brownouts, not to mention the occasional full-fledged blackout. Losing power in the middle of a computing session will likely lead to lost documents and might even result in disk or file errors later. With an uninterruptible power supply (UPS), you can rest more easily, knowing that your iMac will have a few minutes more of "ilife."

Most Mac owners know about the backup battery power that a UPS provides, but they don't know about the extra work performed by most UPS units: namely, filtering your AC current. A filtering UPS prevents electronic noise (think about a vacuum being used next to a TV set) and momentary current spikes. These days, you'll find good UPS models for less than $100.

Refurbished Hardware Is No Deal at All

Boy, howdy, do I hate refurbished stuff. To quote someone famous, "If the deal sounds too good to be true, it probably is."

Examine what you get when you buy a refurbished (often called *recertified*) hard drive. It's likely that the drive was returned as defective, of course, and was then sent back to the factory. There, the manufacturer probably performed the most cursory of repairs, perhaps tested the unit for a few seconds, and then packed it back up again. (I should, however, note that Apple sells refurbished Macs and generally has a good reputation for value on these computers.)

Before you spend a dime on a bargain that's *remanufactured* — I can't get over that term — make sure that you find out how long a warranty you'll receive, if any.

If at all possible, I recommend spending the extra cash on trouble-free, brand-new hardware that has a full warranty.

iMacs Appreciate iCleanliness

Clean your machine, including your keyboard, mouse, and trackpad. Your iMac case needs only a thorough wiping job with a soft cloth to stay spotless, but don't be surprised at the primordial nastiness that can build up on your keyboard and the underside of your mouse over time!

Your screen should be cleaned at least once every two or three days. Never spray anything — cleaners, water, **anything!** — directly on your screen or your iMac's case. I highly recommend using premoistened LCD cleaning wipes to safely clean your iMac monitor.

Index

About the Author

Mark L. Chambers has been an author, computer consultant, BBS sysop, programmer, and hardware technician for more than 30 years — pushing computers and their uses far beyond "normal" performance limits for decades now. His first love affair with a computer peripheral blossomed in 1984 when he bought his lightning-fast 300 BPS modem for his Atari 400. Now he spends entirely too much time on the Internet and drinks far too much caffeine-laden soda.

With a degree in journalism and creative writing from Louisiana State University, Mark took the logical career choice: programming computers. However, after five years as a COBOL programmer for a hospital system, he decided there must be a better way to earn a living, and he became the Documentation Manager for Datastorm Technologies, a well-known communications software developer. Somewhere in between writing software manuals, Mark began writing computer how-to books. His first book, *Running a Perfect BBS,* was published in 1994 — and after a short twenty years of fun (disguised as hard work), Mark is one of the most productive and best-selling technology authors on the planet.

His favorite pastimes include collecting gargoyles, watching St. Louis Cardinals baseball, playing his three pinball machines and the latest computer games, supercharging computers, and rendering 3D flights of fancy — and during all that, he listens to just about every type of music imaginable. Mark's world-wide Internet radio station, *MLC Radio* (at www.mlcbooks.com), plays only CD-quality classics from 1970 to 1979, including everything from Rush to Billy Joel to the *Rocky Horror Picture Show.*

Mark's rapidly expanding list of books includes *MacBook All-in-One For Dummies,* 2nd Edition; *MacBook For Dummies,* 4th Edition; *OS X Mavericks All-in-One For Dummies*; *Macs for Seniors For Dummies,* 2nd Edition; *Build Your Own PC Do-It-Yourself For Dummies*; *Building a PC For Dummies,* 5th Edition; *Scanners For Dummies,* 2nd Edition; *CD & DVD Recording For Dummies,* 2nd Edition; *PCs All-in-One Desk Reference For Dummies,* 6th Edition; *Mac OS X Tiger: Top 100 Simplified Tips & Tricks; Microsoft Office v. X Power User's Guide; BURN IT! Creating Your Own Great DVDs and CDs; The Hewlett-Packard Official Printer Handbook; The Hewlett-Packard Official Recordable CD Handbook; The Hewlett-Packard Official Digital Photography Handbook; Computer Gamer's Bible; Recordable CD Bible; Teach Yourself the iMac Visually; Running a Perfect BBS; Official Netscape Guide to Web Animation;* and *Windows 98 Troubleshooting and Optimizing Little Black Book.*

His books have been translated into 15 different languages so far — his favorites are German, Polish, Dutch, and French. Although he can't read them, he enjoys the pictures a great deal.

Mark welcomes all comments about his books. You can reach him at mark@mlcbooks.com, or visit MLC Books Online, his website, at www.mlcbooks.com.

Dedication

This book is dedicated to my youngest daughter, Rose Chambers — she of the Boris Beast and Major Tom — with all the love and happiness I can give her.

Publisher's Acknowledgments

Acquisitions Editor: Aaron Black

Project Editors: Nicole Sholly, Susan Christophersen

Copy Editor: Teresa Artman

Technical Editor: Dennis Cohen

Editorial Assistant: Annie Sullivan

Sr. Editorial Assistant: Cherie Case

Project Coordinator: Erin Zeltner

Cover Image: ©PhotoInc/iStockphoto.com